ANALECTA BIBLICA
INVESTIGATIONES SCIENTIFICAE IN RES BIBLICAS

139

CRAIG G. BARTHOLOMEW

READING ECCLESIASTES

Old Testament Exegesis and Hermeneutical Theory

EDITRICE PONTIFICIO ISTITUTO BIBLICO - ROMA 1998

IMPRIMI POTEST

Romae, die 22 Septembris 1998

R.P. ROBERT F. O'TOOLE, S.J.
Rector Pontificii Instituti Biblici

ISBN 88-7653-139-4

EDITRICE PONTIFICIO ISTITUTO BIBLICO
Piazza della Pilotta, 35 - 00187 Roma, Italia

TABLE OF CONTENTS

ACKNOWLEDGEMENTS

This work is a revised edition of a doctoral dissertation completed through the University of Bristol in 1996. I wish to acknowledge my indebtedness to several people without whom this project would not have come to fruition.

Thanks to Professor Gordon Wenham for his gracious and facilitating supervision and to Professor Christopher Norris for his willingness to be my second supervisor and for making his encyclopaedic knowledge available so willingly.

Thanks to the Centre for the Study of Religion, Cheltenham and Gloucester College of Higher Education, for their provision of a studentship and for their help in revising my dissertation for publication. Karl Möller deserves particular mention for his help in getting my dissertation into the right format.

My parents and sister have provided lifelong support in all my studies and I would never have reached this point without their sustained support.

Professor Calvin Seerveld for his friendship and help with philosophy.

My colleagues in the Centre for the Study of Religion, Cheltenham and Gloucester College of Higher Education, for making this such a pleasant and stimulating place to work.

Thanks to Albert Vanhoye S.J., the editor of Analecta Biblica, who graciously accepted this work for publication in this series.

The God and Father of our Lord Jesus Christ for his faithfulness.

INTRODUCTION

The economist J.M. Keynes once remarked that those economists who disliked theory or claimed to get along better without it, were simply in the grasp of an older theory. This is also true of literary students and critics.

(T. EAGLETON, *Literary Theory. An Introduction* [Oxford: Blackwell, 1983] viii)

Whether we see a whole text or a defective one involves a range of beliefs. To engage in our work as Biblicists means we must exercise our beliefs.

(E.L. GREENSTEIN, "Theory and Argument in Biblical Criticism," *HAR* 10 [1986] 90)

Sternberg argues that biblical study is not a discipline but the intersection of the humanities par excellence so that "the progress it so badly needs is conditional either on all-round expertise, not given to humans or on a truly common pursuit of knowledge."[1] While it is debatable whether biblical study is *a* discipline or not, Sternberg is right to alert us to the importance of being aware of the different disciplines that impinge upon OT studies. The increased specialisation that characterises modernity makes it harder and harder to look beyond one's own discipline and to take cognisance of broader influences.

Furthermore, as with all disciplines, scholars naturally tend to get on with the hard work at the many work sites in OT studies, operating within the regnant paradigm. However, every now and again it is important to re-examine the larger picture. Indeed there is good reason to suggest that progress in OT studies at present will, as Sternberg suggests, depend on just such a re-examination of the relationship between the discipline and the larger issues. There is a growing sense of hermeneutical pluralism and fragmentation in OT studies. Historical criticism, until recently the dominant paradigm for OT studies, is increasingly being relativised as one approach among many. And there is no consensus among OT scholars about what to do in the contemporary situation. Should we retreat into the familiar grounds of historical criticism?[2] Do we, like Brett, Morgan and Barton, deny the possibility of an integrated hermeneutic and opt for more of a

---

[1] M. STERNBERG, *The Poetics of Biblical Narrative. Ideological Literature and the Drama of Reading* (Bloomington: Indiana University Press, 1985) 21-22.

[2] Cf. J.J. COLLINS, "Is a Critical Biblical Theology Possible?" In: W.H. PROPP, B. HALPERN, and D.N. FREEDMAN (eds.), *The Hebrew Bible and Its Interpreters* (1990).

smorgasbord approach?[3] Do we, like Childs and Levenson, try and keep a foot in the historical critical camp while increasingly shifting our weight to the foot in the literary camp?[4] Do we wait out the present crisis until a new consensus emerges?[5] Or do we reclaim the Bible for the Church?[6] In typical postmodern fashion[7] there is a plurality of responses to the fragmented situation in which OT scholars find themselves, and even advocates of a hermeneutical pluralism like Morgan, Brett and Clines appear to exclude certain approaches from their smorgasbord.

In my view the pluralism in OT studies requires closer attention. There are different aspects to this pluralism and it is problematic when they are confused. There is a *methodological* pluralism which relates to different aspects of texts being focused upon. Thus discourse analysis, form criticism, redaction criticism and feminist criticism *need* not be contradictory – they are legitimate methods which focus upon different aspects of the text under consideration. Then there is a *deeper philosophical* pluralism in OT hermeneutics which is problematic. This is often less visible than methodological pluralism because it operates at the subterranean level which still receives relatively little attention. This philosophical pluralism shapes methods of exegesis, and cannot so easily be seen in complementary terms. Often these philosophies are rooted in antithetical views of reality. Thus, for example, Derrida's philosophy of language is irreconcilable with Ricoeur's, and OT hermeneutics shaped by these are not just different ways to arrive at a larger truth; one has to decide between them.[8]

Consequently an examination of the relationship between OT studies and the larger philosophical issues that impinge upon it is crucial if a constructive way

---

3   Cf. M. BRETT, *Biblical Criticism in Crisis? The Impact of the Canonical Approach on Old Testament Studies* (Cambridge: CUP, 1991). R. MORGAN with J. BARTON, *Biblical Interpretation* (Oxford Bible Series; Oxford: OUP, 1988); stresses that in reading the balance of power shifts to the reader so that readers' aims become decisive in interpretation. See pp. 269-296 for a nuanced presentation of his position. See J. BARTON, *Reading the Old Testament. Method in Biblical Study* (London: DLT, 1984) 198-207; who argues that a basic flaw in much OT hermeneutical discussion is the expectation that the question 'How *should* we read the OT?' can be answered. Barton argues for a focus on literary competence rather than normative hermeneutic.

4   B.S. CHILDS, *Introduction to the Old Testament as Scripture* (Philadelphia: Fortress, 1979); and J.D. LEVENSON, *The Hebrew Bible, the Old Testament and Historical Criticism* (Louisville: Westminister/John Knox, 1993).

5   A South African theologian, A.G. VAN AARDE, "Historical Criticism and Holism. Heading Toward a New Paradigm," In: J. MOUTON, A.G. VAN AARDE, and W.S. VORSTER (eds.), *Paradigms and Progress in Theology* (1988) 49-64, has suggested that the emerging paradigm may be holism. Although van Aarde is somewhat critical of this 'emerging' paradigm, he implies that we need to wait and see what paradigm emerges.

6   See, for example, C.E. BRAATEN and R.W. JENSON (eds.), *Reclaiming the Bible For the Church* (Edinburgh: T&T Clark, 1995).

7   See chapters one and six for a discussion of postmodernity.

8   Cf. M.J. VALDÉS (ed.), *A Ricoeur Reader: Reflection and Imagination* (Harvester Wheatsheaf: London, 1991) 6.

forward is to be found for OT studies. In terms of the larger issues that impinge upon OT studies there are two that I have identified as crucial and which are the focus of this study, namely philosophy and literary theory. Both these elements are key means by which movements in the broader academy impinge upon OT studies and they are the focus of our attention under the rubric of 'hermeneutical theory'.[9] At a theoretical level an OT hermeneutic will always carry with it philosophical i.e. epistemological, ontological and anthropological, presuppositions. These are like the scaffolding in a building and are always present in theory construction, whether acknowledged or not.[10] And because of its textual character, OT studies is particularly vulnerable to the influence of literary theory, which has in any case recently exercised a powerful influence way beyond its disciplinary 'boundaries'.

This book is an attempt to examine how these major elements of the larger picture do and should shape work at one OT work site, namely the reading of Ecclesiastes. Ecclesiastes has been chosen for the focus of this study in order to give it exegetical bite. Ecclesiastes is reasonably short and a limited amount of secondary literature has developed in relation to it, thereby making this kind of cross-disciplinary work feasible. Ecclesiastes is also most intriguing in terms of the reading process, because, despite all the historical critical work done on it, there is still no agreement about its message. Scholars remain divided as to whether it is basically a positive book or decidedly negative. In this sense Ecclesiastes cries out for analysis of the different elements that constitute the reading process and how they shape the result.

As Sternberg points out in the above quote, the sort of expertise required for an integral investigation of this sort is "not given to humans." Indeed a danger of this investigation is that the range and the word limit conspire to make it impossible to be comprehensive at either the hermeneutical or the exegetical poles of the investigation. Nevertheless I regard the context described above as justifying the attempt to explore the interface between these two poles, and every attempt has been made to be as thorough as possible.

There is at present a growing recognition that one's presuppositions shape one's scholarship. This is certainly so with this investigation. A starting point is that Christianity is public truth and that it is unhelpful to bracket out one's ultimate beliefs in one's scholarship. As Greenstein points out, "To engage in our work as Biblicists means we must exercise our beliefs." This will be argued for in the course of the book and particularly at the outset of chapter seven, but it is as well for the reader to note my orientation at the outset. Theory, as Eagleton points out, is indispensable in scholarship, and I would argue that for the Christian

---

9   Or 'philosophical hermeneutics.'

10   Note the quote from Eagleton at the outset of this introduction. Ignoring theory will not make it disappear, it simply goes underground as it were!

scholar this theory ought at root to be shaped by a religious (Christian) perspective.

The course of our investigation is as follows:

Chapter one surveys the terrain of philosophical hermeneutics as an inescapable background of contemporary OT interpretation. Chapter two surveys the history of the reading of Ecclesiastes. Chapter three examines the origin of the historical critical method in the context of modernity and the readings of Ecclesiastes that this has produced. Chapter four investigates the reactions to mainline hermeneutics embodied in Canon criticism, New Criticism (NC) and structuralism and their implications for OT studies and the reading of Ecclesiastes. Chapter five examines the narrative turn in OT studies and its application to Ecclesiastes. Chapter six explores the postmodern turn and its effect upon hermeneutics and OT studies. Chapter seven tentatively maps out an OT hermeneutic and applies it to Ecclesiastes.

CHAPTER 1

PHILOSOPHICAL HERMENEUTICS,
THE CONTEXT FOR READING ECCLESIASTES TODAY

*For we see ... how decisive is our underlying theory of knowledge and our
theory of the ontological status of a work, for they determine in advance the
shape of our theory and practice in literary interpretation.*

(R.E. PALMER, *Hermeneutics. Interpretation Theory in Schleiermacher, Dilthey,
Heidegger, and Gadamer* [Evanston: Northwestern UP, 1969] 80-81)

1.1 Introduction

It is only during the last three hundred years that hermeneutics has become a
discipline in itself.[1] This development is the inescapable context in which biblical
interpretation now takes place, so that any academic interpretation of Ecclesiastes
has to take account of contemporary philosophical hermeneutics and its
relationship to OT exegesis, and more specifically to the exegesis (reading) of
Ecclesiastes. In this chapter our concern is to survey the philosophical
hermeneutical context which forms the backdrop of contemporary biblical
interpretation.

By 'hermeneutics' we understand the theory of text-interpretation which we
take to *include* the relationship between the general problem of understanding and
the specific focus of text interpretation.[2] Our orientation is of course towards the
'theory of biblical text interpretation.' This understanding of hermeneutics differs
from traditional ones in its integration of the historicity of the interpreter as well
as the historicity of the text into its approach.[3] This is what we mean by the
'general problem of understanding,' and it is the recognition of this second
horizon of the reader in interpretation that undermines the naive realism that has
dominated much of modern biblical interpretation, and problematises the process
of 'correct' interpretation. As Thiselton says, "hermeneutics in the more recent
sense of the term begins with the recognition that historical conditioning is two-

---

[1]   K. MUELLER-VOLLMER (ed.), *The Hermeneutics Reader* (NY: Continuum, 1992) 2.

[2]   See R.E. PALMER, *Hermeneutics. Interpretation Theory in Schleiermacher, Dilthey,
Heidegger, and Gadamer* (Evanston: Northwestern UP, 1969) 33-71, for a useful discussion of six
modern definitions of hermeneutics and an examination of the meaning and scope of hermeneutics.

[3]   See A.C. THISELTON, *The Two Horizons. New Testament Hermeneutics and Philosophical
Description* (Carlisle: Paternoster; Grand Rapids: Eerdmans, 1980) 10-12, on the difference
between this understanding of hermeneutics and the traditional one of hermeneutics as method of
biblical exegesis.

sided: *the modern interpreter, no less than the text, stands in a given historical context and tradition.*"[4] Interpretation thus involves the fusion of the two horizons of reader and text in the reading process, the process which hermeneutics seeks to understand.[5]

Hermeneutics in this sense "bears the signature of modernity."[6] We will therefore briefly examine relevant aspects of premodern biblical interpretation, deal succinctly with the emergence of modern hermeneutics with particular reference to Spinoza, Kant and Schleiermacher, and then focus on Gadamer and post-Gadamerian hermeneutics.[7] Hermeneutics covers a vast terrain; our intention is to survey the most important developments as they relate to biblical interpretation.[8]

1.2 'Pre-modern' Hermeneutics

There are three major periods in the history of Western hermeneutics:[9] firstly that of classical Greek literary theory and philosophy. Secondly that of Jewish and Christian theories of biblical interpretation and finally that of modernity. *Post*-modernity might suggest a further period but these developments are better seen as part of modernity.[10]

Greek philosophy is the major source from which Western philosophy is derived, as the Greek revival in the Renaissance and Enlightenment demonstrates. As regards textual hermeneutics, the Greek contribution arose from the need to determine the meaning of literary texts, and especially Homer, in ancient Greek society. Indeed, as Jeanrond points out, "Homeric criticism may be called the

---

4   Ibid., 11.
5   Such an understanding of hermeneutics raises the important question of whether any room is left for a meaningful distinction between *Hermeneutik* and *Rezeptionsgeschichte*. Is there a way of discerning a right from a wrong interpretation? As will become apparent I believe that it is possible and important to make such distinctions but that we cannot escape the historicity of interpretation.
6   J. GRONDIN, *Introduction to Philosophical Hermeneutics* (Yale Studies in Hermeneutics; New Haven; London: Yale UP, 1994) 17.
7   I am well aware that this is to privilege Gadamer. On the centrality of Gadamer for philosophical hermeneutics see ibid., 2.
8   Aspects of this history that receive detailed attention in later chapters will be dealt with briefly and forward references given in footnotes.
9   W. JEANROND, *Theological Hermeneutics. Development and Significance* (London: SCM, 1994) 13. I am aware that periodisation is not a straightforward issue. Postmodern theory has made this clear (cf. D. PREZIOSI, *Rethinking Art History. Meditations on a Coy Science* [New Haven; London: Yale UP, 1989], for example). I have put pre-modern in quotation marks to indicate awareness that my periodisation revolves around modernity, and that this may not be satisfactory. On the one hand it privileges the 'modern' too much, and secondly it is far too blunt a tool for the surgical work that cultural analysis requires. For an example of a Christian (Reformational) analysis of modernity see D. STRAUSS, "The Modern Scientific Dispensation and the Spiritual Climate of Contemporary – 'Postmodernism'" (unpubl. paper, 1995).
10   The significance of 'the postmodern turn' is discussed later in this chapter and in ch. 6.

cradle of literary theory: it offered a scope, a terminology and a methodology for all future literary criticism in the West."[11] Two distinct methods of reading developed in this context, allegorical interpretation[12] and grammatical interpretation, both of which played a dominant role in early Christian interpretation.[13]

At the centre of Christian biblical hermeneutics stands the Jesus event. Jesus clearly saw himself as fulfilling the OT, thereby ensuring that typology constituted an important part of Christian hermeneutics from the outset. The establishment of the canon focused the hermeneutical question for the Christian church, with two major hermeneutical schools developing: the allegorical school associated with Alexandria, and the literal, grammatical school associated with Antioch. These schools were not necessarily kept apart; Augustine's influential hermeneutic represents a synthesis of the two approaches.[14] All this interpretation took place within a theistic, communal perspective with a trust in the contextual framework of tradition.[15] This trust hardened into a rigid control in the Middle Ages,[16] but prior to this there was a careful balance between tradition and Scripture in interpretation.[17]

The Reformation, building on the humanist rediscovery of ancient languages and texts, represented the triumph of literal, grammatical interpretation over allegorical interpretation and theological speculation.[18] Sola Scriptura meant that correct interpretation became a critical issue in the life of the church. Scripture was regarded as self-interpreting but this did not mean that reason had no role to play. The Reformers recovered the tradition-Scripture balance witnessed in

---

[11] JEANROND, *Theological Hermeneutics*, 13-14.

[12] Allegorical interpretation became dominant among Stoics in order to yield a philosophically acceptable meaning to the myths of Greek popular religion. Philo of Alexandria popularised the same method in interpretation of the OT for similar reasons. See GRONDIN, *Introduction to Philosophical Hermeneutics*, 23-32.

[13] For an overview of Jewish hermeneutics see JEANROND, *Theological Hermeneutics*, 15-17, and R. LOEWE, "Jewish Exegesis," in: R.J. COGGINS and J.C. HOULDEN (eds.), *A Dictionary of Biblical Interpretation* (1990) 346-354.

[14] JEANROND, *Theological Hermeneutics*, 22.

[15] See A.C. THISELTON, *New Horizons in Hermeneutics* (Grand Rapids: Zondervan, 1992) 145-173, for a discussion of the nature of tradition in pre-modern Christian interpretation. This communal emphasis of pre-modern Christian interpretation has a parallel in postmodern trends, as Thiselton points out, in contrast to the individualism of modernity. A difference is that whereas for pre-modern Christians their corporate values and beliefs were to be respected and trusted, for post-modern thinkers these corporate values are often thought to need unmasking.

[16] JEANROND, *Theological Hermeneutics*, 26.

[17] Jeanrond argues that Augustine's hermeneutic is a model of such balance (ibid., 22-26). See GRONDIN, *Introduction to Philosophical Hermeneutics*, 32-39, on the contemporary importance of Augustine's hermeneutics. Heidegger and Gadamer revert to Augustine.

[18] MUELLER-VOLLMER (ed.), *The Hermeneutics Reader*, 2, and GRONDIN, *Introduction to Philosophical Hermeneutics*, 42-44, regard Illyricus as the most important Protestant theorist of biblical interpretation.

Irenaeus and Augustine. Thus, "Luther's hermeneutics is circular: the Scriptures provoke first a principal existential decision for or against 'spirit', and secondly, only on the basis of such a principal decision in favour of spiritual existence can the reader embark on the detailed task of interpreting the Scriptures."[19] Calvin[20] and Luther are both agreed that correct Scriptural interpretation arises out of a life lived *coram deo*.

1.3 Modern Hermeneutical Theory

Mueller-Vollmer discerns four streams that flow together into modern hermeneutics.[21] They are the hermeneutics of the Reformers, the resurgence of interest in Greek and Roman classical texts and the resultant philological developments, the development of a special hermeneutics of jurisprudence resulting from renewed interest in Roman law and finally the influence of Enlightenment philosophy. The latter was particularly significant since it was only as philosophers focused on hermeneutical problems that general hermeneutics emerged as a discipline in its own right. Certainly for biblical hermeneutics the philosophical paradigm shift that modernity entailed was fraught with significance since it effectively called into question the role of Christian tradition in interpretation, as is particularly clear in the hermeneutics of Spinoza and Kant in which human autonomy is central.

In the seventeenth century an initial universal hermeneutics was developed by Dannhauer, Meier and Chladenius along rationalist lines.[22] However, Kant's critique of reason "dissolved the rationalism to which Dannhauer, Spinoza, Chladenius, and Meier owed their allegiance" and in Kant's "distinction between phenomena and things in themselves lies one of the secret roots of Romanticism and the emergence of hermeneutics."[23] The Romantic hermeneutics of Schleiermacher made room for religion but very much within the emerging paradigm of modernity and still in an ahistorical way. Droysen and Dilthey were key thinkers in setting in motion a focus upon the historical dimension of hermeneutics,[24] which is developed by Heidegger and brought to fruition by Gadamer, who has in the process thoroughly resurrected the notion of tradition and prejudice in hermeneutics. And Gadamer is *the* central figure of philosophical hermeneutics in the twentieth century.

---

[19] JEANROND, *Theological Hermeneutics*, 33.

[20] See T.F. TORRANCE, *The Hermeneutics of John Calvin* (Edinburgh: Scottish Academic Press, 1988) on Calvin's hermeneutics.

[21] MUELLER-VOLLMER (ed.), *The Hermeneutics Reader*, 1-5.

[22] See GRONDIN, *Introduction to Philosophical Hermeneutics*, 45-62. Note that Dannhauer preceded Schleiermacher in universalising hermeneutics.

[23] Ibid., 64.

[24] See ibid., 76-90.

We cannot review this history in detail, and shall confine ourselves to examining the crucial Enlightenment figures of Spinoza and Kant, with particular reference to the role they assign religion epistemologically. We will then move on via Schleiermacher and Heidegger to Gadamer and the main reactions to his hermeneutics.

1.3.1 Spinoza

In contemporary texts on biblical hermeneutics little attention is given to Spinoza (1632-1677).[25] Norris by contrast insists that Spinoza is of major significance not just for Scriptural interpretation but because he anticipates and gives a helpful perspective upon many of the issues that concern literary theorists today.[26] Spinoza's Jewish background and his conflict with his Jewish co-religionists and Dutch Calvinism ensured that he gave sustained attention to religion and the interpretation of Scripture, and particularly the OT. This combination makes him particularly interesting with respect to philosophy and OT hermeneutics.

According to Spinoza the world is understandable by reason, and falsity is the result of privation of knowledge resulting from inadequate ideas. Adequate ideas are universal ideas which are logically connected with other ideas. The key to successful human life, according to Spinoza, is the development of adequate ideas. Democratic society, which protects freedom of inquiry is the best political context for such ideas to develop, and Spinoza is concerned to undermine anything that subverts adequate ideas and tolerance. Thus it is not surprising that his detailed consideration of Scripture and its proper interpretation occurs in his *Tractatus Theologico-Politicus*. Spinoza was well aware that concepts of reason, religion and Scriptural interpretation have immense implications for society.

---

25 In his two volumes *The Two Horizons* and *New Horizons in Hermeneutics*, Thiselton has only six references to Spinoza. JEANROND, *Theological Hermeneutics*, has one brief reference. Most remarkably H. Graf REVENTLOW, *The Authority of the Bible and the Rise of the Modern World* (London: SCM, 1984) has no reference to Spinoza whatsoever in his nearly seven hundred pages on the authority of the Bible and the rise of the modern world! R.M. GRANT with D. TRACY, *A Short History of the Interpretation of the Bible* (2nd ed.; Philadelphia: Fortress, 1984) devotes four pages to Spinoza and notes that "Spinoza's method is very much like that followed in modern introductions to the Bible. It is clear and rational. It avoids all the theological questions involved in the interpretation of scripture; for scripture has no authority over the interpreter's mind" (ibid., 108). An important exception is the useful chapter on Spinoza in R.A. HARRISVILLE and W. SUNDBERG, *The Bible in Modern Culture. Theology and Historical-Critical Method from Spinoza to Käsemann* (Grand Rapids: Eerdmans, 1995) 32-48.

26 C. NORRIS, *Spinoza and the Origins of Modern Critical Theory* (The Bucknell Lectures in Literary Theory; Oxford: Basil Blackwell, 1991), in a remarkably interesting text, seeks to show how Spinoza continues to influence current debates in literary theory and is relevant to gaining a perspective upon the postmodern turn.

Spinoza's Scriptural hermeneutic is shaped by his philosophy, although he does insist that "the Bible must not be accommodated to reason, nor reason to the Bible."[27] He rightly makes the point that a high view of Scripture should result in a method of interpretation that ensures it is Scripture that is heard and not just our prejudices and traditions. For Spinoza this is particularly important since Scripture often contains what cannot be known to reason, but only by revelation. Spinoza aims to read Scripture in a fresh and impartial manner and argues for a literal reading by means of natural reason. A major element of such an approach is the historical dimension of Scriptural texts: "The universal rule, then, in interpreting Scripture is to accept nothing as an authoritative Scriptural statement which we do not perceive very clearly when we examine it in the light of its history."[28] Spinoza eschews the sort of allegorisation undertaken by Maimonides which seeks through subtle means to secure agreement between Scripture and reason. Meaning and truth must be clearly distinguished,[29] and Scriptural meaning must be judged by reason.

There is a tension here since while on the one hand Spinoza acknowledges that Scripture regularly contains what can be known only by revelation, on the other hand he is opposed to submitting reason to Scripture. Much of this tension is defused by his distinguishing between the Word of God and Scripture[30] and by his categorisation of much of the OT historical and prophetic material as imaginary and adjusted to the masses. Spinoza prefers the NT to the Old, since it contains more intelligible argument. Furthermore Spinoza distinguishes between theology and philosophy by arguing that although Scripture contains a small core of ideas "the sphere of theology is piety and obedience" whereas "[t]he sphere of reason is … truth and wisdom."[31] "Philosophy has no end in view save truth: faith, as we have abundantly proved, looks for nothing but obedience and piety."[32] The practical limits of theology are made quite clear in Spinoza's statement that

> [t]heology tells us nothing else, enjoins on us no command save obedience, and has neither the will nor the power to oppose reason: she defines the dogmas of faith … only in so far as they may be necessary for obedience, and

---

[27] B. SPINOZA, *A Theologico-Political Treatise. A Political Treatise* (trans. ELWES; NY: Dover, 1951) 195.

[28] Ibid., 101.

[29] See NORRIS, *Spinoza and the Origins of Modern Critical Theory*, 194ff, for a critique of Kermode's appropriation of Spinoza as one who blurs the distinction between meaning and truth, thereby generating a plurality of meanings. See HARRISVILLE and SUNDBERG, *The Bible in Modern Culture*, 265-266, for the longterm influence of this distinction on historical criticism.

[30] SPINOZA, *A Theologico-Political Treatise*, 169-170.

[31] Ibid., 194.

[32] Ibid., 189.

leaves reason to determine their precise truth: for reason is the light of the mind, and without her all things are dreams and phantoms.[33]

Although Spinoza thus maintains that "the Bible leaves reason absolutely free"[34] and argues that reason should not be submitted to Scripture nor vice versa, in practice his philosophy determines the understanding of Scriptural ideas, as for example his treatment of the OT theme of election makes clear. By 'the help of God' Spinoza understands the fixed order of nature and since no one can do anything except by this order "it follows that no one can choose a plan of life for himself, or accomplish any work save by God's vocation choosing him for the work or the plan of life in question, rather than any other."[35]

Spinoza's hermeneutic is an important early opponent of the orthodox model which subjugated critical reason to religious or doctrinal truth. In practice he reverses this relationship, making the meaning of Scripture accountable to the bar of critical reason. Although a rationalist Spinoza's historical emphasis anticipates many elements of the historical critical method of biblical interpretation that would develop in nineteenth century Germany.[36] Already at the end of the seventeenth century Spinoza is stressing the need to re-evaluate traditional authors of biblical books and their contexts of origin. For example, he rejects Mosaic authorship of the Pentateuch and argues that Ezra is the author of the larger narrative of the history of the Jews from their beginning down to the destruction of Jerusalem.[37] And he insists that these types of historical questions are crucial for correct understanding of the OT. Finally it is refreshing to note that Spinoza was well aware that a critical issue in the debate over the interpretation of Scripture is that of the relationship between faith and reason, theology and philosophy. It is rare to find biblical scholars addressing this issue nowadays, but it is a foundational issue that shapes the direction any biblical hermeneutic takes.

---

[33] Ibid., 194, 195.

[34] Ibid., 9.

[35] Ibid., 45.

[36] See J.S. PREUS, "A Hidden Opponent in Spinoza's Tractatus," *HTR* 88/3 (1995) 361-388, for a useful analysis of the difference between Meyer's philosophical hermeneutic and Spinoza's historical one. Preus comments that "Spinoza's definitive substitution of history for philosophy as the categorial matrix for biblical interpretation makes the *Treatise* paradigmatic in the sense of an exemplary work that systematically formulates a new historical, critical, and comparative approach to the Bible" (ibid., 367).

[37] At an elementary level Spinoza in this way anticipates debates such as that over the deuteronomistic history.

1.3.2 Kant

> *No thinker ever placed greater emphasis on reason's boundaries than Kant; at*
> *the same time, none has ever been bolder in asserting its unqualified title to*
> *govern our lives.*
>
> (A.W. WOOD, "Rational Theology, Moral Faith, and Religion," in: P. GUYER [ed.], *The*
> *Cambridge Companion to Kant* [1992] 414)

The issue of the relationship between faith and reason was central to German philosophy in the second half of the eighteenth century.[38] Enlightenment rationalism received strong opposition from the Pietists who saw rationalism as a threat to faith and in the 1740's and 1750's their opposition received new impetus through the writings of Crusius. The effect of this controversy was that the rationalists seemed to be faced with the dilemma of either a rational scepticism or an irrational fideism. The main task of Kant's philosophy in the 1750's was to provide a new foundation for metaphysics in the light of Crusius' criticisms, and although he later became sceptical about the possibility of metaphysics the question of the vindication of reason remained central to his mature philosophy. Kant sought to secure reason through a synthesis of the best insights of rationalism and empiricism.[39]

For Kant the human mind is the ultimate source of meaning and understanding; objective reality can only be known as it conforms to the structures of the knowing mind. In this way Kant acknowledges both the value and limitations of reason. The world can never be known as it is in itself, but only through the point of view by which it is perceived. "The world is as we think it, and we think it as it is."[40] Kant's Copernican revolution consisted in making our cognitive capacities primary over nature.

As the quote above from Wood indicates, if Kant stressed the limitations of reason he also stressed its autonomy. Rationalism is too ambitious, in his view, and he compares it to the builders of the tower of Babel.[41] However, the desire for autonomy that motivates the project is quite right; what is required is a more modest plan. We need to ask what can be built with the labour and materials available to us.

> Kant represents attempts to ground practices of reason as a matter of
> proceeding with the 'materials' and 'labor power' that our daily practice of

---

[38] This was made particularly clear to me by F.C. BEISER, *The Fate of Reason. German Philosophy From Kant to Fichte* (Cambridge, Mass.: Harvard UP, 1987).

[39] R. SCRUTON, *Kant* (Past Masters; Oxford: OUP, 1982) 11-21, indicates that Leibniz (1646-1716) and Hume (1711-1776) form the particular background to Kant's thought in his *Critique of Pure Reason*. Scruton maintains that one might call Kant's synthesis an attempt to give a fully enriched account of the objectivity of the physical world (ibid., 38).

[40] Ibid., 23.

[41] O. O'NEILL, "Vindicating Reason," in: P. GUYER (ed.), *The Cambridge Companion to Kant* (1992) 289-290.

defective reasoning has made available to us, and rebuilding these in ways that reduce dangers of collapse or paralysis in thought or action.[42]

Kant proposes that we think of reason as a discipline which rejects external authorities, and is reflexive in that it involves self-discipline and is lawlike.[43] In terms of the relationship between reason and faith/religion the character of reason as negative in the sense of rejecting external authorities is particularly significant. For Kant autonomy is a fundamental characteristic of reason: "Reason is indeed the basis of enlightenment, but enlightenment is no more than autonomy in thinking and acting – that is, of thought and action that are lawful yet assume no lawgiver."[44] Judgement is possible with phenomenal objects alone, and not the noumenal. The latter can be used only negatively in order to demarcate the limits of experience. This limitation arises from the fact that all attempts to embrace the noumenal world in a rational system will ultimately fail since they always end in unresolvable contradictions or antinomies.

Religion is made subservient to morality in Kant's scheme which defines religion as "the cognition of all duties as divine commands."[45] Kant was opposed to religious ceremonies and regarded creeds as an imposition upon our inner freedom of thought. Morality leads to religion and we can be justified practically in holding religious propositions, but religious beliefs are necessary only in so far as they support our sense of morality. Religious tutelage is strongly rejected by Kant and as Scruton puts it, "Kant's writings on religion exhibit one of the first attempts at the systematic demystification of theology."[46] Worship of God is translated into veneration of morality, and faith into certainty of practical reason. "The object of esteem is not the Supreme Being, but the supreme attribute of rationality."[47] In this way Kant's philosophy epitomises the move from providence to progress.[48]

Plantinga argues that Kant's understanding of reality represents a turning on its head of a Christian perspective, especially if taken to its logical conclusion in what Plantinga calls "creative anti-realism."[49] From a Christian perspective God's knowledge is creative; from a Kantian perspective our knowledge is creative. Plantinga suggests that it is an easy step from the view that we are responsible for

---

42 Ibid., 291-292.

43 See O'NEILL, "Vindicating Reason," for a very useful discussion of Kant's mature view of reason.

44 Ibid., 299.

45 See A.W. WOOD, "Rational Theology, Moral Faith, and Religion," in: P. GUYER (ed.), *The Cambridge Companion to Kant* (1992) 406-408.

46 SCRUTON, *Kant*, 78.

47 Ibid.

48 See D. LYON, *Postmodernity* (Concepts in the Social Sciences; Buckingham: Open UP, 1994) 5, for the description of modernity as a move from providence to progress.

49 A. PLANTINGA, "Christian Philosophy at the End of the 20th Century," in: S. GRIFFIOEN and B.M. BALK (eds.), *Christian Philosophy at the Close of the Twentieth Century* (1995) 30-37.

the way the world is to the postmodern view that we do not all live in the same world. Thus Plantinga suggest that the creative anti-realism of postmodernity has its roots in Kantian idealism and that this tendency is profoundly unchristian.[50]

Kant's idealism does take account of human finitude but his insistence on human autonomy makes it difficult to reconcile his account of reason with a Christian perspective. In the latter sense he reinforces the essential Enlightenment belief in the authority of reason. The extent to which this is at odds with a view of Christianity as public truth is well captured by the title of Wolterstorff's *Reason Within the Bounds of Religion*.[51] Gruenler is right that

> the biblical interpreter who accepts the Kantian dichotomy will confine religious experience to the domain of personal, transcendental faith (which cannot be touched by historical criticism) and confine the historical-critical method to analysis of natural cause and effect without recourse to matters of faith or supernatural revelation.[52]

The subjective realm of the transcendental ego is reserved as the one area of freedom where God can be experienced but only subjectively, so that "encounter with God will be confined to the subjective realm, while the Bible will be subjected to naturalistic criticism according to the rational canons of purely historical research."[53] Such a shift is evident in Kant's own readings of Scripture,[54] and amply supported by de Wette and other OT theologians who were deeply indebted to Kant.[55]

Kant shares with Spinoza an emphasis on human autonomy, but his articulation of the limits of reason undermined the rationalist presupposition that the mind could penetrate the logical construction of the world. As Grondin points out this problematising of *rational* access to the world dissolved the rationalism of Dannhauer and Spinoza and opened the door to the subjectivism of

---

[50] Compare this with the suggestion by C. NORRIS, "Criticism," in: M. COYLE, et al., *Encyclopaedia of Literature and Criticism* (1990) 27-65, that postmodern indeterminacy has its roots in Christian readings of the Old Testament. For a very different analysis of Kant by a Christian philosopher to that of Plantinga see M. WESTPHAL, "Christian Philosophers and the Copernican Revolution," in: C.S. EVANS and M. WESTPHAL (eds.), *Christian Perspectives on Religious Knowledge* (1993) 161-179.

[51] N. WOLTERSTORFF, *Reason Within the Bounds of Religion* (Grand Rapids: Eerdmans, 1984).

[52] R.G. GRUENLER, *Meaning and Understanding. The Philosophical Framework for Biblical Interpretation* (Foundations of Contemporary Interpretation 2; Grand Rapids: Zondervan, 1991) 38.

[53] Ibid., 40.

[54] See, for example, A. EDGAR, "Kant's Two Interpretations of Genesis," *Literature and Theology* 6/3 (1992) 280-290.

[55] See J. ROGERSON, *W.M.L. de Wette. Founder of Modern Biblical Criticism* (JSOTSup 126; Sheffield: JSOT Press, 1992) 26-32, for the major influence of Kant upon de Wette, the father of OT criticism.

Romanticism, in which, along Greek lines, the unity of the whole is discovered through 'intuition'.[56]

1.3.3 Schleiermacher

Schleiermacher's significance lies in the synthesis he developed between religion and human autonomy in a context that increasingly saw religion as irrelevant.[57] Religious reality is to be understood, according to Schleiermacher, through an analysis of human consciousness focused on feeling and intuition.[58] In this way Schleiermacher developed a romanticist interpretation of religion which fits with the Enlightenment insistence upon human autonomy. As Reardon points out,

> overall the impression he leaves in the mind of the reader is that of a theology subtly transformed into a philosophy of idealist monism. ... The traditional landmarks are all there: revelation, the Bible, the articles of faith, the church. Yet all show up in a perspective new and somehow altered. ... The viewpoint has shifted, that is, from a theocentrism to an anthropocentrism, so that what really has happened, one begins to suspect, is that Christian dogmatics has been covertly translated into a philosophy of the religious consciousness, for which a variety of elements have been drawn upon.[59]

In line with Romanticism[60] Schleiermacher recognised the limits of reason in achieving understanding. Authors were understood as creators and their productions as works of art so that understanding involved re-living and re-thinking the thoughts and feelings of an author.[61] Thus Schleiermacher speaks of interpretation as an art and compares the process to that of getting to know a friend.[62]

---

[56] GRONDIN, *Introduction to Philosophical Hermeneutics*, 63ff.

[57] For a useful discussion of this see H. VANDER GOOT, "The Modern Settlement: Religion and Culture in the Early Schleiermacher," in: J. KRAAY, and A. TOL (eds.), *Hearing and Doing* (1979) 173-197. He points out that Schleiermacher's *Reden* "effected a resolution of the problem of the relation of culture and religion, or reason and faith, that became widely acceptable to Christians in the nineteenth century" (ibid., 177). B.M.G. REARDON, *Religion in the Age of Romanticism* (Cambridge: CUP, 1985) and Vander Goot stress Schleiermacher's indebtedness to Kant and in particular to Spinoza.

[58] Schleiermacher's understanding of religion and Christianity is more complex than this brief description. See REARDON, *Religion in the Age of Romanticism*, 29-58.

[59] Ibid., 57, 58. Reardon points out that the Romantic understanding of religion with its subjectivising tendency marks the start of "that process of immanentizing religious reality which was characteristic of the nineteenth century in general and which, despite the neo-orthodox reaction, has continued through the present century as well" (ibid., 10).

[60] On the nature of Romanticism see ibid., 1-28. Cf. THISELTON, *New Horizons in Hermeneutics*, 209-216, for the diverse influences upon Schleiermacher.

[61] REARDON, *Religion in the Age of Romanticism*, 8, points out that it was in the personal imagination that the romantics located the real creative principle.

[62] This implies a very positive approach to a text: "We may assume that the author is at fault only when our overview of the text uncovers evidence that the author is careless and imprecise, or

The transcendental turn to Schleiermacher's hermeneutics is significant. "For Schleiermacher, hermeneutics was ... above all concerned with illuminating the conditions for the possibility of understanding and its modes of interpretation."[63] This universalisation of hermeneutics was not new;[64] Schleiermacher's original contribution lay in his "universalisation of misunderstanding," whereby he stressed that understanding needs to proceed *kunstgemäss* at every point.[65] This transcendental turn has received increasing attention among twentieth century philosophers, and it is here that Schleiermacher's major contribution lies.

Understanding a text involves re-experiencing the mental processes of the author. Schleiermacher discerns two aspects to such understanding, a grammatical and a psychological or technical one. The first concerns the understanding of an expression solely in terms of its relationship to the language of which it is a part. The second concerns the expression as part of the author's life-process and involves the comparative and the divinatory method.[66] As Thiselton points out,

> Schleiermacher therefore explicitly raised for the first time a question which remains of permanent importance for hermeneutics: can we interpret the meaning of texts purely with reference to their language, or purely with reference to their author's intention, *or does textual meaning reside somehow in the inter-relation or inter-action between both?*[67]

With Schleiermacher we are also well on the way to a developed understanding of the hermeneutical circle.[68] The process of understanding must begin with a preliminary attempt to understand the whole, only then can one apply oneself to the details. This spiral moves between the grammatical and psychological, between the general and the particular and between the divinatory and comparative. Schleiermacher believes that through this process it is possible to understand a text better than its author; indeed this is the task of interpretation.

Schleiermacher's focus of hermeneutics upon the process of understanding is to be welcomed but there is a tendency in his approach to make the real focus of interpretation the author's thoughts and experience which lie behind the text rather than the text itself.[69] The divinatory aspect of interpretation is related to Schleiermacher's romantic tendency to focus on human subjectivity as the key to

---

confused and without talent" (Schleiermacher in MUELLER-VOLLMER (ed.), *The Hermeneutics Reader*, 88).

[63] MUELLER-VOLLMER (ed.), *The Hermeneutics Reader*, 9.
[64] See GRONDIN, *Introduction to Philosophical Hermeneutics*, 50.
[65] Cf. ibid., 63-75.
[66] For an explanation of the divinatory and comparative by Schleiermacher see MUELLER-VOLLMER (ed.), *The Hermeneutics Reader*, 96.
[67] THISELTON, *New Horizons in Hermeneutics*, 206.
[68] Already Wolf and Ast had developed this idea.
[69] GRONDIN, *Introduction to Philosophical Hermeneutics*, 71-72.

understanding reality so that the intuition of the reader is privileged as the means – and the subjective experience behind the text become the focus – of interpretation. This is evident in Schleiermacher's approach to Scripture, which is seen as a symbolic account of religious consciousness. This experience is the crucial element and can be reproduced because it is in our consciousness as well. Thus Scripture is only a mausoleum, a monument that a great spirit who once was there is there no longer.

Schleiermacher's reading of Scripture through the grid of his analysis of religious consciousness alerts us to the extent to which his understanding of religion operates within the modern worldview. His perspective on reality is Kantian in its starting with an analysis of reality as we experience it, and then finding room in this for religion. Hence Thielicke's description of his theology as 'Cartesian'.[70] Thus, although Schleiermacher makes room for religion, it is very much within the bounds of human autonomy.

Palmer correctly alerts us to the atemporal dimension in Schleiermacher's hermeneutic.[71] Dilthey sought to introduce a critique of historical reason through his development of the psychological emphasis in Schleiermacher's hermeneutic.[72] This historical turn in hermeneutics is of great significance for biblical hermeneutics, for as Nicholson explains, it was nineteenth century *historical* philosophy which shaped the historical critical method.

> To a remarkable extent, indeed to a greater extent than has often been realized or acknowledged, it was this historical thinking that provided the basis of biblical hermeneutics in the nineteenth century, and more than the theologians and biblical scholars themselves it was the leading figures of the German historical school – Barthold Gustav Niebuhr, Wilhelm von Humboldt, Leopold von Ranke, Johan Gustav Droysen, Theodor Mommsen, and others – who created the interpretive framework and provided the method.[73]

In chapter three we will examine this historical turn in more detail. In this survey we proceed to Heidegger who introduced the element of radical historicity into hermeneutics.[74]

---

70 See H. THIELICKE, *The Evangelical Faith. Volume One. Prolegomena. The Relation of Theology to Modern Thought Forms* (Edinburgh: T&T Clark, 1974) 38-45, and cf. THISELTON, *New Horizons in Hermeneutics*, 230ff, for a critical assessment of Thielicke's view. Overall I think Thielicke is correct.

71 PALMER, *Hermeneutics*, 75.

72 See J. BLEICHER, *Contemporary Hermeneutics. Hermeneutics as Method, Philosophy and Critique* (London: Routledge and Kegan Paul, 1980) 16-26, for a brief discussion of this development in hermeneutics.

73 E. NICHOLSON, *Interpreting the Old Testament: A Century of the Oriel Professorship* (Oxford: Clarendon, 1981) 16. See GRONDIN, *Introduction to Philosophical Hermeneutics*, 76-90, on historicism and hermeneutics.

74 Heidegger built in this respect upon Dilthey's historical hermeneutic. For a discussion of Dilthey's view of history and hermeneutics see ibid., 84-90, and T. PLANTINGA, "Dilthey's Philosophy of the History of Philosophy," in: J. KRAAY and A. TOL (eds.), *Hearing and Doing*

1.3.4 Heidegger

Heidegger's philosophy[75] is strongly ontological and his epistemology is rooted in his ontology of *Dasein*. *Sein* can only be investigated if one begins with *Dasein*, which does not have a viewpoint outside of history. In this sense "[t]he phenomenology of *Dasein* is a hermeneutic."[76] This approach allowed Heidegger to rethink the subject-object relationship in knowing along historical lines, and it is here that his most significant hermeneutical contribution lies.[77] "Worldhood" refers to that whole in which the human person finds herself immersed. It is ontological and apriori, given along with Dasein and prior to all conceptualising. To conceive of objects as merely "present-at-hand" involves secondary conceptualisation. The primary relationship of humans to objects is as "ready-to-hand." This contrasts with the Cartesian scientific orientation which makes secondary conceptualisation primary.[78]

Understanding is related to interpretation in that interpretation is not the acquiring of information about what is understood but the working out of the possibilities projected in understanding. What is understood has the structure of something *as* something. Interpretation is grounded in a "fore-having" (*Vorhabe*). "An interpretation is never a presuppositionless apprehending of something presented to us."[79] When this as-structure becomes explicit the object has become meaningful for us. Interpretation thus inevitably involves the hermeneutical circle: "Any interpretation which is to contribute understanding, must already have understood what is to be interpreted."[80]

In this way Heidegger opened the way for the recognition of the radical historicity of hermeneutics; indeed the question of Being can only be asked within time in his view. Gadamer says of Heidegger: "But the concept of substance is in fact inadequate for historical being and knowledge; *Heidegger* was the first to make generally known the radical challenge of thought implicit in this inadequacy. He was the first to liberate Dilthey's philosophical intention."[81]

(1979) 199-214, and idem, *Historical Understanding in the Thought of Wilhelm Dilthey* (Toronto: University of Toronto Press, 1980).

[75] We focus here on Heidegger's philosophy as represented by *Being and Time*. For the significance of *Being and Time* and the later developments in his philosophy for hermeneutics see J.D. CAPUTO, *Radical Hermeneutics. Repetition, Deconstruction and the Hermeneutic Project* (Bloomington; Indianapolis: Indiana UP, 1987).

[76] M. HEIDEGGER, *Being and Time* (Oxford: Basil Blackwell, 1962) 62.

[77] Speaking of the tension between objectivity and prejudice THISELTON, *The Two Horizons*, 27, comments that "Heidegger has paid closer attention to the two-sidedness of this problem than perhaps any other thinker."

[78] Cf. ibid., 157-161, 187-191.

[79] HEIDEGGER, *Being and Time*, 191-192.

[80] Ibid., 194-195.

[81] H. GADAMER, *Truth and Method* (2nd ed.; London: Sheed and Ward, 1989) 242-243.

This historicity of the interpreter has radical implications for hermeneutics and is central to Gadamer's hermeneutic.

1.3.5 Gadamer

Gadamer ascribes primary importance to understanding and insists on the historical nature of understanding itself:

> Heidegger entered into the problems of historical hermeneutics and critique only in order to explicate the fore-structure of understanding for the purposes of ontology. Our question, by contrast, is how hermeneutics once freed from the ontological obstructions of the scientific concept of objectivity, can do justice to the historicity of understanding.[82]

Schleiermacher understood hermeneutics as the means of overcoming the historical distance between the interpreter and the object of his interpretation. However, for Gadamer "[a]ny interpretations of the past, whether they were performed by an historian, philosopher, linguist, or literary scholar, are as much a creature of the interpreter's own time and place as the phenomenon under investigation was of its own time and period in history."[83]

Part one of Gadamer's *Truth and Method* is concerned with the question of truth as it emerges in the understanding of art. Gadamer argues that experience and not abstraction is the key to understanding art. He attacks the Enlightenment exaltation of theoretical reason, as articulated by Descartes in particular, and appeals to Aristotle's notion of practical knowledge and the *sensus communis*. This has significance for hermeneutics in general; hermeneutics must be so understood as to do justice to the experience of art.

In part two of *Truth and Method* Gadamer analyses the hermeneutic tradition stemming from Schleiermacher and develops his own historical approach. In contrast to Enlightenment attitudes Gadamer sees all interpretation as always guided by its own prejudice.[84] This prejudice is not just negative and it cannot be simply discarded: "Using Heidegger, Gadamer rejects the Enlightenment prejudice against one's having presuppositions and working prejudgements, and the concomitant Enlightenment emasculation of tradition – as if one who does not question the prejudices of his own age is therefore a model knower."[85] The Enlightenment manifests a prejudice against prejudice whereas Gadamer refuses to set reason in opposition to tradition. Indeed understanding takes place as an event within a tradition. In contrast to existential thinking Gadamer tries to locate meaning in the larger context of the community, as his view of tradition demonstrates.

---

[82] Ibid., 265.
[83] MUELLER-VOLLMER (ed.), *The Hermeneutics Reader*, 38.
[84] GADAMER, *Truth and Method*, 265-285.
[85] C. SEERVELD, "Review of H.-G. Gadamer, *Truth and Method*," *Criticism* 36/4 (1978) 488.

In the light of the historicity of all interpretation, how is understanding possible? Certainly for Gadamer, the historicity of all interpretation makes Schleiermacher's aim of reconstructing the original world of the text impossible. What makes understanding possible is *Wirkungsgeschichte*. This refers to the overriding historical continuum and cultural tradition of which both interpreter and historical object are part. Thus hermeneutics aims at prejudgements that will foster a fusion of the past with the present which facilitates the miracle of understanding, the sharing of a common meaning by temporally distant consciousnesses. In this fusing of horizons distance and critical tension are never completely obliterated; indeed the hermeneutic task is to foreground the tensions. Nevertheless interpretation always involves application.

Interpretation proceeds through a dialectical process of question and answer. Gadamer is opposed to trying to fix once and for all the meaning of a text. Our interpretation is only one actualization of the historical potential of a text so that correct interpretation will be characterised by unending dialogue. Knowledge is inherently dialectical and we humans *are* conversations. The interpreter is to melt into the continuing, enlarging, ever-interacting-history of tradition, or risk hubris.

This does not mean that the interpreter is free to simply dominate the text with imposed meanings. The good interpreter lets the text speak and convince the receiving interpreter.

> One could say that Gadamer is pointing out the philosophical reason why so much literary criticism ... and critical analysis of 'the other's' scholarship is judgmental rape of the text, when it should be a love affair, if hermeneutical activity is meant to be humane. Interpretation in the humanities went wrong, and remains obstinately wrongheaded, for Gadamer when it tried to understand art, literature, and research in the cultural sciences as if it were dissecting bugs and smashing atoms.[86]

In part three of *Truth and Method* Gadamer offers a draft for an ontology of language-in-action. He proposes an ontology in which all understanding rests in language itself and seeks to explore systematically the universal conditions for just interpretation which will not presume interpretation can be ahistorical.

Since Gadamer's approach no other really ground-breaking hermeneutical innovations have appeared, but his hermeneutics has generated numerous debates. Indeed Gadamer is a pivotal figure between modern and postmodern paradigms of thinking. Thiselton draws attention.

> to Gadamer's role in focusing for hermeneutics, and addressing, a cluster of metacritical questions concerning the *basis* of understanding and of our possible relation to truth. Gadamer's distinctive way of addressing these questions not only constitutes a point of transition towards a new paradigm of

---

[86] Ibid.

hermeneutical theory; it also places him firmly on the boundary-line between modern and post-modern thought.[87]

According to Thiselton the focus on metacritical issues that one finds in Gadamer emerges from three directions: firstly the problem of radical historical finitude; secondly the problem of the constitutive role of language in understanding and thirdly the unease that has beset academic disciplines as they submit to reappraisal what have been regarded as foundations for their methods.[88]

In the remainder of this chapter we will make some further comments about the postmodern turn and then examine the main ways in which Gadamer has been appropriated in contemporary hermeneutics.

1.3.6 Postmodernity

Gadamer is appropriated by Habermas who wants to get the project of modernity back on track, by a postmodernist pragmatist like Rorty,[89] and by Ricoeur. We will briefly explore the nature of the postmodern turn before examining the different ways in which Habermas, Rorty and Ricoeur develop Gadamer's thought. The specifically 'postmodern' debate began as a reaction to modernism in the arts in the 60's and was extended to a critique of Western culture in its entirety in the 80's as philosophers joined the debate in earnest.[90] There are cultural, social (late capitalism) and philosophical elements to the 'postmodern condition'. Philosophically postmodernity involves a foundational crisis in the project of modernity. A marked pluralism characterises epistemology, ontology and anthropology as the modern 'consensus' is increasingly questioned. This pluralism has major implications for hermeneutics, as the writings of Rorty, Derrida, Foucault and Lyotard demonstrate. The relativistic extremes of the postmodern debate, exemplified by Baudrillard and Lyotard, are however only one stream in the contemporary philosophical scenario. Habermas, Ricoeur, Norris and many others discuss many of the same issues but from a perspective of refining the project of modernity.

The philosophical diversity of 'the postmodern turn' has been powerfully experienced in biblical hermeneutics, as in virtually all disciplines. Within biblical studies this influence has generally been mediated through literary theory which has itself come over the past decades to exercise a powerful influence far beyond its disciplinary boundaries.[91] The turn to literary theory is related to the crisis in the nature of philosophy as it has been practised in the Western tradition.

---

[87] THISELTON, *New Horizons in Hermeneutics*, 314.

[88] Ibid., 318.

[89] I have found G. WARNKE, *Gadamer. Hermeneutics, Tradition and Reason* (California: Stanford UP, 1987) particularly useful in terms of the reactions of Habermas and Rorty to Gadamer.

[90] See ch. 6 for a more detailed discussion of the postmodern turn.

[91] Cf. Norris' reference to literary theory's colonizing drive into other disciplines (C. NORRIS, *Truth and the Ethics of Criticism* [Manchester: Manchester UP, 1994] 114). In the process of this

The effect of the literary turn, especially in biblical hermeneutics, should not be underestimated. It provides the most radical challenge to traditional models which has yet arisen. The very possibility of determinate and true readings of texts has been called into question by much postmodern literary theory. Author, reader and text and their interrelationships have come under fresh scrutiny and a variety of positions has developed. Hirsch maintains that textual meaning is inseparable from authorial intention;[92] Barthes, Foucault and others have pronounced the author dead.[93] Burke has recently declared the return of the author![94] The reader and his/her role in the construction of meaning has received close attention with a whole variety of proposals made.[95]

The nature of textuality itself has become highly problematic. New Criticism (NC) focused literary theory on the text itself, and as a result of structuralism, deconstruction and poststructuralism the nature of textuality has come under close scrutiny. Up until recently the classical-humanist paradigm of textuality had dominated the history of biblical interpretation. According to this tradition, texts are stretches of language which express the thoughts of their authors, and refer to the extra-linguistic world. Texts were seen as mediating inter-personal communication. The new approaches have called every aspect of this tradition into question.

1.3.7 Ricoeur

> *Beyond the desert of criticism, we wish to be called again.*
>
> (P. RICOEUR, *The Symbolism of Evil* [Boston: Beacon Press, 1969] 349)

---

colonizing activity the boundary between philosophy and literary theory has been blurred, so that literary conferences have often become predominantly philosophical. This blurring serves as a reminder that in reality literary theory has mediated and actively promoted the influence of certain philosophies rather than literary theory per se being the origin of the postmodern 'literary' turn. This is important, because as Thiselton says, "If there is any area at all in theology and biblical studies where attention to *method* and to *theory* is crucial, it is here" (THISELTON, *The Two Horizons*, 472).

[92] E.D. HIRSCH, *Validity in Interpretation* (New Haven; London: Yale UP, 1967). Cf. Betti's hermeneutic. See GRONDIN, *Introduction to Philosophical Hermeneutics*, 125-129.

[93] R. BARTHES, "The Death of an Author," in: D. LODGE (ed.), *Modern Criticism and Theory* (1988) 167-171; M. FOUCAULT, "What is an Author?" in: P. RABINOW (ed.), *The Foucault Reader* (1984) 101-120.

[94] S. BURKE, *The Death and Return of the Author. Criticism and Subjectivity* (Edinburgh: Edinburgh UP, 1992).

[95] Cf. S.R. SULEIMAN, "Introduction: Varieties of Audience-Oriented Criticism," in: S.R. SULEIMAN and I. CROSMAN (eds.), *The Reader in the Text. Essays on Audience and Interpretation* (1980) 3-45; E. FREUND, *The Return of the Reader. Reader-response Criticism* (London; NY: Methuen, 1987); and R.C. HOLUB, *Reception Theory. A Critical Introduction* (New Accents; London; NY: Routledge, 1984).

Ricoeur is particularly significant for his understanding of interpretation as a semantic event, of the fusion of text and interpreter through the interplay of metaphor and symbol in a reading along the lines of a second naiveté.[96] In contrast to Gadamer, Ricoeur seeks to bring together *explanation* and *understanding*.[97] For Gadamer, in Ricoeur's view, the two collapse into each other so that there tends to be no space for critical testings of understandings. For Ricoeur 'explanation' embodies a hermeneutic of suspicion: the willingness to expose and to abolish idols which are mere projections of the human will. Ricoeur is critical of the Enlightenment insofar as it locates meaning in the subject; he professes

> a permanent mistrust of the pretensions of the subject in posing itself as the foundation of its own meaning. The reflective philosophy to which I appeal is at the outset opposed to any philosophy of the Cartesian type ... the understanding of the self is always indirect and proceeds from the interpretation of signs given outside me in culture and history ... the self of self-understanding is a gift of understanding itself and of the invitation from the meaning inscribed in the text.[98]

However, Ricoeur has no desire to be pre-modern. We cannot, nor should we, try to escape the lessons of the masters of suspicion, Nietzsche, Marx and Freud. Hence 'explanation' is an imperative part of interpretation.[99] However explanation alone is inadequate: "to smash the idols is also to let symbols speak."[100] An effect of Cartesian epistemology is that Western civilisation has lost a sensitivity to symbolic language.[101] Secularisation has led to an estrangement from the kerygmatic situation so that we need to move beyond suspicion to recover this sensitivity: "Myth's literal function must be suspended, but its symbolic function must be affirmed."[102] 'Understanding' entails a

---

[96] The range of Ricoeur's work is staggering and it is impossible to do justice to the breadth and development of his thought in this section. S.H. CLARK, *Paul Ricoeur* (London; NY: Routledge, 1990) is a helpful survey of Ricoeur's thought, and I have found J. FODOR, *Christian Hermeneutics. Paul Ricoeur and the Refiguring of Theology* (Oxford: Clarendon, 1995) and K.J. VANHOOZER, *Biblical Narrative in the Philosophy of Paul Ricoeur. A Study in Hermeneutics and Philosophy* (Cambridge: CUP, 1990) helpful in terms of Ricoeur's approach to and significance for biblical hermeneutics.

[97] On this issue see P. RICOEUR, *Hermeneutics and the Human Sciences* (Ed. and trans. J.B. THOMPSON; Cambridge: CUP, 1981) 145-164.

[98] P. RICOEUR, Preface to D. IHDE, *Hermeneutic Phenomenology: The Philosophy of Paul Ricoeur* (Evanston: Northwestern UP, 1971) xv. Note here the phenomenological rootage of Ricoeur's philosophy (cf. L.S. MUDGE, "Paul Ricoeur on Biblical Interpretation," in: P. RICOEUR, *Essays on Biblical Interpretation* [1980] 9-15).

[99] See P. RICOEUR, "The Critique of Religion", in: C.E. REAGAN and D. STEWART (eds.), *The Philosophy of Paul Ricoeur. An Anthology of His Work* (1978) 212-222, for a concise statement of Ricoeur's insistence upon demystification in interpretation.

[100] Ibid., 219.

[101] MUDGE, "Paul Ricoeur on Biblical Interpretation," 4.

[102] Ibid., 8.

willingness to listen with openness to symbols and to indirect language in such a way that we experience being called again.

In his later writings Ricoeur focuses particularly on metaphor and narrative. Unlike conceptual language which reflects already-perceived actualities, metaphors create possible ways of seeing. Ricoeur develops a theory of metaphor in which the basic unit is the sentence and in which metaphor makes new connections through the use of creative imagination. His more innovative and influential contribution emerges in the way he connects metaphor with narrative. For Ricoeur the synthesis of the heterogeneous brings narrative close to metaphor. Narrative orders scattered sequential experiences and events into a coherent structure of human time. This refigured world becomes revelatory and transformative. Narrative constructs a world of the possible.

There is good reason for the positive appropriation of Ricoeur by theologians.[103] Ricoeur's positive stance towards symbol makes him open to religious experience, and although Ricoeur retains a commitment to the autonomy of 'responsible thought',[104] he also wants to secure a fundamental place for religion and theology. Not only has Ricoeur written extensively about literary theoretical and hermeneutical issues[105] but he has specifically focused on biblical interpretation.[106]

Remarkably Ricoeur specifically addresses the issue of a hermeneutic of Scripture as revelation.[107] He recognises that revelation is the first and last word for faith and seeks to develop a hermeneutic of revelation which overcomes the opposition between an authoritative understanding of revelation and an autonomous view of reason. He rightly insists that such a hermeneutic must focus on the originary level of revelation as confession of faith rather than on the derived propositional levels. Scripture contains an ensemble of genres of discourse: prophetic, narrative, prescriptive, wisdom and hymnic. Ricoeur focuses his attention on the 'last' text, i.e. the final form and understands the Bible as a whole as testimony. Testimony generates revelatory discourse and Ricoeur explores just how a revelatory text comes to be. Central to Ricoeur's

---

[103] Fodor and Vanhoozer are two such examples. FODOR, *Christian Hermeneutics*, appropriates Ricoeur's philosophy for the development of an adequate understanding of reference in theological statements. VANHOOZER, *Biblical Narrative in the Philosophy of Paul Ricoeur*, appropriates Ricoeur to explore how biblical narrative functions.

[104] P. RICOEUR, *Essays on Biblical Interpretation* (Philadelphia: Fortress, 1980) 156. Fodor repeatedly refers to Ricoeur's concern to keep theology and philosophy distinct and to preserve the autonomy of philosophy. Frei's insistence upon a theological hermeneutic forms an interesting comparison with Ricoeur. See FODOR, *Christian Hermeneutics*, 258ff.

[105] P. RICOEUR's *Interpretation Theory: Discourse and the Surplus of Meaning* (Texas: Texas Christian UP, 1976) is a concise statement of his theory of interpretation.

[106] Cf. RICOEUR, *Essays on Biblical Interpretation*, and note that his Sarum lectures, *Time and Narrative in the Bible: Toward a Narrative Theology*, have still to be published.

[107] RICOEUR, *Essays on Biblical Interpretation*, 73-118.

notion of Scripture is its capacity to poetically disclose an alternative world and thereby to name God for us:

> Apprehended as a whole, the Bible forms one large living intertext where its constitutive heterogenous elements are allowed to work on one another, simultaneously displacing their respective meanings but also mutually drawing upon their overall dynamism. These various modes of biblical discourse ... are not merely juxtaposed with the result that the meaning of the Bible is cumulative ... Rather, a veritable augmentation of meaning occurs by virtue of these intertextual dynamics.[108]

In OT study Ricoeur's approach has been explored in relation to Job, and especially Job 38.[109] Clearly Ricoeur's metacritical hermeneutic phenomenology is of great significance for biblical hermeneutics, as theologians and biblical scholars are starting to realise. Not only has Ricoeur addressed virtually every major theoretical issue in literary criticism, but his irenic approach mediates the interests of Gadamer and Habermas, and possibly redirects hermeneutics away from Derridean extremes.[110] Ricoeur shares a central ontological concern with Gadamer but his hermeneutics is focused on the written text and contains a clearer critical moment.

1.3.8 Socio-critical Hermeneutics: Habermas

Habermas has used Gadamer's understanding of the hermeneutic process to clarify the conditions of social scientific knowledge. In opposition to positivism in the social sciences Habermas used Gadamer to stress that it is not possible to create a neutral language since all understanding is historically situated. And in opposition to Wittgensteinian influence in the social sciences Habermas could invoke the Gadamerian understanding of translation as the resaying of the same thing in *one's own* language to deny the view that one could only really understand a language game if one was resocialised within it. However Habermas has strongly criticised Gadamer's understanding of hermeneutics as a fusion of horizons leading to consensus because, in Habermas' view, it fails to take account of the possibility of systematic distortion in the communication process.[111] This

---

[108] FODOR, *Christian Hermeneutics*, 252.

[109] See J.D. CROSSAN (ed.), *Semeia 19. The Book of Job and Ricoeur's Hermeneutics* (Chicago: Scholars Press, 1981).

[110] On the relationship between Gadamer, Habermas and Ricoeur see CLARK, *Paul Ricoeur*, 110-115. Clark suggests that Ricoeur's provision of a *modus vivendi* with structuralism may indicate that Anglo-American literary theory has been unhelpfully distracted from the main issues by the French intellectual debate centred on post-structuralism (ibid., 110).

[111] W. JEANROND, *Text and Interpretation as Categories of Theological Thinking* (Dublin: Gill and Macmillan, 1988) 8-37, focuses on this issue in relation to textual interpretation time and again. NORRIS, *Spinoza and the Origins of Modern Critical Theory*, 201, says of Gadamer's hermeneutic that "this version of the hermeneutic paradigm ends up in a prison-house of its own elaborate devising where there is no longer any role for the values of truth and falsehood, since everything is

has led to an ongoing debate between Habermas and Gadamer which has highlighted the meta-critical (or lack thereof) dimension of Gadamer's hermeneutic. Habermas is deeply concerned that our understanding of 'understanding' be able to account for the complexity and deeply entrenched nature of ideologies. Habermas describes Gadamer's approach as a linguistic idealism which needs a reference system outside of itself to analyse systems of power and domination in society. Habermas uses the analogy of psychoanalytic theory to show how such a reference system would work in relation to the hermeneutic process.

Gadamer denies that one can escape the hermeneutical process in this way and stresses that Habermas' account of the rational structure of communication is itself traditioned.[112] Habermas acknowledges this but maintains that this does not necessarily imply that a universalistic concept of rationality is fictitious. Indeed Habermas suggests that Gadamer overemphasises what 'we' can learn from 'the author' in the process of understanding; this needs to be balanced by a sense of what the author could learn from 'us.'

Habermas' response to his critics has been his project of universal pragmatics in which he seeks to establish that the possibility of ideal speech is implied in the structure of language. Any act of raising validity claims implies the possibility of unrestrained communication so that the communicative practice of everyday life assumes the possibility of discourse in which speakers examine arguments in idealised conditions. In appealing to reasons speakers assume that their claims could be substantiated through rational discourse alone. Thus communication in general points to something like Habermas' ideal-speech situation.

In terms of the debate about modernity Habermas has reacted strongly to the post-modern notion of its end, proposing instead that we think of modernity as an unfinished project.[113] Modernity is in crisis but the answer is to get it back on track, not to abandon it. Habermas acknowledges the problem of logocentrism and foundationalist understandings of rationality but still argues that politically a privileging of rationality is indispensable. Problems have developed in modernity because theoretical, practical and aesthetic reason have become separated from each other, and capitalist modernisation has resulted in theoretical reason dominating the other two modes. The structures of language itself offer a way out

---

decided by preemptive appeal to beliefs that hold good for us (or our own 'interpretive community'), and which therefore operate to screen out any evidence that doesn't fit in with the prevalent consensus-view." Norris describes this type of approach as "the hermeneutic hall of mirrors" (ibid., 230). THISELTON, *The Two Horizons*, 326, is more optimistic that Gadamer's hermeneutic has the resources for the maintenance of critical distance in interpretation.

[112] See WARNKE, *Gadamer*, 107-138, for a summary of the debate between Gadamer and Habermas.

[113] See J. HABERMAS, *The Philosophical Discourse of Modernity* (Cambridge: Polity, 1987) and R.J. BERNSTEIN (ed.), *Habermas and Modernity* (Cambridge: Polity, 1985).

of this impasse. Habermas elaborates on this with his philosophy of intersubjectivity revolving around communication and consensus. "Progress comes about by untiring attempts to achieve an ever more enlightened consensus on the basis of reasoned debate, not by way of a permanent crisis that refuses to resolve itself."[114]

Within theology and biblical studies Habermas' work has been appropriated in a variety of ways. It is particularly relevant to those approaches to the text which seek to get beneath its surface-function in order to expose its role as an instrument of power, domination or social manipulation. Habermas' type of hermeneutic is distinct from the pragmatism of Rorty in that it seeks to establish a metacritical or universal dimension distinct from the texts or traditions in question, on the basis of which their power functions can be exposed. Thus while it shares in the post-modern critique of positivism it does not abandon the search for universals.

1.3.9 Socio-pragmatic Hermeneutics: Rorty

Rorty uses Gadamer to support his project of overcoming what he sees as the false distinctions between all forms of knowledge, between natural and human sciences and also between these and creative enterprises in general.[115] The value of hermeneutics, according to this view, is that it shows that all knowledge is traditioned and that the idea of the accurate *representation* of reality that underlies the Western concern with epistemology is a myth. All forms of knowledge are closer to making than to finding and have this in common with creative enterprises in general. Consequently the legitimation obsession of Western epistemology is irrelevant and wedded to an outmoded metaphysic.

According to Rorty we ought not to think of science as progressing towards a more accurate description of reality as it is; different scientific paradigms are better thought of as ways of coping. Here Rorty stresses Gadamer's notion of *Wirkungsgeschichte*, whereas Habermas and Apel stress the dialogical element in Gadamer's hermeneutic.[116] The idea of ever-interacting history appears to fit with Rorty's pragmatism in which one is not interested so much in what happened in history or what is out there but what we can use for our own purposes.[117] In place

---

114 H. BERTENS, *The Idea of the Postmodern* (London; NY: Routledge, 1995) 117.

115 See WARNKE, *Gadamer*, 156-166. Warnke's chapter five is a useful critique of Rorty's appropriation of Gadamer. See also C. NORRIS, *Contest of Faculties. Philosophy and Theory After Deconstruction* (London; NY: Methuen, 1985).

116 See K.-O. Apel's essay in MUELLER-VOLLMER (ed.), *The Hermeneutics Reader*, esp. 333-335.

117 Comparing Rorty with Hayden White, K. JENKINS, *On 'What is History?' From Carr and Elton to Rorty and White* (London: Routledge, 1995) 132, says that "Like Rorty, White has no time for the idea that we know what history really is, therefore freeing it up to be whatever we want it to be, a history that, for White, is useful for his own notion of utopia. This is not to say – yet again –

of the epistemological concerns of the Western tradition Rorty proposes the goal of 'edification.' He sees this as the equivalent of Gadamer's *Bildung*. Rather than trying to justify our beliefs we should foster conversations in which we are exposed to and can explore other options and thus find better ways of coping.

Rorty denies that his approach is relativistic or irrational. He openly acknowledges that it cannot be philosophically legitimated but insists that its merits become clear from its practical advantages. We cannot escape being traditioned; we can only defend our commitments by continuing to think and explain them as important to have until shown otherwise. Rorty thus develops Gadamer's notion that there can be no determinate criteria of interpretation along thoroughly pragmatic lines. For Rorty hermeneutics is not a way of knowing but a way of coping.

Similarly Rorty has expounded a pragmatic version of postmodernity, which Bertens describes as fitting between Lyotard and Habermas.[118] What is required is not a new quest for legitimation but a detheoreticized sense of community. From such a position one could accept Habermas' privileging of undistorted communication without needing to ground it in a theory of communicative competence. Thus for Rorty postmodern bourgeois liberalism is "the Hegelian attempt to defend the institutions and practices of the rich North Atlantic democracies without using [the traditional Kantian] buttresses".[119]

For such postmodern liberalism morality is stripped of its transcendent grounding and becomes equivalent to loyalty to a society. Rational behaviour is simply behaviour which conforms to that of other members of a society. This implies a modest understanding of the self as a network of beliefs and desires with nothing behind it and the necessity of an ungrounded communitarian solidarity. As Rorty explains, liberals disown cruelty, but liberal ironists (i.e. like himself), while they too disown cruelty have no answer to the reason for not being cruel! Bertens rightly critiques Rorty's pragmatic postmodernism for his easy and imaginary optimism. Rorty's position lacks the political edge that Lyotard seeks to retain and, as Norris has clearly pointed out, Rorty's position easily becomes a buttress for the political right.[120]

1.4 Conclusion

This survey alerts us to the complex factors that have shaped the discipline of hermeneutics and the diversity of approaches that have developed. Issues like

---

that the actuality of the past did not exist exactly as it did, but it does mean that White thinks it can be (as it always has been) used as people desire."

[118] BERTENS, *The Idea of the Postmodern*, 141.

[119] R. RORTY, "Postmodernist Bourgeois Liberalism," *Journal of Philosophy* 80/10 (1983) 584-585.

[120] C. NORRIS, *What's Wrong with Postmodernism?* (London: Harvester Wheatsheaf, 1990) 1-48.

one's view of reason and the human person, one's view of history and tradition, one's philosophy of language, one's understanding of religion – these all influence the shape of the hermeneutic one adopts. And there is no consensus on any of these issues. In the context of modernity the relative philosophic stability allowed a tacit set of philosophical presuppositions to be easily taken for granted. That is no longer possible today as some of the assumptions of modernity have increasingly been problematised in the context of the postmodern turn.

But this lack of consensus should not detract from the decisive importance of philosophical hermeneutics for biblical interpretation. It is especially clear from our discussion of Spinoza and Kant that philosophical hermeneutics has decisive implications for biblical hermeneutics. Enlightenment rationalism and idealism which exempted religious prejudice from the interpretive process and insisted that Scripture should be read in terms of the modern worldview resulted in very different ways of reading Scripture. Gadamer, however, reverses much of this in his call for prejudice to be appropriated positively as part of the hermeneutic process. And Ricoeur argues that Christians will require a hermeneutic of revelation for the interpretation of Scripture.

Thus there are a plurality of philosophical hermeneutical approaches, and different ones will result in one approaching and interpreting the OT differently. These different hermeneutics have been, and are, active in OT studies so that, if we are to understand different readings of Ecclesiastes and to find a way ahead in the diversity of contemporary OT studies, then we must attend to the different hermeneutical options available and their influence within OT studies.

In chapter two we will review the history of the interpretation of Ecclesiastes and then in chapters three to six we will explore the theories of interpretation that have been at work in this history from the Enlightenment onwards.

CHAPTER 2

HOW ECCLESIASTES HAS BEEN READ:
THE HISTORY OF THE INTERPRETATION OF ECCLESIASTES

Research into the book also shows that it reflects the interpreter's world view. That is why, I think, opinions vary so widely with regard to such basic matters as Qoheleth's optimism or pessimism, his attitude towards women ... and his advocacy of immoral conduct.

(J.L. Crenshaw, *Ecclesiastes* [OTL; London: SCM, 1988] 47)

It is always interesting to see where the 'interpretative sweat' breaks out in dealing with such an iconoclastic book; moreover, the history of interpretation of Ecclesiastes sheds an important light on contemporary exegesis.

(C.A. NEWSOM, "Job and Ecclesiastes," in: J.L. MAYS, D.L. PETERSEN, and K.H. RICHARDS [eds.], *Old Testament Interpretation. Past, Present, and Future* [1995] 191)

2.1 Introduction

Just as an academic reading of Ecclesiastes cannot ignore today's hermeneutical context, so too awareness of the tradition of approximately 2300 years of readings of Ecclesiastes is vital. In all sorts of ways the post-Enlightenment period represents *the* watershed in the interpretation of Ecclesiastes, and its historical critical fruit presses in upon the reader of Ecclesiastes as the immediate and weighty scholarly context in which to read the text. Nevertheless there are continuities in the interpretation of Ecclesiastes between pre-critical and critical readings,[1] and since the progressive relativising and questioning of modernity[2] in the context of the post-modern turn, there are signs of a re-appropriation of pre-critical readings of Ecclesiastes, albeit in a post-critical mode.[3]

In this chapter we examine the dominant ways in which Ecclesiastes has been read during the past 2300 years. A vast amount of literature has emerged on

---

[1] Cf. R.E. MURPHY, "Qoheleth Interpreted: The Bearing of the Past on the Present," *VT* 32 (1982) 331-337.

[2] I use 'modernity' to refer to the Enlightenment legacy in the West. See ch. 3 for a full discussion.

[3] B.S. CHILDS, *Introduction to the Old Testament as Scripture* (Philadelphia: Fortress, 1979) and K.J. DELL, "Ecclesiastes as Wisdom," *VT* XLIV/3 (1993) 301-329, are good examples of this post-critical reassessment.

Ecclesiastes and it is not possible to review this history in detail. Our concern is to map out the main contours of the history of the interpretation of Ecclesiastes.[4] Although certain links with the hermeneutic history described in chapter one will be obvious, our intent at this stage is not to trace such links. That is the concern of the rest of this investigation.

2.2 Pre-critical Interpretation of Ecclesiastes

2.2.1 Inter-testamental Interpretations[5]

Ecclesiasticus (approximately 180 BC) and the Wisdom of Solomon[6] are both wisdom texts and chronologically fairly close to Ecclesiastes. Their relationship to Ecclesiastes has been much discussed[7] but according to Murphy there is no serious sign of dependency between Ecclesiasticus and Ecclesiastes,[8] and although the Wisdom of Solomon is often seen as anti-Ecclesiastes "[t]he general run of claims and counter-claims has the appearance of being more impressionistic than substantive."[9] Holm-Nielsen seeks access to early interpretations of Ecclesiastes through analysing the LXX and the Peshitta.[10] However neither these versions nor the Qumran fragments[11] yield much in terms of how Ecclesiastes was read at this early stage.[12]

---

[4]   Note that C.D. GINSBURG, *The Song of Songs and Coheleth* (NY: KTAV, 1970) has written a thorough overview of Jewish and Christian interpretation of Ecclesiastes up to 1860, which I have regularly drawn on in this chapter. In chs. 3, 4, 5 and 6 of this thesis we focus in more detail upon readings of Ecclesiastes from 1860 onwards.

[5]   I have not included a section on the interpretation of Ecclesiastes in the biblical canon because in the OT the relationship is one of Ecclesiastes 'reading' other OT material and not vice versa, assuming that Ecclesiastes' origin is around the third century BC. As regards the NT there are no unequivocal references to Ecclesiastes.

[6]   According to L.G. PERDUE, *Wisdom and Creation. The Theology of Wisdom Literature* (Nashville: Abingdon, 1994) 291, the author probably lived in Alexandria as early as the first century. See B. WITHERINGTON, III, *Jesus the Sage. The Pilgrimage of Wisdom* (Edinburgh: T&T Clark, 1994) 100-103, for a brief discussion of the background.

[7]   Cf. R.E. MURPHY, *Ecclesiastes* (WBC; Texas: Word, 1992) xlv-xlviii.

[8]   Ibid., xlvi.

[9]   Ibid., xlvii; cf. J.L. CRENSHAW, "Ecclesiastes, Book of," in: D.N. FREEDMAN (ed.), *ABD* Vol. II (1992) 278.

[10]   S. HOLM-NIELSEN, "The Book of Ecclesiastes and the Interpretation of It in Jewish and Christian Theology," *Annual of the Swedish Theological Institute* 10 (1976) 38-96.

[11]   See J. MUILENBURG, "A Qoheleth Scroll from Qumran," *BASOR* 135 (1954) 20-28.

[12]   For a useful, brief discussion of these early texts and versions see MURPHY, *Ecclesiastes*, xxiv-xxv.

2.2.2 Pre-critical Readings of Ecclesiastes

Murphy argues that because of common presuppositions of exegesis there is a real homogeneity in the history of interpretation of Ecclesiastes.[13] This is certainly true of the pre-critical era. Murphy identifies three such common assumptions: Solomonic authorship, the interpretation of הבל הבלים against the perspective of immortality in the next life and the recognition of tensions within the book. The assumption and foregrounding of the immortality of the soul is more dominant in Christian than in Jewish interpretation of Ecclesiastes, where the stress is rather on obedience to God and the blessings of the afterlife.[14] However in both cases this difference in nuance alerts us to a deeper assumption which they share, namely their recognition of Ecclesiastes as Scripture. This is a powerful assumption which dominates the interpretation of Ecclesiastes up until the end of the nineteenth century. As regards interpretative method Jewish and Christian exegetes use both literal and allegorical interpretative approaches, and of course mixtures of both.

2.2.2.1 Pre-critical Jewish Readings of Ecclesiastes[15]

That the literal sense was not neglected by the Rabbis is indicated by the well known Rabbinic disputes as to whether or not Ecclesiastes "pollutes the hands" and whether or not it should be "stored away."[16] This controversy about the divine inspiration of Ecclesiastes centred around its secular character, the great difficulty of harmonising its contradictions,[17] and the passages with heretical tendencies like 1:3 and 11:9.[18] The Mishnah reports the difference on Ecclesiastes between the Pharisaic schools. Beth Shammai maintained that Ecclesiastes does not make the hands unclean but Beth Hillel the reverse. These two groups were the disciples of the two great Pharisaic teachers who taught up to about 10 AD. Their disciples were active throughout the first and into the second century, although after the destruction of the temple in 70 AD, the house

---

[13] MURPHY, "Qoheleth Interpreted".

[14] Cf. MURPHY, *Ecclesiastes*, liv, where he argues that the Rabbis reinterpreted Ecclesiastes in the light of the Torah whereas Christians reinterpreted it in the light of their beliefs. With its strong emphasis on creation the OT and Jewish tradition were less amenable to the influence of Greek dualism, which strongly influenced Christianity at an early stage.

[15] The pre-critical history of the interpretation of Ecclesiastes is thoroughly investigated by GINSBURG, *The Song of Songs and Coheleth*, on whom I am dependant for much that follows.

[16] See R. BECKWITH, *The Old Testament Canon of the New Testament Church* (London: SPCK, 1985) 274-337, for a thorough discussion of the early disputes over Ecclesiastes' canonicity.

[17] The Talmud mentions the conflicts between Ecclesiastes 7:3 and 2:2 and between 8:15 and 2:2 (Bab. Shabbath 30b). BECKWITH, *The Old Testament Canon*, 284-287, rightly points out that the rabbis were experts at Scriptural harmonisation so that their problems with Ecclesiastes meant that they found its contradictions especially difficult to harmonise.

[18] These verses are instanced in the Peskita of Rab Kahana 68b; Leviticus Rabbah 28.1.

of Hillel gained the upper hand. The origin of this particular dispute is uncertain[19] but the rabbinic debate about the inspiration of Ecclesiastes indicates the tendency to read it literally in the period of intense exegetical activity in the second century BC to the third century AD.

However, from Jerome's commentary it is evident that by the fourth century the Jews largely allegorised Ecclesiastes.[20] The allegorical and spiritual approach dominated Jewish reading of Ecclesiastes in the following centuries, as is evident from the Talmud and the Chaldee paraphrase; the latter was the first entire commentary on this book. In it, for example, the *carpe diem* passage in 2:24 is explained as the gathering of strength for the service of God.

A breakthrough for literal interpretation came with Rashbam (1085-1155). He interprets according to the principle that the text has only one, single meaning. Rashbam displays great sensitivity to the literary nature of Ecclesiastes[21] and was the first to realise that Qoheleth was set within a framework; 1:1-2 and the last seven verses were written by those who edited the book.[22] Rashbam locates the essence of the argument of Ecclesiastes in 1:2-11. Ecclesiastes here contrasts the transience of human life with the permanence of nature, thus showing the latter's advantage. None of the experiments in Ecclesiastes are successful in dispelling this melancholy; the only adequate response is to live in conformity to traditional values, to enjoy life calmly while resigned to providence. Present mysteries will be rectified in the future life.

In the following centuries as literal interpretation progressed the sceptical passages in Ecclesiastes attracted closer attention from Jewish exegetes. In the thirteenth century the Zohar argued that in Ecclesiastes Solomon quotes ignorant unbelievers in order to expose their folly. However, this foregrounding of the sceptical passages in Ecclesiastes also drew forth an allegorical and spiritualising response, particularly evident in the Kabbalistic interpretation of Loanz (1631) and Landsberger (1724). Loanz defends the retention of Ecclesiastes in the canon by proposing a spiritualistic interpretation of it. In the introduction to his commentary he writes,

> Now, why the sages did not burn it, but intended to hide the book, is because Solomon was no infidel; on the contrary, if his words are properly examined, it will be seen that they are perfectly true, and becoming such a wise man as he was. That an empty-headed man may shelter himself under the literal meaning

---

[19] See BECKWITH, *The Old Testament Canon*, 297-302.

[20] GINSBURG, *The Song of Songs and Coheleth*, 34.

[21] See S. JAPHET and R.B. SALTERS (eds.), *The Commentary of R. Samuel Ben Meir Rashbam on Qoheleth* (Jerusalem: Magnes; Leiden: Brill, 1985).

[22] See ibid., 34ff. They point out that R. GORDIS, *Koheleth the Man and His World: A Study of Ecclesiastes* (NY: Schoken, 1968) 349, attributes the recognition of this framework to Döderlein, but that it is Rashbam who first reached this conclusion.

of the words, is no reason why the wise men should have burned a book of such sublime sentiments.[23]

Loanz argues, for example, that the reference to rejoicing in one's youth is to be understood as referring to the mind, which reaches its highest stage by studying the law.

In the tradition of Rashbam Herzfeld (1838) strongly reasserted the literal interpretation of Ecclesiastes. Herzfeld argues that Qoheleth seeks to show the universal vanity of life and thereby to comfort the Israelites in their experience of life as vain. It is a sign of the developing ethos of biblical criticism that seventeen years later in 1855 Herzfeld felt free to explore the tradition of upholding the Solomonic authorship of Ecclesiastes. Herzfeld argues that Solomon could not be the author of Ecclesiastes and that it was written shortly before the era of Alexander the Great.[24]

By the end of the nineteenth century those assumptions common to pre-critical Jewish reading of Ecclesiastes were beginning to unravel. Rosenthal in his work on Qoheleth published in 1858 still maintains Solomonic authorship. Solomon, in his view, wrote the book to demonstrate that wisdom is only useful when combined with the fear of God and the keeping of his commands. By contrast in 1860 Professor Luzzatto developed a strikingly contemporary view of Ecclesiastes. In his view it denies the immortality of the soul and recommends carnal pleasure as all that is left. It was written in the post-exilic period by one Coheleth who ascribed it to Solomon in order to give it authority. Contemporary sages recognised this forgery, deleted 'Solomon', inserted 'Coheleth' and left in 'son of David, king in Jerusalem,' knowing that such a juxtaposition would ensure recognition of the book for what is was. Later sages never knew this and thinking it to be Solomonic, they added verses to make it more orthodox.

2.2.2.2 Pre-critical Christian Readings[25]

Ecclesiastes is passed over in silence in the first, second and early part of the third centuries AD by the early Christian writers.[26] Gregory Thaumaturgus' (210-

---

[23] Quoted in GINSBURG, *The Song of Songs and Coheleth*, 76.

[24] See ibid., 94-96, for Herzfeld's reasons.

[25] See ibid., 99-243.

[26] Because of the relative silence on Ecclesiastes in the first two centuries, it is harder to determine whether, as with the interpretation of the Proverbs 31 woman, there is first of all a literal interpretation, later replaced by an allegorical one. Commenting on the interpretation of Proverbs 31 A. WOLTERS, *The Song of the Valiant Woman (Prov 31:10-31): A Pattern in the History of Interpretation (To 1600)* (Unpublished MA thesis: McMaster University, 1987) 58, says, "it is remarkable how similar the patterns are in both the Jewish and Christian traditions. Both began with a literal understanding, both moved to a variety of allegorical interpretations, and both developed a standard allegorical reading in the Middle Ages which crowded out the others. For the Jews the Valiant Woman represented the Torah; for the Christians she symbolized the Church. For more than a thousand years, in both traditions, there was an overwhelming consensus that the Valiant Woman

270) *A Metaphrase of the Book of Ecclesiastes* is the earliest extant Christian work on Ecclesiastes. In his view Solomon speaks to the whole Church of God and shows them the vanity of servitude to transient human things in order to lead them to contemplation of heavenly things. In his comments Gregory recognises the unorthodox sayings in Ecclesiastes but seeks to defuse them. In his comments on chapter one he presents Solomon as reflecting on a time when he thought that he was an expert on the nature of things but that he now realises that such pursuits achieve no purpose. In chapter two on the discussion of pleasure Gregory presents Solomon as coming to the orthodox conclusion that "the perfect good does not consist in eating and drinking, although it is true that it is from God that their sustenance cometh to man ... But the good man who gets wisdom from God, gets also heavenly enjoyment."[27]

The tendency to allegorise the reference to joy and eating is evident in the above quote. However, there is a tension in Gregory's understanding of the *carpe diem* passages in Ecclesiastes. On the one hand they are allegorised to refer to heavenly enjoyment, but on the other they are read as a manifestation of folly. At the same time Gregory recognises that a Christian understanding of creation necessitates a positive approach to eating and drinking. In his paraphrase of chapter five he attempts to reduce this tension: "I am persuaded, therefore, that the greatest good for man is cheerfulness and well-doing, and that this shortlived enjoyment, which alone is possible to us, comes from God only, *if righteousness direct our doings*."[28] Not surprisingly, the epilogue is understood by Gregory as Solomon's apt conclusion to Ecclesiastes.

The affirmation of Solomonic authorship of Ecclesiastes is very early in Christian interpretation. It goes back at least to Origen (185-254)[29] who in the preface to his commentary on the Song of Songs notes that in Proverbs Solomon taught moral science, in Ecclesiastes natural science – by distinguishing the vain from the profitable and essential he counsels us to forsake vanity and cultivate things useful and upright, and in the Song of Songs inspective science in which he instils into the soul the love of heavenly things.

The tradition of Solomonic authorship is affirmed by Jerome whose interpretation dominated the patristic and mediaeval period. The preface to Jerome's commentary informs us that some five years previously he had interpreted Ecclesiastes to one Blesilla in order to "provoke her to contempt of

---

should be understood allegorically. It was this consensus which was challenged by the Reformation." Christians in touch with Jewish discussion would have been aware of literal readings of Ecclesiastes (see 2.2.2.1 above). Theodore of Mopsuestia read Ecclesiastes in a literal way but he lived c. 350-428. On Theodore cf. MURPHY, *Ecclesiastes*, xxiii.

[27] GREGORY THAUMATURGUS, "A Metaphrase of the Book of Ecclesiastes," *The Ante-Nicene Fathers*. Vol. VI (Grand Rapids: Eerdmans, 1978) 10.

[28] Ibid., 11 (italics mine).

[29] ORIGEN, *The Song of Songs. Commentary and Homilies* (Trans. R. Lawson; Maryland: Westminister, 1957) 41.

the world" and thus encourage her to adopt a monastic vocation. In the process Jerome asserts the vanity of every enjoyment under the sun and the necessity of an ascetic life devoted to the service of God. The references to eating and drinking are allegorically interpreted as references to partaking of the sacrament, and inconvenient passages are put into the mouths of sceptics and opponents. Jerome's commentary was widely influential; for example, his equating of eating with the Eucharist is followed by Philastrius (380), Ambrose (333/40 – 397) and Augustine (354 – 430).[30]

Tradition dominated mediaeval interpretation of Scripture and so it is not surprising that allegorical interpretation characterises most mediaeval exegesis of Ecclesiastes.[31] However, just as the early Christians were influenced by secular methods in their reading of Scripture,[32] so too were theologians in the Middle Ages, and towards the end of the Middle Ages this led to a renewed interest in the literal sense. Smalley points out that for theologians in the mediaeval schools the rediscovery of Aristotle's *Politics* led to a renewed interest in politics and ethics,[33] and thus to a fresh examination of the sapiential OT literature which shared these interests.[34] The result was an increased output of commentaries on all the sapiential books in the thirteenth century. The neoplatonic influence mediated by Augustine and Jerome privileged the spiritual reading whereas the influence of the rediscovery of Aristotle favoured the literal reading. Thus, in his postill on Ecclesiastes, Bonaventura (1221-1274) exploits the possibilities in the literal sense that Guerric had opened up as a result of the growing influence of Aristotle.[35] He reads Ecclesiastes as teaching contempt for the world, but makes more use of speculative philosophy to do so. Bonaventura expounds his favourite theme, wisdom as the means to sanctification. He discusses contempt of the world and in an effort to explain how the world can be regarded as vanity compares the world to a wedding ring. The wife must regard the ring as nothing relative to her love for her husband, and our attitude to the world must be the same.

The main difference that the Reformation made to the interpretation of Ecclesiastes, accompanying its insistence on the literal sense as *the* method of interpretation,[36] was its reassessment of Qoheleth's attitude to the earthly,

---

[30] On these three see GINSBURG, *The Song of Songs and Coheleth*, 103-105.

[31] On the interpretation of the Bible in the Middle Ages see G.W.H. LAMPE (ed.), *The Cambridge History of the Bible. Vol. 2. The West from the Fathers to the Reformation* (Cambridge: CUP, 1969) and B. SMALLEY, *The Study of the Bible in the Middle Ages* (3rd ed.; Oxford: Blackwell, 1983).

[32] See ch. 1.2.

[33] SMALLEY, *The Study of the Bible in the Middle Ages*, xxxi.

[34] See ibid., 308-328.

[35] See ibid., 292ff.

[36] Melanchton took the lead in rejection of the allegorical method of interpretation.

material realm. This reassessment is apparent in the first Protestant commentary
on Ecclesiastes by John Brentius (1528). Brentius comments,

> There is nothing better than to be cheerful, and enjoy one's life; to eat, drink,
> and delight in one's employment; ... Some foolish persons, not understanding
> these things, have absurdly taught contempt for and flight from the world, and
> have committed many foolish things themselves; as we read in the lives of the
> Fathers that there were some who even shut themselves up from ever seeing
> the sun ... living above the world is not living out of the world.[37]

The fresh understanding of Ecclesiastes that emerged out of the Reformation
results from a new emphasis upon the text in its original language interpreted
literally, and a strong recovery of the doctrine of creation with a corresponding
stress on the priestly vocation of all believers in all spheres of life. The resulting
reassessment of Qoheleth's attitude to the earthly and material is evident also in
Luther,[38] Melanchton and Piscator (1612). According to Melanchton (1556),
Ecclesiastes "shows us that we are to be submissive in every station of life, and
perform the duties of our calling ... that we should know that to follow our
calling is pleasing to God."[39] Catholic interpretations of Ecclesiastes continued to
stress the contempt for the earthly.[40]

Luther is also significant in his anticipation of the modern rejection of
Solomonic authorship. In contrast to his commentary,[41] in his *Tabletalk* he
maintains that "Solomon himself has not written the book of Ecclesiastes, it was
compiled by Sirach at the time of the Maccabees. ... It is like the Talmud, made
up of many books, which perhaps belonged to the library of King Ptolemy
Euergetes in Egypt."[42]

So as not to be outdone by Protestant commentators J. van de Pineda
produced a volume of 1079 pages on Ecclesiastes in 1620. Although it does not
break new ground in the interpretation of Ecclesiastes and interprets it as
directing our minds away from the earthly to the heavenly, Pineda's volume is a
thorough digest of what the Fathers and others said of each verse.

Although it is only at the end of the nineteenth century that the historical
critical method was resolutely applied to Ecclesiastes, modern biblical criticism
has much earlier roots,[43] and these roots gradually become manifest in readings

---

[37]   GINSBURG, *The Song of Songs and Coheleth*, 112.

[38]   M. LUTHER, *An Exposition of Salomons Booke, Called Ecclesiastes Or the Preacher*
(Aldergate: John Draye, 1573) 11-12, insists concerning Qoheleth's vanity assessment that, "All
this he speaketh not against creatures themselves, but against the heart of man, that abuseth the
creatures to his own hindrance."

[39]   Quoted in GINSBURG, *The Song of Songs and Coheleth*, 113.

[40]   Ibid., 123ff.

[41]   See LUTHER, *An Exposition of Salomons Booke*, 9, where he affirms Solomonic authorship
of Ecclesiastes.

[42]   Quoted by GINSBURG, *The Song of Songs and Coheleth*, 113.

[43]   See ch. 3.

of Ecclesiastes. Grotius (1644) argues that we have in Ecclesiastes a collection of different opinions concerning happiness which the author mixes up with his own arguments before giving his final opinion. Grotius is particularly significant with respect to the authorship of Ecclesiastes. He is the first since Luther to argue against Solomonic authorship: "I believe that the book is not the production of Solomon, but was written in the name of this king, as being led by repentance to do it. For it contains many words which cannot be found except in Ezra, Daniel, and the Chaldee paraphrasts."[44]

After Grotius the view that Solomon was not the author gradually gained ground. In 1751 Michaelis argued that Ecclesiastes was written by a post-exilic prophet who wrote the book in Solomon's name so as to be able to philosophise more tellingly about the vanity of happiness. Similarly Bishop Lowth (1753) maintained that Solomon is 'personated' in Ecclesiastes and that the language of the book is 'low'.[45] Herder (1778) by comparison knew of no book in antiquity which describes the sum of human life more impressively than Ecclesiastes. He defended the interruption theory first advanced by Dean Yeard whereby two voices are distinguished in Ecclesiastes, the enquirer and the teacher. Döderlein (1784), Jahn (1793), Schmidt (1794) and Ewald (1826, 1837) also rejected Solomonic authorship of Ecclesiastes.

In 1838 an intriguing article on "The Philosophy of Ecclesiastes" by Nordheimer appeared in the *American Biblical Repository*.[46] Nordheimer anticipates Michael Fox's[47] recognition of the need to examine Qoheleth's epistemology. Nordheimer argues that Ecclesiastes is a philosophic didactic poem which seeks to determine the duties of man. Ecclesiastes entails a warning against philosophical investigation of human relations without first examining the limits and powers of the human mind. If the epistemological limitations of human reason are not observed at the outset such an investigation is liable to lead one to scepticism.

> To set bounds to this sinful endeavour, and to warn mankind of the danger attendant upon it, appear to have been the principal aim of the author of this book. ... he adopted ... the Socratic, or sceptical method of induction. The main feature of this method consists in a suspension of the final decision until the truth has been rendered perfectly evident, and the writer has it in his power to make assertions that shall be incontrovertible; hence it is the most perfect mode of attaining absolute certainty that can be conceived. In this manner it is that the author of Ecclesiastes institutes his examination into the powers of the human mind, which he carries to such fearful lengths that reason itself

---

[44] Quoted in GINSBURG, *The Song of Songs and Coheleth*, 146.

[45] Cf. ibid., 178.

[46] I. NORDHEIMER, "The Philosophy of Ecclesiastes," *American Biblical Repository* XII (1838) 197-219.

[47] See chs. 5, 6 for a discussion of Fox's approach to Ecclesiastes. In drawing this analogy with Nordheimer I am thinking in particular of Fox's analysis of Qoheleth's empiricism.

threatens to totter from its throne. All this is done in order to test its strength, and to bound its sphere of action accordingly.[48]

The father of modern OT criticism, de Wette, published his mature views of Ecclesiastes in 1844 in the final edition of his introduction to the OT. De Wette maintains that Qoheleth asserts the vanity of all things and the reality of enjoyment alone. Qoheleth gives no hope of a future life and his life-view inclines towards fatalism, scepticism and epicureanism. Although far more positive in his assessment of the message of Ecclesiastes, Hengstenberg was the first to deny Solomonic authorship of Ecclesiastes in an orthodox English encyclopaedia.[49] In his commentary on Ecclesiastes Hengstenberg argues that the aim of Ecclesiastes is to encourage the fear of God in the difficult circumstances of its hearers.[50]

As an example of the state of Ecclesiastes-scholarship prior to the application of the historical critical approach at the end of the nineteenth century we will examine Plumptre's commentary on Ecclesiastes. Plumptre finds Ecclesiastes enigmatic, yet fascinating.[51] He regards it as remarkably and providentially relevant to his day "to meet the special tendencies of modern philosophical thought, and that the problems of life which it discusses are those with which our own daily experience brings us into contact."[52]

Plumptre has an extensive discussion of Solomonic authorship but concludes that the evidence is against it.[53] He takes 'Qoheleth' to mean 'debater', and suggests that Qoheleth was a debater in the Museum at Alexandria. He dates the book between 240 and 181 BC. Plumptre describes Ecclesiastes as "autobiographical confession"[54] and devotes twenty pages to a 'biography' of Qoheleth. He suggests *inter alia* that

> [t]he wealth of his parents had attracted a knot of so-called devout persons round them, and his mother had come under their influence, and in proportion as she did so, failed to gain any hold on her son's heart, and left no memory of a true pattern of womanhood for him to reverence and love.[55]

The hypocritical religion of Qoheleth's wealthy parents and their friends was disillusioning for him. As he entered his adult years Qoheleth travelled to

---

[48] NORDHEIMER, "The Philosophy of Ecclesiastes," 207.

[49] In an 1845 article on Ecclesiastes in Kitto's Cyclopaedia. E.W. HENGSTENBERG, *Commentary on Ecclesiastes, With Other Treaties* (Edinburgh: T&T Clark, 1860) 6ff, insists that the picture of Qoheleth and Israel in Ecclesiastes could only come from the time when the Persians had dominion over Israel. He discerns strong affinities between Ecclesiastes and Malachi.

[50] HENGSTENBERG, *Commentary on Ecclesiastes*.

[51] E.H. PLUMPTRE, *Ecclesiastes* (The Cambridge Bible for Schools; Cambridge: CUP, 1881) 7.

[52] Ibid., 11.

[53] Ibid., 19-34.

[54] Ibid., 35.

[55] Ibid., 37.

Alexandria, where he was exposed to the royal court. He lived an extravagant life and indulged in reckless sensuality. Qoheleth experienced one great love, but had been terribly disillusioned by this woman; she had proved to be 'more bitter than death.' Deeply effected by this broken relationship he sought meaning in Greek philosophy, where for a time he found solace. However the dark days returned and finally he reawakened to the fear of God with the help of a male friend who was a great help to him at this and other times.

Ecclesiastes is thus in Plumptre's view an intensely personal book whose main purpose is to warn those in quest of the chief good against the quicksands in which Qoheleth nearly sank. Qoheleth desires to deepen the fear of God in which he at last found the anchor of his soul in his readers. Plumptre discusses the relationship between Ecclesiastes and Ecclesiasticus and the Wisdom of Solomon,[56] and has sections on Jewish and patristic interpretations of Ecclesiastes,[57] plus an analysis of the text.[58] At the conclusion of the commentary are three appendices: the first on Shakespeare and Koheleth, the second on Tennyson and Koheleth, and the third on a Persian Koheleth of the twelfth century!

Although Plumptre denies Solomonic authorship[59] and in this sense agrees with the modern critical consensus, in most ways his work remains within the pre-critical framework. The type of speculative biographical analysis of Qoheleth he develops is rare in twentieth century works,[60] and his introduction addresses none of the source, form and tradition critical questions that are common place in twentieth century commentaries. In line with the pre-critical tradition Plumptre's reading is an orthodox one theologically in which the epilogue provides the key to the message of the book and resolves the tensions in the text. Commenting on the epilogue (12:13-14) Plumptre writes,

> This is what the Teacher who, as it were, edits the book, presents to his disciples as its sum and substance, and he was not wrong in doing so. In this the **Debater** himself had rested after his many wanderings of thought ... From the standpoint of the writer of the epilogue it was shown that the teaching of Ecclesiastes was not inconsistent with the faith of Israel ... From our standpoint we may say that it was shown not less convincingly that the book, like all true records of the search after Truth, led men through the labyrinthine windings of doubt to the goal of duty, through the waves and winds of conflicting opinions to the unshaken rock of the Eternal Commandment.[61]

---

[56] Ibid., 56-74.

[57] Ibid., 75-97.

[58] Ibid., 97-101.

[59] Note however that he feels the need to devote 15 pages to the issue in his relatively small commentary.

[60] F. ZIMMERMAN, *The Inner World of Qoheleth* (NY: KTAV, 1973) is a notable but eccentric exception.

[61] PLUMPTRE, *Ecclesiastes*, 229, 230.

2.3 Critical Readings of Ecclesiastes

In the second half of the nineteenth century the critical reading of Ecclesiastes gathered momentum, but it was only with the source-critical commentaries of Siegfried,[62] Laue,[63] McNeile,[64] Podechard[65] and Barton[66] that historical critical reading of Ecclesiastes emerged in the way that it had done for the Pentateuch during the nineteenth century.[67] By the end of the nineteenth century pentateuchal criticism had already accrued the contributions of de Wette and Wellhausen. Driver published his *An Introduction to the Literature of the Old Testament* in 1898. A comparison of his extensive treatment of the source criticism of the Pentateuch with his treatment of Ecclesiastes is instructive. The source criticism of Ecclesiastes is still in its infancy.[68]

There were reasons for this relative lack of interest in Ecclesiastes and wisdom literature in general. Wellhausen paid almost no attention to wisdom literature since he regarded it as late and secondary. He was especially concerned with the history of Israel's religious institutions and there was no clear indication how wisdom was related to these. Duhm also affirmed the secondary status of wisdom; wise men were heirs of the prophets because they took the great moral principles of justice and applied them to everyday life.[69]

Two developments challenged the belief in the secondary and late emergence of wisdom. Firstly there was the application of form criticism to wisdom by Gunkel. The forms and character of wisdom teaching were discerned to be so distinctive that they could not be derived from prophecy or law. They must have emanated from a special class of wise men who were concerned with education and man's general progress and advancement in life.[70] Form criticism has been particularly important in identifying wisdom as a specific genre of literature within the OT. This is taken for granted nowadays, but it was really

---

[62] C. SIEGFRIED, *Prediger und Hoheslied* (HAT; Göttingen: Vandenhoeck and Ruprecht, 1898).

[63] P. LAUE, *Das Buch Koh. und die Interpretationshypothese Siegfrieds* (Wittenberg, 1900).

[64] A.H. MCNEILE, *An Introduction to Ecclesiastes With Notes and Appendices* (Cambridge: CUP, 1904).

[65] E. PODECHARD, *L'Ecclésiaste* (Paris: Gabalda, 1912).

[66] G.A. BARTON, *A Critical and Exegetical Commentary on the Book of Ecclesiastes* (ICC; Edinburgh: T&T Clark, 1912).

[67] Cf. for example the development of the historical critical approach to Deuteronomy in the nineteenth century. See C.G. BARTHOLOMEW, *The Composition of Deuteronomy: A Critical Analysis of the Approaches of E.W. Nicholson and A.D.H. Mayes* (Unpublished MA thesis: Potchefstroom University, 1992) 13-19.

[68] Cf. S.R. DRIVER, *An Introduction to the Literature of the Old Testament* (Gloucester, Mass.: Peter Smith, 1972) 1-159 and 465-478.

[69] R.E. CLEMENTS, *A Century of Old Testament Study* (Guildford; London: Lutterworth, 1976) 100.

[70] Ibid., 102.

only at the beginning of the twentieth century that wisdom was 'discovered'.[71] The second stimulus was the discovery in 1888 of the Teaching of Amen-em-ope. Erman recognised the original of Proverbs 22:17-23:11 in this text,[72] and this led to a heightening of interest in wisdom literature against its background in the ANE, especially during the years 1924-1936.[73]

However, towards the end of the 1930's this interest waned. OT wisdom literature might have early and international roots but it seemed to have little to contribute to the theology of the OT.[74] Zimmerli had argued that its central concerns were exclusively anthropocentric, and the notion that earlier wisdom had been secular and utilitarian was widely endorsed.[75] Recent decades however have seen a re-awakening of interest in OT wisdom literature. Zimmerli showed that creation was fundamental to OT wisdom[76] and it became increasingly apparent that like ANE wisdom OT wisdom was deeply religious.[77] Von Rad himself came to argue that wisdom is a branch of Yahwism.[78] These developments have led to renewed interest in the ideology of wisdom, its development within the OT and its relationship to other strands of OT thought.[79] Scholars are divided over how to understand wisdom and its relationship to the

---

[71] Cf. J.L. CRENSHAW, "Studies in Ancient Israelite Wisdom: Prolegemonon," in: J.L. CRENSHAW (ed.), *Studies in Ancient Israelite Wisdom* (1976) 3-5. The debate has continued throughout the twentieth century as to what exactly constitutes a wisdom writing in the OT. See R.N. WHYBRAY, *The Intellectual Tradition in the Old Testament* (BZAW 135; NY; Berlin: de Gruyter, 1974); J.L. CRENSHAW, "Method in Determining Wisdom Influence upon 'Historical' Literature," *JBL* 88 (1969) 129-142; and idem, "Studies in Ancient Israelite Wisdom," 3-5.

[72] See H. Graf REVENTLOW, *Problems of Old Testament Theology in the Twentieth Century* (London: SCM, 1985) 172-173, for bibliographic references.

[73] Cf. CRENSHAW, "Studies in Ancient Israelite Wisdom," 5-6.

[74] Or at least to the theological interests of contemporary OT scholars. Especially through von Rad's influence the doctrine of creation which is fundamental to wisdom literature was made subsidiary to redemption. Only in the last few decades has there been a renaissance of interest in creation in the OT (cf. REVENTLOW, *Problems of Old Testament Theology*, 134-186).

[75] W. ZIMMERLI, "Concerning the Structure of Old Testament Wisdom," in: J.L. CRENSHAW (ed.), *Studies in Ancient Israelite Wisdom* (1976) 175-207 (originally published in 1933); cf. G.E. WRIGHT, *God Who Acts. Biblical Theology as Recital* (SBT 8; London: SCM, 1952) 102-105; and W. MCKANE, *Prophets and Wise Men* (SBT 44; London: SCM, 1965) 48ff.

[76] W. ZIMMERLI, "The Place and Limit of Wisdom In the Framework of Old Testament Theology," *SJT* 17 (1964) 146-158.

[77] See REVENTLOW, *Problems of Old Testament Theology*, 174-178.

[78] G. VON RAD, *Wisdom in Israel* (London: SCM, 1972).

[79] REVENTLOW, *Problems of Old Testament Theology*, 181, suggests that "[i]t is at this point, i.e. over the question of the relationship between the various areas of Old Testament thought, that the discussion will have to be continued: in other words, between the conception of order which is characteristic of wisdom (and not just wisdom) and the areas governed by the tradition of salvation history."

rest of the OT, but at the end of the twentieth century it is firmly on OT and theological agendas.[80]

The interpretation of Ecclesiastes in the twentieth century needs to be seen against this background. All the issues that have dominated wisdom study have had their impact on the interpretation of Ecclesiastes. Characteristic methods of historical criticism have been source, form, redaction and tradition criticism. These were applied to Ecclesiastes at the end of the nineteenth and beginning of the twentieth century, and their influence remains strong in the most recent commentaries on Ecclesiastes, albeit in modified form.[81] As we outline the application of these methods to Ecclesiastes we shall note their continuing legacy before going on to note reactions to historical critical readings during this century.

Siegfried pioneered the source critical approach to Ecclesiastes,[82] identifying nine different sources in the book. Within English-speaking circles McNeile and Barton developed more moderate source-critical approaches to Ecclesiastes.[83] As the twentieth century has progressed a radical source critical approach to Ecclesiastes has become rare, and the book has come to be seen more and more as a unity,[84] with the exception of the epilogue, which is almost universally seen as a later addition. The prime legacy of source criticism in the interpretation of Ecclesiastes is this tendency to read the book without the epilogue. By comparison, in almost all pre-critical interpretation of Ecclesiastes the epilogue provides the interpretative key.

Gunkel initiated form critical analysis of wisdom literature,[85] and assessment of the forms used in Ecclesiastes has continued to play a fundamental

---

[80]   A number of overview essays have been published this century which help one to get a feel for the development of wisdom study. See W. BAUMGARTNER, "The Wisdom Literature," in: H.H. ROWLEY (ed.), *The Old Testament and Modern Study* (1951) 210-237, R.B.Y. SCOTT, "The Study of the Wisdom Literature," *Interpretation* 24 (1970) 20-45, CRENSHAW, "Studies in Ancient Israelite Wisdom," J.A. EMERTON, "Wisdom," in: G.W. ANDERSON (ed.), *Tradition and Interpretation* (1979) 214-237, and REVENTLOW, *Problems of Old Testament Theology*, 168-186. Most recently see J. DAY, R.P. GORDON, and H.G.M. WILLIAMSON (eds.), *Wisdom in Ancient Israel. Essays in Honour of J.A. Emerton* (Cambridge: CUP, 1995). Recent monographs on wisdom are those by VON RAD, *Wisdom in Israel*, R.E. CLEMENTS, *Wisdom in Theology* (Carlisle: Paternoster; Grand Rapids: Eerdmans, 1992), PERDUE, *Wisdom and Creation*, and WITHERINGTON, *Jesus the Sage*. For a useful overview of the current issues on the 'wisdom agenda' see R.E. MURPHY, "Wisdom in the Old Testament," in: D.N. FREEDMAN (ed.), *ABD* Vol. VI (1992) 920-931.

[81]   Very little redaction criticism has been done on Ecclesiastes. It has been suggested that Childs' approach is really a redactional one, but see R.E. MURPHY, "The Old Testament as Scripture," *JSOT* 16 (1980) 41, for a contrary view.

[82]   SIEGFRIED, *Prediger und Hoheslied*.

[83]   MCNEILE, *An Introduction to Ecclesiastes*; BARTON, *Ecclesiastes*. Note that the readings of Ecclesiastes in modernity and late modernity are dealt with in detail in the following chapters.

[84]   GORDIS, *Koheleth the Man and His World*, 73, notes the growing recognition of the unity of Ecclesiastes.

[85]   CLEMENTS, *A Century of Old Testament Study*, 101-102.

role in the interpretation of the book.[86] Crenshaw suggests that the dominant literary type in Ecclesiastes is reflection arising from personal observation.[87] He notes that scholars have also drawn attention to mashal, diatribe and royal testament forms, and that Qoheleth also uses autobiographical narrative, example story, anecdote, parable, antithesis and proverb.

Galling developed a form critical interpretation of Ecclesiastes in which he divided Ecclesiastes up into a large number of originally independent sayings.[88] Such an approach clearly militates against reading Ecclesiastes as a strongly unified text. However on the macro level of the form of Ecclesiastes no consensus has been reached as regards its genre and structure,[89] although Wright's New Critical analysis of the structure has convinced a number of scholars.[90] The problem of whether Ecclesiastes is prose or poetry remains, with the majority of scholars treating it as a mixture of both.[91]

The tradition history of Ecclesiastes has been a matter of concern throughout this century.[92] Within the OT wisdom tradition Ecclesiastes has regularly been seen as a negative, sceptical reaction to mainline wisdom as represented by Proverbs.[93] Gese identified Qoheleth with a crisis of wisdom in Israel,[94] but scholars remain divided over the existence and extent of this 'crisis'.[95] To what extent do we have a rigid doctrine of retribution in the OT and to what extent is Ecclesiastes a reaction to this?[96] At the end of this century there is no consensus about the development of the wisdom tradition and how Ecclesiastes fits into that development. Using sociological analysis Brueggemann has suggested that

---

[86] Cf. D. MICHEL, *Qoheleth* (Erträge der Forschung; Darmstadt: Wissenschaftliche Buchgesellschaft, 1988) 76-81; J.L. CRENSHAW, "The Wisdom Literature," in: D.A. KNIGHT and G.M. TUCKER (eds.), *The Hebrew Bible and Its Modern Interpreters* (1985) 377-378; R.E. MURPHY, *Wisdom Literature* (The Forms of the Old Testament Literature XIII; Grand Rapids: Eerdmans, 1981).

[87] CRENSHAW, "Ecclesiastes, Book of," 275.

[88] K. GALLING, "Kohelet-Studien," *ZAW* 50 (1932) 276-299; idem, *Der Prediger* (HAT 18; Tübingen: J.C.B. Mohr, 1940).

[89] A.G. WRIGHT, "The Riddle of the Sphinx: The Structure of the Book of Qoheleth," *CBQ* 30 (1968) 313-334; and A. SCHOORS, "La structure littéraire de Qohéleth," *Orientalia Lovaniensia Periodica* 13 (1982) 91-116; contain useful overviews of the great variety of structures that have been proposed.

[90] Wright's analysis is for example followed by MURPHY, *Ecclesiastes*, xxxii-xli, and is drawn upon by PERDUE, *Wisdom and Creation*, 203ff; cf. MICHEL, *Qoheleth*, 9-45.

[91] Cf. MURPHY, *Ecclesiastes*, xxvi-xxxii.

[92] Cf. MICHEL, *Qoheleth*, 66-75.

[93] Cf. for example BAUMGARTNER, "The Wisdom Literature," 221-227.

[94] H. GESE, "The Crisis of Wisdom in Koheleth," in: J.L. CRENSHAW (ed.), *Theodicy in the OT* (1983) 141-153.

[95] Cf. CRENSHAW, "The Wisdom Literature," 381-382; and MURPHY, "Wisdom in the Old Testament".

[96] Cf. R. VAN LEEUWEN, "Wealth and Poverty: System and Contradiction in Proverbs," *Hebrew Studies* 33 (1992) 25-36.

"Ecclesiastes articulates a conservative ideology that reflects social control and a concern for stability. ... The emancipatory side of wisdom is reflected in the embrace of creation in the Song of Solomon, the ideological dimension is articulated in Ecclesiastes."[97] This view is a development of Brueggemann's discernment of a royal (order) and a liberative trajectory in the OT.[98]

The relationship of OT wisdom to international wisdom has been an issue throughout this century. Ranston, for example, published a monograph in 1925 in which he explored the relationship between Ecclesiastes and the early Greek wisdom literature. He concludes that

> [t]he evidence strongly suggests that Ecclesiastes was not widely or deeply acquainted with the early Greek *literature*, i.e. he had not *read* much of it. ... The conclusion reached is that Koheleth, in his search for suitable proverbs (ix. 9f.), moved for a time in circles where the minds of the people were stored with the wisdom-utterances of the early sages mentioned by Isocrates as the outstanding teachers of practical morality, Theognis being the most important.[99]

Studies of Ecclesiastes continue to concern themselves with Ecclesiastes' relationship to Mesopotamia, Egypt and Greece.[100] During this century the Jewishness of Ecclesiastes has received greater recognition but its relationship to Greek thought in particular continues to be debated.[101]

As regards the message of Ecclesiastes historical critical scholarship differs notably from pre-critical readings in its general rejection of the need to harmonise Qoheleth with theological orthodoxy. This loss of theological constraint has not

---

[97] W. BRUEGGEMANN, "The Social Significance of Solomon as a Patron of Wisdom," in: J.G. GAMMIE and L.G. PERDUE (eds.), *The Sage in Israel and the Ancient Near East* (1990) 129. On the sociological analysis of Ecclesiastes cf. also F. CRÜSEMANN, "The Unchangeable World: The 'Crisis of Wisdom' in Qoheleth," in: W. SCHOTROFF and W. STEGEMANN (eds.), *God of the Lowly* (1984) 57-77.

[98] W. BRUEGGEMANN, "Trajectories in Old Testament Literature and the Sociology of Ancient Israel," *JBL* 98 (1979) 161-185; cf. Middleton's critique of Brueggemann's view of creation order (J.R. MIDDLETON, "Is Creation Theology Inherently Conservative? A Dialogue with Walter Brueggemann," *HTR* 87/3 [1994] 257-277) and Brueggemann's reply (W. BRUEGGEMANN, "Response to J. Richard Middleton," *HTR* 87/3 [1994] 279-289).

[99] H. RANSTON, *Ecclesiastes and Early Greek Wisdom Literature* (London: Epworth, 1925) 149, 150.

[100] Cf. MICHEL, *Qoheleth*, 52-65; MURPHY, *Ecclesiastes*, xli-xlv.

[101] Cf. for example LOHFINK, *Kohelet*, 7-9, who tends to assume the Hellenistic character of Ecclesiastes, with MURPHY, *Ecclesiastes*, xlv, who is far more cautious. Lohfink thinks that Ecclesiastes may have been written between 190 and 180 BC, just before the Macabbean revolt. In this context Judea belonged to the Hellenistic world and Hellenistic ideas were pervasive and competed with the Jewish tradition. "Das Buch Koh kann nur verstanden werden als Versuch, so viel wie möglich von der griechischen Weltdeutung zu gewinnen, ohne dass dabei die israelitische Weisheit doch ihren Eigenstand aufgeben musste" (LOHFINK, *Kohelet*, 9). Lohfink assumes a high degree of Hellenistic influence whereas C.R. HARRISON, *Qoheleth in Social-Historical Perspective* (Ann Arbor, Michigan: University Microfilms, 1991), argues that it was minimal in Judea. Harrison, however, argues that Ptolemaic economic policy was deeply effecting Judean society.

however produced agreement about the message of Ecclesiastes, as for example, the huge variety of proposals about how to translate הבל indicate.[102] Some like Crenshaw regard Qoheleth as deeply pessimistic,[103] others regard him as also positive but to differing extents.[104] Crenshaw writes,

> Qoheleth taught by means of various literary types that earlier optimistic claims about wisdom's power to secure one's existence have no validity. No discernible principle of order governs the universe, rewarding virtue and punishing evil. The creator, distant and uninvolved, acts as judge only (if at all) in extreme cases of flagrant affront ... Death cancels all imagined gains, rendering life under the sun absurd. Therefore the best policy is to enjoy one's wife, together with good food and drink, during youth, for old age and death will soon put an end to this 'relative' good. In short, Qoheleth examined all of life and discovered no absolute good that would survive death's effect. ... Qoheleth bears witness to an intellectual crisis in ancient Israel.[105]

In similar vein to Crenshaw, Watson describes Qoheleth's vision as "rigorously hope-less."[106] "Nowhere else in holy scripture is there so forthrightly set out an *alternative* vision to that of the gospel, a rival version of the truth. ... In the light of the gospel, nothing could be more illusory than the consolation of Qoheleth's celebrated 'realism'." Loader likewise argues that Ecclesiastes is a negative witness to the gospel.[107]

Whybray by contrast has recently argued that Qoheleth was mainly a preacher of joy.[108] And Ogden asserts that Ecclesiastes' thesis "is that life under God must be taken and enjoyed in all its mystery."[109] Ellul sums up Ecclesiastes' message as: "In reality, all is vanity. In truth, everything is a gift of God."[110]

---

[102] MURPHY, *Ecclesiastes*, sticks with 'vanity', FOX, *Qoheleth and His Contradictions*, proposes 'absurd', G. OGDEN, *Qoheleth* (Readings – A New Biblical Commentary; Sheffield: JSOT, 1987), proposes 'enigmatic', the Good News Bible translates הבל as 'useless', LOHFINK, *Kohelet*, suggests 'Windhauch.'

[103] CRENSHAW, *Ecclesiastes*.

[104] Cf. for example MURPHY, *Ecclesiastes*, with OGDEN, *Qoheleth*.

[105] CRENSHAW, "Ecclesiastes, Book of," 277.

[106] F. WATSON, *Text, Church and World. Biblical Interpretation in Theological Perspective* (Edinburgh: T&T Clark, 1994) 283-287.

[107] J.A. LOADER, *Polar Structures in the Book of Qohelet* (Hawthorne, NY: de Gruyter, 1979); idem, *Ecclesiastes. A Practical Commentary* (Grand Rapids: Eerdmans, 1986). H.W. HERTZBERG, *Der Prediger* (2nd ed.; KAT 17,4; Gütersloh: Gütersloher Verlagshaus Gerd Mohn, 1963) 237-238, concludes his commentary on Ecclesiastes as follows: "Hier war das Alte Testament im Begriff, sich totzulaufen. Hinter diesem völligen Nichts auf der Menschenseite war nur noch die 'neue Kreatur' des NT als Hilfe möglich. Das Buch Qoh, am Ende des AT stehend, ist die erschütterndste messianische Weissagung, die das AT aufzuweisen hat."

[108] R.N. WHYBRAY, "Qoheleth, Preacher of Joy," *JSOT* 23 (1992) 87-98.

[109] OGDEN, *Qoheleth*, 14.

[110] J. ELLUL, *Reason for Being. A Meditation on Ecclesiastes* (Grand Rapids: Eerdmans, 1990) 31.

Despite this polarisation with respect to the message of Ecclesiastes, it should be noted that a certain consensus has emerged out of a historical critical interpretation of Ecclesiastes. Very few scholars nowadays defend Solomonic authorship; most regard Ecclesiastes as written by an unknown Jew around the late third century BC. Most scholars regard the book as a basic unity with the exception of the epilogue. With the possible exception of the discernment of different voices/strands in Ecclesiastes, all three assumptions that Murphy identified as common to pre-critical interpretation of Ecclesiastes have been undermined by historical criticism. However, as regards Ecclesiastes' structure, message, relationship to OT traditions and to international wisdom there is no consensus.

To a great extent historical criticism has sought to exclude theological presuppositions from its methodology by insisting that the OT should be read in the same way as any other ANE text. In the latter half of this century there has been a growing reaction to that tendency.[111] Childs has sought to develop a hermeneutic which takes the OT seriously *as* canon.[112] The intriguing effect of his canonical approach upon his reading of Ecclesiastes is that in what we might call a post-critical move he reappropriates the epilogue as the key to the canonical function of Ecclesiastes, thereby undermining the one universal fruit of source-criticism of Ecclesiastes. In Childs' view the epilogue alerts us to Ecclesiastes' nature as a corrective within the broader wisdom tradition.

Barton has suggested that the canonical approach of Childs stands or falls with NC.[113] We shall argue that it is more likely that Childs' approach is part of a general reaction to positivism in the humanities, but it is important to note that the application of NC to Ecclesiastes has resulted in new insights. Wright has sought to analyse the structure of Ecclesiastes by means of a close reading of the text along New Critical lines,[114] and Lohfink describes his creative approach to Ecclesiastes as that of *Werkinterpretation*, the German equivalent of NC.[115] Although both Wright and Lohfink see the epilogue as an addition to Qoheleth by another hand, their approaches indicate the developing tendency to read Ecclesiastes as carefully crafted literature. Loader also fits with this literary trend in his modified structuralist reading of Ecclesiastes whereby he discerns polar opposites as at the heart of its structure.[116] Fox proposes that we read Ecclesiastes

---

[111] Most recently WATSON, *Text, Church and World*, has pleaded for "Biblical Interpretation in Theological Perspective."

[112] CHILDS, *Introduction to the Old Testament as Scripture*.

[113] J. BARTON, *Reading the Old Testament. Method in Biblical Study* (London: DLT, 1984).

[114] WRIGHT, "The Riddle of the Sphinx".

[115] N. LOHFINK, "Freu Dich, Jüngling – doch nicht, weil du jung bist. Zum Formproblem im Schlußgedicht Kohelets (Koh 11,9-12,8)," *BI* 3/2 (1995) 160.

[116] LOADER, *Polar Structures in the Book of Qohelet*; idem, *Ecclesiastes*.

as a narrative and wisdom text, with an openness to distinguishing between narrator, implied author and Qoheleth.[117]

Perry too has recently argued for a literary reading of Ecclesiastes, but one in which Ecclesiastes is approached as the transcript of a debate between Koheleth (K) and the presenter (P).[118] This dialogical approach, according to Perry, is the correct way to understand the 'contradictions' that have plagued commentators for so long. Ecclesiastes is an essay, a collection, a debate, and the reader's task is to discern the alternating voices, which is what Perry attempts in his translation and commentary. Perry argues that Ecclesiastes elaborates on the paradigmatic contradiction in Hebrew Scripture which is introduced in the creation story of Genesis. It has to do with the way religious consciousness distinguishes itself from empirical or experiential modes of viewing life.

> What seems clear is that, as against the empirically based conclusions of K that all is vanity, P counters with a series of concepts that take on the density of myths of beginnings and ultimate ends, challenging the narrowness of experiential empiricism with notions that cannot possibly be verified by the same methods. P creates a tension by reinterpreting K's devalued image of total vanity with a reenergised version of the same: 'less than All cannot satisfy man' (Blake).[119]

Post-structuralism and postmodernism have yet to impact the reading of Ecclesiastes in a major way. As regards deconstruction Ecclesiastes might appear to be a prime candidate. The failure of twentieth century scholars to reach any kind of consensus about its meaning could indicate radical textual indeterminacy. As regards women's experience and Ecclesiastes, attention has tended to be focused on 7:23ff in particular, in an attempt to determine whether Qoheleth was a misogynist or not.[120]

Psychoanalytic readings are in vogue[121] and there has been a serious attempt to read Ecclesiastes along these lines by Zimmerman,[122] using insights from

---

[117] FOX, "Frame Narrative and Composition".

[118] T.A. PERRY, *Dialogues with Koheleth. The Book of Ecclesiastes. Translation and Commentary* (Philadelphia: Pennsylvania State University, 1993).

[119] Ibid., 36.

[120] See for example N. LOHFINK, "War Kohelet ein Frauenfeind? Ein Versuch, die Logik und den Gegenstand von Koh 7,23-8,1a herauszufinden," in: M. GILBERT (ed.), *La Sagesse de l'Ancien Testament* (1979) 259-287; K. BALTZER, "Women and War in Qoheleth 7:23-8:1a," *HTR* 80/1 (1987) 127-132; O. LORETZ, "'Frau' und griechisch-jüdische Philosophie im Buch Qoheleth," *UF* 23 (1991) 245-264; K.A. FARMER, *Who Knows What is Good? A Commentary on the Books of Proverbs and Ecclesiastes* (International Theological Commentary; Grand Rapids: Eerdmans; Edinburgh: Handsel Press, 1991). P. TRIBLE, "Ecclesiastes," in: B.W. ANDERSON (ed.), *The Books of the Bible: The Old Testament* (1989) 231-239; has written on Ecclesiastes, but her introduction to Ecclesiastes contains no feminist critique.

[121] On psychoanalytic literary criticism see E. WRIGHT, "Modern Psychoanalytic Criticism," in: A. JEFFERSON and D. ROBEY (eds.), *Modern Literary Theory* (1986) 145-165.

[122] ZIMMERMAN, *The Inner World of Qoheleth.*

Freud, Rank, Jung and Adler. Zimmerman maintains that Qoheleth was a court official who had respect for the wealthy but was himself poor. He was married and had a son. Zimmerman analyses his psychological condition as follows:

> He is a pathological doubter of everything, stemming from a drastic emotional experience, a psychic disturbance. He is doubtful about himself as a person of worth and character. He has no self-esteem or value of himself. His doubt has destroyed all values. He is an inferior, of no account, and he demeans himself constantly. His doubt comes from a parapathy, a disease of the mind which he shares with many neurotics.[123]

"A time to murder" in 3:1-8 indicates criminal elements in Qoheleth's makeup. These drives are however repressed but at the cost of the disintegration of his psyche. "To throw stones" indicates Qoheleth's suspicion that his wife was adulterous. "To sow" is indicative of Qoheleth's latent homosexuality. Indeed Qoheleth struggles with sexual impotence as is evident from chapter 12. The picture is of an old man with declining physical powers. The symbols refer to the futility of using aphrodisiacs; 'voice of the bird becomes faint' refers to lost sexual potency. Referring to 11:3 Zimmerman says, "When his gonads fill up, inevitably he experiences an emission … And yet when the tree, a familiar symbol of erection … once falls it lies there prone and inert, and Qoheleth's potency is not aroused even by proximity to a woman."[124] Qoheleth's hostility to women revealed in 7:26 could, according to Zimmerman, only stem from a hostile relationship with his mother. "The hatred which was directed against women (at first his mother, then his wife) enlarges, and then is levelled against all womankind."[125] "The first feminine relationship in his life with his mother/sister, on the other hand, fixated a love which he yearned to find again but could not under society's rule of morality and law."[126]

Crenshaw is surely justified to say of Zimmerman's reading: "Such flights of fantasy possess more entertainment value than truth."[127] Zimmerman's reading presents us with an appropriate point to end our overview of readings of Ecclesiastes.[128] It certainly alerts us to the diversity of readings of Ecclesiastes that have been proposed in the 2300 years of this text's existence.

---

[123] Ibid., 8.

[124] Ibid., 27.

[125] Ibid., 29.

[126] Ibid., 36.

[127] CRENSHAW, "The Wisdom Literature," 382; cf. also Michel's response to Zimmerman (MICHEL, *Qoheleth*, 89-90).

[128] We have not considered the widespread cultural use of Ecclesiastes. L.J. KREITZER, *The Old Testament in Fiction and Film. On Reversing the Hermeneutical Flow* (Sheffield: Sheffield Academic Press, 1994), explores the relationship between Hemingway's *Farewell to Arms* and Ecclesiastes. Bono of U2 asserts that Ecclesiastes is the key to understanding U2's album, 'Achtung Baby.' The cultural use (and abuse) of Ecclesiastes has yet to be thoroughly investigated.

2.4 Conclusion

Up until the Reformation pre-critical interpretation of Ecclesiastes tended to be allegorical; either way Ecclesiastes was always read as Scripture and with the epilogue as determinative. The Enlightenment and post-Enlightenment period marks the watershed in the interpretation of Ecclesiastes. Its effect was to reinforce literal interpretation and to bracket out the constitutive role of faith in the interpretation process. The application of historical method to the OT in the nineteenth century lead eventually to source critical analysis of Ecclesiastes, and then to form critical and traditional critical analyses. Although the second half of the twentieth century has seen a recovery of a sense of the unity of Ecclesiastes, the Epilogue still tends to be regarded as secondary. Newer reading strategies are gradually starting to have an impact on the reading of Ecclesiastes.

Clearly there is a close relationship between the history of the interpretation of Ecclesiastes and that of hermeneutics. Modernity and its hermeneutical legacy has shaped contemporary readings of Ecclesiastes particularly powerfully. However scholars are as disagreed as ever about the message of Ecclesiastes. Crenshaw (see quote at outset of chapter) suggests that this diversity is related to the different worldviews readers bring to the text. If this is at least part of the reason, rather than the 'fault' being that of the text alone, then it becomes apparent just how important it is for us to explore in detail the way in which different worldviews or hermeneutics have shaped the interpretation of Ecclesiastes if we are ever to move towards a correct interpretation of this perplexing book.

Because of the importance of modernity in the interpretation of Ecclesiastes, we will focus our attention there. Chapters three to six will examine the link between hermeneutics and the interpretation of Ecclesiastes in modernity and late/post modernity.[129]

---

[129] See ch. 6, where I express my preference for 'late modernity.'

CHAPTER 3

HISTORICAL CRITICISM AND ECCLESIASTES:
READING ECCLESIASTES IN MODERNITY

The historical critique of Scripture that emerges fully in the eighteenth century has its dogmatic base, as our brief look at Spinoza has shown, in the Enlightenment's faith in reason.

(H.-G. GADAMER, *Truth and Method* [2nd ed.; London: Sheed and Ward, 1989] 182)

Enlightenment critique is primarily directed against the religious tradition of Christianity – i.e., the Bible. ... This is the real radicality of the modern Enlightenment compared to all other movements of enlightenment: it must assert itself against the Bible and dogmatic interpretations of it.

(Ibid., 272)

3.1 Introduction

The historical critical method of biblical interpretation remains the dominant mode of academic biblical study, although its hegemony is no longer as secure as it once was. This method is a product of the Enlightenment and post-Enlightenment era (i.e. of modernity) and can only be understood against this background. Examination of readings of Ecclesiastes in modernity requires therefore, that we explore the origins of the historical critical method in the Enlightenment and attend to its prejudices.[1]

Our approach in this chapter will be as follows. We will first examine modernity as the context in which the historical critical hermeneutic developed. We will then trace the development of the historical critical hermeneutic itself and examine Krentz' articulation of it in particular, before going on to consider the types of readings of Ecclesiastes that it has produced. Finally we will evaluate it as a biblical hermeneutic.

3.2 The Narrative[s] of Modernity

Scholder and Reventlow have stressed the importance of examining the development of the historical critical method in its historical and cultural context. The main figures of the development are well known but "up until now it has not

---

[1]   Like GADAMER, *Truth and Method*, 265-285, I am not using prejudice here in a pejorative sense, but to indicate that pre-judgements are universal and unavoidable. Uncommitted neutrality and objectivity are a myth.

been described in context."[2] Exploring this context will involve examining its philosophical hermeneutical elements closely, as Scholder recognises in his assertion that investigation of this area will result in the theologian finding "himself or herself transported into the largely uncharted area which lies between philosophy and theology."[3] Examination of this context is no simple matter. A legacy of modernity is the standard account of its origins, an account which tends to be assumed in OT studies. However, this account has been steadily undermined in recent decades and especially in the context of postmodernism a variety of narratives of modernity have arisen.

We will enter the discussion of modernity through Toulmin's reassessment of the standard account.[4] This will give us an understanding of the standard account plus a contemporary alternative account, which will assist us in asking critical questions in the following section when we examine the rise of the historical critical method in modernity. Toulmin clearly regards modernity as in a crisis:

> [i]f an historical era is ending, it is the era of Modernity itself. ... What looked
> in the 19th century like an irresistible river has disappeared in the sand, and we
> seem to have run aground. ... we are now stranded and uncertain of our
> location. The very project of Modernity thus seems to have lost momentum,
> and we need to fashion a successor program.[5]

According to Toulmin for most of the twentieth century Western Europeans and North Americans were generally agreed that modernity began in the seventeenth century and that the transition from the Middle Ages to modernity was achieved through the application of rational methods in all areas of intellectual study; by Galileo in physics, Descartes in epistemology and Hobbes in political theory. This understanding represents in a nut shell what Toulmin calls *the standard account of modernity*. In its view modernity was unquestionably a good thing. The seventeenth century recovery of the power of rationality plus the rejection of superstition reshaped Europe. The fragmentation of Christendom freed European nations to embrace their autonomy.

---

[2]   K. SCHOLDER, *The Birth of Modern Critical Theology* (London: SCM, 1990) 1; cf. H. Graf REVENTLOW, *The Authority of the Bible and the Rise of the Modern World* (London: SCM, 1984) 2-3.

[3]   SCHOLDER, *The Birth of Modern Critical Theology*, 5-6.

[4]   S. TOULMIN, *Cosmopolis. The Hidden Agenda of Modernity* (Chicago: University of Chicago Press, 1990). One could, of course, enter the debate about modernity from a variety of directions. I have chosen Toulmin because of his long standing concern with modernity and academic theory and the incisive nature of *Cosmopolis*. W. BRUEGGEMANN, *Texts under Negotiation. The Bible and Postmodern Imagination* (London: SCM, 1993) 3, describes *Cosmopolis* as one of two texts that have particularly shaped his understanding of the postmodern shift.

[5]   TOULMIN, *Cosmopolis*, 3.

Since the 1950's this standard account of modernity has however been increasingly undermined,[6] and Toulmin proposes a revised narrative of modernity which recognises two distinct origins for the modern world, one in the humanism of the Renaissance and a second in the seventeenth century Enlightenment, which lost many of the humanist insights. Humanism emerged within a European culture that was still predominantly Christian and struck a balance between theoretical and practical concerns, all the time aware of its epistemological limitations. However in the 1600's "[t]here is a shift from a style of philosophy that keeps equally in view issues of local, time bound practice, and universal, timeless theory to one that accepts matters of universal, timeless theory as being entitled to an exclusive place on the agenda of 'philosophy'."[7]

This shift from 'Montaigne to Descartes' is closely related to changes in the historical and social context. The religious wars seemed to demonstrate that religion was not an adequate base for stable and peaceful existence. With the assassination of Henry of Navarre in 1610 the search for a solid foundation to life became critical and "[t]he only other place to look for 'certain foundations of belief' lay in the epistemological proofs that Montaigne had ruled out."[8]

Descartes' development is regularly presented in an acontextual, rational way, but it was the context of deep uncertainty in the seventeenth century that shaped and provided a receptive audience for his ideas. "Descartes was convinced that we can build a secure body of human knowledge, if we scrap our inherited systems of concepts and start again from scratch – with a clean slate – using 'rationally validated' methods."[9] This approach spread through all branches of knowledge: law, medicine, political theory and theology, thereby creating an estrangement between philosophy and the humanities.[10] In Toulmin's opinion a worldview developed out of this Cartesian source of modernity which dominated the West for some 200 years.

> After 1660, there developed an overall framework of ideas about humanity and nature, rational mind and causal matter, that gained the standing of 'common sense': for the next 100, 150 or 200 years, the main timbers of this framework of ideas and beliefs were rarely called in question. They were spoken of as 'allowed by men' or 'standing to reason', and they were seen as needing no further justification than that. ... Between them, they defined a system of ideas that we may refer to as the Modern world view, or the 'framework of modernity'.[11]

---

6   Ibid., 17-21.
7   Ibid., 24.
8   Ibid., 55-56.
9   Ibid., 81.
10   Ibid., 77-83.
11   Ibid., 107, 108.

Central to this worldview is the Cartesian dichotomy between humanity and nature. The principal elements of the modern worldview[12] divide into two groups, reflecting this dichotomy.[13] On the nature side of the divide Toulmin finds the following principles:

1. Nature is governed by fixed laws set up at creation.
2. The structure of nature was established a few thousand years ago.
3. The material substance of physical nature is essentially inert.
4. Physical objects and processes cannot think or reason.
5. At the creation, God combined natural objects into stable systems.
6. Higher and lower things are linked so that motion in nature, and action in society, flow from 'higher' to 'lower' creatures.

On the humanity side Toulmin discerns the following assumptions:

1. The essence of humanity is the capacity for rational thought and action.
2. There can be no science of psychology.
3. Human beings also have collective power to establish social systems.
4. Humans are mixed beings – in part rational, in part causal.
5. Reason is mental, emotion is bodily.
6. The emotions frustrate or distort reason.

These presuppositions were like an intellectual scaffolding within which theorists worked. Toulmin refers to 1750-1914 as the time of dismantling the scaffolding of the modern worldview.[14] The denial that nature has a history was first to be questioned. The belief in inert matter took a long time to undermine. It had already been strongly criticised at the end of the eighteenth century but lingered long into the twentieth century. Cartesian dualism has been perhaps the most intractable element of the scaffolding. Even reactions to it like romanticism do not transcend its inherent dualism but assume its categories in their reaction. Romanticism, according to Toulmin, "was rationalism's mirror-image."[15] However, by the mid-nineteenth century the sciences were no longer in practice coldly value free and from the 1860's in Germany Helmholtz and his colleagues redefined the body-mind relationship to escape Cartesian dualism. "By 1914, then, all the material was ready to hand to justify dismantling the last timbers of the intellectual scaffolding that had, since the late 17th century, established the

---

[12] J.J. VENTER, *Pieke en Lyne In die Westerse Denkgeskiedenis. Band II: 'n Geskiedenis van Moderne Westerse Leidende Ideë* (Potchefstroom: PU vir CHO, 1991) 33, discerns five main characteristics of the Enlightenment. 1. Faith in the development of mankind. 2. A nature-culture tension. 3. A problematising of the idea of evil. 4. Neo-classicism. 5. Practical and scientific rationality.

[13] TOULMIN, *Cosmopolis*, 109-117.

[14] Ibid., 145.

[15] Ibid., 148.

parameters of acceptable thought."[16] Western Europe was close to recovering the world of tolerance and moderation aspired to by de Navarre and Montaigne.

In 1920-1960, however, this re-Renaissance was deferred,[17] and in fact in this period of uncertainty the tide went into reverse. This reversal is epitomised in logical positivism and Mies' architectural theory. "The ideas of strict 'rationality' modelled on formal logic, and of a universal 'method' for developing new ideas in any field of natural science, were adopted in the 1920s and 1930s with *even greater* enthusiasm, and in an *even more extreme* form, than had been the case in the mid-17th century."[18]

World War II represented the culmination of modernity.[19] It was the last time, according to Toulmin, that the ideals of Modernity could be enacted unselfconsciously.[20] The counter-culture of the 60's represents the deferred reaction to modernity. Within twenty years commitment to the ecosystem, emotional therapy and postmodern architecture were mainstream. The sciences became a confederation of enterprises with methods appropriate to their own field of study.

For Toulmin it is naive to categorise modernity as either a failure or success. Epistemologically foundationalism has proved an illusion but since the eighteenth century there has been a growing concern for human interests. The way ahead is to humanise modernity. Philosophy and science have to be redeemed by reconnecting them with the humanist side of modernity. Practical philosophy must be recovered.

Toulmin's revised narrative of modernity is not the new standard account,[21] for there is no new standard account but a plurality of accounts. How to interpret modernity is at the heart of the postmodern debate, and there is no consensus here.[22] We shall not evaluate Toulmin's account in detail. For our purposes the significance of his narrative lies in its demonstration that the standard account is but one account among many, and that it has its own prejudices. Toulmin maintains that "[b]oth the received view of Modernity, and the standard narrative of its origins, were thus rationalist constructions."[23] Especially in the light of the

---

[16] Ibid., 150.

[17] See ibid., 152-160.

[18] Ibid., 159.

[19] See Z. BAUMAN, *Modernity and the Holocaust* (Cambridge: Polity, 1989), for a penetrating study of the connection between the holocaust and modernity. "The truth is that every 'ingredient' of the Holocaust ... was normal ... in the sense of being fully in keeping with everything we know about our civilization, its guiding spirit, its priorities, its immanent vision of the world" (ibid., 8).

[20] TOULMIN, *Cosmopolis*, 160.

[21] Cf. J. CARROLL, *Humanism. The Wreck of Western Culture* (London: Fontana, 1993) 117, for example. Carroll argues, contra Toulmin, that the Enlightenment was the fulfilment of humanism.

[22] See the discussion of postmodernity in ch. 6.

[23] TOULMIN, *Cosmopolis*, 81.

plurality of accounts of modernity, the rationalist prejudices of the standard account can no longer be assumed; if they are to be presupposed then a case has to be made for adopting them rather than alternatives.

As we examine the emergence of the historical critical method in modernity it is thus vital that we not only recontextualise it but that we critically evaluate the context within which it emerged and interrogate its prejudices in this way.

3.3 The Development and Nature of the Historical Critical Method

'Historical' and 'critical' both identify key elements of the historical critical method of biblical interpretation. *Critical* signifies the subjection of the biblical tradition to examination on the basis of the modern worldview. As Scholder points out, this was clearly understood by F.C. Baur, who in a discussion with a colleague at Jena, Karl Hase, asserts that "in the end only that view can prevail which brings unity, connection and rational consistency to our world-view, our understanding of the history of the Gospel, our whole consciousness."[24] Scholder comments: "'Unity, connection and rational consistency': that means, quite simply, honest exegesis – honest to the degree that in principle it must be carried on with a concern for the understanding of reality 'which has been gained by the spirit in modern times'." *Historical* indicates that it is particularly Enlightenment historical method which is applied to the Bible by the historical critical method, especially as it came to maturity in the nineteenth century.[25]

Our approach in this section will be as follows. Firstly we will briefly outline the development of the historical critical method. Secondly we will examine Krentz's explication of the method as an example of a proponent of historical criticism.

3.3.1 The Origins of the Historical Critical Method

Rogerson describes Germany as the home of the historical critical method,[26] and indeed, it was in nineteenth century Germany that the historical critical method reached maturity. However, prior to the second half of the eighteenth century Germany had hardly been touched by critical theology, whereas a century earlier orthodoxy was forced onto the defensive in all other Western European

---

24 SCHOLDER, *The Birth of Modern Critical Theology*, 2-3. For a discussion of Barr's hermeneutic see R.A. HARRISVILLE and W. SUNDBERG, *The Bible in Modern Culture. Theology and Historical-Critical Method from Spinoza to Käsemann* (Grand Rapids: Eerdmans, 1995) 111-130.

25 Cf. E. NICHOLSON, *Interpreting the Old Testament: A Century of the Oriel Professorship* (Oxford: Clarendon, 1981). E. KRENTZ, *The Historical-critical Method* (London: SPCK, 1975) 1, comments that "historical criticism ... introduced into biblical interpretation a new method based on a secular understanding of history."

26 J. ROGERSON, *Old Testament Criticism in the Nineteenth Century. England and Germany* (London: SPCK, 1984) ix.

countries.[27] Thus, if the mature adulthood of the historical critical method is to be found in Germany, this is not true of its early and adolescent years; generally they are found elsewhere.

Exactly how far back one goes to discover the roots of the historical critical method is debatable. In one sense the roots of the historical critical method go back further than the start of modernity since the Enlightenment has its roots in early Greek philosophy. However, the emergence of the modern worldview and the rejection of a synthesis of nature with grace[28] was something new and unprecedented in its scale. Consequently, it seems wise to follow Krentz and Scholder in focusing analysis of the rise of the historical critical method on the seventeenth century and following.[29] Renaissance rediscovery of antiquity and the development of the printing press were crucial ingredients in the recipe of modernity. But, as Toulmin's distinction between the two origins of the modern world indicates, it was a particular approach to and use of antiquity which produced the modern worldview, and not just its rediscovery.

And this particular approach emerged through the emancipation of reason from all constraints in philosophy and its penetration of science and history. The scientific and historical revolutions of the Enlightenment gave birth to the historical critical method. It was Descartes who emancipated reason, and "like a young stallion locked up in stables for winter set free in spring pasture, it galloped far and wide with a wild and virile exuberance. The main shackle to be cast off was that of religion. ... Out of the scientific explosion the decisive blow against religion was struck by history, which now replaced myth."[30] The changes that came about in the seventeenth century and became focused on the Bible in the historical critical method began with philosophy (Descartes), exploded in the ongoing scientific revolution (Newton) and developed in history from where they were focused hermeneutically on the Bible. Richardson expresses this most clearly:

> The thought of our own times has been shaped by the two great intellectual revolutions of the modern period – the scientific revolution of the sixteenth and seventeenth centuries, and the revolution in historical method which was the great achievement of the nineteenth century. The two revolutions are not indeed separate and distinct things; perhaps we should think rather of one great reorientation of the human mind, which began with the Renaissance and is still continuing. It began with the rise of what we today call the natural sciences;

---

27 SCHOLDER, *The Birth of Modern Critical Theology*, 4-5.
28 See W. WINDELBAND, *A History of Philosophy* (London; NY: Macmillan, 1901) 310-351.
29 REVENTLOW, *The Authority of the Bible*, 3, locates the starting point of historical critical theology in late mediaeval spiritualism.
30 CARROLL, *Humanism*, 120.

and by the nineteenth century it had embraced the sphere of history and what are now called the human sciences.[31]

Shifts in historiography are harder to identify than scientific ones, with the result that the changes in historiography are regularly subordinated to the scientific revolution. "That is certainly a mistake; for which insight in the end changed our understanding of reality more deeply is a completely open question."[32] As early as the mid-seventeenth century de la Peyrère in his *Pre-Adamites* raised the question of how the nations and their religion could be reconciled with the Bible. "There is no more impressive evidence than this remarkable book of what a profound problem the old view of history had already become by the middle of the seventeenth century. With it – almost a century before Voltaire – the development of the new universal-historical conception of world history begins."[33]

The mediaeval view of history did not collapse overnight; historical consciousness was slowly restructured between 1550 and 1650. Jean Bodin's *Methodus ad facilem historiarum cognitionem* produced the first criticism of Melanchton's picture of history.[34] Bodin criticises the scheme of the four monarchies of Daniel, pleads for the notion of human progress, makes chronology the presupposition of all historical understanding, and maintains that the question of whether time is eternal or not must be decided not by tradition but by compelling arguments. "The more marked consideration of political realities, the extension of perspective beyond the limits of the West, the demands for compelling arguments even where tradition has long decided – all this points to the beginning of an emancipation from a purely biblical-theological understanding of the world and the history of nations."[35] The result was a shift similar to that in philosophy and science. History gradually became autonomous from theology. The Scriptures were treated more and more as ordinary historical documents. "The process of objectification had begun."[36]

The eighteenth century was the heyday of the Enlightenment. The critical approach towards the Bible was consolidated in Deism,[37] but the triumph of abstract reason restrained the move towards a fully historical approach to the Bible. However, already in the seventeenth century Spinoza had argued for an

---

[31] A. RICHARDSON, "The Rise of Modern Biblical Scholarship and Recent Discussion of the Authority of the Bible," In: S.L. GREENSLADE (ed.), *The Cambridge History of the Bible. The West from the Reformation to the Present Day* (1963) 295.

[32] SCHOLDER, *The Birth of Modern Critical Theology*, 65.

[33] Ibid., 67.

[34] No fewer than 12 editions of this text were published up to 1650.

[35] SCHOLDER, *The Birth of Modern Critical Theology*, 75.

[36] KRENTZ, *The Historical-critical Method*, 16.

[37] Ibid., 16-17; cf. REVENTLOW, *The Authority of the Bible*, 289ff.

historical approach to the Bible.[38] Now through the labours of scholars like Turrentinus, Wetzstein, Ernesti, Astruc, Semler, Eichhorn, Gabler and Michaelis there was a slow but steady move towards a more historical interpretation of the Bible. A particularly significant figure in the latter half of the century was Semler. He was the first German Protestant theologian to approach the Bible through the history of religion and to insist upon a critical rather than a dogmatic reading of it. The interpreter must seek to discover what the original author meant by the text.[39] Keil likewise stressed that an interpreter must think the author's thoughts after him without judging them. The exegete should only establish the facts. "The standard for subsequent commentaries was formulated."[40]

By the end of the eighteenth century in Germany, most Old Testament professors were either Neologists or Rationalists. Semler and Michaelis were the founders of Neologism. Brought up as Pietists they abandoned Pietism through the influence of Spinoza and Deism. As the eighteenth century moved into the nineteenth, Neologism was increasingly replaced by Rationalism and Supranaturalism, both responses to the Kantianism which penetrated most of the theological faculties in the 1790's.[41] Source criticism of the Pentateuch was advanced through the labours of Eichhorn in particular, but there was no radical reconstruction of the history of Israel.[42]

The historical thought of the Enlightenment, as we explained above, was more philosophical than historical. The eighteenth century fostered an understanding of history dominated by the idea of progress.[43] This philosophy of history continued on into the nineteenth century, but was displaced by German historicism and Hegelian philosophy. Historicism refers to that sort of historical thought which dominated Germany from the rise of romanticism at the end of the eighteenth century down to the mid-twentieth century. It represents a reaction to the idea of progress and is characterised by a belief that all cultures are moulded by history, a privileging of intuition as the means whereby we understand groups other than our own, and a denial of history as linear.[44] It was bound up with Kantian and romantic reactions to the Enlightenment.

Niebuhr's *Römische Geschichte* (1811-1812) was a major early historicist work. Krentz assesses it as follows: Two questions dominated his method: what is the evidence? and what is the value of the evidence? In this way Niebuhr sought

---

[38] See our discussion of Spinoza in ch. 1 and especially J.S. PREUS, "A Hidden Opponent in Spinoza's Tractatus," *HTR* 88/3 (1995) 361-388.

[39] W. JEANROND, *Theological Hermeneutics. Development and Significance* (London: SCM, 1994) 39.

[40] KRENTZ, *The Historical-critical Method*, 19.

[41] ROGERSON, *Old Testament Criticism in the Nineteenth Century*, 16-18.

[42] Ibid., 19-27.

[43] D. BEBBINGTON, *Patterns in History. A Christian Perspective on Historical Thought* (Leicester: Apollos, 1979) 68-91.

[44] Ibid., 92-94.

to separate poetry from truth in his sources and to reconstruct what happened in a more believable narrative.[45] As Collingwood points out, the classic example of this is Niebuhr's treatment of Livy.[46] Niebuhr argues that much of what was taken for early Roman history is patriotic fiction of a later period, and that even the earliest stratum is not sober fact but a national epic of the ancient Roman people. Niebuhr detects the historical reality of early Rome, a society of peasant farmers, behind the epic.[47] As Bebbington makes clear, Niebuhr's approach was more nuanced than Krentz suggests.

> Niebuhr blended the fragmentary sources for early Roman history ... into a coherent story of a perennial struggle for power between patricians and plebians, an interpretation that was to enjoy a remarkable longevity and that has not yet been exorcized from the text books. It was, for its day, a *tour de force*, replacing the traditional accounts of brief phases of republican history based on the ancient historians with a unitary and vivid narrative. Niebuhr could not have achieved his feat without making the typical historicist assumption that poetry and myth express the inner spirit of a nation, and so treating as sound evidence what would now be approached with great caution.[48]

Von Ranke, another historicist, concentrated on collecting the facts of history – commitment to detail being a characteristic of this school – but also sought the unity of history. The historian must penetrate to the inwardness of events. Every moment in history is equidistant from God. This approach assumed some sensible idea or divine presence moving through all history, whether it was Hegel's spirit, von Ranke's governing God, Droysen's ethical progress or Humboldt's pantheistic truth. After 1850 historical enquiry became more immanentist, a turn well represented by Eduard Meyer,[49] for whom the historian should describe happenings and not seek laws and general ideas.

It was during the early nineteenth century that the turning point for critical study of the OT occurred.[50] De Wette was the first scholar to rewrite the history of Israelite religion radically. His approach to the OT was deeply influenced by Kantian thought, which was mediated *inter alia* through J.F. Fries (1773-1843).[51] Just how influential Kant was upon de Wette is apparent from de Wette's semi-

---

[45] KRENTZ, *The Historical-critical Method*, 22.
[46] R.G. COLLINGWOOD, *The Idea of History* (Oxford: OUP, 1946) 130.
[47] Collingwood notes that this method goes back via Herder to Vico, and that by the mid-nineteenth century it was the common property of all competent historians, at least in Germany (ibid., 130).
[48] BEBBINGTON, *Patterns in History*, 106.
[49] KRENTZ, *The Historical-critical Method*, 24.
[50] ROGERSON, *Old Testament Criticism in the Nineteenth Century*, 28-49.
[51] Cf. Rogerson's more recent position on the chronology of Fries' influence upon de Wette (J. ROGERSON, *W.M.L. de Wette. Founder of Modern Biblical Criticism* [JSOTSup 126; Sheffield: JSOT Press, 1992] 19-26, 65-85), compared with his earlier views (idem, *Old Testament Criticism in the Nineteenth Century*, 28-49).

autobiographical novel *Theodore*, in which he describes Kant's influence upon him as follows:[52]

> Theodore heard at the same time some lectures on morals from a Kantian philosopher, through which a completely new world was opened up to him. The notions of the self-sufficiency of reason in its law-giving, of the freedom of the will through which he was elevated above nature and fate, ... all these notions gripped him powerfully, and filled him with a high self-awareness. Those shadowy ideas about the love of God and Christ, about the new birth, about the rule of God's grace in the human mind ... these he translated now into this new philosophical language, and so they appeared to him clearer and more certain.[53]

Fries' notion of the intuition of eternal ideas through myth caught de Wette's imagination as a means of positively approaching the OT as a religious book. A critical approach to the OT demonstrated that it has little to offer in terms of authentic history. In this de Wette was deeply influenced by Fries: "it was the unwillingness of the Friesian system to allow that history is a purposive process that enabled de Wette to make such radical proposals about the history of Israel; to suggest that there was a radical divergence between the Old Testament story and what could be known about the actual facts."[54] Through his exposure to Fries de Wette arrived at an articulate view of religion, and in his study of the Old Testament he brought this to bear on it comprehensively.

Gesenius, Gramberg and George developed de Wette's reconstruction of the history of Israel.[55] Vatke published his *Biblical Theology* in 1835. In the critical interpretation of the OT he was mainly guided by de Wette and Gesenius but his work is deeply influenced by Hegel. The first 170 and the last 120 pages of his text are devoted to the nature of religion. The principle of evolutionary development shapes Vatke's thought throughout.

Under the influence of contemporary philosophical trends and secular historical research, biblical criticism refined its techniques. Schleiermacher had given historical criticism a positive place in his analysis of understanding, and his prestige gave respectability to the use of historical method in biblical studies, which now came to be increasingly practised at the German universities, where OT was studied on a large scale.[56] The *Biblia Hebraica* soon appeared, and in 1829 Heinrich Meyer produced the first volume of his *Critical and Exegetical Commentary*. For Meyer exegesis was to be free of dogmatic and party spirit, not

---

[52] Cf. ROGERSON, *W.M.L. de Wette*, 27-30, for a description of the content of a lecture given at the University of Jena by Kant the year before de Wette arrived there. This lecture gives one an insight into the view of religion Kant was expounding at this time.

[53] Quoted by ROGERSON, *Old Testament Criticism in the Nineteenth Century*, 37.

[54] Ibid., 49.

[55] ROGERSON, *Old Testament Criticism in the Nineteenth Century*, 50-68. He mentions but does not explore the philosophical influences upon all three.

[56] Ibid., 138.

captive to any 'ism', and the exegete should simply determine what the author said. By the end of the century the ICC and the *Handkommentar* were also in production. By this time even the conservative scholars used the historical method to determine the facts. They differed only in their attempt to keep revelation close to the facts.[57]

Probably the most significant OT figure of the nineteenth century was Wellhausen. His documentary hypothesis became the virtual consensus, as did his understanding of the history of Israel. Above all else he was a historian of Israel's religion.[58] Wellhausen recognised the influence of philosophy upon many of his predecessors but denied such influence upon himself:

> Philosophy does not precede but follows [biblical criticism], in that it seeks to evaluate and systematise that which it has not itself discovered. The authors of the two great works of 1835 [Strauss's *Life of Jesus* and Vatke's *Biblical Theology*] were Hegelian, it is true. But that which is of scholarly significance in them does not come from Hegel.[59]

With this statement we see a significant shift from de Wette and Vatke. Their extensive treatments of the nature of religion indicate a strong awareness of the influence of worldviewish questions upon their OT work. Wellhausen's decontextualisation of OT research is a good example of Toulmin's characterisation of modernity, and indicates a direction which became ever stronger in OT studies. Indeed, up to the present, it is rare to find an OT scholar who finds it necessary to grapple with these broader issues in his/her research. We would be most surprised to find a contemporary OT scholar starting a book with a chapter on the nature of religion!

Rogerson does grapple with the broader philosophical issues, and he acknowledges that biblical criticism has been far more influenced by philosophy than Wellhausen allows, but he too removes the heart of historical criticism from philosophical influence:

> If biblical criticism is defined as the investigation of the literary processes which brought the books of the Bible to their extant form, together with a critical evaluation of the history and culture of ancient Israel and Judea so as to interpret biblical material in its original historical and cultural setting, it is difficult to see how philosophy, even defined very broadly, can affect such investigations. Surely, the reconstruction of the history of Israel, or of the apostolic period, involves the use of an historical method unaffected by philosophy. Further, the conclusion, based upon the alteration of the divine names and other criteria in the 'Flood' narrative of Genesis 6-9, that this

---

[57] Cf. KRENTZ, *The Historical-critical Method*, 27-28.

[58] R.E. CLEMENTS, *A Century of Old Testament Study* (Guildford; London: Lutterworth, 1976) 8.

[59] Quoted by J. ROGERSON, "Philosophy and the Rise of Biblical Criticism: England and Germany," In: S.W. SYKES (ed.), *England and Germany. Studies in Theological Diplomacy* (Studies in Intercultural History of Christianity 25; Frankfurt: Peter Lang, 1982) 63.

narrative is a combination of two originally separate written accounts, is something else that in no way depends upon philosophy. ... I am happy to agree that in many of its technical procedures, biblical criticism is not affected by philosophy.[60]

The problem of the relationship between faith and historical knowledge became acute towards the end of the nineteenth century with the emergence of the history of religions school, which sought to explain the Bible in terms of its surrounding cultures. Gunkel was the key OT figure in the history of religions school. "Its basic outlook was positivistic. The Bible, firmly anchored in its own world, was interpreted as an amalgam of various borrowed motifs, and became a book strange to modern men."[61]

With Germany at the forefront, historical criticism dominated Protestantism on the continent by the end of the nineteenth century. England and America embraced the historical critical method much later than Germany, but by the end of the nineteenth century its success there was also ensured. As Krentz points out,

It is difficult to overestimate the significance the nineteenth century has for biblical interpretation. It made historical criticism *the* approved method of interpretation. The result was a revolution of viewpoint in evaluating the Bible. The Scriptures were, so to speak, secularized. ... The Bible was no longer the criterion for the writing of history; rather history had become the criterion for understanding the Bible. ... The Bible stood before criticism as defendant before judge. The criticism was largely positivist in orientation, immanentist in its explanations, and incapable of appreciating the category of revelation.[62]

From one angle the whole of twentieth century theology can be seen as an attempt to relate modernity and faith.[63] World War One called historicism and evolutionary thought into question, generating *inter alia* a strong reaction to the straitjacket of positivism in biblical interpretation. Barth called for theological interpretation while also finding a place for historical criticism. Krentz captures the tension of biblical interpretation in Barth and the twentieth century when he points out that "[b]y the end of the Second World War historical criticism was firmly established, not to be dislodged by any attack. But the dangers of historicism to faith were also clear. The central problem of the relation of faith and historical method was posed as strongly as ever."[64] Throughout the twentieth century there have been strong reactions to the historical critical method in Old Testament studies. These reactions will be our concern in chapter four.

---

60 Ibid., 64; cf. CLEMENTS, *A Century of Old Testament Study*, 3-4.
61 KRENTZ, *The Historical-critical Method*, 28; cf. H.F. HAHN, *The Old Testament in Modern Research* (Philadelphia: Fortress, 1966) 83-118.
62 KRENTZ, *The Historical-critical Method*, 30.
63 Cf. H. ZAHRNT, *The Question of God. Protestant Theology in the Twentieth Century* (London: Collins, 1969).
64 KRENTZ, *The Historical-critical Method*, 32.

3.3.2 Krentz's Articulation of the Historical Critical Method

It is apparent from the above that historical method in modernity is diverse. Different historical methods handled the Old Testament differently so that it seems impossible to pin down *the* historical critical method in biblical interpretation. Krentz recognises this ambiguity: "Today historical criticism is taken for granted ... Yet it is anything but clear just what we mean when we use the phrase *historical method*".[65] The effect of modernity, however, has been to decontextualise the method and to promote the assumption that there is one historical critical method.[66] Thus, even Krentz, who recognises this problem, does not face it but quotes Wilckens with approval and then follows his advice.

> The only scientifically responsible interpretation of the Bible is that investigation of the biblical texts that, with a methodologically consistent use of historical understanding in the present state of its art, seeks via reconstruction to recognise and describe the meaning these texts have had in the context of the tradition and history of early Christianity.[67]

For Krentz history is systematic (analytical) knowledge of the past.[68] The historical critical method in biblical interpretation "produces history in the modern sense, for it consciously and critically investigates biblical documents to write a narrative of the history they reveal."[69] The modern historian, like the historical critical biblical scholar seeks to explain what happened and why. History involves interpretation and the biblical scholar must explain how the diversity of thought arose in Israel. His first task is to hear the text on its own terms: "This basic respect for the historical integrity of a text is inherent in all criticism."[70] The text has hermeneutical autonomy and the exegete must go where the text leads. Thus "the critical biblical scholar will not only question the texts, but himself – his methods, his conclusions, and his presuppositions – and the others who share in the same task."[71] His work is his own judgement and yet he submits to the text: "where that text deals with the profundities of man, that calls for a submission to the autonomy of the text that calls the historian forth for

---

65   Ibid., 33.

66   This tendency is recognised in a fascinating article by J. MCINTYRE, "Historical Criticism in a 'History-Centred Value System,'" In: S.E. BALENTINE and J. BARTON, *Language, Theology and the Bible. Essays in Honour of James Barr* (Oxford: Clarendon, 1994) 370-384. His opening sentence is as follows: "One circumstance which, more than any others, has controlled the discussion of the relation of faith to history, has been the assumption, held by both the theologians and the historical critics with whom they have been debating, that historical criticism is a single, and fairly simply identifiable entity."

67   Wilckens quoted by KRENTZ, *The Historical-critical Method*, 33.

68   Ibid., 34.

69   Ibid., 35.

70   Ibid., 39.

71   Ibid., 53-54.

judgement and knowledge of himself. Then history performs its humane (or in the case of the biblical texts) its theological function."[72]

Krentz argues that historical criticism is conservative in its privileging of the text and refusal to privilege traditional interpretations.[73] The historian listens to the text and interrogates it in order to assess it as a testimony to history. All the linguistic tools available are used to determine the meaning of the text for its original hearers. "Concern for literary figures … are used by the historian to judge the historical usefulness of material, not to achieve a literary appreciation of it *per se*."[74] Historical method evaluates its sources to determine what really happened and what the significance of those events is. It does not exclude specifically Christian goals for the critical interpretation of the Bible because the historian also seeks to understand himself through a study of the past.[75] However, "[t]he differences between biblical scholarship and secular history derive from the major source, the Bible, and not the methods used. Biblical scholars use the methods of secular history on the Bible to discover truth and explain what happened. The methods are secular. The procedures may be modified to fit the Bible, but are not essentially changed."[76] Krentz lists the following as the main methods of historical critical interpretation of the Bible: textual criticism, philological study, literary criticism, form criticism, redaction criticism, historical criticism and perhaps *Sachkritik*.[77]

With regard to presuppositions Krentz acknowledges that "[h]istorical method is anything but a carefully defined and agreed on set of axioms and presuppositions."[78] Troeltsch's 1898 essay articulated the principles of historical criticism and continues to haunt theology. According to Troeltsch there are three principles of historical method: firstly that of methodological doubt, secondly that of analogy and thirdly that of correlation. Troeltsch recognised that the third principle rules out miracle and salvation history, but it is inescapable. By the principle of analogy and correlation Christianity loses its uniqueness. All current historiography affirms Troeltsch's first principle. The second one is generally affirmed although "[a] problem arises when this uniformity is raised to a universal principle that makes some evidence inadmissible."[79] The third principle is very complex. Historicism only allowed causation that is not transcendental or theological, and although historicistic and positivistic philosophies of history are

---

72 Ibid., 54.
73 Ibid., 39.
74 Ibid., 44.
75 Ibid., 41.
76 Ibid., 48.
77 Ibid., 49-54.
78 Ibid., 61.
79 Ibid., 57.

presently in demise this does not mean that a theological interpretation of history is being rehabilitated.[80]

Despite contemporary disagreements about the nature of historiography, theology cannot, according to Krentz, return to a precritical age – "Christian theologians ... can in the present only seek to use historical criticism in the service of the Gospel."[81] Historical criticism does not pose a threat to Scripture because it is congruent with its object, the Bible. The Bible is an ancient text and historical criticism positions the Bible in our history and "makes the 'full brightness and impact of Christian ideas' shine out."[82] To refuse to use historical criticism would be docetic and a denial of faith in Jesus as the Lord of history.

How does faith relate to this method of biblical interpretation? For Krentz it is a mistake to think that there is a sacred method of interpretation: "A method does not have faith or unbelief; there are only believing or unbelieving interpreters. As little as there are sacred engineering and architecture used in the construction of a church building, so little is there a sacred method of interpreting a text."[83] However there are real tensions between faith and secular historical method. Within the Christian community the ideal is biblical interpretation in the service of the gospel. Within historical study the aim is verifiable fact in a significant narrative. A number of proposals for dealing with this tension have been made.[84] For Krentz the tension

> can be resolved only in the person of the interpreter living in the community of faith, who combines dedication to historical truth with the recognition of his own humanity and need for forgiveness. Historical research, like all of man's efforts, is also perverted by sin. But in the community of scholarship that lives in the fellowship of the people of God, the errors that arise from human frailty can be corrected and sin forgiven by God's grace. Then biblical criticism will grow together with faith into the full measure of the stature of Christ, his Gospel, his Word, and his Holy Scripture.[85]

3.4 Readings of Ecclesiastes in Modernity

During modernity many commentaries on Ecclesiastes have been produced. One effect of the historical focus of the historical critical hermeneutic was however to marginalise wisdom literature. Wellhausen paid virtually no attention to wisdom literature, regarding it as late and secondary.[86] He was particularly concerned with the history of Israel's religious institutions and did not see

---

[80] Ibid., 58-61.
[81] Ibid., 61; see pp. 63-67 for his list of ten positive results of the historical critical method that make it worthwhile.
[82] Ibid., 61.
[83] Ibid., 68.
[84] Cf. ibid., 67-72.
[85] Ibid., 72.
[86] CLEMENTS, *A Century of Old Testament Study*, 100.

wisdom literature as an integral part of this. Consequently the thorough application of the historical critical method to 'historical' Old Testament literature occurs far earlier than it does to wisdom literature, as we observed in chapter two. It was the development of form criticism by Gunkel that alerted scholars to the *Sitz im Leben* of wisdom in Israel and its connections with the ANE, thereby leading, at the time when *Religionsgeschichte* was in vogue, to a renewed interest in wisdom. It is thus only at the end of the nineteenth and beginning of the twentieth century that fully historical critical works on Ecclesiastes appear.

Our approach in this section will be as follows. We will focus our exploration of the application of the historical critical method to Ecclesiastes on the commentaries of McNeile[87] and Galling, because these are early major examples of the application of source and form criticism to Ecclesiastes. We will also note how the core of the historical critical method continues to dominate study of Ecclesiastes up to the present by looking briefly at several other important commentators on Ecclesiastes.

As a means of focusing our study exegetically we will repeatedly look at how scholars see Ecclesiastes 12:8ff in relation to the rest of the book. Up until the end of the nineteenth century the epilogue was read as an integral part of Ecclesiastes.[88] Source criticism separated it off from the central section of 'distinctively Qoheleth' material. This has deeply affected the reading of Ecclesiastes so that examination of the relationship between the epilogue and the body of the text foregrounds important hermeneutical issues.

3.4.1 McNeile on Ecclesiastes

The source/literary critical approach to Ecclesiastes was pioneered by Siegfried in Germany.[89] As was typical of early literary criticism of Ecclesiastes, Siegfried thought in terms of a supplementary hypothesis, whereby an original and radically pessimistic text was supplemented with material from different perspectives. This supplementary hypothesis differed from the sort of documentary hypothesis that Wellhausen formulated for the Pentateuch, but the

---

[87] Barton's literary critical approach to Ecclesiastes (in G.A. BARTON, *A Critical and Exegetical Commentary on the Book of Ecclesiastes* [ICC; Edinburgh: T&T Clark, 1912]) is very similar to McNeile's, and so we have selected McNeile's earlier and lesser known commentary as a representative example.

[88] According to R. GORDIS, *Koheleth the Man and His World: A Study of Ecclesiastes* (NY: Schoken, 1968) 349, Döderlein was the first to note that the last six verses are not from Qoheleth's hand, but see our comments on Rashbam in chapter two.

[89] C. SIEGFRIED, *Prediger und Hoheslied* (HAT; Göttingen: Vandenhoeck and Ruprecht, 1898). GORDIS, *Koheleth the Man and His World*, 6, notes that "[t]entatively advanced by Haupt, the theory of multiple sources was meticulously worked out by Siegfried." See R.K. HARRISON, *Introduction to the Old Testament* (Grand Rapids: Eerdmans, 1969) 1079-1083, for an overview of some of the earliest critical approaches to Ecclesiastes.

historical methodology was the same, and Siegfried divided the book among nine sources (Q1, Q2, Q3, Q4, Q5, R1, R2, E1, E2).

In Siegfried's schema Q1 stands for Qoheleth himself, a deeply pessimistic philosopher whose book would have disappeared if it hadn't become associated with Solomon's name. Q2 was an Epicurean Sadducee who recommends eating and drinking as the way to handle life. Q3 is a wise man who highly values wisdom; many of the proverbs in Ecclesiastes come form this source. Q4 is a *Hasid* who strongly opposed Qoheleth's view of God's government of the world. Q5 stands for several other interpolators who propose general moral maxims. The whole writing 1:2-12:7 was edited by a redactor (R1) with a heading 1:1 and a conclusion 12:8. 12:9-10; 12:11-12 and 12:13-14 are three further additions. 12:13-14 betray the hand of a Pharisee which Q4 was unaware of. 12:9-10 and 12:11-12 come from two other epilogists (E1, E2).

Laue,[90] Jastrow,[91] Podechard[92] and others followed Siegfried's type of literary critical approach to Ecclesiastes, but generally it was regarded as too extreme. Kraetzschmar was right when, in reviewing Siegfried's work, he said "it is questionable whether Siegfried will find many followers in his extreme interpolation theory. It is a right idea overstrained in the endeavour to explain all the difficulties in the book ... But the unravelling is done with energy, and will incite to further investigation from this view."[93] Few would follow Siegfried in such an extreme source critical analysis, but his 'right idea' continues to influence study of Ecclesiastes today. At the heart of Siegfried's approach is the principle that in order to understand the text we have to reconstruct the different sources. In the latter part of the twentieth century there has been a strong reassertion of the basic unity of Ecclesiastes with the significant exception of 12:8ff. Unlike commentaries before Siegfried, there are few critical commentaries in the twentieth century which read Ecclesiastes as an integral whole including 12:8ff, so that in this sense at least Siegfried's right idea continues to influence research into Ecclesiastes.

Within English speaking circles (UK and North America) Siegfried's approach was mediated in a modified form *inter alia* through McNeile[94] in Cambridge and Barton in Pennsylvania. As McNeile says in his preface, when he wrote

> very few students have analysed it [Ecclesiastes] by the critical methods which
> have opened up a new world of study in the Hexateuch, the historical books

---

90 P. LAUE, *Das Buch Koh. und die Interpretationshypothese Siegfrieds* (Wittenberg, 1900).

91 M. JASTROW, *A Gentile Cynic. Being the Book of Ecclesiastes* (Philadelphia; London: Lippincott, 1919).

92 E. PODECHARD, *L'Ecclésiaste* (Paris: Gabalda, 1912).

93 Quoted in A.H. MCNEILE, *An Introduction to Ecclesiastes With Notes and Appendices* (Cambridge: CUP, 1904) 31.

94 McNeile says of his own analysis of Ecclesiastes that it "is an attempt at further investigation, incited by Siegfried's interesting commentary" (ibid.).

and the prophets. The following pages have been written with two chief aims: firstly, to disentangle the strands which go to form the 'three-fold' cord of the writing; and secondly, to estimate the position which Koheleth occupied with regard to the religious and philosophical thought of his day. ... neither of these can be accurately studied unless the writing be placed in its historical and literary perspective.[95]

McNeile is clearly conscious of applying the sort of critical approach that had been applied to the Pentateuch to Ecclesiastes. Nearly a third of McNeile's text is devoted to introductory issues, in which he deals with the name Qoheleth, canonicity, the circumstances of the writer, an outline of his thought, the integrity of Ecclesiastes, the style and vocabulary, the relation of Qoheleth to Ben Sira and the Book of Wisdom, and finally the relationship between Ecclesiastes and Greek language and thought.

For McNeile Ecclesiastes has been well described as a "Hebrew journal intime."[96] It is not a thesis, a sermon or a collection of aphorisms but the outpouring of the mind of a wealthy Jew who has seen much suffering and is serious in his wrestling with the meaning of life. Little can be gleaned with any certainty about Qoheleth.[97] Reflection upon nature first made Qoheleth question life. He could not find a key to the riddle of nature and so turned to luxury and elegance; however this too is vanity. His avoidance of Yahweh in his writing alerts us to his attitude towards religion: "'The Deity' is to him 'Nature', the sum-total of the irresistible and inscrutable forces which govern the world. But at the same time he has not quite lost his Semitic belief that God is more than Nature."[98] For Qoheleth Nature involves a mass of misery but he should not be called a pessimist because of his strong conviction that humankind should be and could be better if the circumstances were different. Eschatological expectations are of no help to Qoheleth with the notion of an ideal Israel fading day by day. "There are left him only the shreds of the religious convictions of his fathers, with a species of 'natural religion' which has fatalism and altruism among its ingredients."[99] Qoheleth's conclusion is that since the work of God is inscrutable and allows universal injustice and misery, man can come to no conclusion about life. One can only make the most of the present.

Nowhere does McNeile attempt a structural analysis of Ecclesiastes. His commentary notes follow chapter divisions. In his discussion of Qoheleth's thoughts he divides the text from 2:13-10:20 up into a "series of pictures illustrating the troubles of men."[100] This analysis assumes his source critical analysis of Ecclesiastes, to which we turn now.

---

95 Ibid., v, vi.
96 Ibid., 8.
97 Ibid., 9.
98 Ibid., 15.
99 Ibid., 16.
100 Ibid., 13-21.

In McNeile's view Qoheleth would have been rejected as heretical if it had not been *edited* by an unknown admirer, who emphasised the Solomonic authorship. The statement in 1:12 enabled him to add 1:1. This editor then summed up the burden of the book in 1:2 and 12:8, speaking of Qoheleth in the third person and using the strengthened expression "Vanity of vanities", which does not occur in the body of the text. He finally added 12:9-10 as a postscript in which he elaborates upon the value of Qoheleth's-Solomon's teaching.

Even the edited version would have caused much discussion. Instead of it being dismissed as heretical, attempts were made to improve it, first of all by one of the wise men. He was attracted by the sections of the book with a gnomic and philosophical character and tried to improve the book by adding *mashalim*. Some of these are suggested by Qoheleth's words and either correct or develop them. Many, however, seem to be random additions. McNeile lists the following as the wise man's additions: 4:5; 4:9-12; 6:7; 6:9a; 7:1a; 7:4-6; 7:7; 7:8-9; 7:10; 7:11-12; 7:19; 8:1; 9:17-10:3; 10:8-11; 10:12-15; 10:18; 10:19; 12:11-12.[101]

Although the wise man's proverbs were orthodox, they were not specifically religious. Far more was required to make Qoheleth acceptable for the orthodox. This was the task of a pious Jew, one of the Hasidim. He is responsible for the additions to Ecclesiastes relating to the duty to fear God and the certainty of judgement to those who do not fulfil this duty. McNeile attributes the following verses to this editor: 2:26ab; 3:14b; 3:17; 4:17-5:6; 7:18b; 7:26b; 7:29; 8:2b, 3ab, 5, 6a; 8:11-13; 11:9b; 12:1a; 12:13-14.[102]

McNeile is well aware of the 'innumerable' attempts to read Ecclesiastes as a unity.[103] Most defenders of the unity of the text understand Qoheleth to have gone through different phases of thought, alternating between doubt and faith with faith ultimately triumphing. However, for McNeile the contrasts are too stark for this to be the case. There is also the problem of explaining the miscellaneous proverbs in chapters 4-10 which exhibit neither faith nor doubt. In relation to Greek language and thought McNeile argues that it is very difficult to find any Graecisms in Ecclesiastes.[104] Qoheleth was not directly influenced by any one school of Greek philosophy but

> the natural development of the two religions, Hebrew and Greek, proceeded (broadly speaking) on the same lines, and produced certain affinities between them. Before Christ came ... it was inevitable that all religious thought which was unrestrained by orthodoxy and ancient tradition should tend towards Pantheism- and its necessary corollary Fatalism.[105]

---

[101] Ibid., 22-24.
[102] Ibid., 24-27.
[103] Ibid., 27-30.
[104] Ibid., 39-55.
[105] Ibid., 52.

In 12:8-14 McNeile discerns the editor's closing formula plus three postscripts.[106] 12:8 contains the admiring editor's closing formula with the strengthened 'vanity of vanities'. In 12:9-10 this same editor commends Qoheleth's teaching. In the second postscript 12:11-12 the wise man reflects upon the value of short, incisive proverbs. In 12:13-14 the *Hasid* sums up his own teaching.

McNeile's approach to Ecclesiastes is best described as a literary critical one, with 'literary critical' understood as source criticism. Barton notes that there are also elements of redaction criticism in his approach.[107] Barton examines the effect of wisdom redaction in 4:7-12 and of *Hasid* redaction in 11:9-12:14. As he demonstrates, there is potential to move in this direction. But in his notes on the text McNeile does not pursue this direction; these interpolations are simply omitted and detailed consideration is not given to how they reshape the meaning of the text.

3.4.2 Galling on Ecclesiastes

According to Galling, "[d]as 222 Verse umfassende Buch ist jetzt in 12 Kapitel eingeteilt, die jedoch keine Sinneinheiten darstellen. In Wirklichkeit handelt es sich um eine Reihe von in sich geschlossenen Sentenzen zumeist geringen Umfangs."[108] Qoheleth recorded the sentences[109] which were edited by one of his disciples (QR1) around 300 B.C. "Die bald nach Q.s Tod erfolgte postume editio princeps (mit dem ersten Nachwort) wurde gegen Ende des 3. Jh.s von QR2 mit einem zweiten Nachwort (12:12-14) versehen."[110]

All attempts to discover an overall structure in Ecclesiastes must fail because "der Autor nicht ein Buch (einen Traktat *de vanitate rerum*) geplant hat, sondern seine jeweilige Erkentniss in einer auf ein bestimmtes Thema zugespitzen Sentenz zum Ausdruck bringt."[111] The individual sentence is the primary literary unit and must be interpreted as such. However, behind the sentences Qoheleth's thought again and again revolves around the happenings of fate and death. "In den Sprüchen Q.s ist die Einheit der Lebenssicht Q.s unverkennbar wie die Individuation durch die Ich-Aussage."[112] In this respect the sentences are so close that no overarching structure is required to discern the separate sentences. The

---

[106] Ibid., 91-94.

[107] J. BARTON, *Reading the Old Testament. Method in Biblical Study* (London: DLT, 1984) 69-72.

[108] K. GALLING, *Der Prediger* (2nd ed.; HAT 18; Tübingen: J.C.B. Mohr, 1969) 74.

[109] GALLING, *Der Prediger*, 74, refers to the twenty seven sections he discerns in Ecclesiastes as "Sentenzen" although he acknowledges that in most cases "Reflexionen" would be more appropriate.

[110] Ibid., 75-76.

[111] Ibid., 76.

[112] Ibid.

relative independence of the sentences does not mean that they are randomly mixed up like play cards are shuffled. The order most probably stems from QR1; 1:4-11 and 1:12-2:11 were probably deliberately placed at the beginning by QR1, and 11:7-12:8 at the end. Nevertheless, the relatively free ordering of the sentences must be allowed for. Galling rejects the attempts by Bickell and Siegfried to discern a strict order by making changes and separating out sources.

QR2 has also made various corrections in the text. These stand contrary to the scopus of their respective sentence and are readily recognisable as from the same hand as the second epilogue. Examples are 3:17aβ; 8:5, 12b-13; 11:9b-12:1a. QR2 equated Qoheleth with Solomon by expanding 1:1-3 which is originally from the hand of QR1.

Qoheleth's thought does represent something of a crisis in wisdom but QR1 exaggerates the negative element of Qoheleth's message by summing it up in 1:2 and 12:8 as he does.[113] Against the background of a static view of creation order that had developed in wisdom circles Qoheleth stresses the limitations of wisdom for man. הבל expresses the transience of human experience in the context of human seeking for stability and endurance.

Barton uses Galling as his example of a form critical approach to Ecclesiastes.[114] Galling did however think, as Barton acknowledges, that Qoheleth was the author of these sayings. A more radical form critic might argue that many of these sayings were ancient and anonymous proverbs with histories of their own. However, as Whybray (see below) points out, this sort of form criticism is methodologically unable to deal with the individual genius of a writer. For example, the examination of quotations in Ecclesiastes is related to form criticism because these quotes would have had a life in Israel outside of the text of Ecclesiastes. However, the actual utilisation of the material in Ecclesiastes is something that form criticism cannot account for. But even from Galling's conservative position, it is apparent that form criticism has potentially radical implications for the interpretation of Ecclesiastes. The criterion of consistency in content would be of no use in literary analysis of such an anthology so that Barton and McNeile would be approaching Ecclesiastes quite incorrectly.[115]

3.4.3 Gordis on Ecclesiastes

Gordis' commentary on Ecclesiastes was first published in 1951. In it we get a feel for the shift towards a much stronger sense of the basic unity of Ecclesiastes that has characterised later twentieth century scholarship on Ecclesiastes. Indeed Gordis notes that the few decades preceding his commentary

---

[113] Ibid., 80.

[114] BARTON, *Reading the Old Testament*, 67-68; cf. K. GALLING, "Kohelet-Studien," *ZAW* 50 (1932) 276-299; idem, *Der Prediger* (HAT 18; Tübingen: J.C.B. Mohr, 1940).

[115] Cf. BARTON, *Reading the Old Testament*, 67.

have seen a growing recognition of the unity of Ecclesiastes.[116] Whereas in the nineteenth century the unity of the book was maintained among critical scholars only by Genung and Cornill, it has now been recognised by Levy, Hertzberg, MacDonald, Galling and Weber.[117] Only the epilogue is clearly from another hand.[118]

Gordis rejects the notion of Ecclesiastes going through a number of redactions in order to make it acceptable.[119] Such an hypothesis is contradicted by the history of the Apocrypha and the Pseudepigrapha after their composition. Many of these books were less objectionable to orthodoxy than Ecclesiastes and yet no attempt was made to rework them in order to fit them into the Canon. Chronologically, such an hypothesis is also unlikely because the complex process of writing, popularisation and interpolation would have to take place in a century or less. Detailed study of individual passages confirms that the hypothesis of various editors is unnecessary. Gordis finds that most of the Hasid passages are authentically Qoheleth.[120] In others Qoheleth is citing conventional doctrine. Because of their mashal form the Hokma passages are generally most congenial to Qoheleth's standpoint, or are cited as text for his commentary. "The various Hakam glossators and Hasid interpolators are merely figments of the scholarly imagination."[121]

Within the canon Gordis stresses that whereas Torah and prophecy focused on the group, wisdom focused on the individual.[122] Song and wisdom are both expressions of hokmah as technical wisdom so that the Ketubim is a unity, the deposit of wisdom. Wisdom in Israel has extensive contacts with the ANE but is nevertheless an indigenous development. Gordis explores aspects of the intertextuality of the Old Testament in relation to Ecclesiastes and argues that Qoheleth makes creative use of Genesis and Deuteronomy. Gordis rejects any notion of strong Greek influence:

> Koheleth has two fundamental themes – the essential unknowability of the world and the divine imperative of joy. His unique achievement lies in the skill and the sensitiveness with which he presents his world-view. He has attained to

---

[116] GORDIS, *Koheleth the Man and His World*, 73.

[117] Ibid., 379. Cf. L. LEVY, *Das Buch Qoheleth. Ein Beitrag zur Geschichte des Sadduzäismus* (Leipzig: Hinrichs, 1912); H.W. HERTZBERG, *Der Prediger* (2nd ed.; KAT 17,4; Gütersloh: Gütersloher Verlagshaus Gerd Mohn, 1963); D.B. MACDONALD, *The Hebrew Literary Genius* (Princeton: Princeton University Press, 1933); GALLING, *Der Prediger*; and J.J. WEBER, *L'Ecclésiaste: Le livre de Job-L'Ecclésiaste. Texte et commentaire* (1947).

[118] Cf. R.E. MURPHY, *Ecclesiastes* (WBC; Texas: Word, 1992) xxxiv: "It is preferable to explain the book as generally of one piece … with the obvious exception of the epilogue."

[119] GORDIS, *Koheleth the Man and His World*, 71-72.

[120] Ibid., 378.

[121] Ibid., 73.

[122] Ibid., 14-21.

this plane of vision principally through his ancestral Hebrew culture, modified by some general contact with Greek ideas.[123]

He is a linguistic pioneer in that he is the first to use Hebrew for quasi-philosophical purposes. However, Ecclesiastes is not a debate, a dialogue, or a philosophical treatise. For Gordis it is best described as a *cahier* or notebook, in which the author jotted down his reflections during the leisure of old age.[124] There is no logical progression of thought in the book, and efforts to find it result in far-fetched exegesis. Nor is the book concerned with a single topic. Its unity is not one of logical progression, but of mood and world-view. Like much Jewish literature, it is organic, not syllogistic in structure.

Gordis' commentary is significant in the close attention he plays to quotations in Ecclesiastes. Levy and Galling had independently recognised the presence of quotations in Ecclesiastes but Gordis was the first to tackle the subject systematically.[125] Fox and Whybray have since developed the discussion further.[126] For Gordis failure to recognise quotations is disastrous for they play a fundamental role in wisdom literature, where there is no supernatural revelation but only patient observation used as the basis of reasonable conclusions.[127] Gordis defines quotations as "words which do not reflect the present sentiments of the author of the literary composition in which they are found, but have been introduced by the author to convey the standpoint of another person or situation."[128] He discerns four types of quotation in Ecclesiastes. Firstly there is the straightforward use of proverbial quotations (e.g. 10:18). Secondly there is the sort in which Qoheleth buttresses his argument with a proverb, part of which is relevant but the proverb is quoted in full for the sake of completeness (e.g. 5:3). Thirdly there is the use of proverbial quotations as a text (as e.g. in 7:1-14). Fourthly there is the use of contrasting proverbs as a way of contradicting accepted doctrines (e.g. 4:5-6).

On the relation of 12:9ff to the rest of Ecclesiastes Gordis follows the tradition that the epilogue is from another hand.[129] The use of the third person plus distinctive vocabulary indicate this. It is possible that these concluding verses are not a unit but they do not contradict each other, and there is a

---

[123] Ibid., 51-58.

[124] Ibid., 110.

[125] R. GORDIS, "Quotations in Wisdom Literature," *JQR* 30 (1939-40) 123-147.

[126] M.V. FOX, "The Identification of Quotations in Biblical Literature," *ZAW* 92 (1980) 416-431; and R.N. WHYBRAY, "The Identification and Use of Quotations in Ecclesiastes," *VTSup* 32 (1981) 435-451. However, there is no agreement concerning the presence of quotations in Ecclesiastes. See T.A. PERRY, *Dialogues with Koheleth. The Book of Ecclesiastes. Translation and Commentary* (Philadelphia: Pennsylvania State University, 1993) 4, for example, who regards Gordis' approach as "[a]nother attempt to palliate K's radical condemnation of creation."

[127] GORDIS, *Koheleth the Man and His World*, 95-108.

[128] Ibid., 96.

[129] Ibid., 349ff.

satisfactory progression of thought. "The entire epilogue is best regarded as a unit. ... The editor ... has selected those aspects of Koheleth which were most congenial to him. While he has not done full justice to the temper and world-view of Koheleth, the ideas he stresses ... are part of Koheleth's outlook."[130]

3.4.4 Crenshaw on Ecclesiastes

Since the 1950's the worldview of modernity has increasingly come under attack and this has affected the historical critical method. In the next two chapters we will explore some of the twentieth century reactions to historical criticism. Up until the present however the main commentaries on Ecclesiastes remain historical critical. The sort of shift in type of commentary signalled by Clines' commentary on Job has not yet happened with Ecclesiastes.[131] We will, therefore, conclude our examination of the reading of Ecclesiastes in modernity by briefly examining some of the major contemporary commentaries on Ecclesiastes.

Amidst all his work on wisdom literature, Crenshaw published his commentary on Ecclesiastes in 1988.[132] His assessment of the message of Ecclesiastes is very negative: "Life is profitless; totally absurd. This oppressive message lies at the heart of the Bible's strangest book. ... The deity stands distant, abandoning humanity to chance and death."[133] According to Crenshaw, Qoheleth wrote against a background of a religious/intellectual crisis in which it was very difficult to see any connection between external circumstances and inner worth, as did Job. Qoheleth is more radical than Job; he discerns no moral order at all, although he refuses to carry this position through to its logical conclusions. To those with the ability to enjoy life Qoheleth recommends pleasure so that "[l]ittle room exists here for a scrupulous conscience or for anxiety concerning religious duty."[134]

Ecclesiastes represents no one genre, but reflection arising from personal observation dominates the book. As regards the integrity of Ecclesiastes, Crenshaw acknowledges that the epilogist in 12:9-10 believed that Qoheleth had stamped his teaching with a recognizable design rather than bequeathing a legacy of random thoughts.[135] This seems to be confirmed by the unifying refrain that unifies the text. However, scholars have been unable to agree on this design or on the main message of the text. Crenshaw examines the different attempts to get at the structure of Ecclesiastes[136] and concludes that

---

[130] Ibid., 351.
[131] D.J.A. Clines, *Job 1-20* (WBC; Texas: Word, 1989). See ch. 6 for a discussion of Clines' latest approach to OT study.
[132] See the bibliography for Crenshaw's publications on wisdom.
[133] J.L. CRENSHAW, *Ecclesiastes* (OTL; London: SCM, 1988) 23.
[134] Ibid., 27.
[135] Ibid., 34-35.
[136] Ibid., 35-49.

[t]his discussion of Qoheleth's structure has failed to resolve a single issue, but it demonstrates the complexity of the problem. In my judgement no one has succeeded in delineating the plan of the book, for it certainly has characteristics inherent to a collection of sentences. ... Research into the book also shows that it reflects the interpreter's world view. That is why, I think, opinions vary so widely with regard to such basic matters as Q's optimism or pessimism, his attitude towards women (Lohfink 1979), and his advocacy of immoral conduct.[137]

Crenshaw analyses Ecclesiastes' structure loosely into 25 sections.[138] For him the tensions of the book are best explained as the fruit of a lifetime's research. "Qoheleth bares his soul in all its twistings and turnings, ups and downs, and he invites readers to accompany him in pursuit of fresh discovery."[139] He identifies as secondary materials the following: 1:1; 12:9-11, 12-14; 2:26a; 3:17a; 8:12-13; 11:9b, perhaps 5:18 and 7:26b, and perhaps 1:2 and 12:8. The first epilogue derives from a close student of Qoheleth's and reads almost like an epitaph. The second introduces wholly alien categories as it assesses the unorthodox teacher.

3.4.5 Murphy on Ecclesiastes

Murphy, like Crenshaw, has published mainly on wisdom literature.[140] His commentary on Ecclesiastes is characterised by cautious, sane scholarship within the historical critical tradition.[141] Ecclesiastes was probably published in Palestine rather than Egypt but there is no compelling evidence either way. As regards the integrity of Ecclesiastes "[i]t is preferable to explain the book as generally of one piece ... with the obvious exception of the epilogue."[142] Murphy follows Wright's analysis of Ecclesiastes fairly closely.[143]

Ecclesiastes is intensely Jewish and draws especially on creation theology in the Old Testament. Its relationship to the ANE must also be recognised but Murphy is reluctant to specify influences. He devotes considerable space to the history of the interpretation of Ecclesiastes and concludes that selective emphasis is common to all periods, quoting Pedersen with approval:

---

[137] Ibid., 47.

[138] Ibid., 48.

[139] Ibid., 49.

[140] See the bibliography in K.G. HOGLUND, et al. (eds.), *The Listening Heart. Essays in Wisdom and the Psalms in Honour of Roland E. Murphy, O. Carm* (JSOTSup 58; Sheffield: JSOT, 1987), for a list of Murphy's works up until 1985.

[141] MURPHY, *Ecclesiastes*.

[142] Ibid., xxxiv.

[143] Cf. A.G. WRIGHT, "The Riddle of the Sphinx: The Structure of the Book of Qoheleth," *CBQ* 30 (1968) 313-334. See ch. 4 for our discussion of Wright's New Critical approach to Ecclesiastes.

very different types have found their own image in Ecclesiastes, and it is remarkable that none of the interpretations mentioned is completely without some bias. There are many aspects in our book; different interpreters have highlighted what was most fitting for themselves and their age, and they understood it in their own way. But for all there was a difficulty, namely that there were also other aspects which could hardly be harmonised with their preferred view.[144]

Murphy points out that this contextualises historical critical research:

If we do not accept Solomonic authorship, what is the concept of authorship that we are working with today? Is it Q1 and Q2 and Qinf? Will a future generation find this position unsatisfactory, and centre its attention on the book instead? How many far-fetched theories have been hazarded by modern writers who are locked up in their own crippling presuppositions? Even the vagaries and extravagances of ancient exegesis can have a sobering effect on current scholarship. We need not repeat the mistakes of the past, and we can be made more aware of our own presuppositions.[145]

For Murphy the message of Ecclesiastes has suffered from excessive summarising and he approaches its message by studying the text's major words.[146] Qoheleth is in conflict with traditional wisdom but he should not be set in radical opposition with other biblical wisdom by suggesting that he is deeply pessimistic and ultimately nihilistic. Folly is never an option for Qoheleth and although he couldn't grasp wisdom he believed it was there. If Qoheleth's teaching is sometimes in conflict with traditional wisdom his method is not. As regards historical Old Testament literature, Murphy argues, we have no evidence of what Qoheleth thought about the salvation history, and we should not try to speculate on this.

The epilogue of 12:9-14 is an addition to the book, and is probably best regarded as a unity, although "it was somehow not fitting that the enigmatic book of Ecclesiastes should come to an end without the subtlety and open-ended character that the epilogue shows."[147] 12:13-14 do not fit well with Qoheleth. With respect to the fear of God and importance of obedience "[t]he epilogue is obviously putting forth an ideal which has been developed elsewhere and which is not a concern in Ecclesiastes."[148]

3.4.6 Whybray on Ecclesiastes

For Whybray Ecclesiastes is a wisdom text but in order to express his ideas Qoheleth had to develop a new style of discourse. His use of the first person singular is unique and betrays the influence of the Greek cult of the individual.

---

[144] MURPHY, *Ecclesiastes*, lv.
[145] Ibid., lv-lvi.
[146] Ibid., lvi-lxix.
[147] Ibid., 130.
[148] Ibid., 126.

"Q is an 'intellectual' in a sense otherwise unknown to the OT. In his remorseless determination to probe the nature of things he belongs to a new world of thought, though ... his sense of God's transcendence ... is a Jewish inheritance which distinguishes him quite radically from the secular philosopher."[149] Ecclesiastes was written in the Ptolemaic period which was a time of intense economic development; hence Qoheleth's preoccupation with financial matters. It is a work of the later post-exilic period, when the old values of Israelite society had been displaced because of the intellectual influence of Hellenism and the new spirit of commercial enterprise.

Ecclesiastes is not a systematic treatise and there is generally no progression of thought from one section to the next, but rather a cyclical tendency. Whybray accounts for the tensions as ones existing within Qoheleth's own mind: "Qoheleth was attempting to reconcile his own experience of life and of the world with the traditional wisdom tradition which he inherited, and ... he offers no universal or satisfactory answer to these problems."[150] Form critical criteria are insufficient to determine the structure, especially as they do not make room for individual genius. As regards the structure of Ecclesiastes Whybray argues that there is no uniformity in the way the book has been put together. Some sections are random collections, others show formal and logical continuity. Section divisions between these two types of sections are not clear. Exegetes must be content to leave the questions open. The different themes are closely related in Ecclesiastes but there is no co-ordinating theme. 1:2 and 12:8 are from an editor, and not from Qoheleth. Whybray takes the view that 1:4-12:7 is the work of Qoheleth, while stressing that complete consistency in a work like Ecclesiastes is hardly to be expected.[151]

Qoheleth is not a systematic philosopher. There are inconsistencies in his thought but this is because his problems are insoluble. He is a seeker after truth about man and his fate in the world, and is concerned to test the wisdom tradition by experience. He is not a teacher but one who presents problems to his reader, thereby inviting them to pursue these questions for themselves. It is uncertain whether Qoheleth's thought is ultimately optimistic or pessimistic, but he is certainly a realist. More recently Whybray has argued for the dominance of the exhortation to joy in Ecclesiastes.[152]

In 12:9-14, which is universally acknowledged as not from Qoheleth, Whybray discerns two different hands.[153] The first praises Qoheleth uncritically

---

[149] R.N. WHYBRAY, *Ecclesiastes* (NCBC; London: Marshall, Morgan and Scott; Grand Rapids: Eerdmans, 1989) 6, 7.

[150] Ibid., 18, 19.

[151] Ibid., 169.

[152] R.N. WHYBRAY, "Qoheleth, Preacher of Joy," *JSOT* 23 (1992) 87-98. We will discuss this view in detail in ch. 7. It may indicate a stronger structure to Ecclesiastes than his earlier work recognises.

[153] WHYBRAY, *Ecclesiastes* (NCBC), 169.

whereas the second appears to be softening the effect of his teaching. We can not determine further editorial hands in the text. V. 9-10 contain the only direct information about Qoheleth and are probably from a personal acquaintance who was a former student or admiring colleague.

3.4.7 The Fruit of Historical Critical Readings of Ecclesiastes

On a number of issues a consensus has emerged out of historical critical study of Ecclesiastes. There is near universal agreement that Solomon was not the author and that the book was written in the third century BC or thereabouts. Throughout the twentieth century there has been a growing commitment to the basic unity of Ecclesiastes with the exception of the epilogue. Any notion of strong Greek influence on the book tends to be rejected although broad connections with Greek thought are recognised. Generally Qoheleth is thought to be rooted in Hebraic thought and part of the wisdom movement in Israel.[154] However there is no agreement about the structure of Ecclesiastes, nor about its message. There is widespread agreement that Qoheleth is distancing himself from certain biblical traditions but scholars are not agreed as to whether Ecclesiastes is basically positive or extremely pessimistic in its outlook.

As regards tradition criticism there has been an ongoing debate about Ecclesiastes' relationship to the biblical wisdom and other traditions. Generally it is assumed that while Ecclesiastes is rooted in the biblical wisdom tradition, Qoheleth is subjecting it to a radical critique and distancing himself from parts of it. Qoheleth makes little or no mention of Israel's covenant traditions and scholars disagree as to how to interpret this. Some take him to be highly critical of these traditions and especially of the blessing/curse tradition while others, like Murphy, refuse to make a judgement from his silence. Redaction criticism has never come into its own in historical critical research into Ecclesiastes. Childs' canonical approach to Ecclesiastes is regarded by some as an example of redaction criticism, and we will examine this in the next chapter.

3.5 Re-thinking Historical Criticism

3.5.1 The Importance of Recontextualising Historical Criticism

Historical criticism has dominated the interpretation of Ecclesiastes this century. As we have shown the historical critical method emerged out of and has been deeply shaped by modernity. However, part of the legacy of modernity in Old Testament study has been the tendency to decontextualise this method of

---

[154] Although, as we noted in ch. 2, there are some like N. LOHFINK, *Kohelet* (NEB; Würzburg: Echter Verlag, 1993), who argue for strong Greek influence upon Ecclesiastes.

interpretation so that it is simply regarded as normal.[155] We noticed this with Wellhausen, to an extent with Rogerson, and it is clearly present in Krentz's account of the historical critical method, which assumes the standard account of modernity. Some indications of this are Krentz's assumption that there is such a thing as *the* historical critical method, his understanding of history as objective, systematic knowledge of the past, his failure to take the role of the reader seriously in interpretation, his reluctance to see faith and the historical critical method as in conflict, thereby privatising faith, his understanding that the historical critical method will allow us to hear the OT *ideas* and his privileging of the present state of historiography, thereby affirming the idea of progress.

The historical critical method is however always related to an epistemology, and if we are to assess its significance it must be assessed in its larger philosophical and cultural context. Indeed this tendency to decontextualise the historical critical method is itself an indication of how deeply it has been shaped by modernity. Toulmin notes that "one aim of 17th-century philosophers was to frame all their questions in terms that rendered them *independent of context*" and demonstrates how this aspiration towards neutral objectivity permeates Enlightenment thought.[156] A vital part of our investigation has, therefore, been to recontextualise the historical critical method and to demonstrate that it has been deeply shaped by modernity.[157]

3.5.2 The Importance of Recognising the Diversity Within Modernity

Recontextualisation increases our understanding of historical criticism but we still have to evaluate this deeper understanding. And in the process of evaluation it is important to remember that although there is a common underlying paradigm or worldview which informs modernity, the standard account tends to suppress the diversity of approaches within the unity. It is common, for example, for historical criticism to be referred to as a unitary entity. And it does have a certain unity insofar as the philosophies of history informing it are all modern. However, the diversity of modern philosophies of history

---

[155] J. BARTON, *People of the Book? The Authority of the Bible in Christianity* (2nd ed.; London: SPCK, 1993) 8, says of the historical critical method that "[i]t is a particular attitude towards the study of the biblical text, which became usual in German biblical study in the nineteenth century, and until recently was *normal* in most university faculties of theology" (italics mine).

[156] TOULMIN, *Cosmopolis*, 21.

[157] Wright's distinction between basic and consequential beliefs is relevant here (cf. N.T. WRIGHT, *The New Testament and the People of God* [Minneapolis: Fortress, 1992] 126). The consequential philosophies of history are shaped by the basic Enlightenment beliefs. Cf. Botha's view that the epistemic paradigm remains constant (M.E. BOTHA, "Understanding Our Age. Philosophy at the Turning Point of the 'Turns'? – the endless search for the universal," *Tydskrif vir Christelike Wetenskap* 30/2 [1994] 16-31).

informing the historical critical method rarely receives attention. McIntyre is one of the few scholars who recognises this diversity:

> It is such considerations which lie at the back of my opening remarks in this essay, for they are the justification for the rejection of what has become accepted dogma, not only in history and those disciplines associated with it, but in theology itself, namely, that there is a single identifiable entity called historical criticism, which operates a simple criterion of historicity, in judging and validating historical claims, implicit in those statements which refer to the past. This dogma has dominated not only the unsympathetic critic's approach to the historicity of events described in the Bible, but even the attempts of theologians to understand and express the historical passages of the Christian faith.[158]

Even within modernity it is legitimate to ask of a biblical scholar which philosophy of history undergirds his historical critical methodology. Thus Gabler's rationalistic hermeneutic[159] is very different to Herder's historicist approach,[160] even if at a certain level they both work with a modern idea of progress. And de Wette's Kantianism is different to Vatke's Hegelianism. And in the context of the postmodern turn philosophy of history has become more diverse and fragmented so that, one can no longer, like Krentz, simply give an account of the current state of historiography with an assumed idea of progress. Historiography, like most disciplines nowadays, is pluralistic[161] and one must account for one's particular philosophy of history as opposed to others. The main types of philosophy of history in the nineteenth century all tend to operate within the modern worldview, but nevertheless they will and do produce different results when applied to the OT, and it is important to bear this diversity in mind when evaluating historical criticism. Thus even if one was to assume the standard account of modernity it would still be necessary for an OT scholar to account for his particular approach to history and thus to the historical critical method.

3.5.3 The Importance of Evaluating the Context in Which the Historical Critical Method Emerged

However, as we have seen, the standard account of modernity can no longer be assumed. Modernity has given birth to the historical critical method, and the latter bears all the marks of family resemblance. What are we to make of modernity? Our answer to this question will be determinative for the direction we propose in OT studies in all sorts of ways. One can approach the question of

---

[158] McINTYRE, "Historical Criticism," 374.

[159] See M. BRETT, *Biblical Criticism in Crisis? The Impact of the Canonical Approach on Old Testament Studies* (Cambridge: CUP, 1991) 82-85.

[160] On Herder's view of history see COLLINGWOOD, *The Idea of History*, 88-93.

[161] Cf. K. JENKINS, *Re-thinking History* (London: Routledge, 1991); and idem, *On 'What is History?' From Carr and Elton to Rorty and White* (London: Routledge, 1995), for an indication of the present state of debate about philosophy of history.

modernity from many directions, and I would not want to underestimate its achievements or suggest that reverting to a pre-modern position is possible or warranted. In this section we will evaluate only one aspect of modernity, namely its attitude to religion. Clearly this is relevant to the interpretation of the OT and it will give us an idea of the extent to which a critical stance is required in relation to modernity.

Toulmin does not make a lot of the anti-Christian nature of the Enlightenment, although he does recognise that humanism emerged within a predominantly Christian Europe. Gadamer, however, alerts us to the centrality of the religious implications of modernity. He argues that the Enlightenment critique is directed primarily against Christianity and that historical criticism has its roots in the Enlightenment's faith in reason.[162] The anti-Christian aspect of modernity is also foregrounded by Gay in *The Enlightenment. An Interpretation. Vol. 1: The Rise of Modern Paganism*.[163] In his view the Enlightenment philosophers' claim to distance themselves from Christianity has not generally been taken seriously.[164] He acknowledges some truth in the view that modernity is a secularised version of Christianity but rejects the image of the two as connected by a bridge:

> it fails to evoke the essential hostility between eighteenth-century religion and eighteenth-century secularism: the philosophes rudely treated the Christian past rather as Voltaire treated the plays of Shakespeare – as a dunghill strewn with diamonds, crying out to be pillaged and badly needing to be cleaned out.[165]

The Christian era was regarded by the Enlightenment thinkers as a period of darkness and retreat from reason. Christianity was criticised for its contempt of antiquity, and even those mediaevals who preserved the classics were criticised because, "while they held grimly on to the ramparts of antiquity, they surrendered its citadel – the autonomy of critical thought."[166] It was well recognised that belief in revelation undermined the autonomy of reason, and that, in reviving antiquity a worldview was being espoused poles apart from traditional Christian perspectives. Cassirer perceptively alert us to the fact that the Enlightenment does not so much reject religion as appropriate a new form of faith;[167] however this is faith judged by reason:

> The relations between the concept of God and the concepts of truth, morality, law are by no means abandoned, but their direction changes. An exchange of index symbols takes place, as it were. That which formerly had established other concepts, now moves into the position of that which is to be established,

---

[162] See quotes at outset of chapter.

[163] P. GAY, *The Enlightenment. An Interpretation. Vol. 1: The Rise of Modern Paganism* (London: Norton, 1977).

[164] Ibid., 322.

[165] Ibid., 323; cf. also CARROLL, *Humanism*, 117, 120-121.

[166] GAY, *The Enlightenment*, 226.

[167] E. CASSIRER, *The Philosophy of the E   htenment* (Princeton: Princeton UP, 1951) 134ff.

and that which hitherto had justified other concepts, now finds itself in the position of a concept which requires justification.[168]

A logical extension of this is *Religion Within the Bounds of Reason.* Epistemologically modernity is clearly rooted in views which appear incongruent with Christianity.[169] Toulmin's narrative alerts us to the centrality of human autonomy and rational analysis in modernity. This is nothing new, but his contextualising of this aspiration helps us to understand Enlightenment despair over Christianity and the desperate need for certainty. The answer was found in secular reason. For reasons described above, Toulmin finds this to be an understandable but wrong move. From a Christian perspective Newbigin agrees, but for very different reasons.[170]

Newbigin alerts us to modernity's espousal of secular reason as a reaction to appeals to revelation and tradition as sources of authority.[171] Observation of facts and critical reflection upon them are the source of reliable knowledge, not faith and revelation. Newbigin contrasts Locke's view of faith – "a persuasion of our minds short of knowledge", with Augustine's *"credo ut intelligam"*. For Augustine faith is the path to knowledge, for Descartes doubt. In Newbigin's view Cartesianism is inherently self-destructive;[172] to privilege doubt epistemologically inevitably (and ironically) leads to scepticism and nihilism. Furthermore secular reason has not escaped tradition and faith. Tradition and faith inevitably affect epistemology:

> Reason is a faculty with which we try to grasp the different elements in our experience in an orderly way, so that as we say 'they make sense'. It is not a separate source of information about what is the case. It can only function within a linguistic and cultural tradition. ... All rationality is socially and culturally conditioned.

> In the 'Age of Reason' ... 'reason' was used to denote conformity with a set of assumptions derived from the science and philosophy of the time. ... Reason operates within a specific tradition of rational discourse, which is carried by a specific human community. No supra-cultural 'reason' can stand in judgement over all human traditions of rationality. All reason operates within a total

---

[168] Ibid., 159.

[169] As an example of how strong this privileging of reason was in opposition to religion cf. ROGERSON, *W.M.L. de Wette*, 27-30, for a description of a lecture given by Kant in Jena in 1798. As Rogerson notes, "There are, not surprisingly, radical implications for biblical interpretation in this position" (ibid., 29).

[170] L. NEWBIGIN, *Foolishness to the Greeks* (London: SPCK, 1986); and idem, "Truth and Authority in Modernity," In: P. SAMPSON, V. SAMUEL, and C. SUGDEN (eds.), *Faith and Modernity* (1994) 60-88.

[171] NEWBIGIN, "Truth and Authority in Modernity," 61. Cf. Gunton's view of modernity as the secularisation of Christianity (C. GUNTON, *The One, the Three and the Many. God, Creation and the Culture of Modernity* [Cambridge: CUP, 1993]).

[172] NEWBIGIN, "Truth and Authority in Modernity," 62-64; cf. CARROLL, *Humanism*, 124-125.

worldview which is embodied in the language, the concepts and the models which are the means by which those who share them can reason together.[173]

Part of the Enlightenment's view of reason is its rejection of tradition as formative and belief in rational progress. For Descartes "[t]he task of reason begins on *terra nullius*, to create the world again from the ground up. The building blocks themselves must also be created out of nothing, by the power of the mind alone. ... The palace of Reason will be constructed only from propositions that are clear and distinct. The rest is rubbish."[174] In fact, in its appropriation of antiquity modernity reveals its positioning in a particular tradition. This non-neutrality is widely accepted today and once again raises the question of the pedigree of the historical critical method and its appropriateness for biblical interpretation. Clearly this is a very different approach to faith seeking understanding.

Modernity is under attack from a variety of directions today. Carroll, for example, subtitles his text on humanism, "The Wreck of Western Culture" and concludes that

> [h]umanism failed because man is not the centre of creation, in the sense of being creature and creator in one. ... human reason is powerful only on a narrow front within strict limits. ... Our story is told. Its purpose has been simple, to shout that humanism is dead, has been so since the late nineteenth century, and it is about time to quit. Let us bury it with appropriate rites, which means honouring the little that was good, and understanding what went wrong and why.[175]

Not all would agree with Carroll.[176] His position does, however, indicate that the assumptions of modernity can no longer be taken for granted. This aside, our point in this section is that the historical critical method was shaped within an ethos of suspicion towards Christianity. With the modern worldview now itself a target of suspicion, the question is again foregrounded of the extent of pagan[177] influence upon biblical studies and its appropriateness. It is not just that a theological, a literary and an historical hermeneutic have different *aims* – if that were the case they could easily be seen as complementary. The problem is a deeper one of basic views about the world which shape the theological, literary or

---

[173] NEWBIGIN, "Truth and Authority in Modernity," 79, 80.

[174] CARROLL, *Humanism*, 119.

[175] Ibid., 228-232.

[176] Cf. J. HABERMAS, *The Philosophical Discourse of Modernity* (Cambridge: Polity, 1987); C. NORRIS, *Spinoza and the Origins of Modern Critical Theory* (The Bucknell Lectures in Literary Theory; Oxford: Basil Blackwell, 1991); idem, *Truth and the Ethics of Criticism* (Manchester: Manchester UP, 1994); and E. GELLNER, *Postmodernism, Reason and Religion* (London: Routledge, 1992), as examples of philosophers who are very positive towards the "project of modernity".

[177] I use pagan here in the sense in which R. CLOUSER, *The Myth of Religious Neutrality. An Essay on the Hidden Role of Religious Belief in Theories* (Notre Dame; London: University of Notre Dame Press, 1991) 36-40, uses it.

historical hermeneutic. As it has developed the historical critical hermeneutic tends to operate with very different basic beliefs to most theological hermeneutics, beliefs which occupy the same terrain as religion, viz. questions like who are we, how we know in a reliable way etc. And these basic beliefs of different hermeneutics tend to be antithetical, so that it is hard to believe that a synthesis of views stemming from opposed starting points will lead one to the truth about the OT.

This is particularly relevant with the widespread, renewed recognition of the Bible as much more than just an ancient text.[178] If the Bible is taken seriously as *the story* how would that reshape the historical critical method? What would a contemporary biblical hermeneutic look like developed in an ethos sympathetic to Christianity and shaped by the biblical story? Modernity has tended to privatise religion and to insist that the Christian narrative not be allowed to shape life in its wholeness. The problematising of this privatisation[179] reopens the question of how the Christian narrative would shape a biblical hermeneutic in a postliberal context.

3.5.4 The Importance of Showing the Link Between Philosophies of History (the Context) and Particular Approaches to the Old Testament

Clearly there is a link between modern philosophies of history and OT interpretation. However, as we seek to evaluate modernity and the historical critical method an important part of the evidence is the way in which particular philosophies of history give rise to particular approaches to the OT. These approaches could then be evaluated to see if they do justice to the OT. This is a vast area of investigation, and we will only use one example to indicate the direction such research might take.

We have already noted that in general modern philosophy of history yielded inter alia a source critical approach in OT studies. This was firstly applied to the Pentateuch and the prophets and then later to Ecclesiastes, as we have seen. Within the prophets this approach manifested itself as a concern to identify the authentic words of the prophet from later accretions. Brett argues persuasively that this approach to the prophets is connected with romantic idealism in

---

[178] Cf. Childs, Newbigin, Lindbeck, Frei, etc.

[179] Modernity has privatised religion but from a Christian perspective this is inadmissable. Wright expresses this very clearly: "The reason why stories come into conflict with each other is that worldviews, and the stories which characterise them, are in principle *normative*: that is, they claim to make sense of the whole of reality. ... It is ironic that many people in the modern world have regarded Christianity as a private worldview, a set of private stories. Some Christians have actually played right into this trap. But in principle the whole point of Christianity is that it offers a story which is the story of the whole world. It is public truth. Otherwise it collapses into Gnosticism" (WRIGHT, *The New Testament and the People of God*, 41, 42).

historiography.[180] Such an approach to history focused its investigations on the inner life of great individuals as the key to history. The result of this approach in studies of the prophets is that reconstruction of the exact words of the prophet and their interpretation becomes the goal of exegesis, with little attention being paid to later additions and to the final form of the text. Brett cites Wellhausen and Gunkel as examples of this and notes Gunkel went so far as to contrast the artificial, written stages of the tradition with the vital original context in the life of the nation.

Below we will note the relationship of this link to readings of Ecclesiastes. Suffice it to note here that different philosophies of history shape OT interpretation in decisive ways. Contra Rogerson, the results of historical criticism cannot be distinguished from philosophy, and the question arises as to what type of approach to history would be most appropriate to an OT hermeneutic.

3.5.5 The Importance of Developing a Christian View of History and Biblical Interpretation

As we argued above, that type of approach to the OT which focuses interpretation upon the person or event behind the text is connected to a particular romantic idealist philosophy of history. Thus, if we are to evaluate such an OT hermeneutic we will have to ask at some point, is this a right understanding of history and is it appropriate for understanding the OT? Many OT scholars, like Krentz, when faced with a question like this simply refer to the current state of historical scholarship. Clearly this is important but the evaluative issue will not go away; one still has to account critically for one's philosophy of history and anyway, philosophy of history is increasingy pluralistic. And the point we wish to make in this section is that such evaluation will inevitably involve one's view of religion. If one is to follow Gunkel in locating revelation in the peculiarity of the Hebrew Spirit then that is to assume a certain understanding of religion. Our argument is that biblical interpretation is best served by a philosophy of history shaped by the Christian narrative.[181] We will argue for this approach in this section and then give some indication of the shape of such an approach in the next section.

Throughout Krentz's account of the historical critical method there is a tension between reading Scripture as Scripture and the handling of it by historical

---

[180] BRETT, *Biblical Criticism in Crisis?*, 89-93.

[181] In his evaluation of Childs' hermeneutic, P.R. NOBLE, *The Canonical Approach. A Critical Reconstruction of the Hermeneutics of Brevard S. Childs* (Biblical Interpretation Series 16; Leiden; New York: Brill, 1995) 369, makes the same point. Cf. also R. MORGAN with J. BARTON, *Biblical Interpretation* (Oxford Bible Series; Oxford: OUP, 1988) 187, who rightly makes the point that religious interpretation requires a theoretical framework which integrates religion and human existence. Our argument is that such a framework should be shaped by the Christian narrative.

criticism as another ancient text. Krentz notes this tension but seems to hope that somehow faith and the historical method are reconcilable. The mistake he makes, in my opinion is to place faith and the historical critical method on the same level, whereas they function at different levels. The historical method is always tied to some philosophy of history and to some epistemology, which in turn is rooted in some worldview.[182] In its pre-theoretical sense faith is akin to this level of worldview. In assessing the relationship between historical criticism and faith, the important question is how the 'worldviewish' and philosophical underpinnings of the particular historical critical method being used compare to the Christian story or worldview.

Different worldviews may work with the historical critical method but they will shape it in different ways. Hence the serious mistake of assuming one type of historical critical method. Thus Christian faith conflicts with the modern historical critical method, not in its concern to take history seriously but in *the way in which* it takes history seriously.[183] Brueggemann states this most clearly:

> The claim that 'God acts in history' is not compatible with our Enlightenment notions of control, reason, objectivity, and technique. Indeed, if one begins with the assumptions of modernity, history can only be thought of as a bare story of power, in which the God of the Bible can never make a significant appearance. The claim that 'God acts in history', that God's word impinges upon the human process, requires a very different beginning point.[184]

As Wright says of biblical literature, "The language functions as a lens through which historical events can be seen as bearing the full meaning that the community believed them to possess. However foreign to post-Enlightenment thought it may be to see meaning within history, such language grows naturally out of Israel's basic monotheistic and covenant theology."[185] Thus Christian faith and the historical critical method need not be antithetical, provided the narrative informing and shaping the particular historical critical method is Christian. Even today, however, OT scholars are very reluctant to move in this direction.

> Many have felt the pressure in recent decades to engage in scholarly work, including specialist study of the Bible, from within the post-Enlightenment modernist perspective, putting specifically Christian perspectives on hold while the exercise is going on. This has been helped by the impression that ... matters of religious opinion are simply private options which do not engage with the public world. ... this way of conceiving the problem is based on a

---

[182] This is of course from my thetical-critical position.

[183] MCINTYRE, "Historical Criticism," 378, expresses a similar point: "there are elements in the Christian faith which are not amenable to description in terms that would be admitted by a secular or positivist historian."

[184] W. BRUEGGEMANN, "Response to J. Richard Middleton," *HTR* 87/3 (1994) 279.

[185] WRIGHT, *The New Testament and the People of God*, 425-426.

mistake. All worldviews, including both the modernism of the Enlightenment and Christianity, claim to be public and comprehensive.[186]

No one has exposed the antithesis between the modern-historical critical approach to the Bible and the traditional Christian approach more clearly than Levenson.[187] He argues that a modern historical critical reading is altogether at odds with a 'literary' reading. In the process he exposes the synthetic nature of much contemporary Protestant OT scholarship. It claims to be purely historical-critical but is in fact constrained by Christian (and often anti-Semitic) perspectives in all sorts of ways. Krentz, incidentally, is a good example of this. Consider his reference to the Bible as *Scripture* throughout his text. Ironically, Levenson, even as he exposes the tension between these two ways of reading the Bible, himself articulates his "own intuition … that the two seemingly opposite directions in which these essays move are each indispensable avenues to the larger and more encompassing truth. The dignity both of traditional interpretation and of modern criticism depends on a careful separation of the two and a reengagement on new terms."[188] What Levenson does not recognise is that different worldviews inform these different readings and these worldviews are antithetical. In terms of their starting points there is not going to be a larger and more encompassing truth. To suggest there is betrays an anachronistic idea of progress.

Thus, for a number of reasons the time is ripe for a reassessment of the epistemological (and historical) foundations of OT study. Firstly historical criticism is not a neutral hermeneutic but has been shaped by perspectives suspicious of the public nature of Christianity. Secondly, there is no single historical critical method but a variety of approaches informed by different philosophies of history. And thirdly, as we will discuss below, historical ciritical methods tend to overlook the literary and theological aspects of the OT texts. Within NT study Wright is attempting such a reconstruction along the lines of critical realism. Suffice it to note at this point that such reconstruction does not involve a reversion to pre-modernity.[189] One of the historical critical approach's great contributions has been to focus the historicity of the Old Testament. Some reactions to the historical critical method such as Frei and Lindbeck are in danger of jettisoning this insight, which is a mistake. In my view historical questions are a key element in any biblical hermeneutic, since Scripture is undoubtedly a text developed in and embedded in history. Thus source, form, tradition and redaction

---

[186] Ibid., 137.

[187] J.D. LEVENSON, *The Hebrew Bible, the Old Testament and Historical Criticism* (Louisville: Westminister/John Knox, 1993).

[188] Ibid., xiv, xv.

[189] Cf. WRIGHT, *The New Testament and the People of God*, 9, "I think, that the heirs of the Enlightenment have been too shrill in their denunciation of traditional Christianity, and that Christianity has often been too unshakeably arrogant in resisting new questions."

criticism will always be valid parts of the hermeneutic enterprise. What will need reconsideration is one's understanding of history and how this shapes these disciplines. This is precisely the sort of activity Wright engages in. He defends the historical focus of the historical critical method and the legitimacy of form criticism, for example, but critiques the assumptions that have informed form criticism of the NT through the influence of Bultmann.[190]

Thus it seems to me that what is urgently required in Old Testament study is a reassessment of its epistemological (and historical) foundations from a Christian perspective and an exploration of how that would shape source, form, redaction and tradition criticism differently, as well as how that would relate historical to other types of interpretation.[191] But these are very complex questions. In the 60's Stephen Neill recognised the need for biblical interpretation to be informed by a theology of history which would not by itself solve the historical problems but would "hold the ring within which a solution can be found."[192] And Thiselton and Pannenberg have likewise stressed the need for a philosophy of history that is theologically informed.[193] However, Wright notes that there has been little progress in this area over recent decades.[194]

In narrative texts like the Pentateuch the historical aspect of the text is a more central issue than in a text like Ecclesiastes, and so we will not pursue the question of the referential nature of OT texts. Suffice it to note here that some of the philosophies of history that have shaped the historical critical method have focused interpretation away from the biblical text. Romantic idealism is an example that we have considered. In this way the literary and theological dimensions of the text have been obscured. If the aim of interpretation is understanding of the text then an understanding of history and a hermeneutic is required which will faciliate the bringing into focus of the different aspects of biblical texts and their interrelationships. And it could be argued that, with its transcendent focus a Christian understanding of history is less likely to be reductionistic in the way that some historical criticism has been.[195] This brings us to the next point.

---

[190] Cf. ibid., 418-443.

[191] It is important to note that I am recommending this agenda in the context of a genuine pluralism in OT studies. In this respect see ch. 7.

[192] S. NEILL and N.T. WRIGHT, *The Interpretation of the New Testament. 1861-1986* (Oxford: OUP, 1988) 366.

[193] Cf. A.C. THISELTON, *The Two Horizons. New Testament Hermeneutics and Philosophical Description* (Carlisle: Paternoster; Grand Rapids: Eerdmans, 1980) 51-84.

[194] NEILL and WRIGHT, *The Interpretation of the New Testament*, 366.

[195] The Dutch Christian philosopher, H. DOOYEWEERD, *A New Critique of Theoretical Thought I-IV* (Amsterdam; Philadelphia: Presbyterian and Reformed Publishing Company, 1953-1958); idem, *In the Twilight of Western Thought* (New Jersey: Craig Press, 1960), stressed the non-reductionistic attitude of a consistent Christian perspective on reality. The latter should refuse to make any immanent aspect of creation, like history, the key to understanding the whole.

3.5.6 The Importance of a Comprehensive Biblical Hermeneutic

In chapter seven we will give further attention to the overall shape that a
Christian biblical hermeneutic might take. For the moment we note the overly
historical emphasis of the historical critical hermeneutic, which makes one
wonder whether an *historical* hermeneutic is equipped to allow Scripture to speak
on its own terms? Certainly there is an historical aspect to Scripture and this is
what the historical critical method identifies so clearly. However, before Scripture
is a source for history writing it is literature and highly ideological literature at
that, as our designation of it as *Scripture* indicates. "The theologian," and we
might say 'the biblical scholar,' "has more to think about than the application to
his subject-matter of the canons of historical inquiry. ... The historical method is
not to be taken as the sole component of theological method for the simple reason
that theology and the Christian faith from which it draws its material includes
more than history."[196] The historical critical method focuses on the text as
coming into being at a particular time and place but, at best it relegates to second
place the text as literature and kerygma.

A good example of this is the reduction of literary criticism in biblical
studies to source criticism. As Barton notes, literary scholars are surprised that
Old Testament *literary* criticism should refer to source criticism.[197] Barton
defends the legitimacy of such 'literary' criticism against the criticism that it
comes looking for sources and finds them, by maintaining that source criticism
has its roots in 'observable discrepancies' in the Pentateuch.[198] At this point
Barton makes a typically modern move by reducing the problem to the facts *of
the text*. What about the mode of observation? The origin of Old Testament
literary criticism cannot be reduced to the text or to observation; it is an
interaction between the two. Observation is, however, far from neutral and was
deeply shaped by historical research of the day as we have demonstrated.[199] And
this approach, as Sternberg and Ouweneel recognise, subordinates literary
criticism (in the true sense of the word) to historical criticism and makes the latter
depend on whatever historical philosophy is followed, often nineteenth century
evolutionistic philosophy.[200] Commenting on the documentary hypothesis,
Ouweneel says that "[i]nstead of the evolutionistic approach being the *result* of

---

[196] McINTYRE, "Historical Criticism," 379.

[197] BARTON, *Reading the Old Testament*, 20.

[198] Ibid., 21ff.

[199] Cf. HAHN, *The Old Testament in Modern Research*, 1-43; W.J. OUWENEEL, *A Critical
Analysis of the External and Internal Prolegomena of Systematic Theology* (Unpubl. DTh thesis,
University of the Orange Free State, 1993) II: 384-427.

[200] Cf. Sternberg's very useful discussion on the interrelationship between source and
discourse (M. STERNBERG, *The Poetics of Biblical Narrative. Ideological Literature and the Drama
of Reading* [Bloomington: Indiana University Press, 1985] 13-23); and OUWENEEL, *A Critical
Analysis*, II: 391).

careful historical criticism, the latter itself being based on literary criticism, in reality things are reversed: literary criticism is subordinated to historical criticism, and the latter is made to depend on evolutionistic prejudice."[201]

If Wright is correct that "[t]he NT ... must be read so as to be understood, read within appropriate contexts, within an acoustic which will allow its full overtones to be heard,"[202] then a biblical hermeneutic must correlate with the ontology of the Bible and take its literary, ideological *and* historical nature into account, and accurately interrelate these. What Wright says of Shakespeare is true of the Old Testament:

> A volume of Shakespeare may be used to prop up a table leg, or it may be used as a basis for a philosophical theory. It is not difficult, though, to see that using it as the foundation for dramatic productions of the plays themselves carries more authenticity than either of these ... There is a general appropriateness about using Shakespeare as a basis for staging plays which justifies itself without much more argument.[203]

3.6 Evaluating Historical Critical Readings of Ecclesiastes

How then are we to evaluate historical critical readings of Ecclesiastes? Have they been a success or a failure? Undoubtedly there have been huge advances, as the thorough philological, linguistic, structural and intertextual elements of the range of contemporary commentaries on Ecclesiastes make quite clear. It must also be remembered that more recent historical critical study of Ecclesiastes, like that of Murphy,[204] is somewhat different from that of Barton and McNeile. Other influences have come to bear on the historical critical method which have modified it considerably. Murphy, for example, has followed Wright's New Critical analysis of Ecclesiastes as we noted above. Recent works on Ecclesiastes such as Ogden and Fredericks manifest a much greater concern for the literary shape of the text.[205] These new directions are still in their early days, but show much potential in helping one to understand the text as a whole. And, if this is the test of interpretation, then much of the historical critical work of this century on Ecclesiastes must, despite all the advances, be judged a failure. Different reconstructed texts have tended to be the focus of interpretation and these have yielded a confusing variety of views about the message of Qoheleth.

---

[201] Ibid.

[202] WRIGHT, *The New Testament and the People of God*, 6.

[203] Ibid.

[204] MURPHY, *Ecclesiastes*.

[205] G. OGDEN, *Qoheleth* (Readings – A New Biblical Commentary; Sheffield: JSOT, 1987); and D.C. FREDERICKS, *Qoheleth's Language: Re-evaluating its Nature and Date* (Lewiston: Edwin Mellen, 1988); idem, *Coping with Transience. Ecclesiastes on Brevity in Life* (The Biblical Seminar; Sheffield: JSOT Press, 1993).

It is with McNeile that it is most apparent that a reconstructed text has become the focus of interpretation and not the final form of the text as we have it. There has been widespread agreement among scholars this century that the text as we have it is basically reliable. Yet, in his "Notes on select passages," McNeile makes no comments about the 'interpolations' apart from the epilogue so that the reconstructed text has become the focus of comment.[206] It was Siegfried who set this type of source critical approach to Ecclesiastes in motion. Subsequent return to the substantial unity of Ecclesiastes raises the question of whether his idea was a 'right one' after all. If recent trends are anything to go by, then it would certainly seem as if Siegfried pointed study of Ecclesiastes in a wrong direction. This source critical approach represents the unhelpful dominance of a particular diachronic method which is applied at the expense of the complex literary contours of the text. Surprisingly McNeile still express hope about the positive value of the overall shape of the text. According to McNeile

> it may be gladly admitted that, under these successive hands, Koheleth's *Journal* has been not spoilt but enriched. By the annotations of two contemporary thinkers its value has been multiplied historically and doctrinally. It became a 'three-fold cord' whose drawing and attracting power has been 'not quickly broken.' It is in this triple form that Jews and Christians alike have counted it inspired.[207]

Barton concludes his section on Qoheleth's thought as follows: "It is a teaching which is to a Christian chilling and disappointing, but Qoheleth's negative work had, no doubt, a function to perform in clearing away outworn conceptions before a new, larger, truer, and more inspiring faith could have its birth."[208] Barton fails to consider the message of the text as a whole and assumes that his reconstructed message of Qoheleth is what counts. McNeile is aware of the larger three-fold cord and assumes that this contradictory three-fold voice can be heard positively. What he fails to pay attention to is the cord itself. If the three strands have been woven into a cord it would seem important to attend to the final product! The attempts by McNeile and Barton to synthesise a historical critical view with some kind of positive approach to Ecclesiastes as a three-fold cord or a negative precursor of the positive gospel are not convincing.

The confident division of Ecclesiastes into sources by Siegfried, Barton, McNeile etc., and the almost complete undermining of this approach by later historical critical scholarship acutely focuses the question of the validity of the source critical method. How did these scholars go so wrong in their handling of Ecclesiastes? At one level they seem to have not taken the difference between narrative genre and wisdom seriously enough, and to have applied what seemed to work with the Pentateuch directly to Ecclesiastes. However, source critical

---

[206] MCNEILE, *An Introduction to Ecclesiastes*, 56-94.
[207] Ibid., 27.
[208] BARTON, *Ecclesiastes*, 50.

analysis of the Pentateuch has come under increasing fire this century and it also seems to have been applied without any strong sense of the genre of narrative literature. The deeper problem with this type of source criticism seems to be its weddedness to a historical method which looks for scientific style and precision in literary texts and focuses interpretation on the reconstructed actual words of the historical Qoheleth behind the text in romantic idealist fashion. It is in the *way they observed* Ecclesiastes that the problem lies, contra Barton's notion of observed discrepancies.[209] Barton is, I think, correct that source criticism begins with an intuition about the text.[210] However, intuition is not a neutral category but is informed by one's assumptions and one's cultural context. In the grip of a scientistic and positivistic mindset, McNeile and Barton observed and intuited the sources they discerned. Source criticism remains an important tool for the interpretation of Ecclesiastes. However, as we mentioned earlier it will need to be shaped very differently and in close interaction with discourse analysis.

It is important to note that while most of the source critical reconstruction of Ecclesiastes has been rejected by contemporary scholars, one glaring omission remains: the epilogue. Across the critical board there is agreement that Qoheleth and the final editor differ from each other. Paradoxically, while no one is quite sure what Qoheleth's message was, all are sure that it was not what 'the editor' says it was! In this respect the source critical assumptions of Barton and McNeile live on, for contemporary historical critical scholars assume as strongly as they did that they can distinguish distinctively Qoheleth material from editorial material and assess the relationship between the two. This emphasis is also the legacy of the romantic idealism that we discussed above. The idea that if we can only isolate the historical Qoheleth material then we have the real data for interpretation has been most persistent.

However, while it does seem to me that we can discern editorial comment in 12:9-14 and 1:1, it is impossible to determine with any precision the limits of such activity, or to know whether the editor arranged the Qoheleth material in any particular way, what he left out and what he included and so on. With its repetition structures, Ecclesiastes shows signs of strong overall shaping, as Crenshaw acknowledges (see above). One wonders, therefore, on what basis one can assume that one can easily distinguish Qoheleth from editorial material. One can do this only if one assumes that overt editing is the only real editing in the text; an assumption which seems rather naive.

The near consensus that Qoheleth calls much of the Old Testament tradition into question and that the epilogue counteracts this tendency thereby making Qoheleth acceptable to orthodoxy seems to me questionable. Intuitively I am cautious on this direction, because of my thetical-critical position. On a straightforward reading the epilogue appears to contextualise Qoheleth's work –

---

[209] BARTON, *Reading the Old Testament*, 22.
[210] Ibid., 26.

he was a wise man who was engaged in the typical work of the wise – and to focus its message in terms of the call to fear God and obey his commands. The historical critical approach rather naively assumes that most Israelites were taken in by this epilogue which is clearly at odds with the main body of the text. We now, however, see the contradiction clearly. However, as Gordis points out, the canonical process was by no means so simplistic. It does seem to me therefore, that a recognition of the wrong path that Siegfried initiated in study of Ecclesiastes needs to be followed by a recognition of the literary nature of Ecclesiastes which will reopen the discussion of the relationship between the epilogue and the main body of the text. In the final chapter I present my suggestions in this critical area. It will not do to label 12:9-14 an addendum or epilogue, and then think that one can ignore it in interpreting the text, as most historical critical research has done this century.

The historical critical reading of Ecclesiastes this century has marginalised the poetics of wisdom literature. This is only now starting to come into its own but has still to be applied in detail to Ecclesiastes.[211] There is a great deal of work to be done on literary characteristics of Ecclesiastes-like repetition in a way comparable to Sternberg's work on repetition in narrative.[212] Source criticism will need to work with such discourse analysis to arrive at a more accurate view of the nature of Ecclesiastes.

3.7 Conclusion

In this chapter we have seen that historical criticism is a product of modernity and more particularly of nineteenth century philosophies of history. In particular the undermining of the standard account of modernity has alerted us to the need to attend to these philosophical presuppositions of historical criticism in our evaluation of it and historical critical readings of Ecclesiastes. Especially in early historical critical readings of Ecclesiastes there is a strong tendency to reconstruct the original words of Qoheleth and to focus upon these in interpreting Ecclesiastes. We have argued that this approach is connected with a romantic idealist philosophy of history. The legacy of this approach remains in the near universal tendency of modern commentators to bracket out the epilogue in their interpretation of Ecclesiastes.

Clearly one's view of history plays an important part in shaping one's hermeneutic for reading the OT and in the current context OT scholars will need to account for the philosophy of history that they bring to the OT. Views of religion will inevitably play a part here, and we have argued that Christian scholars ought to seek consciously to allow their philosophy of history and their epistemology to be shaped by the Christian narrative or worldview. What such

---

211 See chs. 5 and 7 for consideration of the poetics of wisdom texts.
212 Cf. STERNBERG, *The Poetics of Biblical Narrative*, 365-440.

shaping would involve for a philosophy of history and for a biblical hermeneutic needs much more consideration, but it was stressed that such a Christian hermeneutic would resist the historical reductionism of historical criticism. In the twentieth century several scholars have recognised this reductionism and sought to correct it. It is to these reactions that we now turn.

CHAPTER 4

BETWEEN EARLY AND LATE MODERNITY:
THE CANONICAL APPROACH, NEW CRITICISM, STRUCTURALISM
AND THE READING OF ECCLESIASTES

4.1 Introduction

Childs' canonical approach to reading the OT is an important but controversial reaction to the historical critical method. Childs denies any particular literary pedigree for his method, claiming only a theological motivation,[1] but this has been questioned.[2] Blenkinsopp says of Childs' *Introduction to the Old Testament as Scripture* (IOTS), "Much of what he has to say reflects recent and not so recent trends in literary criticism to which he makes only passing reference. There is also a shading off into hermeneutical and philosophical issues involved in deciding what is the 'real meaning' of a text."[3] Barton has more specifically noted the close similarity of the canonical method to the New Critical school of literary criticism and maintains that "we may expect new criticism and canon criticism to stand and fall together."[4] Barton also notes the close relationship between New Criticism (NC) and structuralism,[5] and by implication between canon criticism and structuralism.[6]

At the end of chapter three we noted historical criticism's failure to account for the theological and literary aspects of the OT. Not surprisingly Childs and proponents of a literary approach to the OT focus on these neglected aspects. As a professed *theological* reaction to historical criticism which nevertheless raises

---

[1]   B.S. CHILDS, *Introduction to the Old Testament as Scripture* (Philadelphia: Fortress, 1979) 74.

[2]   For the reactions to IOTS see *JSOT* 16 (1980); *Horizons in Biblical Theology* 2 (1980) 113-121; J. BARR, *Holy Scripture. Canon, Authority, Criticism* (Philadelphia: Westminster, 1983).

[3]   J. BLENKINSOPP, "A New Kind of Introduction: Professor Childs' *Introduction to the Old Testament as Scripture*," *JSOT* 16 (1980) 24.

[4]   J. BARTON, *Reading the Old Testament. Method in Biblical Study* (London: DLT, 1984) 153-154.

[5]   Ibid., 180-184. Although of course Barton recognises the reaction of structuralists to NC he also notes five resemblances between them: i. the focus upon the text itself. ii. emphasis on the non-referential character of literature. iii. heightened concern for shape, form and genre. iv. denial of the existence of true synonymity. v. recognition of the meaning of texts as determined and publicly accessible.

[6]   J. BARR, "Childs' *Introduction to the Old Testament as Scripture*," *JSOT* 16 (1980) 20, suggests that those interested in structuralism as an alternative to the historical critical method will be disappointed by Childs' IOTS.

literary questions about final-form readings of the text, Childs' canonical approach provides a convenient entry point into an exploration of reactions to an overly (and particular) historical emphasis in the interpretation of texts. In this chapter we will examine the canonical approach, NC, and structuralism in relation to Old Testament exegesis and the reading of Ecclesiastes. Childs has written briefly about a canonical approach to Ecclesiastes, and at least indirectly NC and structuralism have had a significant impact upon studies of Ecclesiastes. Wright and Loader are prominent exegetes who have fruitfully developed New Critical and structuralist insights in relation to Ecclesiastes.[7] Structuralism is also significant as a pre-cursor of the post-structuralism of postmodernism. Hence the title of this chapter.

In this chapter we will firstly describe Childs' canonical approach and then examine its application to Ecclesiastes. Secondly we will explore NC and the ways in which it has been applied to the OT. We will use Wright's work as an example of its application to Ecclesiastes. Thirdly we will outline structuralism and examine its application in OT studies, using Loader as an example of a structuralist reading of Ecclesiastes. Finally we will consider the implications of the canonical approach, NC and structuralism for reading Ecclesiastes and thus for OT hermeneutics.

4.2 Childs' Canonical Approach as a Reaction to Historical Criticism

Brett has outlined the stages in the development of Childs' canonical hermeneutic.[8] He discerns a growing tension in Childs' published works between diachronic and synchronic interests in interpretation. The tension is there in Childs' 1974 commentary on Exodus, but five years later in his IOTS it has erupted into a polemic against diachronic approaches. In terms of our focus upon Ecclesiastes, Childs' IOTS will be our main concern because it is here that he outlines his canonical approach in most detail and applies it to Ecclesiastes.

In IOTS Childs focuses his problems with historical critical interpretation on the modern discipline of OT introduction. He outlines the history of the development of modern introduction to the OT and notes that the real point of controversy is not the main lines of this history but how one evaluates this history.[9] For Childs it is important that "[t]he rise of the modern historical study of the Old Testament must be seen in connection with the entire intellectual

---

7 . Lohfink, who has published a commentary and a number of articles on Ecclesiastes, also describes his approach as New Critical.

8 M. BRETT, *Biblical Criticism in Crisis? The Impact of the Canonical Approach on Old Testament Studies* (Cambridge: CUP, 1991) 27-57. For a useful analysis and evaluation of Childs' hermeneutic see also P.R. NOBLE, *The Canonical Approach. A Critical Reconstruction of the Hermeneutics of Brevard S. Childs* (Biblical Interpretation Series 16; Leiden; New York: Brill, 1995).

9 CHILDS, *Introduction to the Old Testament as Scripture*, 30, 39.

revolution which occurred during the late sixteenth and early seventeenth centuries, and which issued in a radically different understanding of God, man and the world."[10] In OT studies this revolution led to the modern discipline of OT introduction, a development which can be traced through Cappellus, Spinoza, Simon and Semler. Semler replaced the theological view of the canon as a unified corpus with a strictly historical interpretation which deeply influenced the father of modern introduction to the OT, Eichhorn, for whom "it would have been desirable if one had never used the word canon".[11]

In Childs' view the modern approach to the OT has brought gains and losses. Undeniably the historical critical method has brought great advantages in the areas of philology, textual and literary criticism, historical knowledge and exegetical precision. Negatively however it has meant that the focus of OT interpretation is not the canonical literature of the Hebrews and the church but the stages of development of OT literature. Consequently "there always remains an enormous hiatus between the description of the critically reconstructed literature and the actual canonical text which has been received and used as authoritative scripture by the community."[12] This predominantly historical concern fails to understand the peculiar dynamic of Israel's religious literature and does not relate the nature of the OT literature correctly to the community which treasured it as Scripture. A key issue for Childs is the nature of the historical categories applied; if the OT is read with a historical referential approach as the dominant method then justice is not done to OT as the literature which formed Israel and vice versa.

In Childs' view the development of this modern introduction and the conservative reaction has lead to a number of false dichotomies in the discipline of OT studies: liberal versus conservative, scientific versus ecclesiastical, objective versus confessional. What underlies this confusion? "In my judgement, the crucial issue which produced the confusion is the problem of the canon, that is to say, how one understands the nature of the OT in relation to its authority for the community of faith and practice which shaped and preserved it."[13] By the nineteenth century in critical circles the canon had come to be seen solely in terms of an external ecclesiastical validation and without any significance for the shaping or interpretation of the biblical literature. Historical critical scholars had no room for the notion of canon in their scholarship; conservatives took 'canon' very seriously but had no room for the historical critical method. In Childs' opinion "the crucial task is to rethink the problem of Introduction in such a way as to overcome this long established tension between the canon and criticism. Is it possible to understand the OT as canonical scripture and yet to make full and

---

10 Ibid., 34.
11 Ibid., 36.
12 Ibid., 40.
13 Ibid., 41.

consistent use of historical critical tools?"[14] It is this that his canonical approach seeks to do.

Defining 'canon' and understanding the process of its formation is no easy task. For Childs it is important that there is a historical and a theological aspect to the development of the canon. "The authoritative Word gave the community its form and content in obedience to the divine imperative, yet conversely the reception of the authoritative tradition by its hearers gave shape to the same writings through a historical and theological process of selecting, collecting and ordering."[15] For Childs Israel did not testify to its own self-understanding, but by means of a canon bore witness to God, as is evidenced by the canon's conscious obscuring of its editors. The decisive force at work in the formation of the canon emerged in the transmission of a divine word in such a form as to lay authoritative claim upon successive generations so that adequate interpretation of the biblical text depends on taking the canonical shape seriously.

What is the relationship between the literary and canonical histories of the OT? For Childs the two processes are distinct although they do belong together. The former involves a much broader history than the latter. With regard to both histories caution is required; we lack sufficient historical evidence for much certainty about these processes. Clearly the role of the canon is fundamentally important to understanding the OT but the history of the canonical process does not seem to be an avenue through which one can greatly illuminate the present text. Child's canonical approach seeks to overcome this methodological impasse by relating the significance of the canon to its complex history but in a very different way from the historical critical method.

Childs' proposed approach is that of a canonical analysis of the Hebrew Bible. This is a descriptive task: "It seeks to understand the peculiar shape and special function of these texts which comprise the Hebrew canon. Such an analysis does not assume a particular stance or faith commitment on the part of the reader because the subject of the investigation is the literature of Israel's faith, not that of the reader."[16] This literature has had a special history as Israel's religious corpus and thus requires a hermeneutic which will do justice to its peculiar features. Canonical analysis focuses upon the final form of the text with a view to examining the features of this corpus in relation to its usage within ancient Israel. Without making any dogmatic claims for the literature this approach seeks to take its religious function seriously: "the approach seeks to work within that interpretative structure which the biblical text has received from those who formed and used it as sacred scripture."[17]

---

[14] Ibid., 45.
[15] Ibid., 58-59.
[16] Ibid., 72.
[17] Ibid., 73.

Childs distinguishes his method from the newer literary critical methods such as NC and structuralism, from the kerygmatic exegesis popularised by von Rad and his students and from the traditio-critical approach.[18] The canonical approach is distinguished from the new literary approaches by its concern with the theological shape of the text rather than with an original literary or aesthetic unity. In Child's view the kerygmatic type of exegesis of von Rad is too closely bound to authorial intention. Often the assumption that the theological point must be related to an original intention within a reconstructed historical context runs directly in the face of the literature's explicit statement of its function within the final form of the biblical text. Israel's religious use of her traditions unleashed a force which shaped the literature as it was collected, selected and ordered. Particular editors, groups and parties were involved but, "basic to the canonical process is that those responsible for the actual editing of the text did their best to obscure their own identity."[19] Consequently the process by which texts were reworked is very obscure. "But irrespective of intentionality the effect of the canonical process was to render the tradition accessible to the future generation by means of a 'canonical intentionality', which is coextensive with the meaning of the biblical text."[20] Canonical analysis also differs from traditio-critical analysis in its evaluation of the history of the formation of the text by assuming the normative status of the final form of the text.

This assumption of the normative status of the final form of the OT text is justified, according to Childs, in that it alone witnesses to the full history of revelation. Only in the final form in which the normative history has been concluded, can the full effect of the revelatory history be seen. Certainly earlier stages were regarded as canonical prior to the final form but to take the canon seriously means taking its critical handling of the earlier stages seriously as well. This is not to become ahistorical but to make a critical, theological judgement regarding the process. The ANE historian is justified in reading the OT differently but in the interpretation of sacred Scripture one ought to stay with the final form. This final form is hermeneutically significant in setting up a particular profile for a passage and attempts to shift this canonical ordering ought to be resisted. Childs recognises that much of his polemic is against forms of historicism which make the use of the Bible dependent upon reconstructed

---

18 Since the publication of IOTS scholars have regularly tried to expose a link between the canonical approach and contemporary literary and theological developments. In the main Childs has continued to deny these. In his most recent *Biblical Theology* he distances himself from narrative theology, from the functional approach to the Bible of Kelsey, Lindbeck, Meeks and Ollenburger, and from the literary approaches which detract from reading the Bible as sacred scripture pointing to the extra-biblical reality of the resurrected Christ (see B.S. CHILDS, *Biblical Theology of the Old and New Testaments* [Minneapolis: Fortress, 1992] 18-23, 719-727).

19 CHILDS, *Introduction to the Old Testament as Scripture*, 78.

20 Ibid., 79.

historical events rather than the text.[21] However he notes that his canonical approach is equally incompatible with Ricoeur's philosophical hermeneutics, because Ricoeur does not take the canon seriously in its grounding of the biblical metaphors in Israel's historical context.

Childs dislikes the term 'canonical criticism' for his method since this puts it alongside source and form criticism etc. as simply another historical critical tool. "The issue at stake in relation to the canon turns on establishing a stance from which the Bible can be read as sacred scripture."[22] In delineating the scope of exegesis the canonical method relativises the claims to priority of the historical critical method by resisting the notion that every biblical text has to be filtered through a historical critical mesh before interpretation can begin. Positively it challenges the exegete to focus on the received form and to discern its function for the community of faith: "A canonical Introduction is not the end, but only the beginning of exegesis. It prepares the stage for the real performance by clearing away unnecessary distractions and directing one's attention to the main activity which is about to be initiated."[23]

4.3 Childs' Canonical Approach to Ecclesiastes

Childs' brief treatment of Ecclesiastes is divided into three sections.[24] Firstly, under the heading "Historical-critical problems" he outlines five main issues in the study of Ecclesiastes that have engaged critical scholars. On the issue of authorship there is now a consensus that Solomon was not the author. However there is no agreement as to the significance of this. Most scholars agree on a date between 300-200 BC for the book. There is a growing consensus that the book should be approached as a unified composition of one author. There is however no consensus on structure; in Childs' view the truth lies between the views that find no structure and those that detect a unity of progressive thought. As regards Ecclesiastes' theological contribution scholars remain divided as to whether it is primarily positive or mainly pessimistic. Childs detects and strongly disagrees with a broad critical consensus that the key to the book's interpretation lies in discerning the historical and psychological influences on the writer. In Childs' view this fails to deal with the canonical role of the book as sacred Scripture of a continuing community of faith.

In his second section Childs deals with the canonical shape of Ecclesiastes. The epilogue receives most attention, with about the same amount of space devoted to the superscription and the main body of the work. The *superscription* is regarded by many scholars as part of a final redactional stage in the process of

---

21 Ibid., 77.
22 Ibid., 82.
23 Ibid., 83.
24 Ibid., 580-589.

composition of Ecclesiastes. If Galling was right and the editorial framework was based on a misunderstanding of the body of the work[25] then this would have implications for a canonical reading. His view has however received little support and Childs maintains that the identification of a redactional stage is of secondary importance in a canonical analysis; in the final form the superscription is important. What is important is the function of the title; the important hermeneutical question is why the author is identified as Qoheleth and yet described in terms appropriate to Solomon. Childs rejects the hypothesis that Ecclesiastes is pseudepigraphic because Solomon's name is never used, and furthermore, the identification of Qoheleth with Solomon is abandoned within the book itself. Childs prefers the explanation that the superscription serves to identify the book as an official corrective within the wisdom tradition rather than some individual aberration.

For Childs the *epilogue* betrays the most obvious canonical shaping in Ecclesiastes. There has been much debate about the composition of this section but the crucial issue is not the number of redactors but the effect of the epilogue upon the canonical shape of the book. "Few passages in the OT reflect a more overt consciousness of the canon than does this epilogue."[26] Like the superscription, the epilogue in its description of Qoheleth identifies the book as part of Israel's wisdom. Qoheleth is assigned a public and critical role within Israel's wisdom teaching. 12:13 holds wisdom and law closely together under the overarching theological rubric of the judgement of God.

Childs has little to say about the *main body* of Ecclesiastes. It contains collections of sayings in smaller integral units but there is no attempt to present a unified reflection on life. Ecclesiastes arose in reaction to a body of wisdom literature and so treats almost all the themes common to wisdom. Sometimes Qoheleth contradicts this wisdom tradition; at other times he modifies it or affirms it. Apparent contradictions arise from his addressing different contexts. Amidst the diversity Childs' does however find some "effort on the part of the canonical process to tie these strands together."[27]

Childs' third section deals with the theological and hermeneutical implications of his approach to Ecclesiastes. Canonical analysis alerts us to the fact that the authoritative role of Ecclesiastes lies in its function for the Israelite community within the larger canonical context. The person of Qoheleth and the extent to which his views reflect his own struggles are not relevant to canonical analysis. The canonical shaping of Ecclesiastes focuses rather upon the book as a normative critical corrective similar to James in relation to the Pauline corpus. It might be suggested that the epilogue neutralises the biting force of Ecclesiastes

---

[25] See ch. 3 for a discussion of Galling's approach to Ecclesiastes. Galling thinks that QR1 overemphasises the negative aspect of Qoheleth's sayings.

[26] CHILDS, *Introduction to the Old Testament as Scripture*, 585.

[27] Ibid., 587.

and that the canonical approach is deficient in relying too much upon the epilogue. Ought not a hermeneutic make the reader feel the same shock that Qoheleth's first hearers must have experienced? In Childs' view such a theory of actualisation stems from a romantic understanding of history derived from Herder.

> However, from a theological perspective it is far from obvious. Indeed, the purpose of a canon of sacred writings is to propose a very different understanding of actualization. The authority of the biblical text does not rest on a capacity to match original experiences, rather on the claim which the canonical text makes on every subsequent generation of hearers.[28]

Childs' canonical approach to Ecclesiastes is most intriguing in the weight it accords to the often neglected epilogue. As Ecclesiastes has come to be regarded more and more as a unity the epilogue has still tended to be regarded as secondary and as an attempt to correct the heterodoxy of Qoheleth. Rather than as a secondary addition, Childs privileges the epilogue as *the* major sign of canonical shaping. This reverses the general value judgement of the epilogue and foregrounds it as the key to the canonical interpretation of the book.

Childs' attempt to read Ecclesiastes as a unity is attractive. However it is questionable whether he is actually reading the final form as a unity. Concerning the canonical method Barr maintains that

> [i]n effect, then, the emphasis does not fall on the final form of the text: it falls on the historical joins which in the later stages led from the previous forms to the final text. And let us grant the importance of these joins. But – on the basis of the final text itself – these joins are less important than the content which lies between the joins.[29]

This is certainly true of Childs' treatment of Ecclesiastes. He must first identify the signs of canonical shaping, which then become the key to interpreting the text. This neglects the crucial issue of how the epilogue relates to the main body of the text. Indeed it seems to me that Childs subtly builds on historical critical insights in his treatment of Ecclesiastes. One can only see the epilogue as pointing towards Ecclesiastes as a corrective if one first of all has assumed the radical stance that many historical critical scholars discern in the main body of the work. Apart from this the epilogue would indicate Qoheleth as another orthodox wisdom teacher.

Childs' canonical method seems to me to be a synthesis between redaction criticism and a final form reading.[30] Murphy suggests that the canonical method differs from redaction criticism in two ways: firstly it closes the redaction at a point well beyond the usual date that redaction critics would ascribe to a text. Secondly "it locks into a normative broad exegetical understanding that was

---

28 Ibid., 589.
29 BARR, "Childs' *Introduction to the Old Testament as Scripture*," 20-21.
30 On this point see also BARR, *Holy Scripture*, 146.

regnant at the time of the stabilization of the text."[31] Childs himself articulates the difference as follows: "Canonical analysis focuses its attention on the effect which the different layers have had on the final form of the text, rather than using the text as a source for other information obtained by means of an oblique reading, such as the editor's self-understanding."[32] However, what distinguishes Childs' reading from an intrinsic final form one is his concern to see how different layers have affected the final form. Childs is very cautious on getting behind the text and yet discernment of the effects of layers requires just that and in a fairly precise manner. Hence Barr is right in his assessment that

> Childs' actual operation, however, is far more dependent on historical criticism than his account of the latter would suggest. The operation is bipolar: if one pole is the new canonical reading, the other is the situation reached by traditional criticism. He displays, not what a canonical reading, untouched by historical criticism, would be, but the path by which, starting from current positions, one can find one's way to the new canonical reading.[33]

In some ways at least Childs' canonical hermeneutic is thus different to an intrinsic approach like NC (see below). However there is a similarity. Childs locates the crucial development in the history of introduction to the OT in the revised approach to canon in modernity and thus insists that his approach is a theological one. However as we saw in chapter three the shifts that came about in relation to canon are a small part of deeper philosophical changes. One of the effects of these philosophical changes has been an overly historical emphasis in OT interpretation which has led to a neglect of the literary and theological aspects of OT texts. These neglected aspects are closely linked so that Childs concern to recover the theological function of the texts inevitably involves focusing on the final (literary) form of the text. Thus while it is wrong to lump Childs' approach too closely with NC, it does share the latter's reaction to an overly (and particular) historical emphasis in the humanities. The canonical approach, NC, and structuralism are all attempts to recover neglected dimensions of texts.

4.4 New Criticism and Its Application to Old Testament Studies

4.4.1 Introduction: Chronology and Origins

NC "almost certainly constitutes the English-speaking world's major literary contribution to literary theory."[34] It originated in the USA in the 1920's, was a fully developed theory by 1950, and continued to exert a powerful influence until

---

[31] R.E. MURPHY, "The Old Testament as Scripture," *JSOT* 16 (1980) 41-42.
[32] CHILDS, *Introduction to the Old Testament as Scripture*, 68.
[33] BARR, "Childs' *Introduction to the Old Testament as Scripture*," 15.
[34] D. ROBEY, "Anglo-American New Criticism," In: A. JEFFERSON and D. ROBEY (eds.), *Modern Literary Theory* (1986) 73.

the 1960's.[35] NC however, continues to exert its influence in many different ways.[36]

NC began in America with the work of a group of theorists at Vanderbilt University in Tennessee, most notably Ransom, Tate and Pen Warren. The method they developed was *close reading* or *practical criticism*. In 1941 Ransom published a book *The New Criticism* from which title the movement got its name. NC became a national and then international movement through the additional labours of Wellek, Warren, Brooks, Wimsatt and Beardsley.[37]

4.4.2 New Criticism as a Reaction to 'Positivism'

The development of NC is part of an early twentieth century "revolt against positivism in ... literary scholarship."[38] This revolt was predominantly European and with respect to NC was mediated to America through Richards and Eliot. Since this reaction is important for our research we will first explore the nature of positivism in its broader philosophical sense, then look at how this manifested itself in literary studies before investigating the reaction to 'positivism' within literary studies.

4.4.2.1 Positivism in the Broader Philosophical Sense

Comte used the expression 'positive philosophy' and its abbreviated form 'positivism' has remained with us ever since.[39] Positivism has come to designate a philosophical movement that was influential in all countries of the Western world in the second half of the nineteenth century and the first half of the twentieth century. However, there are varieties within this movement. Kolakowski, for example, traces positivism from Berkeley and Hume through

---

[35] F. LENTRICCHIA, *After the New Criticism* (London: Methuen, 1983) 3, argues that 1957 marks the demise of NC.

[36] For example, A. JEFFERSON and D. ROBEY, *Modern Literary Theory. A Comparative Introduction* (2nd ed.; London: Batsford, 1986) 22, in the process of commenting on the most recent literary theories, make the point that the borrowing and adaptation characteristic of these theories "have the effect of taking one back to a reconsideration of Formalism and New Criticism, and demonstrate by implication that despite their apparent bracketing out of the reader, they do contain embryonic theories of reading that could be developed and further elaborated." For a suggested link between NC and postmodern literary theory see C. NORRIS, "Criticism," In: M. COYLE, et al., *Encyclopaedia of Literature and Criticism* (1990) 27-65.

[37] For a more detailed survey of the development of NC see R. RYLANCE, "The New Criticism," In: M. COYLE, (et al.), *Encyclopaedia of Literature and Criticism* (1990) 721-735.

[38] R. WELLEK, *Concepts of Criticism* (ed. and with an introduction by S.G. NICHOLS; New Haven; London: Yale UP, 1963) 256.

[39] According to N. ABBAGNANO, "Positivism," In: P. EDWARDS (ed.), *The Encyclopedia of Philosophy. Vols 5 and 6* (NY: MacMillan and Free Press, 1967) 414, the term 'positivism' was first used by Claude Henri de Rouvroy, Comte de Saint-Simon, to refer to scientific method and its extension to philosophy. Comte appropriated it from Saint-Simon.

Comte, Bernard, Mill and Spencer and via conventionalism and pragmatism to the logical positivists of the twentieth century.[40] This diversity alerts one to the dangers of generalisations about positivism as a whole. Kolakowski nevertheless suggests that the following are more or less true of the tradition of positivism. It is a type of epistemology seeking to clarify rules and criteria for human knowledge and Kolakowski discerns four main characteristics of positivism.[41] Firstly phenomenalism, which opposes any distinction between substance and essence. Secondly nominalism whereby "we may not assume that any insight formulated in general terms can have any real referents other than individual concrete objects."[42] Thirdly positivism refuses to call value judgements and normative statements knowledge. And finally positivism upholds the unity of the scientific method. The methods for acquiring valid knowledge and the stages of theoretical reflection are essentially the same in all spheres of experience. Positivism sought to apply its epistemology to all disciplines.[43] This meant that methods derived from the natural sciences were extended to other disciplines so that a science of literature analogous to the natural sciences emerged.

4.4.2.2 'Positivism' in Literary Studies

Positivism is used here to refer to the sort of literary scholarship against which the reaction since the twenties has been directed and which was generally shaped by positivism in philosophy. Philosophical positivism, especially with its concern to extend scientific method to all areas of life, played an important role in developing these traits but the complexities and diversities of these developments in literary studies must not be overlooked.[44]

In the latter nineteenth century it was common for literature to be studied in terms of "the genesis of the art-work in terms of 'influences' and 'sources'; to search for similar or analogous motifs and themes in earlier literature; to probe the origins of the political, cultural and social background of the period or the biographical background of the author – all in order to give a causal explanation of how the work came into being."[45] Scientific causality was used to explain

---

[40] L. KOLAKOWSKI, *Positivist Philosophy. From Hume to the Vienna Circle* (Penguin: Middlesex, 1968/72).

[41] Ibid., 9-18.

[42] Ibid., 13.

[43] On positivism and Protestant thought in Britain and America see C.D. CASHDOLLAR, *The Transformation of Theology. Positivism and Protestant Thought in Britain and America* (Princeton: Princeton UP, 1989). On the relationship between positivism and philosophy of history see R.G. COLLINGWOOD, *The Idea of History* (Oxford: OUP, 1946) 126-133.

[44] Note, for example, Wellek's references to the interrelationship between historicism and positivism, and to the effect of different views of the methods of the natural sciences (WELLEK, *Concepts of Criticism*, 257-258).

[45] M. WEISS, *The Bible from Within: the Method of Totality Interpretation* (Jerusalem: Magnes, 1984) 2.

literary phenomena in relation to economic, social and political conditions, and Brunetière and Symonds, for example, argued for an understanding of the evolution of genres on the basis of the analogy of biological sciences. 'Positivism' in literary studies is summed up in an exaggerated form in Taine's introduction to his 1863 history of English literature. In his view a literary text is an expression of the psychology of an individual which in turn is an expression of his/her milieu and race, captured in the phrase 'la race, le milieu, et le moment'. Literary scholarship must therefore take as its object the causal explanation of texts in relation to these three factors. By so doing it will become a form of scientific history comparable in status and method to the natural sciences. In an exaggerated way Taine expressed assumptions which guided European and American scholarship in the late 19th and early 20th centuries. Jefferson and Robey sum these up as follows:

> In its pure form positivistic scholarship studied literature almost exclusively in relation to its factual causes or genesis: the author's life, his recorded intentions in writing, his immediate social and cultural environment, his sources. ... It was not interested in the features of the literary text itself except from a philological and historical viewpoint. ... it disregarded questions concerning the value or the distinctive properties of literature, since these could not be dealt with in a factual and historical manner. Or more exactly, while it took for granted that literary texts possessed a special value, in practice it treated them as if they were indistinguishable from other sorts of historical document.[46]

4.4.2.3 Reaction to Positivism

In his essay, "The revolt against positivism in recent literary scholarship", Wellek outlines the reaction to positivism in literary studies across Europe in the early twentieth century.[47] It was widespread and part of a broader philosophical reaction to positivism. Philosophically there was a shift from positivism to a wide variety of idealisms as exemplified in the work of Bergson in France, Croce in Italy and Alexander and Whitehead in England. Whereas in positivism the natural science paradigm was imposed on other disciplines, in philosophy of history this imposition was now questioned and rejected. Several philosophers now offered a defence of the methods of the historical sciences which they sharply distinguished from the natural sciences. In literary studies too it was stressed that literary scholarship is a system of knowledge with its own aims and methods. This called for a methodologically precise criticism that deals with the distinctive properties of literature. Wellek explores the diverse ways in which this common reaction manifested itself across Europe, ranging from Croce in Italy to Richards, Eliot, Empson and Lewis in England to Russian Formalism. NC's roots lie in the

---

[46] JEFFERSON and ROBEY, *Modern Literary Theory*, 9.
[47] WELLEK, *Concepts of Criticism*.

English reaction of Richards and Eliot. We will therefore briefly explore aspects of Richards' and Eliot's approaches before making some comments about NC as a manifestation of this reaction.

For Richards the key to establishing the autonomy of the literary field lies in emphasising the reader's response. He stresses the need for a theory of communication and valuation in literary studies. Towards this end he distinguishes between referential and emotive functions of language. The value of literature lies in its use of the emotive function of language, that is, in its effect upon the reader. In its effect good literature is disconcerting and thereby carries the reconciliation of conflicting values to an exceptionally high level. "They renovate and enhance our reactions to life by disrupting established habits of response, and creating in us a state of equilibrium of a kind that other sorts of experience can rarely achieve."[48] Richards' influence in literary theory is seen above all in the close reading of texts. This approach was developed by his pupil William Empson, who, according to Wellek did in his *Seven Types of Ambiguity* "more than anybody else to inaugurate the subtle and sometimes even over ingenious analyses of poetic diction and its implications which are flourishing today both in England and in the United States."[49]

If NC derives its emphasis on close reading from Richards it derives its anti-affectivity and stress on the objective reality of the poem from Eliot. In his celebrated essay "Tradition and Individual Talent", published in 1919, Eliot attacks that approach to poetry which seeks its significance in the marks of individual talent which set it off from its immediate predecessors.[50] He stresses that a literary work positions itself within the literary tradition, within which it must be understood and that this context depersonalises it and objectifies it. Thus "the poet has, not a 'personality' to express, but a particular medium, which is only a medium and not a personality, in which impressions and expressions combine in peculiar and unexpected ways."[51] Poetry becomes thus, not an expression of emotion and personality but an escape from both of these.[52]

The New Critics shared Richards' and Eliot's reaction to positivism. Allen Tate epitomises this New Critical reaction. A scholar and a critic he was fiercely critical of the "cloistered historical scholarship of the graduate school", with its positivistic assumption that the literary text "expresses its place and time, or the

---

[48] ROBEY, "Anglo-American New Criticism," 76.

[49] WELLEK, *Concepts of Criticism*, 266, Intriguingly, I am told by Christopher Norris that Empson developed an interest in Ecclesiastes late in his life. I have not been able to track down any references to this.

[50] T.S. ELIOT, "Tradition and the Individual Talent", "The Function of Criticism," In: D. LODGE (ed.), *20th Century Literary Criticism* (1972) 71.

[51] Ibid., 75.

[52] On the influence of Eliot on NC see R. SELDEN and P. WIDDOWSON, *A Reader's Guide to Contemporary Literary Theory* (London: Harvester Wheatsheaf, 1993) 11-12.

author's personality" and nothing more.[53] The New Critics also shared with Richards a stress on the need for a theory of literature and his emphasis on close reading of texts. However, in common with Eliot, the New Critics rejected Richards' focus on the reader and the emotive effect of the text as the way into a properly theoretical approach to literary studies. It is to their distinctive understanding of literary theory that we now turn.

4.4.3 Principles of New Criticism

4.4.3.1 The Nature of Literariness

The shift from an extrinsic to an intrinsic approach to literature raises the question of the nature of literature and the difference between it and other types of writing. NC focuses on the distinctive properties of literature and attempts to deal with these theoretically. Thus Wimsatt and Brooks start with Richards' view of literature as characterised by reconciliation of opposites but contra Richards maintain that this characteristic is not an event in the mind of the author or reader but in the text.[54] Complexity and coherence constitute the key considerations in the analysis of literary texts. A literary work is a system of tensions which may operate without ultimate solution; indeed the presence of these tensions is the sign of a truly valuable work of art. Mature works resist easy satisfactions. However the various elements are integrated into a whole. Ransom, for example, separates the structure of a poem into two features: structure (logic or argument) and local texture (density or particularity).[55] Critical interpretation of a poem consists of integrating the two, of discerning how they balance and enable one another.

The New Critical understanding of literature, and especially poetry, as a distinct type of writing needs to be taken seriously because, unlike many postmodern literary theorists, they restrict their methodology to literary texts. Thus, for example, on the whole notion of intentionality, Wimsatt and Beardsley draw a clear distinction between poetry and practical messages: "In this respect poetry differs from practical messages, which are successful if and only if we correctly infer the intention. They are more abstract than poetry."[56]

4.4.3.2 The Focus of Literary Study Should Be Literary Texts Themselves

NC shifts the focus of literary study to the literary text itself:

---

[53] A. TATE, *Collected Essays* (Swallow: Denver, 1959) 7, 54.

[54] W.K. WIMSATT, *The Verbal Icon. Studies in the Meaning of Poetry* (Lexington: University Press of Kentucky, 1954); and C. BROOKS, *The Well Wrought Urn. Studies in the Structure of Poetry* (London, NY: Harcourt Brace Jovanich, 1975).

[55] J.C. RANSOM, *The New Criticism* (Norfolk: New Directions, 1941).

[56] W.K. WIMSATT and M.C. BEARDSLEY, "The Intentional Fallacy," In: D. LODGE (ed.), *20th Century Criticism* (1972) 335; cf. WEISS, *The Bible from Within*, 21-24.

The natural and sensible starting-point for work in literary scholarship is the interpretation and analysis of the works of literature themselves. After all, only the works themselves justify all our interest in the life of an author, in his social environment and the whole process of literature. But, curiously enough, literary history has been so preoccupied with the setting of a work of literature that its attempts at an analysis of the works themselves have been light in comparison with the enormous efforts expended on the study of the environment.[57]

Criticism should focus on the poem/literary work itself, not the reader/author. The objective features of the medium thus become the focus of study; criticism is the study of the form and structure of a text. "Only one who will explain without looking to the right or left, above all without inquiring what is before and what is after, only he will fulfil his obligations to the creation, and only he will refrain from undermining the sovereignty of literary study."[58]

4.4.3.3 Literary Study Should Not Focus upon Authorial Intention or Emotive Affect

Two of the best known products of NC theory are Wimsatt's and Beardsley's "The intentional fallacy" and "The affective fallacy".[59] These two essays are central to NC's attempt to construct a theoretical base which is an alternative to positivism. Although they acknowledge that "[t]he words of a poem … come out of a head, not out of a hat" they nevertheless reject design or intention as a standard by a which to judge a poem; the intentional fallacy is a romantic error.[60] We do not have access to a poet's intention[61] and furthermore, a literary work is an object in the public domain and not the private creation of an individual. The author's experience etc. are only of historical interest and do not determine the meaning or effect of his creation. What counts is what is embodied in the text and that is wholly accessible to anyone with a knowledge of the language and culture to which the text belongs. In this way the significance of authorial intention for literary interpretation is severely curtailed. This is not an ahistorical approach but one which severely restricts the role of history in literary study, "relegating questions about 'how the poem came to be' to a different, and

---

57 R. WELLEK and A. WARREN, *Theory of Literature* (3rd ed.; London: Penguin, 1963) 139.

58 Staiger as quoted by WEISS, *The Bible from Within*, 6.

59 WIMSATT and BEARDSLEY, "The Intentional Fallacy," 334-345; idem, "The Affective Fallacy," In: D. LODGE (ed.), *20th Century Criticism* (1972) 345-358.

60 WIMSATT and BEARDSLEY, "The Intentional Fallacy," 334, 336.

61 WEISS, *The Bible from Within*, 13-17, points out that since the time of Socrates the importance of intention for interpretation has been disputed. From time to time poets themselves have admitted that they did not fully understand their intentions in producing a poem. In the nineteenth century it was suggested that the creative activity of the poet flowed from the unconscious like a prophet who does not know what he is prophesying. Weiss also suggests that intentionality is intellectually focused whereas poetry touches on areas neglected by intellect and memory.

by implication, inferior, branch of enquiry."[62] The 'affective fallacy' refers to the type of approach which Richards represents, judging literature by its effect. This too is rejected.

Weiss recognises that the way in which NC understands a literary work to relate to its historical context of origin is distinctive of NC.[63] All New Critics refuse to allow causal factors to dominate the interpretation of a literary text. However, Weiss does point out that New Critics are divided as to the role of background information in interpretation. Some reject it *per se*, whereas others oppose it as the sole method. The latter group recognise the indispensability of a historical base for interpretation. Wellek and Warren's *Theory of Literature* is a fine example of the balance that this second group of New Critics represents.[64] A good one sixth of their text is devoted to the extrinsic approach to literature compared with two thirds devoted to the intrinsic approach. This makes clear which approach they wish to privilege, but it also shows that they do not reject the extrinsic approach out of hand. Even on the more specific issue of intentionality their position is more refined than is sometimes suggested. They are reacting against a Romantic and intellectual understanding of intention, but are not opposed to what Sternberg calls embodied intentionality.[65] As Wellek and Warren say, "There can be no objections against the study of 'intention', if we mean by it merely a study of the integral work of art directed towards the total meaning."[66]

4.4.3.4 Literature Cannot Be Paraphrased

The reduction of literature to a paraphrase is just that, a reduction and it can never be equivalent to the work itself. Hence Brooks' essay "The Heresy of Paraphrase".[67] The structural properties which draw literature into a unity are of a dramatic and not a logical nature and the form/content distinction that is often applied to literature as though the poetic form is only the vehicle for the message is invalid. This understanding of the integrality of the literary work affects the New Critics' view of the relationship of the art work to its historical context of origin. Source criticism is, for example, severely curtailed. "That ancient text which gave the push to the artist was at the most some raw material in the hands of the creator but in no sense the source of his creation. This new creation … springs completely from the poet's mind and soul. Therefore Knight asserts that

---

62 ROBEY, "Anglo-American New Criticism," 82.
63 WEISS, *The Bible from Within*, 8-12.
64 WELLEK and WARREN, *Theory of Literature*.
65 M. STERNBERG, *The Poetics of Biblical Narrative. Ideological Literature and the Drama of Reading* (Bloomington: Indiana University Press, 1985) 9.
66 WELLEK and WARREN, *Theory of Literature*, 149.
67 In BROOKS, *The Well Wrought Urn*, 192-214.

the expression 'source' is only a misleading metaphor."[68] NC stresses that the literary work, even if entirely constructed from other texts, is in its present form an integral whole and must be understood as such. The literary creation is much more than the sum of its sources. Tate observes how difficult critics find it to focus on the literary work itself:

> For some reason critics have a hard time fixing their minds directly under their noses, and before they see the object that is there they use a telescope to scan upon the whole horizon to see where it came from. They are wood cutters who do their job by finding out where the ore came from in the iron of the steel of the blade of the axe that Jack built.[69]

New Critics do seek objectivity in their interpretation of literary works. "The true interpretation is the outcome of that fortunate occasion when the interpreter does not subjugate the creation but is subjugated by it."[70] The method best suited to such interpretation is close reading; close, attentive reading of the text is regarded as the best key for unlocking the secrets of the literary text.

4.4.4 New Criticism and Old Testament Studies

The reaction to positivism within literary studies has a parallel in biblical studies. Weiss' *The Bible From Within*, published in Hebrew in 1962, presents a New Critical approach to Biblical literature as the key to resolving the distorting influence of what he calls 'historicism' upon biblical studies.[71] Another early advocate of NC as the method for biblical study is Alonso-Schökel,[72] who used NC in studies on prophetic poetry and poetic imagery. Since the 50's and 60's there has been an explosion of literary approaches to the Bible, with the production of a huge amount of literature applying the developing smorgasbord of literary approaches to biblical literature. This explosion occurred at the time when NC was starting to lose its dominance in literary theory, and so it is not surprising that biblical study done along specifically New Critical lines is limited. In many ways the influence of NC remains, but, as it was superseded in literary theory, so too it has been superseded in biblical studies.

---

68 WEISS, *The Bible from Within*, 24.
69 TATE, *The Man of Letters in the Modern World*, 333.
70 WEISS, *The Bible from Within*, 19.
71 What Weiss calls 'historicism' is equivalent to what Wellek calls positivism. Historicism, even more than positivism, is a notoriously slippery word. See M. MANDELBAUM, "Historicism," In: P. EDWARDS (ed.), *The Encyclopedia of Philosophy*. Vols. 3 and 4 (1967) 22-25, for a useful discussion of the diverse ways in which it has been used. The general definition that Mandelbaum proposes fits with Weiss' use: "Historicism is the belief that an adequate understanding of the nature of anything and an adequate assessment of its value are to be gained by considering it in terms of the place it occupied and the role it played within a process of development" (ibid., 24).
72 See L. ALONSO-SCHÖKEL, *A Manual of Hebrew Poetics* (Subsidia Biblica 11; Rome: Editrice Pontificio Istituto Biblico, 1988) 205-206, for a list of his works.

It is thus not easy to find a body of biblical study which is specifically New Critical. Longman refers to Weiss, the "Sheffield School" and Adele Berlin as examples of biblical work which has adopted many of NC's insights.[73] As an example of the Sheffield School he refers to Gunn's work on David and Saul. Clearly Gunn and Berlin's work is influenced by NC, but only in a general way. Berlin herself appeals to other influences as well and Gunn is clearly not New Critical in any strong sense.[74] Weiss and Alonso-Schökel are however, two examples of Old Testament scholars working with a strong commitment to New Critical principles. Weiss' work is particularly interesting since the Hebrew version of his *The Bible From Within* was published in 1962 and the revised, enlarged and fully-updated English edition in 1984. He has had twenty-two years in which to reassess his commitment to NC but has not shifted his position. We shall therefore focus this section on Weiss' New Critical approach to biblical scholarship.

Weiss coined the expression "Total Interpretation" to describe his method of interpretation for the poetic parts of the Bible.[75] This method is 'total' because it seeks to grasp the literary creation in its totality by an explanation based on all the formal elements which work together to create the literary work. Weiss welcomes the reaction to historicism that NC represents since this allowed the literary work itself to become the focus of literary study. Weiss is well aware that nowadays NC tends to be regarded as out of date. However he defends it against structuralism and continues to argue that 'Total Interpretation' is the best method for reading biblical poetry. NC does have a lot in common with structuralism, but it is focused on the individual text whereas structuralism tends to be concerned with underlying and general structures.[76] Criticisms of NC are often either a result of the abuse of the method or stem from a lack of understanding. Indeed,

---

[73] T. LONGMAN, *Literary Approaches to Biblical Interpretation* (Foundations of Contemporary Interpretation 3; Grand Rapids: Zondervan, 1987) 25-27.

[74] A. BERLIN, *Poetics and the Interpretation of Biblical Narrative* (Bible and Literature Series; Sheffield: Almond Press, 1983), is aware of structuralism and refers to Polzin, Todorov and Genette. Her methodology is however not structuralist and does come very close to NC. So, for example, commenting on Genesis 37 she says "we must begin our reading without prior commitment to any theory. The text must speak for itself" (ibid., 117). Berlin's work is more New Critical than D.M. GUNN'S, *The Story of King David. Genre and Interpretation* (JSOTSup 6; Sheffield: JSOT, 1982). He stresses that his reading of the David narrative as story rests on a reconstructed text and not the final form (ibid., 14, 16). As he says, "How the narrative relates to its present context and how this location might affect its meaning are questions of importance, but not questions I have chosen to deal with here" (ibid., 16). Gunn's work on the David narrative represents something of a synthesis of historical critical and narrative methodologies.

[75] WEISS, *The Bible from Within*, 27.

[76] To support this statement Weiss quotes the structuralist Holenstein: "We cannot understand and elucidate something until its appropriate place in its polymorphous and polyvalent universal code has been found, until it is clear which partial system of this general code is to be actualized for its constitution and comprehension" (ibid., 8).

Weiss' *The Bible From Within* is an exemplary example of just how sophisticated a methodology NC can be.

Weiss regards form criticism as wedded to historicist presuppositions and rejects it as an external approach utilising an outmoded notion of form.[77] A good scientific method must be appropriate to its object and Weiss regards the internal method of 'Total Interpretation' as the most appropriate method for interpreting Biblical poetry.

Weiss' carefully nuanced understanding of the relationship between historical context and poetic interpretation is worth noting. In observing that NC is opposed to historicism he distinguishes between two shades of opposition, as we saw above. As an opponent of historical background as the sole method, Weiss is concerned to restore the methodological imbalance resulting from historicism[78] but has no desire to deny the legitimate role of historical concerns in literary studies. This role is however restricted. Biographical and philological data can confirm one's interpretation but cannot replace it. The limitations and problems of historical criticism have to be faced; however good its intentions

> [t]his method seems now to have come to the point where its deficiencies are becoming more obvious than its merit. The keys which have been cut and shaped with such care certainly opened a door; but the door only seems to lead into another room with a door which is locked, and the lock on that door the keys do not fit. And the room we have got into is plainly not the heart of the building, but only another antechamber.[79]

Indeed, historical criticism as practised is not truly historical because of its unbalanced idea of the relationship between literature and history. NC seeks to redress this balance and in so doing argues for a different understanding of literary texts in history; it opposes their reduction to historical documents and recognises their resistance to historical reconstruction. Weiss argues that literature will only yield what it has to give if it is approached as literature.

The strength of Weiss' work is that he is at pains to show how his 'Total Interpretation' bears fruit in actual exegesis. This, in his view, is the ultimate test of a method: "it can only be tested and proved in practice. If the results it produces appear to be *eis*egesis instead of *ex*egesis, then a thorough philological-critical examination of the text should point up the inadequacy and illuminate the source of the error."[80] The major part of Weiss' work is devoted to showing the difference that his method makes in exegesis.

---

[77] Cf. ibid., 47-64 for a thorough critique of Gunkel's form critical approach in relation to Psalm 23:1.

[78] Weiss quotes Brooks: "the danger now, it seems to me, is not that we will forget the differences between poems of different historical periods, but that we may forget those qualities which they have in common ... those qualities that make them *poems*" (ibid., 9).

[79] Gardner as quoted by Weiss (ibid., 64).

[80] Ibid., 73.

4.5 Wright on Ecclesiastes

Wright has been selected as an example of the application of NC to
Ecclesiastes because he specifically appeals to it as providing a methodological
key for breaking the deadlock in studies of Ecclesiastes.[81] Plumptre referred to
Ecclesiastes as "the sphinx of Hebrew literature, with its unsolved riddles of
history and life";[82] Wright argues that NC provides a method for getting at the
structure of Ecclesiastes, and thereby breaking this riddle.[83] "The structure that
the author intended to give to this book has finally been recovered."[84]

Ecclesiastes, according to Wright, is like a maze. However, there is order to
it, and the principles underlying this maze need to be discovered. By 'principles'
Wright means underlying structure. In his view we have access to this through the
patterns of verbal repetition in Ecclesiastes. These provide an objective base for
getting at the underlying structure. "When these patterns are taken as indicating
the framework of the book and when that framework is brought to the material as
an overlay as it were, there emerges out of the apparent disorder a straightforward
presentation of a very simple theme, albeit somewhat reduced in content from
what had previously been seen as the message of the book."[85]

Previous scholarship, in Wright's view, has lacked a scientific approach to
solving the riddle of Ecclesiastes. Historically Wright discerns two major
approaches to the structure of Ecclesiastes; those who find no plan in it and those
who find some unity or progression of thought. The entire debate is, however,
plagued by subjectivity. Phrases like "This is how I read Ecclesiastes ..." dog the
footsteps of the history of interpretation of Ecclesiastes. In this history of research
into Ecclesiastes "[t]he results have been quite disparate, and this lack of
agreement has been viewed by many as the final and conclusive evidence if more
were needed that there is indeed no plan in the book to begin with."[86]

---

[81] Lohfink is also an important representative of a New Critical approach to Ecclesiastes.
Lohfink's indebtedness to NC manifests itself mainly in his commitment to close reading: "Das
ganze Buch durchzieht eine *Leitworttechnik*, die ihresgleichen im alten Orient sucht. Sie bewirkt,
das alles mit allem in einem geheimnisvollen Netz verknüpft ist und alle Ausleger, die einen
einlinigen Gedankenfortschritt suchen, sich in dieser subtilieren Sprachwelt rettungslos
verheddern" (N. LOHFINK, *Kohelet* [NEB; Würzburg: Echter Verlag, 1993] 10). However, at least
as regards structure, he is less consistently New Critical than Wright. Lohfink arrives at his
structure of Ecclesiastes through Greek and Jewish genre comparisons (ibid., 10-11). Wright's
analysis of Ecclesiastes has also been more influential than Lohfink's.

[82] E.H. PLUMPTRE, *Ecclesiastes* (The Cambridge Bible for Schools; Cambridge: CUP, 1881)
7.

[83] A.G. WRIGHT, "The Riddle of the Sphinx: The Structure of the Book of Qoheleth," *CBQ* 30
(1968) 313-334.

[84] A.G. WRIGHT, "Ecclesiastes (Qoheleth)," In: R.E. BROWN, J.A. FITZMEYER, and R.E.
MURPHY (eds.), *The New Jerome Biblical Commentary* (1990) 489.

[85] WRIGHT, "The Riddle of the Sphinx," 314.

[86] Ibid., 316.

Wright reopens the search for objective criteria for the structure of Ecclesiastes and, as mentioned above, finds the impulse in NC. It is the commitment to close reading of NC that Wright finds most attractive. He describes this close reading as "a careful and verbal structural analysis."[87] He refers to Wellek and Warren's *Theory of Literature* but does not carefully distinguish NC from structuralism and other contemporary theories. Indeed Wright sees NC's commitment to close reading as an expression of contemporary structural concerns in the sciences of his day. As examples in biblical criticism of work in the same new critical spirit as his he includes the rhetorical criticism of Muilenberg. He is also cautious about the reactionary nature of NC and particularly of its shift away from authorial intention. Thus it would be wrong to see Wright as a dogmatic New Critic. However it is in NC that he finds the key for an objective close reading which can lift one out of the subjective morass that pervades scholarship on Ecclesiastes.

NC, he maintains, discerns two ways in which one can get at the plan of a work. One can proceed immediately to the content of a work and try and follow the sequence of ideas and thereby construct an outline. This approach is, however, plagued by subjectivity. The second alternative is an objective method:

essentially it is to put attention, first of all, not on the thought but on the form. The critic looks for repetitions of vocabulary and of grammatical forms and thus seeks to uncover whatever literary devices the author may have used, such as inclusions, *mots crochets*, anaphora, chiasm, symmetry, refrains, announcement of topic and subsequent resumption, recapitulation, etc.[88]

Changes in genre, mood etc. and numerical patterns may also provide clues to the author's plan. Patterns thereby discerned are then related to the content of the book and, where development in thought coincides with these patterns, an outline emerges. The subjective element is not purged but is considerably constrained. Where changes in thought regularly converge with multiple patterns relative certainty can be obtained.

Loretz and Castellino have applied this approach to Ecclesiastes. However, according to Wright, the former concentrated on microanalysis rather than macroanalysis, and the latter's plan does not match the thought of Ecclesiastes, and the objective data for his analysis is meagre.[89] This sets the stage for Wright to redo a close reading of Ecclesiastes.

In 1:12-18 Wright finds a double introduction followed in 2:1-17 by two paragraphs which expand on this double introduction. The double introduction is marked out by its form. Each introductory section contains an introductory statement and ends with "all is vanity and a chase after wind" plus a proverb. Wright justifies starting with 1:12 because of a general acknowledgement that

---

[87] Ibid., 317.
[88] Ibid., 318.
[89] Ibid., 319-320.

this is where the book starts. 2:1-11 and 12-17 are also marked off by the phrase "all was vanity and a chase after wind". In this way Wright discerns 4 sections in 1:12-2:17. These sections are generally recognised but in Wright's view, no one has pursued this type of analysis further. This he seeks to do by letting subsequent occurrences of the "vanity" phrase indicate the ends of other units. In this way, he arrives at four additional sections in a short-long-short-long arrangement: 2:18-26; 3:1-4:6; 4:7-16; 4:17-6:9.[90] The "vanity" phrase ends in 6:9 and is not repeated in the remaining six chapters. These four sections are all concerned with evaluating man's toil and would seem to be meaningful units. The main subject of 2:18-6:9 is "toil".

Thus, in 1:12-6:9, Wright finds a continuity of thought. Qoheleth seeks to report the results of his investigation of life. He starts with a double introduction (1:12-15; 1:16-18), and then evaluates pleasure seeking (2:1-11), wisdom (2:12-17) and the results of toil (2:18-6:9). These eight units are tied together not only by the repetition of the evaluation, but also by an interlocking arrangement whereby, once the series begins, each section picks up a motif mentioned two units earlier. For example, in 2:12-17 "wisdom, madness and folly" picks up from 1:17. The four sections on toil are also connected by the idea of there being nothing better to do than to eat and drink and enjoy one's labour. There is development in this idea in that it is heavily qualified in the last section.

6:6-9 contains a number of phrases that recall earlier remarks. This, plus the cessation of the "vanity" phrase, suggests that 6:9 marks a major break. Wright scrutinises 6:10-12 and finds two new ideas introduced: man does not know what is good to do nor does he know what comes after him. In 7 and 8 a pattern occurs with the verbal expressions "not find/who can find", and in 9 and 10 "do not know" and "no knowledge" occur with great regularity. Wright uses these phrases to mark off sections and thereby ends up with the development of man not knowing what is good in four sections in 7:1-8:17, and with the development of man not knowing what is to come in six sections in 9:1-11:6.[91] This brings us to the generally recognised final poem on youth and old age at the end of the book. 1:2 and 12:8, as is generally recognised, is an overall inclusion. The question in 1:3 provides the context in which 1:4-11 is to be read. The epilogue is from the editor. In this way Wright arrives at the following outline.

TITLE	1:1
POEM ON TOIL	1:2-11
I. QOHELETH'S INVESTIGATION OF LIFE	1:12-6:9
Double Introduction	1:12-15
	1:16-18
Study of pleasure seeking	2:1-11
Study of wisdom and folly	2:12-17

---

90   Ibid., 321.
91   Ibid., 323.

Study of the fruits of toil	
one has to leave them to another	2:18-26
one cannot hit on the right time to act	3:1-4:6
the problem of a 'second one'	4:7-16
one can lose all that one accumulates	4:17-6:9
II. QOHELETH'S CONCLUSIONS	6:10-11:6
Introduction: man does not know what God has done, for man cannot find out what is good to do, and he cannot find out what comes after	6:10-12
A. Man cannot find out what is good for him to do	
Critique of traditional wisdom	
on the day of prosperity and adversity	7:1-14
on justice and wickedness	7:15-24
on women and folly	7:25-29
on the wise man and the king	8:1-17
B. Man does not know what will come after him	
he knows he will die; the dead know nothing	9:1-6
there is no knowledge in Sheol	9:7-10
man does not know his time	9:11-12
man does not know what will be	9:13-10:15
he does not know what evil will come	10:16-11:2
he does not know what good will come	11:3-6
POEM ON YOUTH AND OLD AGE	11:7-12:8
EPILOGUE	12:9-14

Wright is sure this is objective: "it seems almost certain that the patterns uncovered are a deliberate device utilized by the author to provide the main structure of the book. ... it is a case of verbal repetitions marking out and exactly coinciding with the repetitions of ideas."[92] The theme of Ecclesiastes is thus the impossibility of understanding what God has done. Qoheleth's only advice is to enjoy life while one can.

Up until this point we have focused our discussion on Wright's 1968 article since this is the one in which he develops his close reading of Ecclesiastes. It should be noted that Wright buttressed this early analysis with two later articles in which he argues that there are intricate numerical patterns in Ecclesiastes which support his proposed structure.[93] His 1968 article received mixed reactions.[94] He examines the criticisms made by Braun, Glasser, Lys and Loader against his reading of Ecclesiastes and concludes that the proposal has suffered nothing from their scrutiny.[95] However he does acknowledge the difficulty in objectively discerning the sorts of pattern he found in Ecclesiastes:

---

[92] Ibid., 324.

[93] A.G. WRIGHT, "The Riddle of the Sphinx Revisited: Numerical Patterns in the Book of Qoheleth," *CBQ* 42 (1980) 38-51; idem, "Additional Numerical Patterns in Qoheleth," *CBQ* 45 (1983) 32-43.

[94] WRIGHT, "The Riddle of the Sphinx Revisited," 39.

[95] Ibid., 42.

A repetition which one interpreter sees as an ending formula another sees as part of a chiasm leading in a different direction and another sees as a *Leitmotiv*. While one critic is impressed by repetitions as indicators of structure in this particular book and allows for irregularities in other stylistic features, another gives primary value to introductory formulae or to discontinuities (change of person, topic, genre) and allows for irregularities in other areas.[96]

To escape the impasse of this subjectivity further evidence is required from Ecclesiastes. "What is really needed at this time is additional data from the book itself which would be of such a nature that it would aid in evaluating the data already in the discussion and aid in weighing in favour of one or other interpretation of that data."[97] Such additional data Wright found in intricate numerical patterns.[98] In his 1983 article he extended the analysis of numerical patterns in Ecclesiastes to the subsections.[99] Since our concern with Wright is as an example of a New Critical reading of Ecclesiastes we shall not describe and evaluate his numerical analysis in any detail.[100] He justifies it not only in terms of its success, but also in terms of similar numerical relations in Proverbs, the fascination of ancients with numbers, numerical patterns in the Book of Wisdom and the practice of the Sopherim of counting letters, words and verses.[101] The numerical preoccupation we find in the book is not bizarre by the standards of the ancients, in Wright's view, and we have to look at their books on their own terms. For our purposes it suffices to note that these patterns confirm Wright's' earlier analysis.

Wright's interpretation of Ecclesiastes is firmly New Critical. He is hesitant about NC's denial of authorial intentionality but in practice works very much with an embodied intentionality stance, which approximates the refined view of NC (see above). Wright's approach to the structure of Ecclesiastes is intrinsic, working with the final form of the text and concentrating his attention on a close reading of the text. Verbal repetitions in particular are the key for Wright to the objective structure of the book.

4.6 Structuralism and Its Application to Old Testament Studies

4.6.1 Introduction

The literature related to the development and application of structuralism is vast and multi-disciplinary.[102] We will firstly outline the development of

---

96 Ibid., 41.
97 Ibid., 42-43.
98 Ibid.; and idem, "Additional Numerical Patterns in Qoheleth."
99 WRIGHT, "Additional Numerical Patterns in Qoheleth."
100 For a summary cf. R.E. MURPHY, *Ecclesiastes* (WBC; Texas: Word, 1992) xxxviii-xxxix.
101 WRIGHT, "Additional Numerical Patterns in Qoheleth," 39-40.
102 See for example the bibliography in T. HAWKES, *Structuralism and Semiotics* (New Accents; London: Routledge, 1977).

structuralism, concentrating on Jakobson's and Greimas's views in particular since they are key figures in relating structuralism to literature. Then we will survey the application of structuralism to Old Testament interpretation and in particular to wisdom literature. This will provide the backdrop for an examination of Loader's work on Ecclesiastes with a view to considering the positive insight that a structuralist approach to Ecclesiastes might provide.

Terence Hawkes begins his study of structuralism with Vico in the eighteenth century.[103] Vico attempted to develop a science of human society by applying the principles of natural science to the world of nations. Primitive man possessed *sapienza poetica* whereby he cast his responses to his context in a metaphysics of metaphor, symbol and myth. Early accounts of creation were not intended to be taken literally but were ways of encoding and shaping reality. Consequently that which man recognises as true and that which he constructs are the same. "When man perceives the world, he perceives without knowing it the superimposed shape of his own mind."[104] This works both ways; humans construct society and society shapes humanity. "That is, man constructs the myths, the social institutions, virtually the whole world as he perceives it, and in so doing he constructs himself. This making process involves the continual creation of recognizable and repeated forms which we can now term a process of *structuring*."[105] Vico's work is one of the first modern attempts to deny a permanent structuring to reality. With the exception of poetic wisdom there is no givenness to human nature or reality.

From a structuralist perspective the world does not consist of independently existing objects which can be perceived. "In fact, every perceiver's *method* of perceiving can be shown to contain an inherent bias which affects what is perceived to a significant degree. ... any observer is bound to create something of what he observes. Accordingly, the *relationship* ... becomes the only thing that *can* be observed."[106] The true nature of things lies in the relationships which we construct and then perceive between them. The common ground with Vico is clear. Structuralists aim to conceptualise these structures constructed by humans.

4.6.2 Structuralism and Linguistics: Saussure

In linguistics structuralism involves the search for linguistic structure. The Swiss linguist Saussure is the originator of structuralist linguistics. He inherited a worldview in which the world consisted of independently existing objects and in which language was thought to have a correspondence relationship with this world. Saussure rejected this and the notion of language that resulted from it in

---

[103] Ibid.
[104] Ibid., 13.
[105] Ibid., 14.
[106] Ibid., 17.

favour of a more relational view. His views are set out in his *Course in General Linguistics*. The extent to which structure is central to his understanding of linguistics is evident from the second of his three main points about the scope of linguistics: "to determine the forces that are permanently and universally at work in all languages, and to deduce the general laws to which all specific historical phenomena can be reduced."[107]

Order within the field of linguistics becomes manifest when one approaches linguistics in the following way: "from *the very outset we must put both feet on the ground of language and use language as the norm of all other manifestations of speech*."[108] Once *Langue* (language) is given priority over *langage* (speech), then order results. This principle is developed into Saussure's distinction between *langue* and *parole*, whereby he distinguishes between the language system and concrete acts of speech.

Language for Saussure is a system of signs that express ideas and his linguistics explores the way in which these signs operate. The linguistic unit is a slice of sound which, to the exclusion of everything that precedes and follows it in the spoken chain, is the signifier of a certain concept. The bond between the two is wholly arbitrary so that in language there are only differences and no positive terms. "Whether we take the signified or the signifier, language has neither ideas nor sounds that existed before the linguistic system, but only conceptual and phonic differences that have issued from the system."[109] Saussure rejects the use of symbol as a synonym for sign because the symbol is never wholly arbitrary, whereas the sign is. Meaning is thus generated not by a correspondence relationship with reality but by differences within the system.

4.6.3 American and European Structuralism

The English translation of Saussure's *Cours* only appeared in 1959 and it was mainly in the 1960's that it experienced the height of its influence, being taken up and developed in a variety of disciplines. Lévi-Strauss extended semiotics to the whole of culture on the basis of his understanding that language constitutes the prototype of cultural phenomena. Thus phenomena like kinship and myth were studied along structuralist lines. And this work on myth was soon extended to include the Old Testament.

In Europe and America three major schools of structuralist linguistic analysis developed.[110] In the USA *descriptive* linguistics developed, originating in the work of Peirce and taken up by Morris. In Prague a functional type developed focusing on the functions language fulfils in society as a distinct

---

[107] F. de SAUSSURE, *Course in General Linguistics* (Trans. W. BASKIN; New York: McGraw-Hill Paperbacks, 1959) 6.
[108] Ibid., 9.
[109] Ibid., 120.
[110] HAWKES, *Structuralism and Semiotics*, 73-76.

structure. Key figures were Troubetskoi and Jakobson. In Copenhagen a *glossematic* school developed which emphasised the formal nature of all language so that for every process there is a system. These three varieties are the major structuralist modes of linguistic analysis in the twentieth century.

Jakobson focused on the poetic function of language and sought to give an account of this within the context of linguistics.[111] To this end he invokes the linguistic notions of polarities and equivalence in order to account for the peculiar nature of poetic language. Jakobson's notion of polarities is derived from Saussure's syntagmatic-associative distinction which is developed in poetry in terms of metonymy and metaphor. The former is associative in character, the latter is syntagmatic. They are binarily opposed and underpin the process of selection and combination by which signs are formed. The distinction between the two modes is fundamental to language.

The *poetic* function of language draws on both the selective and the combinative modes as a means for the promotion of *equivalence*. "The poetic function projects the principle of equivalence from the axis of selection into the axis of combination."[112] Poeticalness is an aspect of all uses of language; poetry arises when 'poeticalness' is raised to a higher degree than other competing functions. Hence, when dealing with poetic function, linguistics cannot limit itself to the field of poetry.[113] We therefore need a poetics of poetry and prose which attends to metonymy and metaphor at all levels and this is what Jakobson seeks to provide. To this end he draws attention to six constituent factors that make up any speech event. All communication entails a *message* initiated by an *addresser* and directed towards an *addressee*. The message requires a *contact* between the two (e.g. oral, visual, electronic) and must be formulated in terms of a *code* (speech, writing, numbers) and refer to a *context* understood by both addresser and addressee. This can be diagrammatically represented as follows.

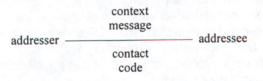

It is important to note that the message cannot be the sole carrier of meaning in this act; rather meaning resides in the total act of communication. All meaning is context-sensitive and thus is not a stable entity which passes untrammelled from sender to receiver. The six constitutive elements are never in perfect balance. One is always dominant so that, if, for example, the act is directed

---

111 For a useful summary of Jakobson's view see ibid., 76-87.

112 R. JAKOBSON, "Closing Statement: Linguistics and Poetics," In: T.A. SEBEOK (ed.), *Style in Language* (1960) 358.

113 Ibid., 377.

towards the context, then the referential function of the act dominates. If towards the addresser the emotive and so on.

Jakobson's work was most strongly directed towards poetic texts. In terms of structuralist analysis of prose Vladimir Propp was most probably the linking figure between the Russian Formalists, of which Jakobson was a member, and structuralists, especially French ones.[114] Propp's work was refashioned and developed by Greimas.

Greimas' primary concern is semantics. He focuses on narrative structure in particular and describes it in terms of a Saussurean linguistic model of an underlying langue generating a parole. Binary oppositions underlie the elementary structure of signification. We perceive differences and thus the world takes shape in front of us. These oppositions form the basis of a deep-lying actantial model from whose structures the surface structures of individual stories derive. Stories spring from a common grammar or enunciation-spectacle so that, although stories differ considerably at a surface level, at a structural level they derive from a common grammar. At a surface level the structure of the enunciation spectacle is manifested through the actants who embody it and these actants operate at a functional/phonemic level rather than in terms of content. An actant may be embodied in a single character or reside in the function of more than one character. "The content of the actions changes all the time, the actors vary, but the enunciation-spectacle remains always the same, for its permanence is guaranteed by the fixed distribution of the roles".[115]

Like Propp, Greimas argues for a grammar of narrative in which a finite number of elements, organised in a finite number of ways, generate stories. Greimas reorganises Propp's seven spheres of action into the following three relationships: subject versus object, sender versus receiver, helper versus opponent.

If these three relationships form a type of phonemic analysis, then a syntactic analysis is required at the surface level which will show how these elements can be joined to form a narrative. Greimas reduces and modifies Propp's thirty-one functions to twenty. Greimas' work on narrative constitutes a refinement of Propp's with the same basic aim; to establish the plot models and to explore their combinatory potential.

It is not easy to generalise about structuralism but we can sum up its approach to literary texts in the following three ways. Firstly, structuralism looks at a text as a manifestation of a deep, underlying structure. This has led to the well known distinction between surface and deep structure. Because of structuralism's fascination with deep structure some have concluded that it is not

---

[114] Cf. HAWKES, *Structuralism and Semiotics*, 87.
[115] Greimas quoted in ibid., 89.

interested in the final form of the text and therefore in interpretation.[116] This has led some to characterise structuralism in terms of 'absence' as opposed to present meaning in texts. One such is Ricoeur, who said to Lévi-Strauss in a public discussion of June 1953:

> there is no 'message', not in the cybernetic sense, but in the 'kerygmatic' sense; you give up meaning in despair; but you save yourself by the notion that if human beings have nothing to say, at least they say it so well that one can subject their discourse to a structural analysis. You save meaning, but it is the meaning of meaninglessness, the admirable syntactic arrangement of a discourse which says nothing. I see you at that point of conjunction of agnosticism and an acute understanding of syntaxes.

Certainly the focus of structuralism is deep, underlying structure but it would be wrong to conclude therefore, that it has no concern with interpretation. Polzin's work on Job (see below) is a fine example of how concern with deep structure may illumine the surface structure and overall interpretation of the message of the text. Polzin correctly comments that "[f]ormulas, methodologies, formal analyses may all have their place in such an enterprise. But they are valuable only insofar as they help to make what one studies a little more intelligible to whoever employs them."[117]

Secondly the model that structuralism constructs is a hypothetical-deductive and not an inductive one.[118] Thirdly, structuralism is conscious of the reader of the text; it emphasises deep-subjectivity. "Structural analysis as sign can be viewed in its dual role as the *meaning* (= content) of an object but the *expression* of a subject. It is the crucial awareness and self-consciousness of the latter role of analysis that most often signals the study of an object as truly structural."[119]

4.6.4 Application of Structuralism to Old Testament Texts

The application of structuralism to biblical studies began in the early 1960's with the work of Leach, who, using methods deeply influenced by Lévi-Strauss, attempted a structural analysis of the creation stories in Genesis.[120] By September 1969 close to two hundred biblical scholars, including Roland Barthes, gathered

---

[116] D.C. GREENWOOD, *Structuralism and the Biblical Text* (Religion and Reason 32; Method and Theory in the Study and Interpretation of Religion; Berlin; NY; Amsterdam: Mouton, 1985) 8-9, notes that structuralists are not *primarily* concerned with the meaning of a text. BARTON, *Reading the Old Testament*, 121, stresses that structuralists are more concerned with analysis than exegesis. They are not so much concerned with providing new interpretations as explaining how an interpretation comes to be appropriate.

[117] R.M. POLZIN, *Biblical Structuralism. Method and Subjectivity in the Study of Ancient Texts* (Philadelphia: Fortress; Missoula: Scholars, 1977) 102.

[118] GREENWOOD, *Structuralism and the Biblical Text*, 112-113; POLZIN, *Biblical Structuralism*, 19ff.

[119] POLZIN, *Biblical Structuralism*, 38.

[120] Cf. GREENWOOD, *Structuralism and the Biblical Text*, 16-22.

at Chantilly to discuss the relationship between structuralism and biblical interpretation. In 1970 Güttgemanns founded the journal *Linguistica Biblica* to promote structuralist approaches to the Bible.

Structuralist interpretation of the Old Testament has produced a sizeable body of literature, although the latter is concentrated on Old Testament narrative texts. Greenwood maintains that the methodologies of Lévi-Strauss, Barthes, Greimas and Güttgemanns are the most established structural procedures for biblical interpretation.[121] Very little structuralist work has been done on Old Testament wisdom literature. Polzin's outstanding work on Job is a notable exception.[122] Although Job has a much stronger narrative aspect to it than Ecclesiastes, there are many parallels between them, and we shall therefore focus our discussion in this section upon Polzin's work on structuralism and Job.

Polzin finds discrepancy and contradiction at the heart of Job. He identifies three major contradictions: firstly there is that between what a person is taught to believe about divine justice and what he experiences in his life. Secondly Job's friends affirm divine retribution for ten chapters but following the words of God in 42:7-8 they sacrifice to God for "not speaking of Him what is right." Thirdly some of God's words seem to contradict his actions. His statement in 42:7 that Job spoke right of him seems to contradict Yahweh's speeches in 38-41 and the reaffirmation of the principle of retribution in the epilogue.

For Polzin, confrontation of these inconsistencies is part of the book's structure and message. "Attempts to remove these inconsistencies can be characterised as academic 'failure of nerve' just as the platitudes of Job's friends are a 'failure of nerve' in the face of Job's problems. By removing the book's inconsistencies, some scholars have succeeded in removing its message."[123] Polzin rejects the usual source-critical and form-critical approaches to Job and works with Job as a unified work. Of the usual form-critical approaches to Job he says that "[s]uch attempts at analysis seem to me ultimately to destroy the message(s) of the book and moreover make impossible the first step towards understanding how, *in its present form*, it has affected men so profoundly down through the ages."[124]

This of course, raises the question of genre at a macro rather than micro level. Polzin is cautious with respect to form-critical analyses of genre.[125] He does, however, recognise the need for a "full-fledged science of discourse" which would include a typology of discourse.[126] Such an approach would examine Job

---

[121] GREENWOOD, *Structuralism and the Biblical Text*. See POLZIN, *Biblical Structuralism*, as well for useful bibliographies relating to the application of structuralism in Old Testament studies.

[122] R.M. POLZIN, "The Framework of the Book of Job," *Interpretation* XXVIII/2 (1974) 182-200; idem, *Biblical Structuralism*.

[123] POLZIN, "The Framework of the Book of Job," 183.

[124] Ibid., 186.

[125] Ibid., 187.

[126] Ibid., 189.

as *a whole* in relation to different types of discourse. Polzin recognises that although the science of discourse is still an infant we may nevertheless discern three main types of discourse, viz. metonymy (e.g. story, narrative, novel), metaphor (e.g. lyric poetry) and enthymeme (e.g. philosophical treatises). Since Job tells a story and falls into the first category Polzin investigates it as a sequence of sentences constituting a narrative. Polzin proposes three stages in a structural analysis of Job. Firstly analysis of the "framework" of the book, secondly consideration of its "code", and thirdly analysis of the "message". This tri-partite distinction is derived from Greimas.[127] "Code" and "message" are concepts from communication theory and correspond to the Saussurean distinction between langue and parole. "Framework" refers to the first step of analysis whereby the discourse is divided up into its basic units that are fundamental to the next two stages.

Analysis of the framework seeks to determine the largest units essential to the story. "Its basic unities are 'cardinal functions', veritable hinges of a story in that they are nucleatic actions or events without which the story would be essentially different."[128] Every story can be described as a series of sequences which can be united into larger 'movements'. Polzin designates the functional role of each movement the *main sequential* function of the movement.[129] In a way analogous to Lévi-Strauss' work on myth, Polzin proposes that the main sequential function in Job is set up to mediate contradictions.

Polzin discerns four movements in Job which involve a dialectical working out of a series of contradictions by means of four major sequential functions. In the first movement (Job 1-37) the sequential function is that of God afflicting Job. This sets up a conflict between the sphere of belief and experience. The friends side with belief, Job with experience. In the second movement (Job 38-42:6) the first contradiction is resolved by the theophany but a new one is set up: by assenting to the vision Job has to deny the validity of his previous experience. The third movement (Job 42:7-8) resolves the second contradiction (Job spoke what is right) but sets up another: how does God's speech in 38-41 relate to 42:7f? The fourth movement (42:10-17) resolves the last conflict and restores equilibrium. By restoring Job's fortunes God confirms his word of 42:7-8 and the affirmation of his power in 38-41. "Far from being a gratuitous 'hollywood ending', the final verses in chapter 42 dialectically resolve the subsidiary conflicts which the central event of the entire book, the theophany of God, had engendered."[130]

For Polzin the framework of Job is the work of a genius. "The genius of this journey is that insight is conferred not by the avoidance of contradiction and

---

[127] Ibid., 187.
[128] Ibid., 189.
[129] Ibid., 190.
[130] Ibid., 198.

inconsistency but precisely by the courageous integration of contradiction and resolution. In other words the story is a paradigm. What is on the surface a diachronic linear treatment of a problem reveals itself as containing an underlying or latent synchronic structure."[131] This pattern provides the material for analysis of the code of Job.

The second stage in Polzin's structural analysis of Job is determination of the code of the text. Interdisciplinary co-operation is vital at this level and Polzin, in an attempt to analyse the code (that which is left of the structure once all the semantic content is removed), makes use of mathematical concepts of group structure.[132] Polzin argues that the framework of Job is made up of a set of transformations which can be thought of as a representation of a Klein group, or more precisely as an Abelian group having four members.

Within each movement in Job there is a before and after element, and a sphere of belief and one of experience. If X and Y symbolise belief and experience then the four movements can be seen in the following way.

Initial situation:	$+X$	$+Y$			
First movement:	$+X$	$+Y$	—	$-X$	$+Y$
Second movement:	$-X$	$+Y$	—	$+X$	$-Y$
Third movement:	$+X$	$-Y$	—	$-X$	$+Y$
Fourth movement:	$-X$	$+Y$	—	$+X$	$+Y$

This analysis alerts us to the fact that only four states are possible but that one of these four never occurs. $-X$ $-Y$ is avoided. "The one state avoided throughout the framework is that state representing somehow a negation both of the sphere of belief and the sphere of experience! It seems to me that this one observation is worth the entire (and tiring) trip."[133] Polzin plausibly argues that it is the one state that Job fervently requested.[134] The conflict between Job and God is ultimately one in which God represents $+X$ $+Y$ whereas Job keeps begging for $-X$ $-Y$, that is to be taken down to Sheol. "The message of the book centres around the courageous affirmation of apparently irreconcilable spheres instead of the insane negation of those spheres to avoid conflict and contradiction."[135]

The third stage in Polzin's structural analysis of Job is the explication of the message. Polzin recognises that if structural analysis is relevant to biblical exegesis then it has to make a difference at this stage.[136] All the characters in the book take up positions which are then challenged. This pushes one to inquire concerning the "situation of discourse" out of which and for which Job was written. The key to the situation of discourse is what Polzin calls "contextualised

---

[131] Ibid., 200.
[132] POLZIN, *Biblical Structuralism*, 89ff.
[133] Ibid., 100.
[134] Ibid.
[135] Ibid., 101.
[136] Ibid., 102.

situation"; textual indexes that would point at aspects of the situation of discourse. Analysis of the situation of discourse particularly through the role of the speeches indicates that ambiguity is avoided in the message of the book by what God is reported to have done and said. These two aspects validate or invalidate everything else in the story.

> The figures of the story, far from being arbitrary, capricious, and mutually contradictory, interrelate with one another to help form a coherent message. There is no absolute answer to the problem of innocent suffering, no stance that is valid for all times and situations of one's life. At certain moments, suffering is so horrendous that any attempt to justify and explain it is 'obscene' … This is the situation with which Job was confronted … it was 'obscene' for his friends to explain away the 'Holocaust' his life had become. But at another moment in his life, after the vision of God out of the whirlwind, faith in redemption of some sort was once again possible for Job and he could now see his way to a belief he had once lost.[137]

4.7 Loader's Reading of Ecclesiastes

Structure is central to Loader's interpretation of Ecclesiastes.[138] Barton invokes Loader's approach as a possible candidate for a structuralist approach to Ecclesiastes, although he does find it wanting in terms of any precise definition of structuralism.[139] For Loader synchronic analysis must precede diachronic analysis of a text.[140] The form and content of Ecclesiastes must first be analysed in their own right before the history of the development of the text is considered. Loader thus suggests five steps to be followed in the analysis of Ecclesiastes. Firstly, the individual pericopes need to be demarcated. Secondly the form of these pericopes should be assessed. Thirdly typical forms or *Gattungen* are to be identified. Fourthly the contents of each pericope are to be interpreted and finally, the composition of the whole book is to be accounted for.

Loader finds the following figures of style in Ecclesiastes: parallelism, chiasmus (particularly suited to the polar tensions in Qoheleth), paranomasia, anaphora, hyperbole and rhyme.[141] He argues that, apart from 1:1 the book as a whole is poetry. He thus rejects the view that the whole book is prose (Masoretes, Podechard) and the view that it is part prose, part poetry. The Masoretes did not apply the accentuation system of the poetical books to Ecclesiastes and thus saw it as prose. The LXX, however, places Ecclesiastes with the poetic books, in Loader's view, correctly. It is poetry with an unusual metre and form.

---

[137] Ibid., 120, 121.

[138] J.A. LOADER, *Polar Structures in the Book of Qohelet* (Hawthorne, NY: de Gruyter, 1979); idem, *Ecclesiastes. A Practical Commentary* (Grand Rapids: Eerdmans, 1986).

[139] BARTON, *Reading the Old Testament*, 130.

[140] LOADER, *Polar Structures in the Book of Qohelet*, 1-2.

[141] Ibid., 9-16.

By *Gattungen* Loader understands typical forms, and not form as the unique structure of a specific literary unit. He identifies the following Gattungen in Ecclesiastes: the royal fiction, the *Wahrspruch* and maxim, the טוב saying, the comparison, the metaphor, the parable, the allegory, the observation, the self-discourse, the woe-saying and benediction, the antilogion, the rhetorical question, and the admonition.[142] Many of the typical literary forms of wisdom literature are used by Qoheleth, but they often become parts of new structural units. Series of literary units may be regarded as a Gattung when they have several characteristics in common and this is the case with some of Ecclesiastes' units containing many of the wisdom forms. Pericopes in Ecclesiastes often contain questioning and reflections; we may therefore speak of an additional Gattung, which Loader refers to as the reflection.[143]

Polar structures occur in virtually every literary unit of Ecclesiastes, according to Loader. Polar structures are "patterns of tension created by the counterposition of two elements to one another".[144] Thus in 3:1-9 for example, which Loader identifies as a pericope, he discerns the underlying polar structure life, conservation (pole), abandonment, death (contra-pole), no security, surrender of helpless man to the eventualities of life (tension).[145] Loader finds this type of polar structure throughout Ecclesiastes.[146]

The style of Ecclesiastes is so uniform and the basic theme so consistently pursued that there can be no question of identifying different sources in terms of Ecclesiastes' composition. There are also, however, so many repetitions in the book that we cannot speak of a progressive development of a theme either. As a volume of poetry Ecclesiastes is neither a random collection nor a scientific treatise. The poems each constitute a unit by themselves but are also held together by more than a common theme. The inclusion (1:2 and 12:8) and the nature of the first poem as a prologue to the entire volume confirm this. The hebel declaration is found throughout the book, and even in chapter ten where the word is not mentioned the idea is present. Thus "[i]t is obvious and certain that this *one conviction* of emptiness and senselessness is the dominant motif in the book."[147] The several separate units function as illustrations, motivations and discussions of this basic hebel idea, and the polar structures express this relationship.

The polar tensions indicate the tension between Qoheleth's views and that of general wisdom.[148] This raises the question of the interpretation and explanation of the polarity. The development of ANE wisdom is one aspect of the background

---

[142] Ibid., 18-28.
[143] Ibid., 28.
[144] Ibid., 1.
[145] Ibid., 29.
[146] Ibid., 29-111.
[147] Ibid., 9.
[148] Ibid., 116.

needed for an understanding of Ecclesiastes. Israelite wisdom developed through the same stages as Egyptian and Mesopotamian wisdom so that a comparison of Israel's wisdom with these other cultures allows Ecclesiastes to fall exactly into place.[149] Once wisdom precepts are encoded a crisis of wisdom follows, and Ecclesiastes represents part of such a crisis. Loader discerns three phases in the development of wisdom: firstly there is a strong appreciation of the relationship between action and the opportune time for action. Secondly there is a loss of the sense of temporal relevance so that a dogmatic system originates. Thirdly there is protest against this petrification. For the first see Prov 10-29. Job's three friends are an example of the second and Qoheleth is an example of the third. Qoheleth never comes to a happy ending; the tension and protest continue to the end.

Another important aspect of the background is the religious history of the time. Loader dates Ecclesiastes to the mid third century BC. After the exile of the sixth century BC profound changes in religious outlook took place in Israel. The God-concept became less personal, a development which was often compensated for by the personification of circumlocutions to fill the gap; this is how Judaism resolved the tension between the growing remoteness of God and the desire to hold onto God. Ecclesiastes is a striking exception to this; God is the distant one with whom Qoheleth cannot speak and he refuses to fill this vacuum. Qoheleth's thinking is rooted in two traditions: on the one hand he wishes to make room for human participation but on the other he wishes to be the dispassionate onlooker. "Involvement and detachment are polar opposites and hence stand in a relationship of tension to each other."[150] He therefore strongly criticises mainstream wisdom and yet appropriates all the typical forms of expression that characterise it. "*He accepts God, but God is far – this is the ground for the polarity in his thought.*"[151] Loader illustrates his conclusions with the following diagram:

1	2	3	4
thought	tension: vanity	involvement	typical genres
counterthought	tension	tension	
	God	withdrawal	criticism

---

[149] LOADER, *Ecclesiastes*, 9.
[150] Ibid., 13.
[151] LOADER, *Polar Structures in the Book of Qohelet*, 129.

Barton is correct in arguing that Loader's interpretation of Ecclesiastes can only be called structuralist in a very limited sense.[152] He certainly is not working with a structuralist methodology. One clear indication of this is his conclusion that there is one contradiction in the book, namely that between the epilogue and the rest of the book. This presupposes some understanding of the redaction of the text and a refusal to work with the final form of the text as a unified whole. He also works with a stronger sense of the historical setting of the text than is normally the case with structuralists. Even Polzin in his discussion of the situation of discourse argues his case intrinsically rather than by trying to relate Job to external developments. His structural concern is also very much a surface structural one, although his polar structural analysis points in the direction of the possibility of a developed structural analysis of Ecclesiastes. Such an analysis remains to be done.

4.8 The Implications of Canonical Criticism, New Criticism and Structuralism for Reading Ecclesiastes and for Old Testament Hermeneutics

Just how successful Childs', Wright's and Loader's analyses of Ecclesiastes are is debatable. However the questions they bring to the text are crucial. All three raise questions about the *literary* unity of the text in the light of its neglect. NC, structuralism and the canonical approach can in this respect all be seen as reactions to 'positivism' as it became obvious that positivism prevented literature from being itself and being studied in a way that is true to its character.[153]

The recovery of reading which the New Critics sought inevitably recentres the question of genre, since reading method must always be appropriate to its genre. Hence the large amount of discussion in NC concerning the nature of literariness. Whatever we may think of their conclusions in this area, their recognition of macrogenre and the necessity of developing methods of interpretation appropriate to the object remains crucial. The danger for OT studies is that NC was developed in relation to literary and particularly poetic texts. Poetic texts are often highly allusive and non-didactic in a way that contrasts with much of the OT where a didactic, kerygmatic focus is much more evident. Even within literary studies the New Critical understanding of 'poeticalness' as essentially paradoxical and incapable of paraphrase has come under strong

---

[152] BARTON, *Reading the Old Testament*, 130-131.

[153] See COLLINGWOOD, *The Idea of History*, 126-133, for a discussion of the effect of positivism upon philosophies of history, and thus upon the historical critical method. Collingwood discerns two negative effects of positivism upon history; firstly it led to "unprecedented mastery over small-scale problems with unprecedented weakness in dealing with large-scale problems" and secondly it prevented scholars from judging the facts with the result that history could only be the record of external events.

criticism.[154] Norris argues that we need an approach which does justice to the literary nature of literature without sacrificing the question of truth. It seems to me that such an approach would be more appropriate to OT texts in comparison with the New Critical stress on poetic texts as 'being' rather than meaning. As we have seen much of the New Critical polemic against intentionality is related specifically to poetic (paradoxical and ambiguous) as opposed to practical texts. OT texts regularly fall more into the practical category than the poetic one, and even from a New Critical perspective this would change the method of interpretation.

This raises the question of the nature of Old Testament texts and of Ecclesiastes in particular. Can we, without further ado, categorise them as literary texts and apply literary methods of interpretation? At very least NC and structuralism rightly alert us to the literary *aspect* of the OT as text. In this respect the recovery of synchronic reading of a text by NC and structuralism seems to me to be particularly valuable. Weiss captures this in his description of his method as *Total* interpretation, and de Man refers to the same thing as the "circular intent at totality."[155] The final form of the text is the only form in which we have a text like Ecclesiastes and it makes sense to devote one's energies to this form. Certainly this is what any *reading* of Ecclesiastes ought to do. As NC stresses, no text is simply the sum of its sources. A text is a new creation and a reading of it must "be judged at the moment of creative art ... by the art of the poem itself."[156] Even if we could recover all the sources of an Old Testament text that is still something very different from understanding the text itself. Source criticism is certainly a legitimate and important enterprise but it should not be equated with the reading of a text.

Childs' approach reminds us that OT texts are also highly theological. Synchronic readings of OT texts will need to account for the relationship between the theological and literary aspects of these texts. Indeed Childs' emphasis on the final form of the text alerts us to the fact that seeking the message of the text will inevitably involve analysis of it as a literary text.

And in this respect NC and structuralism do therefore point one in a host of fruitful directions for reading Ecclesiastes. Wright's and Loader's analyses are a real advance in the quest to understand Ecclesiastes. Wright's work is particularly important in its focus upon the function of repetition in Ecclesiastes. Sternberg has explored this in detail in relation to Old Testament narrative texts.[157] Such work remains to be done in relation to a wisdom text like Ecclesiastes, but Wright's analysis is an important step in the right direction. His analysis of the

---

[154] Cf. NORRIS, "Criticism."

[155] P. de MAN, *Blindness and Insight. Essays in the Rhetoric of Contemporary Criticism* (2nd ed.; London: Methuen, 1983) 31.

[156] WELLEK and WARREN, *Theory of Literature*, 294.

[157] STERNBERG, *The Poetics of Biblical Narrative*, 432-435.

repetition of the hebel sayings has been fruitful in allaying scholarly despair over discerning the structure of Ecclesiastes, as evidenced by the positive reception of Wright's analysis by Perdue, Murphy etc.[158] In my opinion his analysis often incorrectly privileges form at the expense of content,[159] and, as I argue in chapter seven, the hebel repetitions are closely connected with the *carpe diem* repetitions, and these need to be analysed closely together. Form and content need to be held more closely together in the analysis of Ecclesiastes. Fox says, for example, about Wright's use of inclusios, "we can know that a repeated expression is an inclusio only after we find it occurring at the beginning and end of a unit demarcated by other means."[160] This is an overstatement but it serves as a reminder that one cannot escape the hermeneutical circle in analysis of the poetics of Ecclesiastes.

Loader's thesis about the polar opposites in Ecclesiastes is also an important advance in Ecclesiastes' research. Structuralism alerts us to the role of contradictions in literature and taking this seriously prevents one from reconstructing Ecclesiastes because of its contradictions. Personally I think the polar tensions operate somewhat differently in Ecclesiastes and that these tensions are better approached as juxtapositions which create gaps (see chapter seven). However, concern for the literary nature of Ecclesiastes has led Loader to analyse its literary structure and it is this kind of analysis that is crucial if we are to advance in our understanding of the text as a whole. Loader's tentative probing of the underlying structure also suggests that a structural analysis of Ecclesiastes comparable to Polzin's work on Job may be a fruitful area in which to work. A weakness of biblical structuralism has been its focus on deep structure at the expense of exegesis and message. However, as we have seen from Polzin's work on Job, this need not be the case. Structuralism can be a powerful accompaniment to exegesis and I suggest that it could work this way with Ecclesiastes.

NC and structuralism are, however, reminders that such readings would need to take the epilogue seriously as an integral part of the form of Ecclesiastes, an approach which Childs helpfully foregrounded. However Childs did not explore the relationship of the epilogue to the main body of the work; this remains to be done. Wright's and Loaders' analyses of Ecclesiastes move towards a synchronic reading of Ecclesiastes, but even they fail to explore the literary relationship of the epilogue to the text as a whole. Loader, as we saw, regards the epilogue as the one genuine contradiction in Ecclesiastes. Wright regards the epilogue as theologically very close to the main body of the text:

---

[158] Cf. L.G. PERDUE, *Wisdom and Creation. The Theology of Wisdom Literature* (Nashville: Abingdon, 1994); and MURPHY, *Ecclesiastes*.

[159] Cf. for example Ogden's criticism as to whether 6:7-9 does divide the book (G. OGDEN, "Qoheleth's Use of the 'Nothing is Better'-Form," *JBL* 98 (1979) 347-348), and see in particular M.V. FOX, *Qoheleth and His Contradictions* (JSOTSup 71; Sheffield: Almond Press, 1989) 156ff; and A. SCHOORS, "La structure littéraire de Qohéleth," *Orientalia Lovaniensia Periodica* 13 (1982) 97ff.

[160] FOX, *Qoheleth and His Contradictions*, 156.

Qoheleth himself recommended the fear of God (5:6) and expressed belief in judgement (11:9). He does not speak of the commandments of God but he surely promoted them because he never recommends folly. It would seem that the ideas of fear, commandments, and judgement are really presuppositions for Qoheleth as he discusses the concrete problem of how specifically one is to conduct one's life within that religious context; hence, those ideas are not prominent in the book. What the editor does is to give those presuppositions a greater prominence lest anyone misunderstand. From the concluding sentence one might surmise that God's judgement is less mysterious for the editor than it was for Qoheleth.[161]

One would have thought that Wright's mathematical analysis of Ecclesiastes would result in a closer consideration of how the epilogue fits into its literary structure. However, despite Wright's different understanding of the epilogue to Loader's, at this point both scholars have assumed a diachronic analysis of the development of the book and have failed to pursue New Criticism's circular intent at totality.

4.9 Conclusion

As reactions to 'positivism' Childs' canonical approach, NC and structuralism rightly alert us to the literary (and theological) dimensions of the OT texts, aspects which historical criticism tends to neglect. The applications of NC and structuralism to Ecclesiastes have been particularly fruitful in their foregrounding of the poetics of the text. Clearly if we are to advance in our understanding of Ecclesiastes then sustained attention will need to be given to the literary shape of Ecclesiastes. Childs' canonical approach is a reminder that the literary and the theological aspects of OT texts are inseparable; access to the message is gained via the literary shape of the text. Thus a hermeneutic is required which accounts for the historical, literary *and* theological aspects of the OT texts.

In the context of his narrative poetics Sternberg has given sustained attention to the development of a hermeneutic which integrates the historical, theological and literary elements of texts. Fox has given sustained attention to the genre of Ecclesiastes along narrative lines. In the following chapter we will examine these issues in the context of narrative approaches to OT interpretation.

---

161 WRIGHT, "Ecclesiastes (Qoheleth)," 495.

CHAPTER 5

NARRATIVE AND THE READING OF ECCLESIASTES

5.1 Introduction

Biblical narratology is a relatively recent addition to the smorgasbord of biblical hermeneutical approaches, having emerged in the seventies and matured in the eighties. Gunn traces its emergence from the growing awareness of the limitations of the historical critical method through canon criticism and NC (including Muilenberg's rhetorical criticism) to the narratology of Alter and Berlin.[1] Exegetical narrative approaches to the OT are thus part of the reaction to historical criticism and part of the literary turn in biblical hermeneutics. Indeed, as we saw in chapter four, structuralism has devoted considerable energy to laying bare the depth structure of narrative.

In this chapter our concern is with two scholars who articulate narrative approaches concerned more with surface analysis of narrative texts. Sternberg has developed a sophisticated poetics of biblical narrative in which he seeks to integrate the historical, ideological and aesthetic aspects of the text. Fox has argued for the application of a narrative approach to Ecclesiastes. We will begin by outlining Sternberg's poetics of biblical narrative and then examine Fox's argument for a narrative approach to Ecclesiastes. This focuses the question of the genre of Ecclesiastes, and the remainder of this chapter will be devoted to this issue.

5.2 Sternberg's Poetics of Biblical Narrative

In 1981 Alter was able to write that "[o]ver the last few years, there has been growing interest in literary approaches among the younger generation of biblical scholars ... but, while useful explications of particular texts have begun to appear, there have been as yet no major works of criticism, and certainly no satisfying overview of the poetics of the Hebrew Bible."[2] Alter's *The Art of Biblical Narrative* is an overview but Sternberg's *Poetics* is the major work. Gunn, by no means a fan of Sternberg,[3] nevertheless comments when speaking

---

[1] D.M. GUNN, "New Directions in the Study of Biblical Hebrew Narrative," *JSOT* 39 (1987) 65-68.
[2] R. ALTER, *The Art of Biblical Narrative* (NY: Basic Books, 1981) 15.
[3] See D.M. GUNN, "Reading Right. Reliable and Omniscient Narrator, Omniscient God, and Foolproof Composition in the Hebrew Bible," in: D.J.A. CLINES, S.E. FOWL, and S.E. PORTER

about biblical narratology that "Sternberg's recent book on poetics moves such a narratology into a whole new dimension of discrimination and sophistication and will be fundamental to the emerging generation of narrative critics."[4]

The substance of Sternberg's theory of biblical narratology is found in the first three chapters of his *Poetics*. The remaining chapters flesh out this theory in exegetical examples. Since our main concern in this section is with the theory of biblical narratology and its relationship to Ecclesiastes – Sternberg does not deal with wisdom literature – our focus will be particularly upon chapters one to three.

Sternberg defines poetics as "the systematic working or study of literature as such."[5] It is important to Sternberg that biblical narrative is a work of literature so that in a poetics such as his, the discipline and its object come together. He stresses this in opposition to biblical scholars who see 'literary approaches' to the Bible as the conscious imposition of alien categories upon the OT text. For Sternberg the authors of the biblical narratives have used narrative techniques to convey their message, and poetics is a study of *these* techniques. Consequently at the very outset of his *Poetics* he indicates his understanding of narrative as *functional discourse* and sees poetics as research into how this discourse functions.[6] Sternberg's opening paragraph is a ringing affirmation of communication as the context within which narrative interpretation takes place.[7] "Biblical narrative is oriented to an addressee and regulated by a purpose or set of purposes involving the addressee. Hence our primary business as readers is to make purposive sense of it". Recognition of the genre of the text alone is insufficient: "Unless firmly anchored in the relations between narrator and audience, therefore, formalism degenerates into a new mode of atomism."[8]

Sternberg is critical of literary approaches to the Bible which view the text as autonomous. He detects the influence of NC in these approaches. NC was in reaction to the historicism of the historical critical method and this accounts for its being so anti-historical: "their dismissal of historicism makes an ideological rather than methodological reorientation: polemics may at best clear the ground but not substitute for a scholarly alternative."[9] For Sternberg seeing narrative technique as part of the text itself means taking the historical construction of the text seriously if one is going to come to grips with the functional purpose of biblical narrative. Sternberg discusses Wimsatt and Beardsley's intentional

---

(eds.), *The Bible in Three Dimensions* (1990) 53-64, where he critiques Sternberg for being ideological in an 'absolutist' sense.

   [4]   GUNN, "New Directions in the Study of Biblical Hebrew Narrative," 68.

   [5] M. STERNBERG, *The Poetics of Biblical Narrative. Ideological Literature and the Drama of Reading* (Bloomington: Indiana University Press, 1985) 2.

   [6] Sternberg's poetics represents in this sense a sort of textual realism far removed from the pluralism and indeterminacy of postmodernism. For a discussion of the latter see ch. 6.

   [7] STERNBERG, *The Poetics of Biblical Narrative*, 1.

   [8] Ibid., 2.

   [9] Ibid., 8.

fallacy and concludes that their attack focused not so much on authorial intention as on speculative reliance on external intention. We know virtually nothing about external intention as regards biblical authors so that our concern with authorial intention has to be focused on textual indicators, which Wimsatt and Beardsley were not against. This discernment of *objectified or embodied intention* Sternberg regards as crucial: "such intention fulfils a crucial role, for communication presupposes a speaker who resorts to certain linguistic and structural tools in order to produce certain effects on the addressee; the discourse accordingly supplies a network of clues to the speaker's intention."[10]

Taking authorial intention seriously means that source criticism and narratology should not be set against each other. This is especially so considering the gap in sociocultural context between our time and that of the origin of the biblical narratives. Of course we can never fully bridge this gap but this does not mean we cannot try. In fact this is the only alternative: "Once the choice turns out to lie between reconstructing the author's intention and licensing the reader's invention, there is no doubt where most of us stand."[11] The historicity of the text cannot be avoided; at the very least all scholars acknowledge that the language and its meaning require historical reconstruction. Of course the nature of the source criticism we engage in needs careful attention and Sternberg is very critical of much that has been called source criticism. There is an inevitable tension between source and discourse but Sternberg appeals for a closer partnership between the two; indeed he maintains that the two cannot but work together and neither has the primacy over the other.

Frequently it is falsely assumed that the Bible as a religious text is in antithesis to the Bible as literature. For Sternberg this is a false antithesis. In the ancient world highly poetic and literary material was regularly highly ideological and attended to for instruction. "The question is how rather than whether the literary coexists with the social, the doctrinal, the philosophical."[12] Representation is never to be set against evaluation, although the extent to which these aspects dominate in any piece of literature will vary. Only if the Bible were ideological in an extreme form of didactic would taking it seriously as literature be inadmissible. However, "if biblical narrative is didactic, then it has chosen the strangest way to go about its business. For the narrator breaks every law in the didacticist's decalogue. Anything like preaching from the narrative pulpit is conspicuous for its absence."[13] Narrative is the means whereby the Bible presents its message and the two, narrative technique and message are not to be set against each other.

---

10 Ibid., 9.
11 Ibid., 10.
12 Ibid., 35.
13 Ibid., 37-38.

In this respect it is time we stopped seeing the techniques of narrative as *literary* techniques. Those in the literary field have often been in the forefront of examining these techniques but that does not mean that they are confined to literary texts where art may be high and content and message low. "What determines literariness is not the mere presence but the dominance of the poetic function, the control it exerts over all the rest."[14] Narrative techniques are as much the prerogative of the historical biblical narratives as of fictional texts, and the presence of these techniques must not be seen as compromising the texts' ideological nature.

So how does the aesthetic aspect relate to the ideological in biblical narrative? "Biblical narrative emerges as a complex, because multifunctional, discourse. Functionally speaking, it is regulated by a set of three principles: ideological, historiographic, and aesthetic."[15] The ideological is particularly prominent in the law sections of the Pentateuch and in prophetic moralising for example. The historiographic is prominent in the names of places, people and etiologies. The aesthetic is in high profile in the narratives. The relation of these three principles is one of co-ordination and tense complementarity. Sternberg sums up the point at which the three merge as 'the drama of reading.' "They join forces to originate a strategy of telling that casts reading as a drama, interpretation as an ordeal that enacts and distinguishes the human predicament."[16] The ideological principle is seen in the foolproof aspect of the narratives; the aesthetic is seen in the exposition of biblical doctrine in a narrative which has built into it the cognitive antithesis between God and humanity.

Sternberg stresses the need not to impose a poetics upon the biblical narratives but to work so as to allow the biblical poetics to emerge:

> In practice as well as in methodology, the gravest danger to the literary approaches lurks in their imposition of models that do not fit the Bible, nor indeed … literature in general. … In most of the theoretical work I have done, on narrative and other subjects, the Bible has proved a corrective to widely held doctrines about literary structure and analysis, often a pointer to the formation of alternatives.[17]

Sternberg's work is in a class of its own and it will be in the centre of discussion of biblical narrative for a long time to come. No one who has read Sternberg can deny the validity of taking the biblical narratives seriously as narratives. A question which Sternberg does not address is the extent to which his poetics of biblical narrative would apply to biblical wisdom literature, and for our purposes, Ecclesiastes in particular. Fox has, however, recently suggested that

---

[14]   Ibid., 40.
[15]   Ibid., 41.
[16]   Ibid., 46.
[17]   Ibid., 56, 57.

Ecclesiastes has a narrative frame structure and that narrative analysis is the key to accessing its message.

5.3 Fox: Frame-narrative in Qoheleth

Fox's (1972) doctorate is entitled *The Book of Qoheleth and its Relation to the Wisdom School*.[18] This early work contains none of Fox's subsequent theories about Ecclesiastes as narrative or about Qoheleth's methodology as empirical where wisdom's methodology was not. Indeed Fox argues that "[t]he book of Qoheleth is an attack on wisdom starting from wisdom premises and conducted by wisdom methods."[19] Wisdom's epistemology, according to Fox at this point, is empiricism, although it frequently abandoned its empiricism when it did not fit with the doctrines of wisdom. Qoheleth differs from traditional wisdom only in using empiricism more consistently.

By 1977 Fox had begun to focus upon the literary shape of Ecclesiastes. He now maintains that Ecclesiastes is wisdom literature *and* narration.

> It tells something that happened to someone. I would like to take some first steps in the investigation of the literary characteristics of *Qoheleth* as narrative: Who is speaking (the question of *voice*), how do the voices speak, and how do they relate to each other? I will argue that the *Book of Qoheleth* is to be taken as a whole, as a single, well-integrated composition, the product not of editorship but of authorship, which uses interplay of voice as a deliberate literary device for rhetorical and artistic purposes.[20]

Fox argues that while modern scholarship correctly recognises more than one voice in Ecclesiastes, its presuppositions prevent the voice other than Qoheleth's from being listened to carefully. This other voice is the one we hear speaking in 1:2; 7:27 and 12:8 for example. This third person voice is not that of Qoheleth, as is made particularly clear by the way the voices interact in 7:27. It is unlikely, according to Fox, that Qoheleth would speak of himself in the third person in the midst of a first person sentence,[21] while a writer quoting someone else can put a *verbum dicendi* wherever he wishes within the quotation.

But if it is not Qoheleth, who is this other voice? Generally scholars speak of an editor/editors. But, says Fox, what signs are there of editing in Ecclesiastes? Fox suggests that the notion of editorship needs closer examination. The other voice could be that of a passive editor who receives a finished book and only

---

[18] Note that Fox's doctorate is written in modern Hebrew. These comments are dependent upon the extended abstract in English.

[19] M.V. FOX, *The Book of Qoheleth and it Relation to the Wisdom School* (Unpublished PhD thesis: Hebrew University, Jerusalem, 1972) i.

[20] Idem, "Frame Narrative and Composition in the Book of Qoheleth," *HUCA* (1977) 83.

[21] Ibid., 84.

adds glosses. Barton is an example of this view.[22] However 1:2 (the addition of a title), 7:27 and the epilogue make this impossible; whoever is responsible for these 'insertions' is far more active than a mere phrase inserter. Neither could the other voice be that of an editor-rearranger as Loretz suggests. The way the voice appears in 1:2; 12:8 and especially 7:27 betrays activity at the level of sentence formation. Fox wonders by what criteria one could distinguish editorial rearrangement of a previously completed book. Loretz uses the criterion of logical order but, as Fox demonstrates illogical order is not evidence for editorship and in the absence of a strong structure it is difficult to say what violates original structure.

A third possibility is that the other voice is that of the editor as compiler and arranger, as Ellermeier proposes. Ellermeier alone has investigated precisely what this editor did and concludes that Ecclesiastes was compiled by a redactor (QohR1) who wrote 1:1a; 1:2-3; 12:8, 9-12. QohR1 had before him 56 small independent *meshalim* which he joined on the basis of 'thematische Begriffe' and 'Stichwörter'. A second editor QohR2 was responsible for 12:13f and some glossing. Fox finds Ellermeier's view wanting on three accounts.[23] Firstly it is not at all clear whether we can distinguish originally independent units. Secondly it is often not clear whether Ellermeier's 'Begriffe' and 'Stichwörter' join or are internal to units. Thirdly to the extent that there are connections how does one know that these are editorial rather than from the author. "While I agree with Ellermeier that in 1:2 and elsewhere we can hear another voice speaking besides Qoheleth's, I see no evidence that that voice belongs to an editor who arranged numerous units he received from Qoheleth."[24] Fourthly, Qoheleth's words are presented to us as the single search by one man. The language of search and observation are found throughout the book and "provide a matrix that unites the disparate observations that Qoheleth reports."[25]

How then should we understand this other voice speaking in the third person about Qoheleth in 1:2; 7:27; 12:8 and in the epilogue?

> Here we should not ask what Qoheleth or an editor *could* have written, but rather – what are the literary implications of the words? What are we *meant* to hear in the third-person sections? ... I believe the questions raised can best be answered by the following understanding of that voice and its relation to Qoheleth. That certain words are in a different voice does not mean that they are by a different hand. ... I suggest that all of 1:2-12:14 is by the same hand[26] – not that the epilogue is by Qoheleth, but that *Qoheleth* is 'by' the epilogist.

---

22   G.A. BARTON, *A Critical and Exegetical Commentary on the Book of Ecclesiastes* (ICC; Edinburgh: T&T Clark, 1912).

23   FOX, "Frame Narrative and Composition," 88-90.

24   Ibid., 89.

25   Ibid., 90.

26   To an extent Fox had already recognised this in his doctoral thesis. In *The Book of Qoheleth*, xii, he argues that the editor and Qoheleth are the same person.

In other words, the speaker we hear from time to time in the background saying 'Qoheleth said' … this speaker is the teller of the tale, the external narrator of the story of Qoheleth. That is to say, the epic situation of the third-person voice in the epilogue and elsewhere is that of a man looking back and telling his son the story of the ancient wise-man Qoheleth, passing on to him words he knew Qoheleth to have said, appreciatively but cautiously evaluating his work in retrospect. Virtually all the 'story' he tells is a quotation of the words of the wise-man he is telling about. The speaker, whom I will call the *frame-narrator*, keeps himself well in the background, but he does not make himself disappear. He presents himself not as the creator of Qoheleth's words but as their transmitter.[27]

Fox thus understands Ecclesiastes as operating on three levels: the first is that of the frame-narrator who tells about the second (2a), Qoheleth-the-reporter, the narrating 'I', who looks back from old age and speaks about the third level (2b), Qoheleth-the-seeker, the younger Qoheleth who made the investigation in 1:12ff. Level one is a different person from levels two and three; levels two and three are different perspectives of the same person.

Fox's approach leads him to explore in detail the meaning of the epilogue in terms of its relationship to the main body of Ecclesiastes.[28] The didactic tone of the father-son instruction situation would have been easily recognised by the early readers of Ecclesiastes. In this way the epilogist identifies himself as a wisdom teacher. The frame narrator's first function in the epilogue is to testify to the reality of Qoheleth so that we react to him as having lived.

The reader's acceptance of the reality of literary figures is important to certain authors even when writing the most outlandish tales. … What the author seeks is not necessarily genuine belief in the character's existence (though that may be the intention in the case of *Qoheleth*) but *suspension of disbelief* for the purposes of the fiction. … The epilogist of Qoheleth succeeded in convincing many readers that he had an intimate familiarity with Qoheleth, and it is clear that this is one of the epilogue's purposes.[29]

The second function of the frame-narrator in the epilogue is to convey a certain stance towards Qoheleth and his teaching. Qoheleth is acknowledged as a wise man and his goals are praised but the frame-narrator is subtly non-committal about the truth of Qoheleth's words. In v. 10 Qoheleth is said to have sought fine words and truth but it is not said that he succeeded. This caution becomes more pronounced in v. 12 with the warning against excessive writing and speaking, the very activities Qoheleth is engaged in. Fox takes the comparison of the words of the wise with goads/nails to indicate not positive stability but their dangerous nature; they both prick and hurt. And of course the dogmatic certitude with which the overall duty of humans is stated contrasts with Qoheleth's insistence on the

---

27 FOX, "Frame Narrative and Composition," 90, 91.
28 Ibid., 96-106.
29 Ibid., 18.

uncertainty of everything. In a sense the epilogue can be seen as a call to allow expression of unorthodox opinion as long as the right conclusion is arrived at. But

> it is not only in offering a proper conclusion that the frame-narrative makes the book more easily tolerated. The use of a frame-narrative in itself puts a certain protective distance between the author and the views expressed in his work. This distance may be important even when the author is anonymous, because it may prevent the book as a whole from being violently rejected. The author blunts objections to the book as a whole by implying through use of a frame-narrator that he is just reporting what Qoheleth said, without actually rejecting the latter's ideas.[30]

Finally, Fox considers the relationship between the frame-narrator and the implied author, "the voice behind the voices".[31] In a footnote Fox refers to the work of Wayne Booth, who has argued that every work of literature has an implied author which "includes, in short, the intuitive apprehension of a completed artistic whole; the chief value to which *this* implied author is committed, regardless of what party his creator belongs to in real life, is that which is expressed by the total form."[32] This is important because the view of the frame-narrator may not be the same as the implied author, particularly in a book like Ecclesiastes where the conventional view of the frame-narrator does not cancel out Qoheleth's scepticism unless the reader allows it to. In fact, by ending such an unorthodox book with an orthodox epilogue, the author creates an ambiguity which gives the reader freedom to choose which position she will align herself with.

Fox's understanding of the frame-narrator – implied author relationship is questionable. However he has certainly demonstrated the value of a literary approach to Ecclesiastes, and in my opinion, raised one of the most important questions in the interpretation of Ecclesiastes, namely how, in a final form approach, one understands the epilogue to relate to the main body of the text. Fox is the only recent commentator on Ecclesiastes who has focused intensively on this problem. But how does his kind of literary analysis relate to typical, *historical* studies of the genre of Ecclesiastes? This is the question that will occupy us in the following section, before we go on to evaluate in detail Fox's reading of the epilogue in the context of his narrative approach to Ecclesiastes.

5.4 The Genre of Ecclesiastes

The conjunction of autobiography and fiction in actual writing practice is still apt to be felt as something of a scandal.

(A. JEFFERSON, "Autobiography as Intertext: Barthes, Sarraute, Robbe-Grillet," in: M. WORTON and J. STILL [eds.], *Intertextuality* [1990] 108)

---

[30] Ibid., 103.
[31] Ibid., 104.

Part of the problem with Ecclesiastes is that there is no consensus about its genre. Scholars are, for example, disagreed about how unified a book Ecclesiastes is. Galling represents one extreme,[33] Lohfink another.[34] Lohfink acknowledges that "I consciously go against current majority opinion that the book of Qoheleth is no more than a loose agglomeration of single proverbs, sentences, and 'mashals'. … In my opinion the book of Qoheleth is a very organised text." Fox, as we have seen, has argued that Ecclesiastes is best approached as narrative, wisdom literature; an approach which also sees a stronger unity in the book.

Emic analysis of genre in a comparative sense might be expected to produce a stronger consensus, but here again there has been considerable disagreement. Von Rad considered Ecclesiastes a royal testament.[35] Braun argues that it has the genre of a Hellenistic diatribe,[36] and more recently Lohfink suggests that the genre is that of a "Zugleich von Diatribe und Palindromie; ein Buch aus dem Bereich der Bildungsarbeit."[37] Longman maintains that Ecclesiastes is fictional royal autobiography.[38] Not surprisingly Murphy maintains that there is no satisfactory solution to the problem of the literary form of Ecclesiastes.[39] However, in my opinion, comparative genre analysis may provide more insight than the above differences suggest, if, as we will argue below, it works with literary analysis of the text.

The more valuable genre analyses have come from comparisons with ANE texts,[40] one of the most recent of which is that by Perdue.[41] We will use his thorough analysis as an entry point into the detailed discussion of the genre of Ecclesiastes. Perdue points out that scholars usually place Qoheleth in one of two form critical categories; either it is a sayings collection, or a first person narrative. Compared with Proverbs, Ben Sira and Pirke Aboth Ecclesiastes does look like a sayings collection, according to Perdue, with a loose rhetorical structure. However, first person narration is Ecclesiastes' most distinguishing characteristic among the Israelite and Jewish wisdom corpus. Thus Perdue explores the following ANE forms which are all characterised by first person usage, in order to determine the genre of Ecclesiastes.

---

32 W. BOOTH, *The Rhetoric of Fiction* (2nd ed.; London: Penguin, 1983) 73.

33 K. GALLING, *Der Prediger* (HAT 18; Tübingen: JCB Mohr, 1969) 76. See ch. 3.

34 N. LOHFINK, "Qoheleth 5:17-19 – Revelation by Joy," *CBQ* 52/4 (1990) 628.

35 G. VON RAD, *Wisdom in Israel* (London: SCM, 1972) 226.

36 R. BRAUN, *Kohelet und die frühhellenistische Popularphilosophie* (BZAW 130; Berlin: de Gruyter, 1973) 36.

37 N. LOHFINK, *Kohelet* (NEB; Würzburg: Echter Verlag, 1993) 10, 14.

38 T. LONGMAN, *Fictional Akkadian Autobiography. A Generic and Comparative Study* (Winona Lake: Eisenbrauns, 1991).

39 R.E. MURPHY, *Ecclesiastes* (WBC; Texas: Word, 1992) xxxi.

40 It is unlikely that Ecclesiastes is modelled directly on the Greek diatribe as Lohfink suggests, since it lacks its strong dialogical character with opponents who are clearly identified.

41 L.G. PERDUE, *Wisdom and Creation. The Theology of Wisdom Literature* (Nashville: Abingdon, 1994) 194-205.

1. Righteous Sufferer Poems

These are modelled on the style of the individual lament in which a righteous sufferer narrates his trials and calamities, including his questioning of traditional wisdom and cultus. Finally he is redeemed by his personal god. The Sumerian "Man and his God"[42] and the Akkadian "I will praise the Lord of Wisdom"[43] fit into this category. For Perdue these poems differ from Qoheleth in that he experiences a radical gulf between God and the world, a gulf which they do not manifest.

2. The Dialogue of Pessimism[44]

Qoheleth has in common the use of the first person voice and structures that support opposite decisions. However Qoheleth never advocates suicide.

In Perdue's opinion the smell of death surrounds Qoheleth, and he suggests that the following three categories of Egyptian literature which are all set in situations involving death provide the closest form-critical parallels to Qoheleth.

3. The Songs of the Harper

Egyptian banquet songs were sometimes used in funerary contexts. Although in a funerary context they tended not to question the afterlife and not to emphasise the present, as did their secular counterparts, "A Song of the Harper"[45] represents an intriguing difference. Composed at a time of social and political disintegration, this song is sceptical about the afterlife and encourages the reader to:

> Fulfil thy needs upon earth, after the command of thy heart,
> Until there come for thee that day of mourning.

In common with Qoheleth, according to Perdue, this song shares the context of death, first person narration and scepticism about the future life, as well as celebration of present life.

4. Grave Biographies

These were placed in the mouth of the deceased; they are first person posthumous speeches addressed to tomb visitors, and contain an autobiographical narrative, ethical maxims and instructions to visitors.[46] In the later inscriptions the gods act without the constraint of retributive justice; this pessimistic element reveals a remarkable parallel with Qoheleth, according to Perdue, as does the fictional narrator's voice, the above literary features and the pervasive autobiographical style.

---

[42]   ANET, 589-591. The numbers are the relevant page numbers in J.B. PRITCHARD (ed.), *Ancient Near Eastern Texts Relating to the Old Testament* (3rd ed.; Princeton: Princeton UP, 1969).

[43]   ANET, 596-600.

[44]   ANET, 600-601.

[45]   ANET, 467.

[46]   See PERDUE, *Wisdom and Creation*, 365, for bibliographical details.

5. Royal Instructions[47]

The longer form of Egyptian royal instruction inserts an introductory narrative between the title and admonitions. In this way the biography provides the occasion for the instruction. Within the OT royal instructions are found in 1 Kings 12:1-12 and Proverbs 31:1-9. The longer form of royal instruction parallels Qoheleth in terms of the royal voice of the narrator, the list of royal achievements and the giving of instruction.

Perdue concludes that "the book of Qoheleth is best seen as the fictional testament of Israel's most famous king, who is presented as speaking to his audience either in his old age, shortly before death, or perhaps from the tomb."[48] "In Qoheleth we have the fiction of Israel's greatest and wisest king, presumably the one best able to master life and to know by wisdom the meaning of existence, undertaking the quest to determine the 'good' in human living."[49] In Perdue's view Ecclesiastes is thus imaginative wisdom literature with a narrative structure in a form that is close to that of grave biographies and royal testaments – Qoheleth is perhaps presented as a dead person who undertakes to instruct from the tomb!

The fictional autobiographical nature of Ecclesiastes has also been argued for recently by Tremper Longman, but by means of a comparison with Akkadian fictional autobiography.[50] Longman argues persuasively that there is a genre of Akkadian literature which is fictional autobiography. He discerns three sub-groups within this genre; fictional autobiography with a blessing and/or curse ending, fictional autobiography with a didactic ending and fictional autobiography with a prophetic ending. As regards the comparison with Ecclesiastes, Longman maintains that "[w]hat has not been examined before, however, is the close similarity that exists between Qoheleth and the Akkadian genre of autobiography, particularly fictional autobiography with a didactic ending."[51]

Longman argues that 1:1-11 and 12:9-14 are the frame of Ecclesiastes which were provided by a second wisdom figure who is using Qoheleth's sayings to instruct his son. If one removes these, Ecclesiastes may be divided into three sections:

---

[47] ANET, 412-414; 421-425.

[48] PERDUE, *Wisdom and Creation*, 202.

[49] Ibid., 205.

[50] LONGMAN, *Fictional Akkadian Autobiography*, which is a development of idem, "Comparative Methods in Old Testament Studies," *TSF Bulletin* (March-April 1984) 5-9. Surprisingly PERDUE, *Wisdom and Creation*, does not mention Longman, and he does not consider the genre similarities between Ecclesiastes and Akkadian fictional autobiography. LONGMAN, *Fictional Akkadian Autobiography*, 118ff, notes the similarity between Akkadian fictional autobiography with a didactic ending and Egyptian Instruction texts, but does not suggest a comparison with the Songs of the Harper or with Egyptian Grave Biographies.

[51] LONGMAN, *Fictional Akkadian Autobiography*, 120.

1:12-18   a first person introduction
2:1-6:9   an extended first person narrative in which Qoheleth
               describes his search for meaning in life
6:10-12:8   first person instruction from Qoheleth

Analysed in this way, Ecclesiastes exhibits the same three-fold structure as the Akkadian Cuthaean legend, the best preserved Akkadian didactic autobiography. There is also a similarity at the level of form. Qoheleth shares the forms of royal fiction and self-discourse with the Cuthaean legend. Longman concludes that Ecclesiastes has an obvious Akkadian background in terms of genre. "Thus the literary structure and the use of royal fiction and self-discourse in the book of Qoheleth and in the Cuthaean Legend demonstrate a generic relationship between the two."[52]

Longman is well aware that this analysis of Ecclesiastes does not provide a detailed analysis of the whole structure of Ecclesiastes. Without careful analysis of the relationship between 1:12-12:8 and the frame, he argues that the frame is a crucial part of the book since it provides a hermeneutical guide by instructing the reader how to understand the text. Indeed for Longman the frame warns the reader against Qoheleth's scepticism. Longman also suggests that understanding Ecclesiastes as autobiography may help to explain its 'contradictions':

> Perhaps … if there is a development within the structure of Qoheleth, it is that of a temporal thought progression. In other words, the book traces Qoheleth's thoughts on subjects at different periods in his life. The so-called 'contradictions' in the book may thus be explained as being different conclusions reached at different times in his life.[53]

Longman's and Perdue's analyses of the genre of Ecclesiastes are stimulating and helpful in confirming the autobiographical and didactic wisdom nature of Ecclesiastes. Some questions about the detailed comparisons remain. As is widely acknowledged, for example, the royal fiction in Ecclesiastes is soon dropped and this militates to some extent against it being a royal instruction or the testament of Israel's most famous king.[54] The similarity to grave biographies is also dependent upon Perdue's pessimistic reading of Ecclesiastes, something which is far from firmly established. As will become apparent in chapter seven,

---

52 Ibid., 122.
53 Ibid., 121, 122.
54 MURPHY, *Ecclesiastes*, xxxi, says that the proposal of royal testament for the genre of Ecclesiastes is unacceptable because the king fiction disappears after chapter two. See PERDUE, *Wisdom and Creation*, 201-202, for an attempt to defend the royal fiction of Ecclesiastes. Longman refers to all Akkadian autobiography as royal. He acknowledges that while the royal fiction is adopted throughout the Cuthaean legend, some think it is only present in part of Ecclesiastes. According to LONGMAN, *Fictional Akkadian Autobiography*, 122, "This question is not important to adjudicate; it is clear that royal fiction is employed in both Qoheleth and the Cuthaean Legend." However, if the author adopts the fiction and then drops it, this deviation from the form may be significant since the norms of a genre provide a basis for conformity *and* divergence. As a heading to the entire book 1:1 does however confirm the royal fiction.

this is not our reading of Ecclesiastes. Furthermore Ecclesiastes may be closer to righteous sufferer poems than Perdue suggests depending upon how one understands the total message of the book.[55] However Qoheleth does not speak of his own suffering but of his observations and this brings a more philosophical, perhaps Hellenistic element into his discussion which none of the proposed parallels accounts for. Longman points out that all the Akkadian fictional autobiographies are written in prose, and he regards this as an important element of their genre.[56] Very few Akkadian texts were written in prose and fictional autobiography takes this characteristic from non-fictional autobiography which used prose rather than poetry as a means of stressing its authenticity. What Longman does not comment on is the fact that Ecclesiastes is highly poetic, although admittedly scholars are still not agreed as to whether its style is that of poetry or prose.[57]

Isaksson's *Studies in the Language of Qoheleth* confirms the autobiographical and reflective nature of Ecclesiastes.[58] Isaksson argues that the autobiographical feature of Ecclesiastes is one of its central characteristics. Syntactically this trait is manifested through a chain of Suffix Conjugation forms in the first person singular, sometimes preceded by waw. Waw + Prefix Conjugation forms of the verb are very infrequent in Ecclesiastes.

> My conclusion is that the choice of conjunctive SC and wSC forms in the autobiographical thread is due to the special kind of narrative that constitutes this thread. The narrative of the thread is of the résumé type, in which, with the words of F. Rundgren "the events are not given according to the historical process of the (usual) narrative, but are picked out as important single events and then juxtaposed". There are many examples of this kind of résumé narration from all genres of the Old Testament, which means that this special feature of the book is not a valid proof of lateness. ... The infrequent usage of waPC forms is noted. ... My conclusion is that the low frequency of this verbal usage is a matter of literary genre: the philosophical approach of the book and the absence of straightforward historical narration.[59]

---

[55] Perdue's main reason for distinguishing Ecclesiastes from righteous sufferer poems is that in the latter the sufferer is rescued by his personal god, whereas Qoheleth experiences a great gulf between god and the world. In my view the difference is more at the level of the type of problem the sufferer is experiencing rather than the view of God. But see H. FISCH, *Poetry with a Purpose. Biblical Poetics and Interpretation* (Bloomington; Indianapolis: Indiana UP, 1988) 158-159, who distinguishes the subjective, personal 'I' of the Psalms from the autobiographical 'I' in Qoheleth.

[56] LONGMAN, *Fictional Akkadian Autobiography*, 199.

[57] Cf. MURPHY, *Ecclesiastes*, xxviii-xxix.

[58] B. ISAKSSON, *Studies in the Language of Qoheleth With Special Emphasis on the Verbal System* (Studia Semitica Upsaliensia 10; Uppsala: Acta Universitatis Upsaliensis, 1987).

[59] Ibid., 190.

Thus the comparison of the form of Ecclesiastes with that of ANE[60] texts helpfully focuses its autobiographical and instructional nature, but do Perdue and Longman successfully explain how Ecclesiastes *as a whole* fits together? As we saw in chapter 3 a crucial test in this respect is explaining how the epilogue relates to the rest of the book. For Longman the form of the material *within* the frame of Ecclesiastes is that of a fictional autobiography. In his 1984 article, Longman argues that the frame provides an orthodox warning against the sceptical pessimism of Qoheleth.[61] Qoheleth is throughout pessimistic; the *carpe diem* passages represent resignation and not hope. Qoheleth is a sceptic because he has not allowed God to enter into his thinking. In his 1991 text Longman does not explain how he understands the frame as providing a hermeneutical guide to Ecclesiastes,[62] but the introduction to Ecclesiastes in *An Introduction to the Old Testament* makes it clear that Longman still upholds his 1984 view.[63] He quotes Fox's translation[64] of 12:10-12 with approval; it fits with Longman's view that the narrator distances himself strongly from the pessimistic Qoheleth. "Qoheleth's speech (1:12-12:7) is a foil, a teaching device, used by the second wise man in order to instruct his son (vs. 12) concerning the dangers of speculative, doubting wisdom in Israel."[65]

Perdue recognises the need to analyse the literary structure of Ecclesiastes in terms of narrator etc., but he ends up with an uneven mixture of a source-critical and narrative analysis.[66] Nowhere is this more evident than on p. 237 where he mentions in one paragraph that 12:9-14 consists of three parts attached by an editor, and then goes on in the next paragraph to say that, "The narrator then turns to his or her own understanding ..." This type of diachronic analysis cannot simply be juxtaposed with a narrative, synchronic reading in this way!

A weakness of both Longman and Perdue's *comparative* approaches is thus that neither explains in any detailed or satisfactory way how the epilogue relates to the rest of the book.[67] Indeed their comparative approach rests on a diachronic

---

[60] What we have not explored here in detail are comparisons with Greek genres. LOHFINK, *Kohelet*, 10, argues that the form of this *Lehrbuch* results from the confluence of two forms; Greek philosophical diatribe and Hebrew chiasm. For a brief evaluation of Lohfink's view of a close relationship between Ecclesiastes and Hellenistic thought see MURPHY, *Ecclesiastes*, xliii–xlv.

[61] Cf. LONGMAN, "Comparative Methods in Old Testament Studies".

[62] Idem, *Fictional Akkadian Autobiography*.

[63] R.B. DILLARD and T. LONGMAN, *An Introduction to the Old Testament* (Grand Rapids: Zondervan, 1994) 247-253.

[64] See below.

[65] DILLARD and LONGMAN, *An Introduction to the Old Testament*, 254.

[66] PERDUE, *Wisdom and Creation*.

[67] Longman has most recently seconded Fox in support of his view as explained above (cf. DILLARD and LONGMAN, *An Introduction to the Old Testament*). His frame, however, includes 1:1-11 and he would need, even if one accepted Fox's translation of the epilogue, to explain how the opening poem is part of the orthodox hermeneutical guide that Longman takes it to be. It seems to me that Longman's approach fails in terms of that circular intent at totality of NC. The parallel to

analysis of Ecclesiastes, which identifies the first person narration as the main element in Ecclesiastes. Perdue, for example, argues that first person narration is Ecclesiastes' most distinguishing characteristic, and he then looks for parallels to this among ANE literature. For Longman as well self-discourse is utterly central to the parallel with Akkadian autobiography. Thus for both Longman and Perdue comparative genre analysis is done *after* diachronic analysis of Ecclesiastes in which the first person narration is identified as the main characteristic of the book. Diachronic analysis can thus be said to shape their comparative analysis.

One suspects that these underlying diachronic assumptions are an unconscious legacy of historical critical interpretation of Ecclesiastes which ensures that the conjunction of fiction and autobiography in Ecclesiastes remain a scandal for many OT scholars.[68] Diachronic analysis of Ecclesiastes often works on the historical assumption that "[e]ven though in the first part of the book he [Qoheleth] uses the device of pretending to be King Solomon ... there is no doubt that throughout the book this 'I' is a real and not a fictitious 'I'."[69] In the light of this assumption every effort is often made to locate the historical Qoheleth and the text is interpreted on this basis. OT scholars have become increasingly sceptical about source critical analyses of Qoheleth, but the method of finding the real Qoheleth and then reading the book on this basis remains in place and shapes comparative genre analysis.

I am not suggesting that Perdue or Longman would necessarily argue that the 'I' of Ecclesiastes is historical in the sense that Whybray does. Indeed, the comparison of Ecclesiastes with fictional autobiography confirms what literary studies of autobiography alert us to; the 'I' of autobiography can be very elusive.[70] Perdue's and Longman's analyses indicate that the 'I' of Ecclesiastes is fictional. But what they fail to pursue are the implications of the 'I' being fictional, for the presentation of a fictional Qoheleth in the context of a frame narrative raises in an acute way the question of the relationship between the first person narration and the frame narrator. As Fox has argued, Ecclesiastes 7:27 in particular indicates that the frame cannot just be regarded as a frame put on a complete first person narration. The evidence points to deliberate shaping.

There is an important methodological issue at stake here. Comparative genre analysis must be based upon analyses of texts that are, initially at least, performed

---

Akkadian autobiography is not strong enough to warrant taking 1:12-12:7 as an enclosed, unified section. The *carpe diem* sayings should not just be read as representative of resignation. And, as I will argue below, Fox's interpretation of the epilogue is not convincing. Which all points towards the limits of the comparative approach; the nature of Ecclesiastes has to be argued primarily from the text itself.

[68] Note the quote from Jefferson at the outset of this section.

[69] R.N. WHYBRAY, *Two Jewish Theologies: Job and Ecclesiastes* (Hull: University of Hull, 1980) 6.

[70] For contemporary studies of autobiography see L. MARCUS, *Auto/biographical Discourses. Criticism. Theory. Practice* (Manchester: Manchester UP, 1994).

independently of studies of comparative genre.[71] The hermeneutical spiral operates here as well, but the effort has to be made to compare Ecclesiastes with other genres without reading comparative genres into Ecclesiastes at the outset, as part of that continual move between source and discourse that Sternberg describes so well.[72] That Perdue and Longman are in danger of privileging diachronic at the expense of synchronic analysis become apparent when one examines Fox's proposals for ANE texts with a similar genre to Ecclesiastes.

Fox *begins* with a literary analysis of Ecclesiastes as 'frame-narrative' and *then* looks for ANE texts comparable to "[t]he use of an anonymous third-person retrospective frame-narrative encompassing a first person narrative or monologue".[73] Fox finds examples of this style particularly in Egypt but also in Israel. It occurs in various genres, including wisdom literature. Fox lists the following examples.[74]

1. The Instruction for Kagemeni

Only the final portion of this text is preserved but the overall design is clear. In the body of the text the old vizier who is the father of Kagemeni instructs his children and records his instruction. The epilogue speaks about the vizier in retrospect and explains how his son benefited from his instruction and became vizier himself. The narrative frame which surrounds and presents the instruction of the old vizier looks back on the life of the old vizier and evaluates his work.

2. The Prophecy of Neferti

Although written in the reign of Amenemhet I in the twelfth dynasty, this text begins with a frame-narrative presenting itself in the reign of Snefru in the fourth dynasty looking back on the life of the ancient sage Neferti, whose words are respectfully introduced. The work is fictional, presenting a prophecy *ex eventu* of the triumph of Amenemhet I.

3. The Complaint of Ipuwer

The introduction has been lost but, according to Fox, it must have explained the setting that is implied in the ending of the work, i.e. how Ipuwer was called to address the king. The body of the work consists of Ipuwer's lament about the breakdown of the social order. His 'I' occurs only occasionally. Thus the speech

---

[71] A similar example of the importance of correct methodology is that of the comparison between Deuteronomy and ANE treaties. See C.G. BARTHOLOMEW, *The Composition of Deuteronomy: A Critical Analysis of the Approaches of E.W. Nicholson and A.D.H. Mayes* (Unpublished MA thesis: Potchefstroom University, 1992) 203-220.

[72] See ch. 7.3.3.

[73] FOX, "Frame Narrative and Composition," 83-92.

[74] Ibid., 92-96; and idem, *Qoheleth and His Contradictions* (JSOTSup 71; Sheffield: Almond Press, 1989) 312-315. Fox's 1989 list is longer than the 1977 one. The former adds Duachety, Shuruppak and Ahiqar. These additions do not add much to the overall argument and we have ommitted them from our consideration of Fox's examples.

of Ipuwer, which forms the body of the text, is presented within a framework by an anonymous narrator who looks back on the sage, quoting and evaluating him.

4. Onchsheshonqy

Onchsheshonqy consists of an anonymous frame-narrator relating the story of Onchsheshonqy. It opens by explaining how he came to write his Instruction on ostraca while in prison. The body of the book consists of a long quotation of Onchsheshonqy's words. It is uncertain whether Onchsheshonqy ever existed. Fox says that the introductory story is probably fictional and notes that the Instruction contains references to the introduction and is probably contemporaneous with it.

5. Deuteronomy

Fox argues that in its present state, but excluding the additions in 4:41-43; 32:48-52; 34:1-12, Deuteronomy is a first-person monologue by Moses set in a third-person framework. Thus we have a narrator telling about Moses, looking back on him while remaining in the background. In a footnote Fox acknowledges that Haran suggested the parallel between Ecclesiastes and Deuteronomy to him,[75] arguing that the narrative form might be another sign of wisdom influence upon Deuteronomy.[76]

6. Tobit

According to Fox the title and brief identification are not part of the frame narrative. Immediately after this Tobit begins speaking in a reflective manner similar to Qoheleth. The book as a whole is a third-person narrative, as, for example, 3:7ff indicate, in which the author speaks about Tobit. The essential narrative design is the same as Qoheleth. Fox notes with interest that the first person speaker in Tobit can appear immediately after the title without an introduction by the frame-narrator, contrary to the expectations of modern readers who would anticipate that the frame-narrator would be more prominent at the outset. Fox finds this a helpful parallel to Ecclesiastes: "The frame-narrator's voice in *Qoheleth* as in *Tobit* is scarcely heard at the beginning of the work – only 'Qoheleth said' in 1:2. The author allows the first-person speaker to introduce himself in order to establish him immediately as the focal point."[77]

7. Uncle Remus[78]

Fox also employs an analogy from modern literature to help elucidate the function of the narrative framework. He notes the difference between Qoheleth

---

[75] FOX, "Frame Narrative and Composition," 93.

[76] M. WEINFELD, *Deuteronomy and the Deuteronomic School* (Oxford: Clarendon, 1972) 244ff, discusses the relationship between deuteronomic literature and wisdom literature at length.

[77] FOX, "Frame Narrative and Composition," 94.

[78] A series of novels by Joel Chandler Harris. Fox (ibid.) argues that the various volumes really form a single work.

and 'Uncle Remus' and explains that he is concerned only to compare the rhetorical function of the narrative framework as a literary technique. Fox does however note that models from far afield can be helpful in drawing our attention to phenomena we might be unaware of and in helping us to break out of unjustified assumptions that arise from working with a restricted body of texts.

Like Qoheleth, Uncle Remus' words are surrounded by a frame narrative. The words "said Uncle Remus", interrupting a first-person sentence, are equivalent to אמרה קהלת in Ecclesiastes 7:27. As with Ecclesiastes the frame-narrator presents himself not as the creator of the story but merely as the transmitter, "a relatively passive agent between their creator (Uncle Remus) and the reader."[79] The narrator stays well in the background, and indeed the author Harris once referred to this narrator as a "dull reporter." Fox notes that the narrator is not to be identified with the author himself;

> Harris was far more than simply a collector and transmitter of Negro folklore. He utilised old slave tales but altered and polished and sharpened them until the products were far from pure folk tales. He once showed a friend sixteen introductions he had written for a single story.[80]

Why does Harris employ a frame-narrator? According to Fox this is in order to cause the reader to treat Uncle Remus seriously – without the frame it would be too easy to laugh him off – and to create some distance from Uncle Remus. The frame-narrator embodies an attitude of respect at a distance to Uncle Remus. The frame-narrative also attests to the reality of Uncle Remus, thus calling for a suspension of disbelief in the reader since he is a fictional character. "In other words, a bizarre character, one whose voice we are not used to encountering in literature, needs a plausible, normal voice to mediate him to us and to show us how to relate to him. Qoheleth too receives this type of mediation from his frame-narrator."[81]

Remarkably there is no overlap between the ANE texts that Fox invokes and those that Perdue and Longman call upon. This powerfully indicates the extent to which one's initial decisions about Ecclesiastes shape comparative investigations of the genre. What are we to make of these different approaches? If one was forced to choose between them then Fox's approach would be preferable because it seeks to do justice to the genre of Ecclesiastes as a whole. However, I suggest that in accordance with their starting points Fox and Perdue-Longman recognise real but partial aspects of Ecclesiastes, aspects which in my view need not be antithetical. Perdue and Longman are alert to the royal fiction, the dominant first person narrative and Perdue is sensitive to the pessimism and ethos of death that surrounds Qoheleth. And indeed the fictional testament or royal autobiography closely parallels these. Fox is above all concerned with the frame-narrative aspect

---

[79] Ibid., 95.
[80] Ibid.
[81] Ibid., 96.

of Ecclesiastes and he correctly finds that this is a style that extends across particular genres. Fox's comparisons do not however account for the royal fiction and the scepticism in Ecclesiastes. For example, not one of the main characters in his examples is the king.

In my view Fox, Longman and Perdue pick up correctly on different aspects of Ecclesiastes:

- first person narration is a dominant characteristic
- there is a royal fiction and 1:1 relates that to the entire book
- there is a pessimistic element in Ecclesiastes
- death is a dominant feature of Ecclesiastes
- frame-narrative is integral to the book and cannot simply be read as a late addition to a complete text

Any understanding of the genre of Ecclesiastes must do justice to all these features. My suggestion is that we have in Ecclesiastes a developed wisdom form of the royal testament or fictional autobiography cast in a frame narrative. The explosive material in Qoheleth requires careful presentation, and the frame-narrative technique which was common in the ANE would lend itself to such caution and is developed accordingly in Ecclesiastes. Contra Longman and Perdue, however, the fictional autobiographical aspect of Ecclesiastes undermines diachronic analysis which quickly isolates the first person narrative as the 'real Qoheleth.' The recognition of this fictionality should have led Longman and Perdue to see that the way in which Qoheleth is presented and the relevance of the framework to this are integral parts of interpreting Ecclesiastes.

Fox is thus right that it is the *literary* implications of the third person sections, i.e. of the 'editing' in Ecclesiastes that should be focused upon in our interpretation of the book. Further development of our understanding of Ecclesiastes requires that we move beyond comparative genre analysis, but certainly not without the important insights it has brought, to the sort of narrative literary analysis pursued by Fox,[82] as Longman recognises. Comparative genre analysis helpfully alerts us to many of the characteristics of Ecclesiastes, but these must lead us to deepened close analysis of the text itself. This enables the whole text of Ecclesiastes to be taken seriously, and the voice of Qoheleth to be treated as one voice in the text, and not necessarily that of the implied author. In the following section we will examine Fox's literary approach in more detail, especially as it relates to the epilogue.

---

[82] Note that while I am using narrative theory to develop a methodology for discerning the message of Ecclesiastes, I am aware that Ecclesiastes' genre is composite in the sense that it is not 'pure' narrative. The autobiographical and wisdom elements are also important parts of the total genre. Autobiography has however a strong narrative element to it and it does seem to me that a narrative structure constitutes Ecclesiastes, so that a narrative approach provides a useful way into the text.

5.5 Fox's Reading of the Epilogue

The implication of Fox's approach is that we ought to read Ecclesiastes as a narrative unity. The way to discover the message/theology of Ecclesiastes then, is decidedly not by reconstructing original versions of the text but by inquiring after the implied author of Ecclesiastes. In other words the way to arrive at the message of Ecclesiastes is by exploring the following diagrammatically expressed relationships in Ecclesiastes.

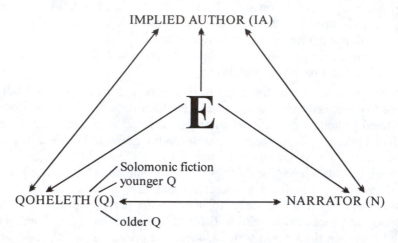

IMPLIED AUTHOR (IA)

E

Solomonic fiction
younger Q

QOHELETH (Q) ←——————————→ NARRATOR (N)

older Q

E = Ecclesiastes

According to this approach the way to discover the message of Ecclesiastes is to inquire after the Implied Author (IA). One inquires after the IA by firstly exploring the characters in the text and their interrelationship; namely the narrator and Qoheleth. Qoheleth himself is represented in a number of ways; as king in Jerusalem (the Solomonic fiction), as a younger man and as the older man who reflects upon all that he has experienced. The relationships between these different representations also need to be explored.[83] Secondly, to discern the message of the text it is important to also ask how the implied author relates to the narrator and to Qoheleth. Sternberg maintains that in biblical narrative the

---

[83] It remains a moot point as to what extent it is possible to discern the relationship between these different representations. I have not pursued this issue further here. In his discussion of the aspectual value of the SC verbs in the autobiographical thread, ISAKSSON, *Studies in the Language of Qoheleth*, 44ff, suggests that while in 2-4 the SC thread may have an historical aspect to it, in later chapters the aspect tends to be neutralised by placing the verb in a subordinate clause. "The neutralized aspect in such passages depicts the author as speaking out of his *present* state of thought, not about conclusions specifically made in the past" (ibid., 45). This kind of data supports the existence of different representations and might help to discern the relationship between them.

implied author and the narrator are the same.[84] Fox and Lohfink[85] suggest that in Ecclesiastes they are not. Fox's case hinges on his reading of the epilogue, to which we now turn. He translates the epilogue as follows:

8   "Utterly absurd," said Qoheleth, "Everything is absurd."
9   Now furthermore, Qoheleth was a wise-man. He constantly taught
     the people knowledge, and weighing and investigating he composed
     many sayings.
10   Qoheleth sought to find fine words and to write the most honest words of
truth.
11   The words of the wise are like goads, and the (words of) masters of
     collections are like implanted nails that are given by a shepherd.
12   And furthermore, my son, beware of these things. It is pointless to
     make a lot of books, and much talking wearies the flesh.
13   Finally, when everything has been heard: Fear God and keep his
     commandments, for that is the whole man.
14   For God will bring every deed into judgement, (judging) even every
     hidden matter, whether it is good or bad.[86]

Below we identify the crucial aspects of Fox's translation and outline his arguments supporting his translation.

1. V. 10 'sought to find fine words and to write'

For Fox this expression is subtly non-committal, the implication being that Qoheleth *sought* to find and to write fine and honest words of truth, but perhaps did not! Essential to this interpretation is the pointing of וכתוב as an infinitive absolute, translated 'to write', which Fox understands as the direct object of בקש. The NRSV translation by comparison (reading either the infinitive absolute form or the alternative reading וכתב the NRSV translates this phrase "and he wrote words of truth plainly") would clearly undermine Fox's interpretation. In support of this non-committal reading of v. 10 Fox also points out that למצא and בקש are two of Qoheleth's theme words which here remind us that seeking does not necessarily mean finding. Fox alerts us to Ecclesiastes 8:17 in this respect, arguing that this verse teaches that God made man unable to comprehend the world and he implies that this teaching underlies למצא and בקש in the epilogue. Just as the human person cannot understand the world no matter how much he searches, so Qoheleth was unable to write truth.

2. V. 11a 'The words of the wise are like goads, and the (words of) masters of collections are like implanted nails.'

According to Fox the words of the wise are like goads and nails not because they goad into right action and provide a stable point of anchorage but because they prick and hurt; they are painful and dangerous and one needs to be cautious

---

84   STERNBERG, *The Poetics of Biblical Narrative*, 74-75.
85   I learnt this in a discussion with Lohfink.
86   FOX, "Frame Narrative and Composition," 96.

of them. Fox maintains that v. 11 is unclear and perhaps deliberately ambiguous. However he argues that if there is parallelism in this verse we would not expect the comparison to refer to completely different things like encouraging better behaviour and being permanent. Fox suggests that the nails like the goads are dangerous.

3. V. 11b 'that are given by a shepherd'
    According to Fox the shepherd is not God, because in the OT God is called 'shepherd' in his capacity as keeper and saviour and these attributes are not relevant here. Furthermore 'shepherd' is never used by itself to refer to God. In Israelite, and Egyptian and Babylonian didactic wisdom literature God is never called 'shepherd.' Indeed he is hardly ever given any metaphorical qualities in wisdom literature. The words of the wise are also never considered as given by God.

    אחד which qualifies רעה cannot be read as indicating that there is only one i.e. divine shepherd, since the weight of the verse would then rest there and not on the similes of v. 11a, and the verse would be a theological declaration totally divorced from its context. Thus Fox argues that רעה is simply a shepherd, any shepherd, and אחד functions simply as an indefinite article, as in 1 Samuel 24:15; 26:20; 1 Kings 19:4-5 and Ezekiel 17:7. "In all these cases numerical qualification is not the point, i.e., there is no need to show unity as opposed to plurality. The modifier could be removed with little effect on the sense of the sentence."[87]

4. V. 12a 'And furthermore, my son, beware of these things.'
    ויתר should, according to Fox, not be translated as 'besides.' Whereas in v. 9 Fox followed the accents,[88] here he proposes going against them, arguing that we ought to pause after ויתר as in v. 9 but here against the accents. In v. 12 the reserve in the epilogist's account becomes pronounced and Qoheleth's words are included in the warning: "And furthermore, my son, beware of these things."

5. V. 12bα 'It is pointless to make a lot of books.'
    Fox rejects the translation of this phrase as "Of making many books there is no end" because 'of' would require beth or lamed before עשות. According to Fox קץ indicates purpose and with אין should be translated as 'pointless.' He argues that הרבה is banal in v. 12bα if קץ means 'end'. Fox compares the use of קץ אין here with Ecclesiastes 4:8 and points out that the lonely man's work had an end-point, death, but that what it lacked was purpose. Fox also argues that syntactically אין cannot negate the predicate nexus in a nominal sentence. קץ אין is a noun phrase meaning literally 'a nothingness of purpose' or 'a lack of purpose'.

---

[87] Ibid., 103.
[88] Ibid., 98.

6. V. 12bβ 'and much talking wearies the flesh'

להג is a hapax legomena. Fox rejects the explanation by comparison with the Arabic *lahija* meaning 'apply oneself assiduously', noting that it is a root which does not appear elsewhere in Hebrew. Fox proposes that we read להגה, which root means 'meditate' or 'study' but which could also mean 'utter, speak' as in Psalm 37:30. The advantage of this interpretation is that in bα and bβ the activities of the wise men are referred to rather than there being a shift to the pupil's activities in bβ.

7. In v. 13-14 the epilogist sets law against wisdom, thereby contrasting dogmatic certainty with Qoheleth's uncertainty of all knowledge. For Fox this relegates the words of the wise to a place of secondary importance.

Evaluation of Fox's reading

1. How strong is Fox's case that the narrator is subtly non-committal in v. 10?

With respect to וכתוב there are a number of possibilities:

a. The passive form could be retained as it is in the Septuagint (και γεγραμμενον ευθητετος) and in Lohfink's recent translation of this verse as "und hier sind diese wahren Worte sorgfältig aufgeschrieben."[89] Delitzsch retains the passive form but translates, "Koheleth strove to find words of pleasantness, and written in sincerity, words of truth."[90] The latter translation has the same meaning as Fox's translation. The difficulty with the passive is that the form is singular whereas 'words' are plural, although that in itself is not conclusive since the 'true words' may be here viewed as a single totality.

b. וכתוב as an infinitive absolute is certainly possible as a proposal for revocalising the text, and this could legitimately be understood as the direct object of בקש. וכתוב could also be revocalised as an infinite absolute but be understood as a continuation of the preceding finite verb in the sense of "He sought ... and he wrote ..."[91]

c. Five Hebrew manuscripts and certain versions (Aquila, Symmachus, Peshitta, and Vulgate) understand the verb actively as וכתב. Such a reading would count strongly against Fox's position, especially if אמת is understood as "in the profound sense of capturing reality."[92]

There is little difference of meaning between Lohfink's translation, which takes וכתוב as an infinitive absolute which continues the preceding בקש, and that which reads וכתב. All these translations count against Fox. However

---

89 LOHFINK, *Kohelet*, 10.

90 F. DELITZSCH, *Commentary on the Song of Songs and Ecclesiastes* (Grand Rapids: Eerdmans, 1970) 432.

91 See GK, 113z. MURPHY, *Ecclesiastes*, 123, argues for such revocalisation. On the infinite absolute as object see GK, 113d.

92 MURPHY, *Ecclesiastes*, 125.

whether the passive form is retained or revocalised to an infinite absolute, both can be translated to support Fox's position. Context alone will determine a decision in this area, but it does seem to me that the tentativeness of Fox's translation at this point makes it less likely. A more positive reading of v. 10 can embrace either translation, but Fox's depends upon translating this verse as "He sought ... to write." Remarkably, although without discussion, even Fox in his 1989 paraphrase of Ecclesiastes 'translates' v. 10b as "and he wrote words that were completely true and honest."[93] Of course, if this is the correct translation, it deconstructs Fox's position!

Fox finds further support for reading v. 10 as subtly non-committal in its use of the theme words בקשׁ and מצא. מצא certainly is one of Ecclesiastes key words; it occurs seventeen times and its wide semantic range is exploited by the author in the rhetorical form of antanaclasis especially in those passages in which it is repeated.[94] Fox may be correct in seeing a link between the use of these words here and in the main body of Ecclesiastes, especially 7:25-29 and 8:16-17, but his understanding of the link is inadequate in my view. In 7:25-29 and 8:16-17 these two verbs are linked with the limitations of Qoheleth's project but the words themselves do not suggest 'not finding'. The negative element in these passages is stressed by negating בקשׁ and מצא, and the search to find is not always unsuccessful in these passages. See for example 7:27-29 for the ironic play on 'finding' and 'not finding'. 8:16-17 has a stronger stress on 'not finding.' It should also be noted that where מצא is used without repetition as in 9:10, 15 and 11:1 it has the meaning of 'to find.'

The use of בקשׁ and מצא in 12:10 resonates with the previous use of this vocabulary in Ecclesiastes by reminding us that they are connected with Qoheleth's encounter with the limitations of human knowledge but this by no means makes v. 10 subtly non-committal. Whenever Qoheleth has wanted the reader to know that his search leads to 'not finding' he has clearly said so, and in the absence of such negating the context alone could suggest, and would need to do so very clearly, that this is how these words are to be read in v. 10. The context however points clearly in the reverse direction, and this on two accounts.

Firstly it should be noted that Fox suggests that the narrator is subtly non-committal in v. 10 because he wants to create some distance between Qoheleth's radical views and his own. In other words it is the 'truth' of Qoheleth's

---

93 FOX, *Qoheleth and His Contradictions*, 348.

94 On the semantic range of מצא see A.R. CERESKO, "The Function of Antanaclasis (ms' 'to find' // ms' 'to reach, overtake, grasp') in Hebrew Poetry, Especially in the Book of Qoheleth," *CBQ* 44 (1982) 551-569, who argues that the wisdom poets in particular exploited the ambiguity inherent in מצא as a form of antanaclasis. The semantic range of מצא extends to such activities as arrive, reach, overtake, seize, grasp, understand, find and acquire.

presentation that the narrator wants to distance himself from to some extent.[95] But v. 10 is about more than the truth of Qoheleth's sayings, it is also about their aesthetic form, as דברי חפץ indicates. As Crenshaw comments, "Qoheleth devoted time and energy both to the aesthetic of his composition and to the reliability of what he said."[96] Like Crenshaw Fox translates חפץ as 'pleasing' but he never claims that the narrator is distancing himself subtly from the truth *and* the aesthetic form of Qoheleth's sayings. But v. 9 is clear that Qoheleth, like other wisdom teachers, was a master of form.[97] However if the narrator is subtly non-committal he would have to be suspicious of both.

Secondly, to read v. 10 as Fox does is to set it against v. 9a, where Qoheleth is described as 'wise.' Contextually it makes far more sense to read v. 10 as Qoheleth achieving what he set out to do, thereby demonstrating his wisdom. That there is a contradiction between the positive affirmation of v. 9a and Fox's reading of v. 10 is confirmed by Fox's discerning a very negative comment about wisdom in general in v. 11 and Qoheleth in particular in v. 12. This takes us on to a second question.

2. Is the point of the comparison of the words of the wise with goads and implanted nails that they are painful and dangerous?

For two reasons I suggest that Fox is on weak ground here. Firstly what is being described is not just the words of Qoheleth but the דברי חכמים,[98] and it seems extraordinary that the narrator would create distance between himself and Qoheleth by describing the whole corpus of the words of the wise as dangerous, especially in the light of his positive statement in v. 9 about Qoheleth being one of the wise! A more plausible strategy would be to distinguish Qoheleth from other wisdom literature, a strategy which most biblical scholars follow today!

Secondly, Fox's argument about parallelism in v. 12 as being better accounted for by having both similes referring to the danger and pain of the דברי חכמים is unconvincing. The traditional interpretation also has both similes referring to one thing, namely the value of the words of the wise, with the two similes developing slightly different aspects of that value, goading in the right direction on the one hand, and providing stability on the other. Indeed, one could argue that the traditional understanding fits better with the dynamic nature of biblical parallelism in which there is invariably movement from one line to the

---

[95] Fox understands ישר דברי אמת as a superlative, which he translates "the most honest words of truth." It is this strong statement of truth that Fox maintains the narrator wants to distance himself from.

[96] J.L. CRENSHAW, *Ecclesiastes* (OTL; London: SCM, 1988) 191.

[97] Cf. Fishbane's understanding of the three verbs in v. 9 as technical terms describing Qoheleth's activity in terms of conventional scribal tasks (M. FISHBANE, *Biblical Interpretation in Ancient Israel* [Oxford: Clarendon, 1985] 29-32).

[98] This expression recalls the titles in Proverbs 22:17; 24:23; 30:1 and 31:1. Galling suggests that v. 11a is a quote.

next. As Alter puts it, "Literature thrives on parallelism … But it is equally important to recognize that literary expression abhors complete parallelism, just as language resists true synonymity, usage always introducing small wedges of difference between closely akin terms."[99] If in this verse we have in the parallelism the characteristic heightening or intensification which Alter proposes,[100] then the heightening is probably to be located in the נטועים qualifying 'nails.' Thus the direction in which the sayings of the wise goad one is a direction which is firm, solid and trustworthy.

3. Is Fox right in understanding v. 11b as not referring to God as the one shepherd who is the source of the words of the wise?

Fox's reading is certainly possible but for a number of reasons it is not as strong as it might appear. Firstly, Fox insists that אחד functions simply as an indefinite article, and he refers the reader to a number of verses where אחד apparently functions this way. Remarkably not one of these verses strongly support Fox's view. We cannot examine each of the relevant verses in detail here but careful examination of the relevant verses bears out the following points. In Ezekiel 17:7 אחד is best translated as 'another' and is not redundant. In 1 Samuel 24:15 אחד is emphatic and should be translated 'a single flea'. The expression is deliberately repeated in 26:20. In 1 Kings 19:4 the NRSV correctly translates אחד as 'solitary' and the expression is repeated in v. 5, although the NRSV does not repeat it.[101] Thus, remarkably, in not one of Fox's examples does אחד function simply as an indefinite article.

Does this mean then that אחד never functions as the indefinite article? No, but it does alert us to the danger of too quickly assuming that we are dealing with the indefinite article when we encounter אחד. GK, to whom Fox refers, notes that "[o]nly in a few passages is a noun made expressly *indeterminate* by the addition of אחד in the sense of our indefinite article",[102] and BDB lists the indefinite article as one of eight possible meanings of אחד. It should be noted, incidentally, that Fox appears to have taken his examples of the use of אחד as the indefinite article straight out of BDB, for BDB lists all Fox's examples plus one other, 1 Samuel 16:7. The latter verse, however, also seems to me a bad example of אחד as the indefinite article. NRSV simply translates it as "'a' new cart", but it seems to me that the numerical sense of 'one' *is* present, being compared to the two milch-cows. This means, if correct, that all BDB's examples of אחד as the indefinite article fail!

---

[99] R. ALTER, *The Art of Biblical Poetry* (Edinburgh: T&T Clark, 1985) 10; cf. chapter one of Alter's book. Fox is in danger of understanding parallelism in biblical verse as "a system for the deployment of synonyms" (ibid., 9).

[100] Ibid., 19.

[101] In the BHS v. 4 reads רתם אחת but several manuscripts read אחד. As mentioned, the NRSV does not translate the אחד in v. 5 as 'solitary', but this is inconsistent, in my opinion.

[102] GK, 190: 401.

There are uses of אחד equivalent to the indefinite article in the OT. Daniel 8:3 seems to me a particularly strong case, and Exodus 16:33; Judges 9:53; 13:2; 1 Samuel 7:9, 12; 22:9 are highly likely cases. It is therefore possible that אחד is the indefinite article in v. 11b, but one ought to be cautious about coming to that conclusion and it seems unlikely that the word is redundant in the compact epilogue of 12:9-14. The idea of 'one shepherd' would make sense as indicating the unified source of the diverse words of the wise if it is understood as referring to God as the ultimate source of such wisdom.

Secondly Fox is wrong that God cannot be metaphorically referred to by מרעה אחד because the ideas of him as keeper and saviour are irrelevant here. Quite the contrary. God as the unified source of the diverse words of the wise would explain their value. Furthermore דרבנות were used by shepherds to goad cattle along the right route, and thus shepherd imagery is already strongly present in this verse,[103] which can be seen to progress naturally to God the shepherd as the one source of wisdom.[104]

4. Is Fox's reading of v. 12 as a warning against Qoheleth and his type of activities convincing?

For a number of reasons, the answer must be 'No.' Firstly in v. 9 Fox uses the accents to argue for translating יתר as 'furthermore.' Here he argues against the accents in order to retain the same translation. This reflects a lack of consistency but makes it possible for Fox to read מהמה as the object of הזהר. The accents however make Murphy's translation more likely: "As for more than these, my son, beware".[105]

---

[103] MURPHY, *Ecclesiastes*, 125, maintains that the precise meaning of the metaphor of nails is not clear. FOX, *Qoheleth and His Contradictions*, 348, strengthens our argument that shepherd imagery dominates v. 11 by paraphrasing v. 11b, "and the words of proverb-collectors may smart like the nails a shepherd uses to prod his sheep." It should be noted that this paraphrase makes the reference to the nails more positive than in his translation in idem, "Frame Narrative and Composition," 96, that we are examining.

[104] In my work on Ecclesiastes I have been struck by the similarities to Deuteronomy. Eating and drinking is a dominant motif in Ecclesiastes and Deuteronomy (cf. J.G. MCCONVILLE, *Law and Theology in Deuteronomy* [JSOTSup 33; Sheffield: JSOT, 1984] on this theme in Deuteronomy), Ecclesiastes 4:17ff is akin to the name theology of Deuteronomy, Ecclesiastes 5:3-4 restates the law of Deuteronomy 23:22-24, the exhortation to beware of anything more than these in 12:12 and that nothing can be taken away from God's work in 3:14 is similar to Deuteronomy's exhortation not to add or take anything away from the law (cf. WEINFELD, *Deuteronomy and the Deuteronomic School*, 261, 362), the exhortation to keep the commandments in Ecclesiastes 12:13 is a characteristic deuteronomistic phrase (WEINFELD, *Deuteronomy and the Deuteronomic School*, 336), the remembrance motif is common to both Deuteronomy and Ecclesiastes, and so on. If the author of Ecclesiastes is keenly aware of Deuteronomy or its theology then it is possible that אחד in Ecclesiastes 12:11 may be related to יהוה אחד in Deuteronomy 6:4. A.D.H. MAYES, *Deuteronomy* (NCBC; London: Oliphants, 1979) 177, also notes that some of the exhortations following Deuteronomy 6:4 have wisdom parallels.

[105] MURPHY, *Ecclesiastes*, 124, acknowledges the difficulty with this phrase but comments, "Here the two words are to be joined in accordance with the Masoretic punctuation".

However, even if Fox is right in understanding יתר as 'furthermore,' זהר in v. 12a need not imply a negative warning as Fox reads it. Ogden translates v. 12a as, "PS. From these things my Son *be instructed*,"[106] and as Görg says, "A similar semantic neutralization obtains in the case of the … imperative in Eccl. 12:12: the son should 'be advised.' That ultimately a 'warning' is involved becomes apparent only from the content of the admonition that follows."[107] זהר is often used in the OT to refer to giving instruction.[108] The context alone can determine whether or not this instruction is a warning.

The context militates strongly against v. 12a being a warning against Qoheleth; such an interpretation would contradict v. 9 in particular. However, it should also be noted that if this is a warning then מהמה most likely relates to דברי חכמים as a whole. This focuses the contradiction with v. 9 even more strongly, and makes Fox's reading even less likely.

In terms of context it should be noted that Fox's understanding of v. 12 and the epilogue in general as warning against Qoheleth is closely related to his translation of הבל as 'absurd'. We do not have time to explore the great variety of proposals for translating הבל but suffice it to note that this negative and in my opinion anachronistic translation has not won broad approval among biblical scholars and by itself fails to do justice to the positive strand within Ecclesiastes.[109] If the positive strand in Ecclesiastes is better accounted for, and if it is the stronger strand or the one that triumphs, then contextually it is much harder to argue that the narrator distances himself from Qoheleth in the epilogue. It is thus better to take זהר as referring to instruction (Ogden) or in the traditional way as a warning against adding to the wisdom writings.[110]

As regards 12bα Fox's translation is possible but not as compelling as he makes out. It is not essential for עשות to be prefaced with a ב or ל in order for it to be translated 'of'. As Whybray points out the rest of v. 12 from עשות onwards has the form of a wisdom saying.[111] This form is pithy and compressed and regularly lacks the sort of prepositions we might anticipate in narrative. Apart

---

[106] Italics mine.

[107] M. GÖRG, "זהר," *TDOT* Vol. IV (1980) 43.

[108] Cf. BDB, 2094. The form הזהר in 12:12 is Niphal imperative m.s. The Niphal infinitive construct form occurs in 4:13, appropriately translated as "take advice" by the NRSV. Cf. also Psalm 19:12. BDB does suggest that in 12:12 הזהר means only 'warn' as in Ezekiel but that of course must be argued from the context.

[109] Ogden translates הבל as 'enigmatic', which seems to me a better grasp of the metaphorical focus of this word. Fox's translation seems to be influenced by modern existentialism and hence in danger of being anachronistic. Qoheleth is not declaring life to be absurd in an existentialist way but shows it to be empirically impossible to grasp. If this empirical epistemology is pushed all the way it would lead to absurdity but Qoheleth always juxtaposes his statements about the enigma of life with confessional affirmations of life.

[110] Cf. MURPHY, *Ecclesiastes*, 125.

[111] R.N. WHYBRAY, *Ecclesiastes* (NCBC; London: Marshall, Morgan and Scott; Grand Rapids: Eerdmans, 1989) 173.

from this, in a compound sentence formed by the juxtaposition of a subject and an independent noun clause, as we have here, it is legitimate to translate, "(And) as for …".[112] 'No end' would thus be a legitimate translation of אֵין קֵץ.[113] It is unconvincing to argue that הרבה is banal in v. 12bα if קֵץ means 'end'; the authors point would simply be that the production of books just goes on and on. However, even if one were to translate אֵין קֵץ as a noun phrase, 'pointless' is only one option. Ogden, for example, proposes 'endless'.

Nor is Fox's translation of להג as 'talking' particularly persuasive. Even on his terms it could mean 'study' and indeed in his 1989 paraphrase he translates this phrase "and too much study just tires one out."[114] Fox's argument that 'speaking' is preferable because then in bα and bβ the activities of the wise men are referred to rather than there being a shift to the pupil's activities in bβ is reminiscent of his argument about parallelism in v. 11, and just as unconvincing. V. 12 starts by addressing בני and in this respect the weariness would be rhetorically apt. Even if one opts for 'talking' it could refer to the response that students make to books just as much as to the activities of scribes.

5. Fox finds a strong opposition between wisdom and law in the epilogue. This is a common view. For many commentators, the language about fearing God and keeping his commandments is so alien to Qoheleth, that 12-14 *must* be read as a critique of Qoheleth.[115] The relationship between these two types of OT material continues to be a matter of discussion among OT theologians.[116] However, this type of 'strong opposition' reading may be in danger of reading a modern antithesis back into Ecclesiastes. Murphy for example, rightly says about v. 12,

---

[112] GK, 143a.

[113] It *is* unusual to have אֵין as part of the predicate nexus in a nominal sentence. I can find no parallel in the OT, but there is no reason why אֵין cannot negate the predicate in a nominal sentence. Murphy, Whybray, Lohfink and Crenshaw all translate it this way. Fox simply states that אֵין cannot negate the predicate in a nominal sentence but presents no evidence or reference to sustain this comment.

[114] FOX, *Qoheleth and His Contradictions*, 348.

[115] Cf. for example A. LAUHA, *Kohelet* (Biblischer Kommentar Altes Testament; Neukirchen: Neukirchener Verlag, 1978) 221-223. The content of v. 12-14 is decisive for Lauha's understanding of v. 12-14 as an independent second afterword. Lauha comments, "Bisweilen ist versucht worden, die beiden Nachworte miteinander zu verbinden …, aber nicht nur die Form, sondern vor allem auch der Inhalt und die Intention sind ganz verschieden, ja sogar entgegensetzt."

[116] See H. Graf REVENTLOW, *Problems of Old Testament Theology in the Twentieth Century* (London: SCM, 1985) 168-186. Recent decades have seen a re-awakening of interest in OT wisdom literature (R.E. Clements, *Wisdom in Theology* [Carlisle: Paternoster; Grand Rapids: Eerdmans, 1992] 13-39), but, as REVENTLOW, *Problems of Old Testament Theology*, 181, says, "It is at this point, i.e. over the question of the relationship between the various areas of OT thought, that the discussion will have to be continued: in other words, between the conception of order which is characteristic of wisdom (and not just wisdom) and the areas governed by the tradition of salvation history." See J. GOLDINGAY, *Theological Diversity and the Authority of the Old Testament* (Grand Rapids: Eerdmans, 1987) 200-239, for a discussion of the wisdom-salvation history relationship.

Lauha and many others regard it as a criticism of Qoheleth. In this view, one can do without books such as Ecclesiastes that are so troublesome and confusing. ... Thus the reader is protected against the upsetting doctrine offered in the book. However, this inference is not at all necessary. It seems to reflect more the problem of moderns who see the presence of the book in the canon as an exceptional thing that must somehow be 'explained.' Were the ancients as easily scandalized as the moderns?[117]

Murphy does note that the conjunction of the fear of God and obedience to the commandments in v. 13 is not found elsewhere in Ecclesiastes; "The epilogue is obviously putting forth an ideal which has been developed elsewhere and which is not a concern in Ecclesiastes."[118] Below (ch. 7) I argue that Murphy's latter statement overstates the case, and that there are indications that Qoheleth is aware of law and that the conjunction of law and the fear of God is not so surprising. This issue is closely connected with one's view of OT theology and the development and relationship between the OT legal and wisdom traditions. Clearly if one sees wisdom and law as radically distinct and opposing traditions then this will lend weight to Fox's view.

6. Finally in our evaluation of Fox's reading of the epilogue it should be noted that it undermines his notion of foolproof composition in Ecclesiastes. Sternberg says that biblical narrative is characterised by foolproof composition so that the central developments are clear to all readers.[119] Fox says that this is also true of Ecclesiastes;[120] in its canonical form it presents a reasonably clear message along the following lines: Everything in life is vanity and there is no point in striving too hard for anything. It is best to enjoy what you have when you have it and to fear God. The essentials, according to Fox, are clear to all readers. In a footnote to this section Fox modifies his position slightly:

> This is so, Sternberg says, because the biblical narrator is completely reliable and does not deal in the esoteric. In the case of this text, the speaker (Qoheleth) is almost entirely reliable, notwithstanding the slight distance that the epilogist, who is probably the author of the book, sets between himself and Qoheleth, his persona.[121]

However Fox seems to me to overstate the reliability of his narrator here. In his view the narrator affirms an orthodox perspective but the implied author wishes to create room for Qoheleth's type of view to be heard. One is thus left uncertain as to precisely where the implied author stands, the implications being, especially when one considers the large amount of space given to Qoheleth, that he is sympathetic to Qoheleth's affirmations of life as absurd! This makes Fox's

---

[117] MURPHY, *Ecclesiastes*, 126.
[118] Ibid.
[119] STERNBERG, *The Poetics of Biblical Narrative*, 41-57.
[120] FOX, *Qoheleth and His Contradictions*, 9-10.
[121] Ibid., 10.

position very similar to the major historical critical readings in which an orthodox editor has added an appendix to a radical text in order to make it more acceptable, and certainly undermines the notion of foolproof composition in Ecclesiastes.

How then is Fox's reading of the epilogue to be evaluated in its totality? As we have seen, in most cases his translation is possible, but not persuasive. Part of the difficulty in evaluating Fox's reading of the epilogue is that most of his arguments *are* possible. A more sophisticated means is required of evaluating their relative strength as arguments. This need in much OT scholarship has been recognised by Wenham who follows Sanders in proposing that the strength of different arguments with which scholars propose positions need evaluation.[122] Wenham's six categories are helpful in assessing the overall strength of Fox's reading of the epilogue. This evaluation can be diagrammatically expressed as follows:

ARGUMENT	CERTAIN	VIRTUALLY CERTAIN	HIGHLY PROBABLE	POSSIBLE	CONCEIVABLE	INCREDIBLE
1. וכתוב				✓		
2. בקש למצא					✓	
3. comparison: goads & nails						✓
4. מרעה אחד					✓	
5. ויתר (v. 12)					✓	
6. אין קץ					✓	
7. להג					✓	
8. law versus wisdom				✓		

Barclay and Sanders have suggested that a consequence of this type of evaluation should be the setting aside of the weaker arguments and focusing upon the stronger ones.[123] It is clear from the diagram above that such an approach makes Fox's reading of the epilogue less than convincing.

It *is* refreshing though, to find a commentator exploring in detail the relationship between 12:9-14 and the main body of the text in the way that Fox does. Debate about the details of 12:9-14 will no doubt continue.[124] In my view v. 9 must be read positively, as most commentators, including Fox, agree. V. 10

---

[122] G.J. WENHAM, "Method in Pentateuchal Source Criticism," *VT* XL/1 (1991) 84-109; cf. E.P. SANDERS, *Jesus and Judaism* (London: SCM, 1985) 326-327.

[123] J.M.G. BARCLAY, "Mirror-Reading a Polemical Letter: Galatians As a Test Case," *JSNT* 31 (1987) 73-93; and SANDERS, *Jesus and Judaism*.

[124] Cf. F. BAUMGÄRTEL, "Die Ochsenstachel und die Nägel in Koh 12,11," *ZAW* 81 (1969) 98; C. DOHMEN, "Der Weisheit letzter Schluß?" *BN* 63/1 (1992) 12-18; G.H. WILSON, "'The Words of the Wise': The Intent and Significance of Qoheleth 12:9-14," *JBL* 103/2 (1984) 175-192; and G.T. SHEPPARD, *Wisdom as a Hermeneutical Construct* (Berlin; NY: de Gruyter, 1980).

should be read with the implication that the teacher sought *and* found pleasing words, as I argued above. If v. 9 is taken seriously as a positive statement about the wise, then Fox's reading of v. 11 as a negative generalisation about the wise is ruled out and a positive interpretation of this verse becomes much more likely.[125] The goads may be painful, but it is their capacity to push in the right direction rather than the negative pain that is in mind here. Likewise the nails or pegs should be read positively as points of stability and anchorage.[126] מהמה in v. 12a refers back to the writings of the wise, and thus, ויתר is best understood as 'In addition to'[127] and v. 12 as a warning against being instructed by books other than the words of the wise like Qoheleth.[128] V. 13 and v. 14 conclude the epilogue and the book. V. 13b is in the second person and sums up the message of Qoheleth in the OT terms of fearing God and keeping his commandments.

Thus in terms of my reading of the epilogue the narrator reads Qoheleth positively and at least as arriving at a point in agreement with fearing God and keeping his commandments, contrary to Fox and Longman's suggestions. In terms of our diagram at the outset of section 5.5 above, this means that the narrator and the implied author occupy the same stance. The critical question is whether or not Qoheleth and the narrator can be shown to be as close to each other as this suggests. I suggest that a careful analysis of Ecclesiastes' literary artistry may provide an answer to this question.[129]

5.6 Conclusion

In this chapter we have examined Sternberg's narrative poetics as an example of literary reactions to historical criticism. Sternberg's poetics is an important attempt to integrate the historical, ideological and aesthetic aspects of

---

[125] The context has to determine what aspect of the image of goads is in mind here, and in my view it can only be the positive aspect of giving direction, especially when one realises that the author is talking about the words of the wise as a whole and not just Qoheleth's words.

[126] Cf. CRENSHAW, *Ecclesiastes*, 190.

[127] Thus Murphy and Crenshaw.

[128] Ogden takes v. 12 to be an exhortation to be instructed by these things (including Qoheleth); and the 'no end' and 'much study' to refer positively to the huge amount of effort such wisdom analysis requires. "He is advising the student that what Q has done is the same endeavour that any who would be wise must undertake for themselves" (G. OGDEN, *Qoheleth* [Readings – A New Biblical Commentary; Sheffield: JSOT, 1987] 211). V. 12 is "a solemn counsel to any who would follow the sage that such a decision calls for a sincere commitment to an endless and all-consuming task. There can be no turning back" (ibid., 212). Ogden's interpretation differs in content from Fox, but both connect מהמה with הזהר. However, as DELITZSCH, *Song of Songs and Ecclesiastes*, 436; and MURPHY, *Ecclesiastes*, 123-124, point out, the Massoretic punctuation holds ויתר and מהמה together and the word order makes it more likely that they belong together. Murphy is right I think, in suggesting that ויתר means more than 'furthermore' (Fox) in v. 12. In v. 9 יתר is separated from the rest of the sentence by Massoretic punctuation marks, whereas in v. 12 מהמה ויתר are held together.

[129] See below in ch. 7.

narrative texts into a hermeneutic. Fox has argued that analysis of the literary (aesthetic) aspect of Ecclesiastes along narrative lines is vital to its correct interpretation. A detailed comparison of his narrative analysis of Ecclesiastes with historical analyses of the genre of Ecclesiastes provided a test case for exploring the relationship between historical and literary analysis of Ecclesiastes. Our research confirms Sternberg's insistence that diachronic and synchronic analysis need to work in close partnership with each other. We shall elaborate more on this relationship in chapter 7.

These reactions to historical criticism that we have examined in this chapter and the previous one all more or less operate within the classical humanist paradigm of textuality.[130] Postmodernism has however raised a variety of questions about this sort of approach. Thus, before we outline a hermeneutic and apply it to Ecclesiastes we will examine the postmodern turn and its implications for OT studies and the reading of Ecclesiastes in the next chapter.

---

[130] See ch. 1.3.5.

CHAPTER 6

POSTMODERNITY AND THE READING OF ECCLESIASTES

The liberal consensus has so successfully established itself as the ideology of Western intellectual culture, that it has become almost invisible as the presupposition of every postmodern debate.

(M. HESSE, "How to be Postmodern Without Being a Feminist," *The Monist* 77/4 [1994] 457)

Creative antirealism is presently popular among philosophers; this is the view that it is human behaviour – in particular, human thought and language – that is somehow responsible for the fundamental structure of the world and for the fundamental kinds of entities there are. From a theistic point of view, however, universal creative anti-realism is at best a piece of laughable bravado. For God, of course, owes neither his existence nor his properties to us and our ways of thinking; the truth is just the reverse. And so far as the created universe is concerned, while it indeed owes its existence and character to activity on the part of a person, that person is certainly not a human *person.*

(A. PLANTINGA, "Advice to Christian Philosophers," *Faith and Philosophy* 1/3 [1984] 269)

6.1 Introduction

Postmodernism constitutes a radical challenge to traditional notions of textual interpretation in which hermeneutics is concerned with the attempt to discern the true meaning of texts. In this sense both historical critical and literary biblical interpretation have been traditional. Postmodernism in certain forms, by contrast, challenges the very possibility of determinate meaning, declares the author dead, and makes textual meaning dependent on the reader.

We have already made some initial comments about postmodernity in chapter one. In this chapter we will supplement these by firstly analysing the philosophical crisis that is central to postmodernism, and then we will examine the manifestation of postmodernism in OT studies and its implication for OT hermeneutics and the reading of Ecclesiastes.

6.2 Theories of the Postmodern

Postmodernity is an unusually slippery word, used nowadays in a bewildering variety of ways. The contemporary debate about postmodernism

begins in the 1950's and 60's as a reaction to modernism in the arts.[1] This
reaction was soon extended to a critique of modern culture as a whole through
theorists like Hassan, Spanos and Jencks. This does not of course mean that the
postmodern debate has no earlier roots. A cursory reading of Baudrillard,
Derrida, Foucault and Lyotard makes their dependence upon earlier theorists like
Nietzsche and Heidegger clear. In his brief summary of the progenitors of
contemporary theorising of the postmodern Lyon singles out Nietzsche, Marx,
Heidegger, Dostoyevsky, Kierkegaard and Simmel as "streams feeding into the
postmodern river."[2] Little in theories of the postmodern is new, but it is the
widespread disillusionment with modernity and the widespread embrace of
previously minority anti-modern positions that makes the present different.

Up until the 80's the debate on postmodernism was generally confined to the
arts and architecture. In 1981-1984 this all changed, when philosophers began to
address the postmodern debate in all seriousness. Habermas set the ball rolling as
it were, with his 1980 Adorno lecture entitled "Modernity versus Postmodernity".
As we saw in chapter one, Habermas has reacted strongly to the post-modern
notion of the end of modernity, proposing instead that we think of modernity as
an unfinished project. Modernity is in crisis but the answer is to get it back on
track, not to abandon it.

At the end of the 80's and beginning of the 90's the postmodern debate was
increasingly bounded on the one side by Habermas and on the other by Lyotard.[3]
Lyotard's *The Postmodern Condition* is a study of "the condition of knowledge in
the most highly developed societies."[4] Knowledge has been profoundly affected
by the replacement of the production of material goods as the central concern in
advanced societies with information. Society has become computerised and

---

[1]   See H. BERTENS, *The Idea of the Postmodern* (London; NY: Routledge, 1995) 20, and M.
ROSE, *The Post-Modern and the Post-Industrial. A Critical Analysis* (Cambridge: CUP, 1991) 3-20,
on the earliest uses of the term 'postmodern'. Bertens points out that after the 1870's "'Postmodern'
resurfaced in 1934, in 1939, and in the 1940's. From then on sightings began to multiply. There is,
however, very little continuity between these early uses and the debate on postmodernism as it gets
underway in the course of the 1960s."
[2]   D. LYON, *Postmodernity* (Concepts in the Social Sciences; Buckingham: Open UP, 1994)
7-11.
[3]   BERTENS, *The Idea of the Postmodern*, 122. Inevitably it is not easy to talk of boundaries
with postmodernity. Contra L. HUTCHEON, *Irony's Edge. The Theory and Politics of Irony*
(London; NY: Routledge, 1994), Lyotard may not be the opposite boundary to Habermas. C.
NORRIS, *What's Wrong with Postmodernism?* London: Harvester Wheatsheaf, 1990) 165, argues
that *no one* is as extreme as Baudrillard in his opposition towards truth claims. He acknowledges
that Lyotard has made similar claims but, "In Lyotard's case there has been a marked shift of
emphasis, from a work like *The Postmodern Condition* where enlightenment values are seen as the
source of manifold errors and evils, to those recent texts where a certain (albeit heterodox) reading
of Kant is applied to questions of history, politics and interpretation."
[4]   J. LYOTARD, *The Postmodern Condition: A Report on Knowledge* (Theory and History of
Literature 10; Manchester: Manchester UP, 1984) xxiii.

performativity dominates others forms of reason. The resulting postmodern condition is characterised by

> incredulity towards metanarratives. ... To the obsolescence of the metanarrative apparatus of legitimation corresponds, most notably, the crisis of metaphysical philosophy and of the university institution which in the past relied on it. The narrative function is losing its functors, its great hero, its great dangers, its great voyages, its great goal. It is being dispersed in clouds of narrative language elements – narrative, but also denotative, prescriptive, descriptive, and so on. Conveyed within each cloud are pragmatic valencies specific to its kind. Each of us lives at the intersection of many of these. However, we do not necessarily establish stable language combinations, and the properties of the ones we do establish are not necessarily communicable.[5]

Thus Lyotard strikes at the heart of the possibility of transcendent, objective legitimation. Language games have replaced metanarratives and these always have only local and limited validity. In his opposition to metanarratives Lyotard has modern science particularly in mind. However science too has to operate within narratives and the postmodern condition is about immanent legitimation. "Narrative is thus for Lyotard the inevitable source of all legitimation, and therefore of all value and truth."[6]

Baudrillard's grim analysis is deeply pessimistic about Western society. In his view consumerism has come to dominate our social order, and, especially through electronic media, this shift has been accompanied in what he calls the third simulacra by the hyperreal replacing and being indistinguishable from the real. Disneyland is, for example, there to conceal the fact that the real Disneyland is America. Baudrillard sees everything in terms of cybernetic control so that we are helpless victims of technological control. Even the masses are the product of information, and the only response is to 'join the objects',[7] since thinking and action have become impossible from the perspective of the subject. This is a bleak picture indeed:

> We are left with a hyperreal that has escaped our control and that is beyond conceptualization in spite of the 'obscene' visibility of every single detail. ... Baudrillard, however, leaves all other theorists far behind in the nightmarish character of his conclusions. ... for Baudrillard that [electronic] revolution has effectively made us the helpless victims of a technological determinism that through its unassailable code serves the interests of a hyperreal, meaningless capitalist order.[8]

In his understanding of consumerism as central to our social order and in his notion of the hyperreal Baudrillard has made a contribution to the debate about

---

5   Ibid., xxiv.
6   BERTENS, *The Idea of the Postmodern*, 126.
7   For a discussion of this see J. BAUDRILLARD, *Simulations* (NY: Semiotext[e] Inc., 1983) and BERTENS, *The Idea of the Postmodern*, 155.
8   BERTENS, *The Idea of the Postmodern*, 156.

postmodernity.[9] However this "apostle of unreason" shows scant regard for facts and paints with a large brush. His analysis of the decay of so much contemporary culture may well be correct, as Norris recognises,[10] but whether this diagnosis pushes truth forever out of reach, as Baudrillard would have it, remains an open question. Norris for one thinks that criteria of truth and falsehood remain, and it is surely true that the more hyperreal the situation the more important such criteria become.

Derrida is synonymous with deconstructive postmodernism. He has been an important figure in promoting the priority of language, suspicion of metaphysics and textual instability; themes which have become central to much postmodernism. The genre of Derrida's writings is not easy to classify and this is related to his radical understanding of the relationship between philosophy and literature. Derrida refuses to privilege philosophy as *the* dispenser of reason and focuses on language with all its disruptiveness as the basis of both philosophy and literature. Philosophy cannot dispense with language and is thus subject to modes of rhetorical analysis as is any discourse. In the history of Western philosophy thinkers have been able to impose their concepts on other disciplines only by ignoring the disruptive effects of language. By undermining/deconstructing this boundary between philosophy and other modes of discourse Derrida "provided a whole new set of powerful strategies which placed the literary critic, not simply on a footing with the philosopher, but in a complex relationship (or rivalry) with him, whereby philosophic claims were open to rhetorical questioning or *deconstruction*."[11] Indeed in so far as literary texts are in touch with their rhetorical nature they are less deluded than philosophers who deny their embeddedness in language.

Derrida's deconstructive approach rests therefore on his philosophy of language. Language as 'writing' is the bottom line of reality and is Derrida's means of opposing logocentrism. It is important to note that he is using writing to mean something different from mere inscription. In *Of Grammatology* he says, "We say 'writing' for all that gives rise to inscription ... cinematography, choreography, ... pictorial, musical, sculptural 'writing'."[12] Norris explains Derrida's notion of writing as follows:

> the term is closely related to that element of signifying *difference* which Saussure thought essential to the workings of language. Writing for Derrida is the 'free play' or element of undecidability within every system of communication. Its operations are precisely those which escape the self-

---

9   The link between capitalist consumerism and postmodernity is also analysed by F. JAMESON, *Postmodernism, or, the Cultural Logic of Late Capitalism* (London, NY: Verso, 1991). See BERTENS, *The Idea of the Postmodern*, 160-184.

10   NORRIS, *What's Wrong with Postmodernism?*, 164-193.

11   C. NORRIS, *Deconstruction. Theory and Practice* (2nd ed.; New Accents; London: Routledge, 1991) 21.

12   J. DERRIDA, *Of Grammatology* (Baltimore; London: John Hopkins UP, 1976) 9.

consciousness of speech and its deluded sense of the mastery of concept over language. Writing is the endless displacement of meaning which both governs language and places it for ever beyond the reach of a stable, self-authenticating knowledge.[13]

If this is difficult to understand that is part of Derrida's intention; he does not want the meaning to be pinned down. Similarlz with *différance*, whose meaning remains suspended between 'difference' and 'deferral'.[14] Derrida applies his understanding of writing to Rousseau's "Essay on the Origin of Languages" and Lévi-Strauss's nature-culture distinction in order to show how their texts suppress writing which nevertheless remains present, and once foregrounded deconstructs their texts.[15] In terms of deconstructive method Norris comments on this work of Derrida that "[o]nce again it is a matter of taking a repressed or subjugated theme (that of writing), pursuing its various textual ramifications and showing how these subvert the very order that strives to hold them in check."[16] Such self-engendered paradoxes in texts Derrida calls 'aporia'.[17]

Language as the bottom line of reality has no underlying ground to support it, or meaning beyond itself. Consequently Derrida resists any attempt to recentre philosophy. The Western tradition has identified a number of different possible centres which provide a foundation for language. However for Derrida all these centres take their place within the universe of signs and they cannot escape the endless chain of signifier and signified. Centres are functionally indispensable but they are always only provisional; Derrida calls this approach *decentering*, and the refusal to acknowledge the provisionality of our centres *logocentrism*. Here we encounter a major theme of postmodern thinking, what Lyotard refers to as incredulity towards metanarratives. Fragmentation and transience characterise postmodernity, accompanied by thorough going pluralism. For Derrida there is no grounding of language; language has no ground external to itself that is not illusory. Here he follows Heidegger in absolutising language and thinking of it as a "bottomless chessboard" to indicate the lack of any foundation and that play has no meaning outside of itself.[18]

---

13 NORRIS, *Deconstruction. Theory and Practice*, 28-29.
14 Ibid., 31.
15 Cf. ibid., 32-41.
16 Ibid., 39.
17 Cf. ibid., 49.
18 'Play' is an important theme in Derrida's comments on interpretation. See, for instance, J. DERRIDA, *The Ear of the Other. Otobiography, Transference, Translation* (ed. by C.V. McDONALD; NY: Schocken Books, 1985) 59ff.

Habermas and Norris disagree strongly about how to evaluate Derrida and how to position him among postmodern theorists.[19] For Habermas "Derrida is particularly interested in standing the primacy of logic over rhetoric, canonized since Aristotle, on its head."[20] Norris argues that Habermas misreads Derrida, who retains a concern for rigorous analytical work and careful philosophical argumentation. This is true but it does seem that there are tensions in Derrida's work between this emphasis and that of language as "the bottomless chessboard."

Our survey of key theories of the postmodern has been all too brief. Theorists of the importance of Foucault and Bauman have not received attention. However the purpose of the survey is simply to put our discussion of postmodernity and OT hermeneutics in this broader philosophical context. These broader issues impinge on OT hermeneutics continually but are often unknown. Before we progress to the implications of 'the postmodern condition' for OT hermeneutics, it is worth pausing to identify central characteristics of postmodernity.

1. Postmodernity has raised all sorts of questions about our capacity to know and how we know and whether we can accurately represent reality i.e. about *epistemology*. The possibility of universal objective knowledge is considered by many to be impossible. Much postmodern theory is strongly anti-realist and considers all knowledge to be local, communal and a human construct. Such epistemological scepticism is captured very clearly in Lyotard's notion of "incredulity towards metanarratives." The corollary of this scepticism has been a profound suspicion of the hidden agendas of 'neutral' modern knowledge; what claimed to be objective and value free has come to be seen by many as a mask for powerful ideologies. The consequence of this scepticism is an awareness of inevitable pluralism in knowledge and consequent fragmentation. Certainty and truth are regarded by many with great suspicion – paradoxically the one thing that radical postmodern thinkers seem quite sure of is that there are no metanarratives! There is widespread disagreement about the role of rationality and whether or not knowledge can be grounded. Some, like Norris, Habermas and Gellner seek to reconstruct the project of modernity. Others would seek a genuinely post-modern position in which rationality is always perspectival. Others like MacIntyre seek to do justice to the perspectival nature of rationality while holding on to more universal perspectives.[21]

2. Epistemology is closely related to *ontology* and here too postmodernity has undermined the broad consensus of modernity. One would expect that incredulity towards metanarratives would leave little room for much ontological

---

[19] J. HABERMAS, *The Philosophical Discourse of Modernity* (Cambridge: Polity, 1987) 161-210); NORRIS, *Deconstruction. Theory and Practice*, 139-158; idem, *What's Wrong with Postmodernism?*, 49-76.

[20] HABERMAS, *The Philosophical Discourse of Modernity*, 187.

[21] A. MACINTYRE, *Whose Justice? Which Rationality?* (London: Duckworth, 1988).

reflection but of course this is unavoidable. All philosophical analysis inevitably carries with it ontological presuppositions whether conscious or not. A common ontological presupposition in postmodern theory is that language is the most fundamental aspect of reality. Derrida is a good example of this view. Lyotard's view of reason as inextricably bound up in power games and needing to be subverted by desire which will get the flow of the libidinal economy going again reflects strong ontological presuppositions.[22] Much postmodern theory has little room for any notion of an order in reality existing apart from human construction. Scepticism about human knowing goes hand in hand with a high view of the human community as constructing the worlds in which we live. This too reflects a particular ontology.

3. Epistemology and ontology are inseparable from *anthropology* in the sense of the nature of humankind. The rationalistic autonomous view of the human which was so dominant in modernity has been undermined and a plurality of alternatives proposed. Rorty, for example, suggests that we should think of the moral self as "a network of beliefs, desires, and emotions with nothing behind it – no substrate behind the attributes. For purposes of moral and political deliberation and conversation, a person just *is* that network."[23] Foucault stresses the extent to which our view of the human person is a construct when he asserts that

> strangely enough, man – the study of whom is supposed by the naive to be the oldest investigation since Socrates – is probably no more than a kind of rift in the order of things, or, in any case, a configuration whose outlines are determined by the new position he has so recently taken up in the field of knowledge ... man is only a recent invention, a figure not yet two centuries old, a new wrinkle in our knowledge, ... that will disappear as soon as that knowledge has discovered a new form.[24]

In several postmodern thinkers Freud's anthropology has been revised and renewed.[25] If thinkers like Baudrillard play down the possibility of the human subject acting in any significant way others stress the possibility of human self-creation.

Epistemology, ontology, anthropology. That so much postmodern theorising is related to these areas indicates the extent to which the philosophical *foundations* of modernity are in crisis. In many respects postmodernity is the name we give to this foundational crisis, which Neil Smith captures poignantly

---

[22] See BERTENS, *The Idea of the Postmodern*, 134-137.

[23] R. RORTY, "Postmodernist Bourgeois Liberalism," *Journal of Philosophy* 80/10 (1983) 585-586.

[24] M. FOUCAULT, *The Order of Things: An Archeology of the Human Sciences* (London: Tavistock, 1970) xxiii. See in this respect also J.G. MERQUIOR, *Foucault* (Modern Masters; London: Fontana, 1985) chs. 3-5.

[25] For example Baudrillard, Deleuze and Guattari, Lacan. See R. SELDEN and P. WIDDOWSON, *A Reader's Guide to Contemporary Literary Theory* (London: Harvester Wheatsheaf, 1993) 136-144, for a brief discussion of psychoanalytic theories in literary studies.

when he writes, "The Enlightenment is dead, Marxism is dead, the working class movement is dead ... and the author does not feel so well either."[26] Postmodernity is characterised by pluralism, uncertainty, instability and fragmentation. The old certainties seem to have gone with no unified vision to replace them even as capitalism hurtles on into a revolutionary information phase.

Personally it seems to me better to refer to what is being called postmodernity as late or high modernity.[27] Harvey suggests that modernity is characterised by a rejection of tradition and embrace of change as well as a confidence in reason to lead to new certain truths.[28] The capacity of reason to do this has been undermined so that we are left with change, flux and instability. In my opinion it is important to note that the roots of modernity have been called into question but not abandoned.[29] Human autonomy tends to remain as firmly entrenched as ever, the difference being that we now simply have to learn to live with the uncertainties. It should also not be forgotten that the nihilistic and relativistic side of postmodern theory is only one aspect of the contemporary situation. Norris already detects something of a reaction to the extremes of postmodernism among some of its proponents, namely Said and Kristeva.[30] Certainly if modernity is a reaction to and immanentising of a Christian worldview, then postmodernity shows little sign of openness to recovering Christian perspectives on reality. Lyon does say that

> [t]oday, the human is being displaced, decentred, and the grip on the future seems once more up for grabs. While this opens the door for everything from Foucault's play of power to the Age of Aquarius, it also renders more possible the possibility that Providence was not such a bad idea after all. Perhaps postmodern apocalyptics will have to make space for a vision of a (re)new(ed) earth, that antique agent of social change, and the original partner of final judgement.[31]

And Milbank has argued that only Christian theology provides an alternative route to contemporary nihilism.[32] However, these voices are in the minority. The fact is that important shifts are taking place and as Lyon says the concept of postmodernity is a valuable 'problematic' that alerts us to key questions concerning our age:[33] "the question of postmodernity offers an opportunity to

---

26   Quoted in D. HARVEY, *The Condition of Postmodernity. An Enquiry into the Origins of Cultural Change* (Oxford: Blackwell, 1989) 325.

27   'High modernity' is Anthony Giddens's expression (A. GIDDENS, *Modernity and Self-Identity. Self and Society in the Late Modern Age* [Cambridge: Polity, 1991] 4, 27-32).

28   HARVEY, *The Condition of Postmodernity*.

29   As the quote from Hesse at the outset of this chapter indicates.

30   C. NORRIS, *Truth and the Ethics of Criticism* (Manchester: Manchester UP, 1994).

31   LYON, *Postmodernity*, 86.

32   J. MILBANK, *Theology and Social Theory. Beyond Secular Reason* (Oxford: Blackwell, 1990).

33   LYON, *Postmodernity*, 84-85.

reappraise modernity, to read the signs of the times as indicators that modernity itself is unstable, unpredictable, and to forsake the foreclosed future that it once seemed to promise."[34] Postmodernity problematises the foundations of modernity and thus of OT studies, and in this way it invites us to debate the nature and direction of present day OT studies, and in particular the interpretation of Ecclesiastes.

6.3 The Postmodern Turn and Old Testament Hermeneutics

In virtually every discipline there is a growing body of "postmodernity and ..." literature. Theology is no exception, nor is biblical studies.[35] That developments in theology are significant for biblical studies and vice versa is receiving new recognition amidst the fluidity of the present.[36] Within modernity it has become commonplace in the university to assume that biblical exegesis should take place in isolation from theology and that it should not be related to Scriptural proclamation. Watson refers to C.F. Evans' proposal that we should strive "to ensure as far as possible that exegesis is studied in such a way that it does not issue in proclamation."[37] This rigid drawing of boundaries between exegesis, theology and proclamation is now open to question in ways that it was not some twenty years ago. However, for the sake of focusing what could become a very wide-ranging discussion we will confine our investigation to postmodernity and Old Testament hermeneutics.[38]

---

34 Ibid., 70.

35 On postmodernity and theology see G. LOUGHLIN, "At the End of the World: Postmodernism and Theology," in: A. WALKER (ed.), *Different Gospels. Christian Orthodoxy and Modern Theologies* (1993) 204-221; and D.R. GRIFFIN, W.A. BEARDSLEE, and J. HOLLAND, *Varieties of Postmodern Theology* (SUNY Series in Constructive Postmodern Thought; Albany: SUNY, 1989). On postmodernity and the Bible see E.V. MCKNIGHT, *Post-modern Use of the Bible: The Emergence of Reader Oriented Criticism* (Nashville: Abingdon, 1988).

36 Cf. F. WATSON, *Text, Church and World. Biblical Interpretation in Theological Perspective* (Edinburgh: T&T Clark, 1994) 1-14; L.G. PERDUE, *The Collapse of History. Reconstructing Old Testament Theology* (Minneapolis: Fortress, 1994) 305, 306, who stresses that "biblical theologians must begin to make the effort to become more theologically literate. As biblical scholars who possess some sense of the importance of public discourse, we must learn to read texts that are not simply behind but also beyond the Bible. This means that we must attempt to become theologically literate in order to become familiar with the horizons of meaning that historical and modern cultures produce. Otherwise, the questions we bring to the text are highly subjective and unavoidably individualistic. ... This does not mean that we should replace contemporary theology with a constructive biblical theology, but it is obvious that serious dialogue between the two groups would enrich them both."

37 WATSON, *Text, Church and World*, 6; cf. C.F. EVANS, *Explorations in Theology 2* (London: SCM, 1977) 82.

38 In this chapter I have focused on philosophical and 'OT' approaches to postmodernity. I see great value in exploring theological approaches to postmodernity but regard philosophy as more fundamental. Postmodern developments in theology and in OT studies echo philosophical views of postmodernity.

If postmodernity is characterised by instability and crisis then according to Rendtorff this is also true of contemporary Old Testament hermeneutics. In an article appropriately entitled "The Paradigm is Changing: Hopes – and Fears" Rendtorff maintains that

> Old Testament scholarship at present is 'in crisis'. The Wellhausen paradigm no longer functions as a commonly accepted presupposition for Old Testament exegesis. And at present, no other concept is visible that could replace such a widely accepted position. ... the shaking of this paradigm is part of a far-reaching shaking of the centuries-old fundamentals of Old Testament scholarship. ... Almost half a thousand years have faded away.[39]

Rendtorff follows Kuhn in using 'paradigm' to refer to a methodological model that has secured consensus in a discipline.[40] According to Rendtorff this is precisely what has happened in OT study this century. Wellhausen's documentary hypothesis has been the paradigm within which OT scholarship has operated. However, Rendtorff uses the notion of paradigm in a somewhat contradictory way. On the one hand he argues that the Wellhausen paradigm dominates OT scholarship during this century, but simultaneously sees Gunkel, von Rad and Noth as undermining this paradigm. For Rendtorff the significant difference between Wellhausen and these other scholars is the latter's concern with the oral history of the material underlying the text. Although Gunkel, von Rad and Noth maintained Wellhausen's sources (this indicates for Rendtorff the existence and strength of the Wellhausenian paradigm), their research actually led in a different direction and Rendtorff implies that this direction heads towards the contemporary focus on the final form of the text.

There is a link between some of von Rad's creative OT exegesis (for example on Genesis) and redaction criticism and final form readings of the text.[41] However a narrative of Gunkel's work leading on to final form readings today is too simplistic.[42] Form criticism, for example, has far more in common with

---

[39] R. RENDTORFF, "The Paradigm is Changing: Hopes – and Fears," *BI* 1/1 (1993) 44. In his *Canon and Theology. Overtures to an Old Testament Theology* (trans. and ed. by M. Kohl; Edinburgh: T&T Clark, 1994) 180, Rendtorff perceptively notes of this crisis that "Kuhn has also convincingly described the varying reactions to such a crisis, once it begins to show itself. If we follow his analysis, we must expect that, for a longer or shorter period, some Old Testament scholars will not recognise the symptoms of crisis at all, or will not be prepared to recognise them. Instead they will expect that solutions to the problems that can be found through an even more rigorous and even more precise application of the old methods. So in the near future we have to reckon with an increasing pluralism of methods, rather than with a unification of the questions asked."

[40] Ibid., 36; cf. T. KUHN, *The Structure of Scientific Revolutions* (2nd ed.; Chicago: University of Chicago Press, 1970).

[41] Von Rad, for example, was involved in the formation of *Interpretation*, a journal which is committed to hearing the message of the OT texts as redactional wholes.

[42] As RENDTORFF, "The Paradigm is Changing," 43, himself notes: "There is a continuity with the present discussion about the final shape of the text, canon criticism and the like ... But I think it

source criticism in its concern with reconstructing earlier stages of texts. Rendtorff is concerned to establish continuity between historical criticism and contemporary readings of the OT and consequently a narrative of continuity fits his purposes well. It fails however to do justice to the strong reaction to modernity that is at the heart of postmodernity. To understand the present crisis in OT studies it is vital to penetrate behind Wellhausen's source criticism and Gunkel's form criticism to discern the common matrix out of which both scholars worked. Rendtorff's analysis does not take sufficient account of the fact that the worldview of modernity underlies both approaches. Rendtorff recognises that Wellhausen was deeply influenced by romanticism but does not pursue the issue of philosophical shaping in discerning the paradigm operative in twentieth century OT scholarship.[43]

Now however Rendtorff is sure that this dominant Wellhausen paradigm has ended: "I do not see any new arguments that could turn back the wheel."[44] What has changed is not the object of study: "the sources are the same as they have always been. What has changed is the scholarly attitude to the sources, in particular to the main core of sources, namely the texts of the Old Testament itself."[45]

In looking at changing attitudes towards the OT and history Rendtorff notes the tendency to try and write histories of Israel without the OT. He dislikes this tendency and even more the tendency by those engaged in such ventures to declare their method the only right one and those who pursue more traditional approaches biblicists or fundamentalists.

> There are many scholarly approaches and methods, in Bible studies as well as in history writing. Nobody will forbid any scholar or group or school to believe their own method to be the best one. Many will be interested in seeing the results and checking their validity and usefulness. But in scholarship there is by definition no heresy. We should rather practice and accept methodological pluralism.[46]

The great advantage in the newer literary methods is, according to Rendtorff, their concern with the text as it is. And indeed, in this respect Rendtorff has made an important contribution to canonical readings of the OT as well as to the revival of interest in biblical theology.[47] For too long and too intentionally OT scholarship has neglected the final form of texts. "Scholars still

---

would be an inappropriate harmonization of the history of research to draw too strong a line from Gunkel through von Rad and Noth to the present discussion; because there are obvious elements of discontinuity, in particular since the mid-seventies."

[43] Ibid., 35. However, see his *Canon and Theology*, 1-16, which takes note of philosophical shaping in German OT scholarship.

[44] RENDTORFF, "The Paradigm is Changing," 44.

[45] Ibid., 46.

[46] Ibid., 47.

[47] See RENDTORFF, *Canon and Theology*.

seem to be proud of knowing things better than the final redactors or compilers. This is a kind of nineteenth-century hubris we should have left behind us."[48] Rendtorff's conclusion is that,

> The paradigm is changing. I believe it has changed already. But the field is open. Many new and fruitful approaches are visible that will lead Old Testament scholarship into the twenty-first century. At the moment there is no new model that could be expected to achieve common acceptance as a paradigm, and there will probably be none in the near future.[49]

Rendtorff correctly recognises that Old Testament studies is increasingly characterised by fragmentation and pluralism; common postmodern themes. But it is not just that the Wellhausen paradigm has lost its power, as Rendtorff correctly asserts, but that the underpinnings of the dominant mode of OT interpretation in modernity seem to many no longer valid. The postmodern turn has called modernity into question and with the dominant method of OT interpretation in modernity, historical criticism, being deeply rooted in the modern world view, it is inevitable that historical criticism should also partake of the crisis of modernity. It is this link that Rendtorff has not adequately explored in his analysis of the contemporary crisis in OT studies. Consequently he too easily speaks of continuity between the historical critical era and the 'postmodern era' in OT interpretation and too easily imagines that a methodological pluralism will solve the problem.[50] It is not that there is no continuity, but the crisis is not just a methodological one, but a *philosophical* one, in which different epistemologies compete for attention.

In this section we will examine the views of three OT scholars who reflect more deeply on the challenge postmodernity constitutes to the foundations of OT study and seek to articulate ways ahead amidst postmodernity, namely Brueggemann, Clines and Perdue.

6.3.1 Clines: Old Testament Consumerism

Clines is one of the most capable and creative OT scholars in the UK today. His writings range across the OT (Pentateuch; Ezra, Nehemiah, Esther; Job) and extend from detailed Semitic study (Hebrew dictionary) to avant garde methods for reading the Old Testament. One gets the impression that he is constantly rethinking his positions and on the move. Currently he is a strong proponent of a

---

48 RENDTORFF, "The Paradigm is Changing," 52.

49 Ibid., 52-53.

50 J. BARTON, *Reading the Old Testament. Method in Biblical Study* (London: DLT, 1984); M. BRETT, *Biblical Criticism in Crisis? The Impact of the Canonical Approach on Old Testament Studies* (Cambridge: CUP, 1991). Rendtorff, *Canon and Theology*, 28, does however perceptively note that "the use of new methods does not make the old questions disappear. We have to ask whether or to what extent the questions posed by traditional Old Testament scholarship have been legitimate and of what relevance they are in a changed framework."

'postmodern' approach to the OT and we shall focus on him in this capacity. In order to put his present moves in context we will briefly outline the development of his OT scholarship.

In his early years of OT scholarship Clines was a conservative proponent of the historical critical method. As he says, "in the olden days I thought we were all doing the same thing, historical-critical scholarship with the goal of arriving at some objectively determinable meaning of the text."[51] However, early on in his career Clines manifested a capacity to go against the dominant currents of OT scholarship, as evidenced by his *The Theme of the Pentateuch*. In this highly creative piece of work Clines criticises the excessive atomism and geneticism in pentateuchal studies and commits himself to ignoring the sources and focusing on the final form of the Pentateuch as a literary work. In the process he identifies his allies as the structuralists, Childs, Alonso-Schökel, Walter Wink and the late von Rad.[52] This is not to say that he denies the need for atomistic work; biblical studies requires both atomistic and holistic work but the ratio has been terribly unbalanced.[53]

The Pentateuch, in Cline's view, is a literary work and requires therefore a method shaped by the humanities and not the sciences. The scientific, pyramid view of knowledge whereby each scholar makes his little contribution which he hopes will contribute to the macrostructure of OT scholarship is inadequate.

> For our discipline belongs firmly in the tradition of humanistic studies, and inasmuch as it occupies itself with the interpretation of data that are already given, has more in common with the criticism of a body of well known literature than with the discovery, accumulation and evaluation of new data. In the sphere of literary criticism knowledge does not accumulate steadily through the industry of objectively distanced scholars, but by means of repeated engagement with the text. When one learns from others, it is as much from the shaft of light the critic has brought to bear on the text, a setting of the text in a new context, that one learns, as from the details of the commentator's explications. The model is that of the guide in a darkened museum who holds up his torch to reveal an unfamiliar object, or a familiar object from a fresh angle, in a new light.[54]

Clines' approach is to seek the 'theme' of the Pentateuch which he defines along literary lines. His conclusion is well known: the theme of the Pentateuch is the partial fulfilment of the promise to the patriarchs.[55] Although Clines is aware of structuralism his approach is clearly not structuralist in any strong sense, but an

---

[51] D.J.A. CLINES, "Possibilities and Priorities of Biblical Interpretation in an International Perspective," *BI* 1/1 (1993) 71.

[52] D.J.A. CLINES, *The Theme of the Pentateuch* (JSOTSup 10; Sheffield: JSOT, 1978) 10-11.

[53] Ibid., 6.

[54] Ibid., 8.

[55] Cf. ibid., 29.

approach to the Pentateuch as a literary-work-of-art.[56] Nor is it redaction critical, at least not in the way in which Clines defines redaction criticism. For Clines, although redaction criticism is concerned with the shape of the work as a whole, such concern is closely linked with authorial/editorial intention, which Cline's thematic approach is not.[57] Clines is critical of Hirsch's insistence that meaning is inseparably allied with authorial intentionality; the theme need not have been in the mind of the author.[58] However Clines does regard the theme as objectively in the text; there can ultimately be only one theme in a literary work like the Pentateuch.[59]

In 1983 Clines contributed the chapter on method in OT study to the text *Beginning Old Testament Study*.[60] This gives a clear indication of where Clines was in terms of methodology at this time. Method, he maintains, is a means to an end and the end is determined by the goals we have in mind in studying the OT. Clines acknowledges that most people have religious goals in mind in their study of the OT. However,

> [t]he academic study of the Bible has been, and must be, one in which people of any religious faith, or of none, can engage, and can co-operate. The immediate goal of biblical study must be one that allows but does not require religious preconceptions; for many, the immediate goal may only be a stage on the way to an ultimate (religious) goal, but for others it may be a sufficient goal in itself.[61]

Thus Clines proposes that in academic study of the Bible our primary goal should be *understanding*.

> Given that there is an Old Testament (or, Hebrew Bible), what else can be done about it in an institution of higher education? It cannot be preached, and it cannot be 'taught' – as doctrine, that is, as what one ought to believe; for a university or college is not the place for that. But neither can it be used simply as a textbook for ancient history or as a source for illustrating social customs in the ancient Near East; for it was self-evidently not for these purposes that the Hebrew Bible was brought together in the form that it has and it does not as a whole have the character of a history or a manual of social customs. Only some description like 'the Scriptures of the Hebrew people', or 'the sacred writings of the Jews which now form part of the Christian Bible', can do justice to its essence. It is a religious document, and the most appropriate way of handling a religious document in an academic setting is to attempt to *understand* it.[62]

---

56 See D.J.A. CLINES, "Methods in Old Testament Study," in: J. ROGERSON (ed.), *Beginning Old Testament Study* (1983) 33-37.

57 Ibid., 31-33.

58 *The Theme of the Pentateuch*, 121.

59 Ibid., 20.

60 "Methods in Old Testament Study," 26-43.

61 Ibid., 26.

62 Ibid., 27.

With the primary goal of OT study as understanding the OT Clines reshapes traditional historical criticism into first and second order methods.[63] The former have understanding as their chief aim whereas the latter are not principally aimed at interpretation but have valuable contributions to make to it. First order methods are divided into two categories: traditional methods (historical-grammatical exegesis, textual criticism, redaction criticism) and methods in literary criticism (close reading, the idea of the literary work of art, engagement). Second order methods are historical criticism, source criticism and form criticism. These second order methods may help interpretation but they are not aimed at it.

Clines is still working with the concepts of a stable text, objective interpretation and the modern university but his reshaping of OT methods is noteworthy and represents an advance upon his 1978 position. In *The Theme of the Pentateuch* equal validity for atomistic and holistic criticism was allowed. Here priority is given to the text in its final form with understanding of that form as the goal. Clines' reshaping is similar to the reaction to positivism which we observed in NC and in Childs. His notion of understanding remains a modern one.

A good example of Clines' 1983 method in action is his *The Esther Scroll. The Story of the Story*.[64] This book contains thoroughgoing textual, source and redaction criticism but pride of place is given to the literary shape of Esther, as indicated by the 'inclusion' of chapters 1 and 10 which deal with the literary shape. However this privileging of literary shape operates in chapter 10 not just with 'the final form' but with the form of the narrative at five different stages that Clines has identified. This combination of source criticism with literary criticism makes Clines one of those rare few about which he speaks in relation to the documentary hypothesis: "very few scholars have used this reconstruction of the sources as a means for interpreting the text that now stands."[65]

Recently Clines has shifted considerably from his 1978-1984 approach towards a postmodern position which embraces textual indeterminacy and methodological plurality. A clear indication of this is his statement that he does "not really want to talk with most redaction critics – about their work, that is – because I do not think what they are doing is very plausible,"[66] and his acknowledgement that he could no longer write a book like *The Theme of the Pentateuch*. In 1984 in *The Esther Scroll* two chapters were devoted to redaction criticism; by 1993 Clines was no longer interested in redaction criticism. The first volume of his commentary on Job further evidences a waning of interest in historical criticism; he simply states that he has not and will not devote much time

---

[63] This reshaping is conscious and deliberate. Cf. ibid., 42.

[64] D.J.A. CLINES, *The Esther Scroll. The Story of the Story* (JSOTSup 30; Sheffield: JSOT, 1984).

[65] "Methods in Old Testament Study," 41.

[66] "Possibilities and Priorities of Biblical Interpretation," 72.

to the history of the text.[67] He does, however, include a vegetarian, feminist, materialist and Christian reading of Job.

Cline's current position is clearly articulated in his 1993 article, "Possibilities and Priorities of Biblical Interpretation in an International Perspective." In respect of his current methodological position he also gave a public lecture in Cheltenham on 7 December 1994 called "Shopping for Methods in the Old Testament Supermarket", and we will use these sources plus some of his most recent publications to outline his contemporary position. His current position is in my opinion best described as *OT Consumerism*.

Clines stresses the actual and, in his opinion, desirable pluralism in OT studies nowadays. He used to think that OT scholars were all doing the same thing in their OT scholarship but now he realises that different scholars have different goals.[68] The Bible furthermore, is a common cultural object and biblical interpretation must make room for the religious and ideological plurality of our societies. It is important for Clines to be able to affirm that the Bible is not just an ecclesiastical object but a cultural one: "my academic context has no connections whatsoever with the church. ... It is not, therefore, surprising that what I want to affirm is that the Bible is a cultural artefact in our society, and not just an ecclesiastical object."[69] A tension thus exists between the church and biblical studies in the academy and Clines considers this healthy. Although in today's economic climate biblical scholars are having to produce products that will sell,

> academic freedom has to mean – not a freedom to research their subject in isolation from the impact their work has on anyone except their fellow academics, but – freedom to choose their own priorities and goals, freedom to resist the magisterium of anyone – church leaders, politicians, and also the senior scholars who distribute research grants – freedom to resist the imposition of the agenda of anyone at all.[70]

It is good for the church to be challenged by the less powerful academy: "The church does not really know, I think, how much it needs to be liberated from the shackles of fundamentalism, or how much it needs to abandon the use of the Bible as a tool for social control. ... The academy's biblical criticism inevitably relativizes the authority of the Bible, and the church can only benefit from such a humanizing of the Bible."[71]

The pluralism in OT studies is related to the recognition nowadays that all interpretation is contextual and cultural. In Clines' view one constructs one's identity out of one's prejudices and presuppositions and it would be a mistake to suppress these in interpretation. This, combined with the postmodern break with

---

[67] D.J.A. CLINES, *Job 1-20* (WBC; Texas: Word, 1989) xxix.
[68] "Possibilities and Priorities of Biblical Interpretation," 71.
[69] Ibid., 76.
[70] Ibid., 77.
[71] Ibid., 77, 78.

Cartesian categories makes for a deeply pluralist situation, but in Anglo-American biblical studies,

> the full impact of the contemporary break with the Cartesian categories has still to register ... most active scholars still write as if they were engaged in a quest for objectively determinable meanings and objectively verifiable history. The shifting of the ground brought about by the philosophical hermeneutics of Gadamer or the deconstructive philosophy of Derrida is bound to bring questions of method to the forefront in biblical and theological studies.[72]

6.3.1.1 A Consumer Product

In response to our changed context Clines proposes an end-user theory of interpretation. Clines says:

> I want to propose a model for biblical interpretation that accepts the realities of our pluralist context. I call it by various names: a goal-oriented hermeneutic, an end-user theory of interpretation, a market philosophy of interpretation, or a discipline of 'comparative interpretation'. ... First comes the recognition that texts do not have determinate meanings. ... The second axis for my framework is provided by the idea of interpretative communities. ... There is no objective standard by which we can know whether one interpretation or other is right; we can only tell whether it has been accepted. ... There are no determinate meanings and there are no universally agreed upon legitimate interpretations.
>
> What are biblical scholars then to be doing with themselves? To whom shall they appeal for their authorisation, from where shall they gain approval for their activities, and above all, who will pay them? ... If there are no 'right' interpretations, and no validity in interpretation beyond the assent of various interest groups, biblical interpreters have to give up the goal of determinate and universally acceptable interpretations, and devote themselves to interpretations they can sell – in whatever mode is called for by the communities they choose to serve. I call this 'customised' interpretation.[73]

Such an end-user approach could entail recycling old waste interpretations which were thought to have been superseded by the progress model of modernity. These discarded interpretations could be revived in a post-critical form to stock afresh the shelves of the interpretational supermarket.

6.3.1.2 Ideological Critique

Clines goes on to say that he regards the literary turn in OT studies as the most important trend since the middle of this century, with its focus upon the text in its final form as a literary artefact, upon the reader and her role in the construction of meaning and upon hermeneutics and the nature of language and texts. Clines particularly commends feminist and ideology criticism. Feminist

---

[72] Ibid., 75.
[73] Ibid., 78, 79, 80.

criticism more than any other form relativises the authority of the Bible because it takes its starting point in an ideological position very different from the patriarchal biblical text. Reading from 'left to right' is Clines' slogan for reading the text against its grain and insisting on addressing one's own questions to the text.

In his recent lecture in Cheltenham Clines advocated a pragmatic, pluralist approach to OT hermeneutics in which a range of interpretive methods are available and OT scholars select those they enjoy and find useful. This represents a marked shift from his 1983 position where understanding as the goal of interpretation governed one's methodology. He acknowledges that

> It is the question whether feminist criticism and ideological criticism are, properly speaking, *interpretational* at all. Perhaps we should be sharply distinguishing between acts of *interpretation*, which seek only to represent the text, to exegete and explicate it, to rehearse it in words other than its own, to understand it – but *not* to critique or evaluate it – and, on the other hand, acts of *criticism*, which judge the text by a norm outside itself. If a feminist or some other ideological point of criticism takes its point of departure from an ethical or ideological position that lies outside the text, one which may indeed be deeply hostile to the text, its goal cannot be mere *understanding*, mere *interpretation*. … Perhaps the almost unchallenged assumption that the task of biblical scholars is essentially to *interpret* the text represent a systematic repression of our ethical instincts. … Will not the most interesting prospects for biblical studies lie precisely in reading against the grain of the texts, in bringing to bear on our texts our own cultural and historical and personal positions, and in evaluating the texts against the hundred and one yardsticks that the pluralist world of international biblical scholarship will inevitably suggest?[74]

An example of this pluralist style in action and its contrast with Clines' previous work is his "Reading Esther from Left to Right" in which he performs a formalist, structuralist, feminist, materialist and deconstructionist reading on Esther and concludes, "I have been impressed in this study by the value of as many strategies as possible for reading a text. As a critic of the text, I should hate to be restricted by a methodological purism. What I have noticed is that different strategies confirm, complement or comment on other strategies, and so help develop an integrated but polychromatic reading."[75]

It is apparent from the above just how far Clines has shifted between 1983 and 1993. Then he argued for a unified hermeneutic, now the stress is on hermeneutic pluralism. Then he worked with a notion of objective textual meaning, now he insists on textual indeterminacy and the role of readers in

---

[74] Ibid., 86, 87.

[75] D.J.A. CLINES, "Reading Esther from Left to Right. Contemporary Strategies for Reading a Biblical Text," in: D.J.A. CLINES, S.E. FOWL, and S.E. PORTER (eds.), *The Bible in Three Dimensions* (1990) 51.

creating meaning along the lines of Stanley Fish's 'interpretive' communities'.[76] Then he stressed understanding as the overarching goal of interpretation, now his great concern is ideological critique. Then he stressed literary reading of texts, now a whole new range of methods are foregrounded and historical criticism is hardly mentioned.[77] Clines continues to be wary of allowing religious presuppositions too much control in biblical studies and insists on the freedom of the academy. Now, however, he has a much greater sense of pluralism.

Although his close exegetical work has remained very traditional (cf. the first volume on Job) Clines has shown a refreshing tendency to go against the flow of historical critical OT scholarship. However his ready espousal of hermeneutic pluralism, textual indeterminacy and consumerism raise all sorts of questions which we will address below.

6.3.2 Brueggemann: Funding Postmodern Imagination

Brueggemann has long been an advocate of the role of imagination in biblical interpretation.[78] However, only recently has he related imagination to the postmodern situation in his *Texts Under Negotiation. The Bible and Postmodern Imagination*.[79] He uses postmodern theorising to validate and develop his previous work on imagination and OT theology.

Brueggemann is emphatic about the change in our epistemological context signified by the postmodern turn and its implications for OT hermeneutics. We are in "a wholly new interpretive situation";[80] "the end of modernity requires a critique of method in scripture study. It is clear to me that conventional historical criticism is, in scripture study, our particular practice of modernity, whereby the text was made to fit our modes of knowledge and control. As we stand before the text, no longer as its master but as its advocate, we will have to find new methods

---

[76] Clines says in his introduction to Job that "meanings are not properties of books, but are understandings created in the minds of readers who are intent upon reading books" (Clines, *Job 1-20*, xxix).

[77] Clines says of his commentary on Job, "I must confess to having spent almost all my time on the book as it now is, without thinking very much about how it came to be in its present form." He does acknowledge the traditional questions of date, source etc. as "interesting" but wishes to focus on the meaning or interpretation of Job and these questions are extrinsic to that purpose (ibid.).

[78] Cf. W. BRUEGGEMANN, *The Prophetic Imagination*. Philadelphia: Fortress, 1978) and idem, *Hopeful Imagination: Prophetic Voices in Exile* (Philadelphia: Fortress, 1986). See PERDUE, *The Collapse of History*, 285-298, for a description of Brueggemann's work prior to his book on postmodern imagination.

[79] W. BRUEGGEMANN, *Texts Under Negotiation. The Bible and Postmodern Imagination* (London: SCM, 1993).

[80] Ibid., vii.

of reading."[81] "What is now required and permitted is a mode of scripture interpretation quite unlike most of what we have practised heretofore."[82]

Brueggemann proposes an epistemology which privileges imagination, which he defines as "my quintessential locus where I receive, process, and order all kinds of input, input that heals and assaults, that subverts and transforms, and I take into it and handle what I am able as I am able. ... It is that operation of receiving, processing, and ordering that transpires when my mind wonders in listening to a text, a reading, in praying, or in any other time."[83] For Brueggemann imagination refers to

> the human capacity to picture, portray, receive, and practice the world in ways other than it appears to be at first glance when seen through a dominant, habitual, unexamined lens. More succinctly, imagination as the quintessential human act is a valid way of knowing. Imagination as a human act does not yield the kind of certitude required by Cartesian anxiety, but it does yield a possible 'home' when we accept a participating role as 'home-maker'.[84]

We thus need a mode of reading the Bible, according to Brueggemann, which funds postmodern imagination. This does not involve constructing a full new metanarrative but interpreting the OT in such a way as to provide the pieces out of which a new world can be imagined. Brueggemann sees the main context for this as the church community and envisions "a place where people come to receive new materials, or old materials freshly voiced, that will fund, feed, nurture, nourish, legitimate, and authorize a *counter imagination of the world*."[85] It is important for Brueggemann that in our postmodern context all worldviews are under negotiation so that

> [r]eality ... is no longer a fixed arrangement inhospitable to theological categories, but is an ongoing, creative, constitutive task in which imagination of a quite specific kind has a crucial role to play. The core of our new awareness is that the world we have taken for granted ... is an imaginative construal. And if it is a construal, then from any other perspective, the world can yet be construed differently. It is the claim of our faith, and the warrant of our ministry, to insist that our peculiar memory in faith provides the materials out of which an alternatively construed world can be properly imagined.[86]

Faith thus plays a central role in Brueggemann's hermeneutic of postmodern imagination, and the Christian community is privileged as the context of interpretation. Although he is very wary of imposing systematic categories upon texts he does want to take the Bible seriously as the Word of God in biblical interpretation and proposes an evangelical infrastructure of memory, covenant

---

[81] Ibid., 11.
[82] Ibid., 64.
[83] Ibid., 62.
[84] Ibid., 13.
[85] Ibid., 20.
[86] Ibid., 17, 18.

and hope to shape interpretation. Furthermore he includes liturgy, preaching and teaching in the enterprise of biblical interpretation.[87]

Brueggemann proposes a dramatic model of biblical interpretation in which reality is taken as a drama and the biblical text as a script for the drama. This model evokes playful open-endedness which is appropriate to our present liminality, and avoids the modern dangers of conservative retreat into propositional absolutes on the one hand, and liberal developmentalism on the other. Such an approach will be strongly text centred, applying itself to one text at a time. Creation, fall, redemption does seem to be the core drama of the Bible but Brueggemann, although very sympathetic to the work of Lindbeck and Frei, is wary of privileging this drama at the expense of the small stories of the Bible.[88] The individual text must be allowed to speak in all its hoary roughness so that it can do its task of subverting our assumed world. In this way the Bible will function as the *"compost pile* that provides material for new life."[89] There is little room for historical criticism in this method of interpretation[90] and the aesthetisising of the new literary criticism also needs to be guarded against.[91] The Bible is treated as an "army of metaphors" with which the listener is called to actively engage.[92]

6.3.3 Perdue: The Collapse of History and the Promise of Imagination

Perdue is particularly interesting on a number of accounts. He is aware of the postmodern shift and explores its implications for OT theology.[93] He follows Brueggemann in privileging imagination as a way ahead for OT theology in the postmodern context.[94] He has published extensively on wisdom literature, and finally he has brought his interests in postmodernity and imagination to bear on wisdom literature.[95] Perdue refers to the postmodern turn in OT studies as "the collapse of history".[96]

> Traditional paradigms and their theological worlds, centred in and constructed by history and historical method, have come under serious assault ... I have chosen to call this destabilization of the dominant paradigm of historical criticism 'the collapse of history.' By 'the collapse of history' I do not mean to argue or even imply that history and historical method are now passé ... But I

---

[87] Ibid., 68.
[88] Ibid., 69-70.
[89] Ibid., 61.
[90] Ibid., 90.
[91] Ibid., 105.
[92] Ibid., 90.
[93] PERDUE, *The Collapse of History*, 3-15.
[94] Ibid., 263-307.
[95] L.G. PERDUE, *Wisdom and Creation. The Theology of Wisdom Literature* (Nashville: Abingdon, 1994).
[96] PERDUE, *The Collapse of History*.

do mean that for at least a generation now active revolt against the domination of history and historical method for Old Testament study in general and Old Testament theology in particular has been under way and in large measure has seceded from the epistemological rule of this once unchallenged strategy of interpretation.[97]

Perdue gives the following four reasons for this collapse.[98] Firstly newer paradigms have challenged history as the dominant paradigm for Old Testament scholarship and it is often argued that these newer paradigms make theological meaning of the OT more accessible. Secondly the current diversity in theology ("the shattered spectrum") has contributed to the diversity in Old Testament theology. Thirdly loss of confidence in Enlightenment epistemology has undermined the dominance of the historical critical method. Fourthly an increasing number of biblical theologians have rejected the descriptive approach in favour of "reflective, critical, constructive, or systematic strategy."[99] All these reasons, according to Perdue, can be subsumed under 'postmodernity.' As with postmodernism in general pluralism characterises contemporary biblical studies as different paradigms compete for attention.

However Perdue is adamant that we must hold on to objective criteria that can weigh the merits "of *any* theological presentation ... In any intellectual inquiry, no theology, or, for that matter, no ideology, should be exempted from the close examination of rational investigation and judicious criticism. Here I speak as an *unrepentant rationalist*."[100] There is a contradiction in his thinking here. On the one hand he acknowledges and welcomes the pluralism and sees no quickly emerging consensus and yet he insists on common legitimating criteria![101] At the heart of much postmodern theorising is specifically the denial of such common legitimation. Perdue's insistence on common legitimation positions him close to Habermas whereas his ready acknowledgement of the demise of Enlightenment epistemology and of pluralism takes him in a rather different direction. One does wonder if Perdue has fully understood the implications of postmodern pluralism – if he had it would be difficult for him to describe himself as an unrepentant rationalist while welcoming pluralism.

Perdue proposes the following four stages in a paradigm for OT theology.[102] The first stage involves explicating the meaning of OT texts in their historical and cultural context. The second stage is "conceptualization of the multiple images, ideas, and themes that leads to the systematic rendering of the multiple theologies of Old Testament texts within the dynamic matrix of creation and history."[103] The

---

[97] Ibid., 4.
[98] Ibid., 7-11.
[99] Ibid., 9.
[100] Ibid., 11 (italics mine).
[101] See section 6.2 above.
[102] PERDUE, *The Collapse of History*, 306-307.
[103] Ibid., 306.

third stage is to examine how OT texts have been understood within the history of interpretation. Finally the theology of the OT and past interpretations must be correlated with contemporary discourse.

In this process Perdue sees a central place for imagination. He deals very positively with Brueggemann's theology of the imagination,[104] and says that "[a] comprehensive Old Testament theology of imagination would be most welcome. ... Especially important is the inclusion of historical criticism, social-scientific analysis, and newer literary methodologies."[105] Perdue does not elaborate in detail how imagination would relate to the four stages in his proposed paradigm for OT theology. In his treatment of Brueggemann he particularly stresses the role of imagination in making the fourth step possible, and presumably this is where it would make most difference in his own paradigm.

If Perdue is not explicit about the centrality of imagination in his paradigm for OT theology he is so in his theology of wisdom. He says of *Wisdom and Creation*, "this book undertakes the task of rendering the theology of the sages by interpreting through a paradigm of metaphor and imagination the five major wisdom books."[106] Imagination is, according to Perdue, the capacity of the human mind to create images.[107] "Imagination is the bridge between perception and thought or sensation and conception."[108] He distinguishes between common imagination (which completes the fragmentary data of the senses or projects objects that are not perceived directly), creative imagination (which represents or redescribes reality) and religious imagination (which imagines God). Perdue says of theological imagination that it

> attempts to create and then interpret divine character and the world of the holy through skilful presentation. The substance and mode of theological discourse is not rational discourse that presents through discursive language a systematic rendering of God, humanity and the world. Rather, through images available indirectly through sense experiences, views of God are presented that are intelligible, that make some sense to human reason and emotions. To move into rational and systematic presentation is a second order of theological discourse.[109]

In Perdue's view the sages used their imaginations in shaping a worldview for wise living.[110] This sapiential imagination has six components: tradition and memory, engagement and reformulation of images of faith and the moral life, redescribing reality, imagining God at the centre of reality, recognition of the historicality and linguisticality of human experience and thereby imagining the

---

[104] Ibid., 285-298.
[105] Ibid., 298; cf. also 302.
[106] PERDUE, *Wisdom and Creation*, 20.
[107] PERDUE, *The Collapse of History*, 263-272; idem, *Wisdom and Creation*, 50-52.
[108] *The Collapse of History*, 264.
[109] *Wisdom and Creation*, 51.
[110] Ibid., 59-62.

nature and destiny of humans, recognising the mystery of human experience. In the cosmological wisdom tradition Perdue discerns the root metaphors of fertility, artistry, word and battle.[111] In the anthropological tradition he finds the metaphors of birth and nurture, artistry, the breath of God, king and slave.[112] The metaphors of reality are kingdom, household, city and garden.[113]

Previous theologies of wisdom have conceptualised the theology of wisdom in rational, discursive language. In the process the imagistic and aesthetic aspects of sapiential language have been neglected. The better procedure would be to attend first to the imagistic qualities of sapiential language and especially the organising metaphors, and then to go on systematically and rationally to set out the sage's conceptions. In *Wisdom and Creation* Perdue's concern is with the first of these approaches.

What does Perdue's imaginative approach yield in terms of Ecclesiastes? Chapter 5 of *Wisdom and Creation* is devoted to Qoheleth. Ecclesiastes, according to Perdue, was probably written by a Hebrew sage in Jerusalem around the end of the fourth century BC. Qoheleth's crisis is one of imagination: the cosmology of traditional wisdom with its root metaphors is not sufficient for his questions about discovering the good in human existence. "What was called for was a new world view shaped by Qoheleth's imagination. To find the resources for this human-centred reality, Qoheleth turns to the anthropological tradition. This tradition is reconceived in this sage's imagination, and central to this reconception is his metaphor of *hebel* ("breath")."[114]

The question of genre, according to Perdue, is vital for understanding Qoheleth's imaginative construction of creation theology.[115] Perdue conducts a thorough investigation of possible genre parallels to Qoheleth and concludes that the closest form-critical parallels are grave biographies and royal testaments, both of which create the fiction of a dead person who undertakes to instruct the living from the tomb.[116] "The book of Qoheleth is best seen as the fictional testament of Israel's most famous king, who is presented as speaking to his audience either in his old age, shortly before death, or perhaps from the tomb."[117]

Drawing in particular upon the work of Wright[118] and Rousseau,[119] Perdue discerns the following structure in Ecclesiastes.[120]

---

[111] Ibid., 330-333.

[112] Ibid., 333-336.

[113] Ibid., 336-338.

[114] Ibid., 194.

[115] Ibid.

[116] Ibid., 194-202.

[117] Ibid., 202. See ch. 5.4 for a more detailed discussion of Perdue's view of the genre of Ecclesiastes.

[118] Cf. ch. 4.5.

[119] F. ROUSSEAU, "Structure de Qoheleth i 4-11 et Plan du Livre," *VT* 31 (1981) 200-217.

[120] Ibid., 204.

Frame   1:1-11; 11:9-12:14

Introduction		Conclusion	
1:1	Title	12:9-14	Epilogue
1:2	Theme	12:8	Theme
1:3	Central question		
1:4-11	Two stanza poem	11:9-12:7	Two stanza poem
	1:4-7 Cosmology		11:9-10 Anthropology
	1:8-11 Anthropology		12:1-8 Cosmology and Death

Internal Structure   1:12-11:8

I. 1:12-5:19 Cosmology, Anthropology and the Moral Order: Human Action

       1:12-18   Two-fold introduction to Sections I and II

    A. 2:1-26   Solomon's accomplishments
                Carpe Diem: Conclusion   2:24-26
    B. 3:1-13   Time: Human Toil and Divine Action
                Carpe Diem: Interlude   3:12-13
    C. 3:14-22   Judgement and Human Nature
                Carpe Diem: Conclusion   3:22
    D. 4:1-5:19   Royal Rule and the Cult
                Carpe Diem: Conclusion   5:17-19

       6:1-9   Interlude: Joy, Appetite and Desire

II. 6:10-11:8 The Sovereignty of God and the Moral Order: Human Knowing

    E. 6:10-8:15   Divine Sovereignty and Human Wisdom (A)
                Carpe Diem: Conclusion   8:14-15
    F. 8:16-9:10   Divine Sovereignty and Human Wisdom (B)
                Carpe Diem: Conclusion   9:7-10
    G. 9:11-11:8   Divine Sovereignty and Human Wisdom (C)

The two poems on cosmology and anthropology (1:4-11; 11:9-12:7) and the repetition of "breath of breath" provide the literary structure of Ecclesiastes. Wright has correctly recognised that the book is divided into two parts ("doing" and "knowing") and Rousseau has correctly recognised that the internal part of the book is divided into seven main sections marked off by the *carpe diem*. There is some progression in the book since the quest for the good proceeds from doing to knowing.

Ecclesiastes contains the imaginative fiction of Solomon, Israel's wisest and greatest king, seeking to determine the "good" in life. The opening and closing poems are an inclusio setting up their two elements, cosmology and anthropology as the context for reality. Within the inclusio we have the quest of the king to find the "good" through doing and knowing. The only good that Qoheleth discovers is *carpe diem*, which may provide joy.

In Solomon's quest to determine this good, the teacher composes a narrative testament embodying moral instruction that constructs a world offered for human habitation. It is not a comforting world, but nevertheless is a new world view that calls for the transformation of the way that sages had conceived of God, reality, and the place and role of humanity.[121]

The dominating metaphor of Qoheleth for life is הבל. Perdue maintains that the root meaning underlying הבל is ephemerality and proposes that we translate the key statement in 1:14c: "all is ephemeral and a desire for life's vital spirit."[122] The paradox of human life is its ephemeral nature combined with the human desire for the spirit that animates life. Thus it is the ephemeral nature of life that Qoheleth laments and not its meaninglessness or absurdity; Qoheleth is obsessed with finding something that endures. In connection with this Perdue proposes that יתרון should be understood as that which remains.[123]

Perdue is emphatic about Qoheleth's opposition to traditional Israelite wisdom. As is particularly evident in the opening poem Qoheleth, according to Perdue, understands creation as enduring but there is no description of God as creating or sustaining the world; "traditional creation theology is absent."[124] The cosmos is beautiful but it is not a just order reflecting God's righteousness. Qoheleth does not believe in the providence of God. In traditional creation theology "remember your creator" evokes a positive image of divine response to suffering. However, "For Qoheleth, God is indeed the powerful tyrant whose power directs the world and determines the fate of human beings, but he is not the redeemer who enters into life to save the human creature. Thus, while students are instructed to remember God, they should not expect God to remember them."[125] Qoheleth does not believe that the universe is made for the well being of humans and ultimately history has no value. "Under the sun" expresses the distance between God and human beings. Jerusalem is no longer the location of God's presence among his people. God is a tyrannical ruler who secretly determines the course of history; his sovereignty is grounded in power alone and not in justice. Humans cannot affect reality in any important way or know God's purposes. "The inability to discern divine activity undercuts both the theologies of salvation history and cultic ritual, which represented and reactualized in sacred drama deeds of divine redemption."[126]

All in all Perdue's view of Qoheleth approximates the pessimistic portrait of Crenshaw, to which the view of the narrator forms a stark contrast. 12:9-14 are from an editor and of 11-14 Perdue says, "The narrator then turns to his or her own understanding … The narrator concludes with his admonition that summarizes his or her own understanding of wisdom."[127]

---

[121] Ibid., 238-239.
[122] Ibid., 207.
[123] Ibid., 208.
[124] Ibid., 210.
[125] Ibid., 234.
[126] Ibid., 217.
[127] Ibid., 237.

6.4 Orientation amidst the Flux

The relativisation of historical criticism, the hermeneutical pluralism and lack of consensus about the way ahead make it clear that the postmodern turn is being felt in OT studies. OT studies are manifesting signs of the crisis that is central to postmodernity. However, for all their talk of pluralism and rejection of metanarratives, proponents of pluralism and indeterminacy cannot and do not avoid positioning themselves philosophically.[128] It is easier to talk about rejecting metanarratives than to practice such rejection! To say, for example, that *all* knowledge is contextual and local, as Brueggemann does,[129] is to position oneself where one can see the whole and thus make such a comprehensive statement. In other words Brueggemann's position conceals a powerful, *autonomous* metanarrative.

This confirms what we argued in section 6.2, namely that postmodernism is not as radically new as it is often presented. Indeed postmodernity is better described as late or high modernity because it represents the outworking of the tensions within modernity. Postmodernism has challenged some of the key assumptions of modernity but as Hesse (see quote at outset of chapter) reminds us it remains deeply rooted in modernity. The belief in human autonomy, for example, remains as entrenched as ever.

Some form of a metanarrative (philosophical positioning) is inescapable and postmodernity has not suddenly produced radically new options. Thus in order to orient ourselves amidst the growing pluralism in OT studies it is important to identify the presuppositions and inconsistencies in the perspectives underlying the views we examined in section 6.3. This will then put us in a position to critique their views more insightfully.

Perdue welcomes the postmodern shift while trying to hold on to universal criteria for legitimating readings, thereby also manifesting a superficial understanding of the extent to which consistent postmodern pluralism undermines rationalism. Clines and Brueggemann are the more perceptive analysts of postmodernity in that they see the implications of the shift that the turn implies in OT studies. Clines embraces methodological pluralism, indeterminacy and the impossibility of validating readings. Brueggemann rejects the possibility of large truth.

What is interesting though is the very different ways in which Clines and Brueggemann have embraced postmodernity. It is broadly recognised now that one aspect of late modernity is the encroachment of capitalist consumerism upon all areas of life.[130] Clines, as we have seen, embraces this aspect of late

---

[128] See in this respect the useful article on pluralism by M.E. BOTHA, "Does Reformational Philosophy Have an Answer to the Many Guises of Pluralism?" *Koers* 60/2 (1995) 171-188.

[129] BRUEGGEMANN, *Texts under Negotiation*, 8-12.

[130] See LYON, *Postmodernity*, 54-69; and Baudrillard in section 6.2 above.

modernity and allows it to reshape the practice and theory of OT hermeneutics. The methods and the product of OT interpretation are to be determined by consumer desire. By contrast, Brueggemann is repeatedly at pains to distance himself from consumerism.[131] In his section on the development of an evangelical infrastructure that will shape interpretation he says that "if this evangelical infrastructure is not carefully constructed, the Christian congregation will rely on the dominant infrastructure of consumerism, and will not even discern until very late (too late) that the infrastructure of consumerism contains little good news."[132]

It is I think a mistake to reconstruct OT hermeneutics along consumer lines. Clines' espousal of indeterminacy, which opens the door for his consumer move, sounds very radical, but, as Norris and Bertens have noted, is politically close to the right wing pragmatism of scholars like Rorty. The debate about the death of the author seems to have come full circle since Barthes' provocative essay[133] and Bertens notes that

> Deriddean postmodernism largely limited itself to texts and intertexts. In its firm belief that the attack on representation was itself an important political act, it was content to celebrate the so-called death of the subject ... without realizing that the end of representation had paradoxically made questions of subjectivity and authorship ... all the more relevant. ... In the absence of transcendent truth it matters, more than ever, who is speaking (or writing), and why, and to whom.[134]

Clines' ready espousal of consumerism and indeterminacy is vulnerable to Norris's critique of

> 'theory' as practised by post-structuralists, post-modernists and other fashionable figures on the current intellectual scene. ... their 'radicalism' has now passed over into a species of disguised apologetics for the socio-political status quo, a persuasion that 'reality' is constituted through and through by the meanings, values or discourses that presently compose it, so that nothing could count as effective counter-argument, much less a critique of existing institutions on valid theoretical grounds.[135]

Both Brueggemann and Clines accept postmodern epistemological pluralism but do so in different ways. Clines' is a pragmatic pluralism in which a smorgasbord of methodologies are available and interpreters use what works for

---

[131] Cf. BRUEGGEMANN, *Texts under Negotiation*, 27, 29, 40, 57.

[132] Ibid., 27.

[133] R. BARTHES, "The Death of an Author," in: D. LODGE (ed.), *Modern Criticism and Theory* (1988) 167-171.

[134] BERTENS, *The Idea of the Postmodern*, 7.

[135] NORRIS, *What's Wrong with Postmodernism?*, 3, 4. It should be noted however that there is a tension in Clines' recent work between doing what sells and his preference to ideological (feminist and materialist) criticism. The latter generally depends on reading texts determinatively and may involve standing against market forces. It is unclear how Clines holds these diverging tendencies together.

them. Brueggemann acknowledges the plurality of hermeneutics but argues for a hermeneutic which is shaped by faith and privileges imagination as the key to knowledge in the local context. Brueggemann's privileging of imagination and the powers he assigns to it contradict his espousal of pluralism. Like Perdue his understanding of the imagination is more Kantian-Romantic than postmodern.[136] And this productive understanding of the imagination has taken a beating in postmodernity.[137] As Kearney says,

> In our Civilization of the Image might we not expect to find imagination accorded a privileged place by contemporary philosophers? The very opposite is the case. Right across the spectrum of structuralist, post-structuralist and deconstructionist thinking, one notes a common concern to dismantle the very notion of imagination. ... The philosophical category of imagination, like that of 'man' himself, appears to be dissolving into an anonymous play of language.[138]

Thus, for Brueggemann to sustain his proposed hermeneutic, he would need to take a far more critical stance in relation to postmodern thinking.

On the surface Clines' pluralism would appear to be more democratic but this is not entirely so. In his Cheltenham lecture on the supermarket of methods he dealt with NC, rhetorical criticism, structuralism, feminist criticism, materialist or political criticism, psychoanalytical criticism, reader response criticism and deconstruction. Conspicuous by its absence was any type of religious (Christian or Jewish) reading of the OT, which may suggest a certain imperialism in his pluralism.[139] Such imperialism manifests itself in much contemporary OT hermeneutic pluralism. Brett, in his work on Childs' canonical approach, argues for a pluralistic understanding of OT hermeneutics and acknowledges the validity of the canonical approach *provided* it be one of the smorgasbord of methodologies, precisely what Childs denies.[140] Similarly Barton argues for a

---

[136] On the modern imagination see R. KEARNEY, *The Wake of Imagination. Toward a Postmodern Culture* (Minneapolis: University of Minnesota Press, 1988) 155-195. R. LUNDIN, *The Culture of Interpretation. Christian Faith and the Postmodern World* (Grand Rapids: Eerdmans, 1993) 104-136, relates the sort of privileging of the creative imagination that we see in Brueggemann and Perdue historically to Emerson's understanding of the romantic imagination. He comments that, "Admittedly, there are distinct differences between an Enlightenment conception of reason and Emerson's romantic stress upon intuition. The one emphasizes law and pattern, while the other stresses spontaneity and freedom; the one enshrines reason, while the other exalts the imagination. Yet in spite of their differences, Cartesian rationalism and Emersonian romanticism share a deep trust in the power of self to unveil the truth and a deep distrust of tradition" (ibid., 131).

[137] On postmodern imagination see KEARNEY, *The Wake of Imagination*, 251-358.

[138] Ibid., 251.

[139] CLINES, *Job 1-20*, does include a Christian reading of Job in his commentary and he has written the commentary on Job for the overtly Christian *New Bible Commentary. 21st Century Edition*. However his recent writings fail to mention such readings as a priority.

[140] BRETT, *Biblical Criticism in Crisis?*

pluralism of approaches to OT texts provided one does not think that there is a correct way to read such texts.[141]

Imperialistic pluralism of this sort reminds us once again that it is hard and perhaps impossible to escape some type of metanarrative and thus some type of unified OT hermeneutic, even if its unity consists in an insistence upon diversity. What is called hermeneutic pluralism often amounts to a consideration of different aspects of the hermeneutic process. Thus feminist readings are often not 'readings' but critiques of patriarchal ideology in texts which first have to be read before the feminist critique can take place. Lategan points out that what is called historical criticism focuses on part of the communication act involved in interpreting a text, namely the relationship between the sender and the text.[142] The new literary criticism by comparison focuses on the text itself and reader response on the role of the reader in interpretation. Clearly historical criticism, 'textual' criticism and reader criticism are not necessarily antithetical but could form part of a hermeneutic seeking to interpret texts as part of a communicative act.

However, hermeneutic pluralism also refers to the interpretation of the OT from conflicting ideological/philosophical perspectives. As our examination has shown these are not absent from proponents of pluralism and indeterminacy, and in their respective appropriations of consumerism and a Kantian view of the imagination Clines and Brueggemann show themselves to be more modern than they acknowledge. The question for OT scholars is not whether they work with a metanarrative (philosophical presuppositions) or not, but which philosophical presuppositions they work with. For OT scholarship postmodernity means that all practitioners should reflect and give an account of their foundational/philosophical presuppositions. In this way the real pluralism in OT studies will become clear.

Clines and Brueggemann are two examples of different ways of grounding OT studies philosophically. Although I am cautious of Brueggemann's too ready acceptance of all truth as local and his privileging of imagination, I do think that his path is more helpful than Clines'. In the context of postmodern pluralism it seeks to formulate an integrated Christian/theological hermeneutic which will allow the Bible to speak as God's Word.

Indeed Clouser has argued that religious beliefs are universal and the deepest type of human belief which shape all of our lives, including our theorising.[143] From a Christian perspective the postmodern context provides us with an opportunity to take that religious shaping seriously and the hermeneutic proposals of Brueggemann, Lindbeck, Frei, Childs, Newbigin, Sternberg and

---

[141] BARTON, *Reading the Old Testament*.

[142] B. LATEGAN, "Hermeneutics," in: D.N. FREEDMAN (ed.), *ABD* Vol. III (1992) 149-154.

[143] R. CLOUSER, *The Myth of Religious Neutrality. An Essay on the Hidden Role of Religious Belief in Theories* (Notre Dame; London: University of Notre Dame Press, 1991).

Lategan seem to me to offer fruitful ways forward in the development of what Ouweneel calls a bibliotropic hermeneutic, i.e. one shaped by a Christian perspective upon reality which does justice to the historical, literary and kerygmatic aspects of OT texts as well as the contextual nature of interpretation.[144] Since this will be developed in the context of the Christian community, as Brueggemann stresses, it will certainly not achieve universal agreement but then the goal of universal public knowledge is no longer credible, as I think MacIntyre has demonstrated.[145] Such an approach would seem to me to do justice to the perspectival nature of truth claims (following MacIntyre and an important insight of postmodernism) while keeping open claims of universal relevance within that perspective.[146] At the outset of chapter seven I will explain my position more fully and outline the sort of hermeneutic I envision. Suffice it to note here that, as Plantinga points out (see quote at outset of chapter), a Christian perspective would be resistant to the sort of creative anti-realism that underlies much postmodernism. In this respect a Christian perspective would be closer to modernity in its commitment to the existence of truth and the possibility of its discovery, although for different reasons.

6.5 Postmodernism and Ecclesiastes

What hope do the sort of postmodern OT hermeneutics that we have looked at hold for reading Ecclesiastes? Very little specifically postmodern work has been done on Ecclesiastes. In chapter two we briefly looked at the feminist, socio-critical and psychoanalytic readings of Ecclesiastes that have been done. None of these have had much of an impact upon the interpretation of Ecclesiastes. Perdue announces the collapse of history and promises much with his imaginative, metaphorical reading of Ecclesiastes, but in practice his work yields little that is new and fails to deal with the text in its final form. He never deals seriously with the question of how the narrator's views in 12:9-14 relate to Qoheleth's unorthodox views, and the position he arrives at is virtually the same as that of mainline historical criticism.

But this lack of postmodern readings of Ecclesiastes should not be taken to mean that postmodernism makes no difference to the interpretation of Ecclesiastes. Clines' supermarket could offer us a smorgasbord of different readings of Ecclesiastes – a deconstructionist reading, a feminist reading, a psychoanalytic reading, a materialist reading – without ever privileging one as the correct reading. A postmodern hermeneutic could insist that we ignore the author and his intentions in interpreting Ecclesiastes, that we regard the text as

---

[144] W.J. OUWENEEL, *A Critical Analysis of the External and Internal Prolegomena of Systematic Theology* (2 Vols.; unpubl. DTh thesis, University of the Orange Free State, 1993).

[145] MACINTYRE, *Whose Justice?*

[146] It should be noted that while I agree with MacIntyre in principle about the location of rationality within traditions, he proposes a recovery of the *Aristotelian* tradition.

inherently indeterminate and that we read Ecclesiastes in whatever ways appeal to us and in whatever ways people will pay us to read it.

In practice, however, it is impossible to operate consistently in this way. Most feminists and liberationists, for example, would be reluctant to see their readings as simply theirs and as legitimate as say a patriarchal reading. Even Clines, after presenting a variety of readings in his introduction to Job, exegetes the text as though it has a single meaning.[147] Furthermore, with many of these 'readings', one first has to read Ecclesiastes determinatively *along the grain* before one can deconstruct it, or perform a feminist or materialist critique. This is not to deny the validity of the important questions these 'readings' raise, but it is to insist that if one is going to suspect something, one first needs a good idea of what it is one is suspicious of. Thus, for example, if Ecclesiastes 7:23ff are to be critiqued as patriarchal, one first needs to be sure of what they are asserting, and this is where the debate is being conducted at present along traditional lines of the meaning of the text.[148]

The real contribution of postmodernism to biblical interpretation, in my opinion, is its insistence that what we bring to the text influences what we get out of the text. This recovery of insight into the historicity of all interpretation derives, as we have seen in chapter one, from Gadamer. Of course the logical implication of this insight *could be* the radical pluralism of postmodernism but it will depend on one's view of history. The attraction of Gadamer's hermeneutic is its radical undermining of Cartesian objectivity, its recovery of the role of prejudice and tradition in interpretation, its dialogical model of understanding and its notion of being addressed by the text. It seems to me that the insistence that hermeneutics involves two horizons is very helpful; it enables much that shapes biblical interpretation to be brought into the light.

Gadamer's hermeneutic has however been consistently criticised for its inability to discern distorted communication or to be able to distinguish a correct from an incorrect understanding. In Klapwijk's words, "How can anyone, after the Holocaust, still unreservedly maintain: 'In understanding we are drawn into an event of truth.'?"[149] The underlying issue is, I think, Gadamer's immanentist perspective on reality (history). The transcendent cannot be taken into account hermeneutically so that it is only through the dialectic of a great diversity of interpretations that the universally valid emerges and the thing itself manifests itself. Klapwijk suggests that only the notion of the God who has revealed himself in Christ is adequate to enable us to hold on to a strong notion of truth in language.

---

[147] CLINES, *Job 1-20*.

[148] See ch. 2.3.

[149] J. KLAPWIJK, "The Universal in Hans-Georg Gadamer's Hermeneutic Philosophy," *Philosophia Reformata* 50 (1985) 127, 123.

Thiselton similarly points out that socio-critical theory raises in an acute form the issue of hermeneutical pluralism because, once it is allowed that 'the world' can/should absorb the text, and a plurality of worlds is acknowledged, a plurality of diverse interpretations will inevitably be generated.[150] Thiselton argues that while hermeneutical pluralism is inevitable, since we cannot assess one reading model in terms of another, this is "not the same as the belief that each life-world is self-contained, and incapable of metacritical ranking in terms of trans-contextual theory". "Would it be the same," asks Thiselton, "in principle, *to de-centre the present situation as a criterion* of theological relevance and truth as *to de-centre the biblical texts and their witness to Christ and to the cross as a criterion* of relevance and truth?"[151]

The answer, from a Christian perspective, is of course 'No!', and Thiselton concurs at this point with those scholars who appeal for the Bible to absorb the world. Certainly when it comes to biblical interpretation one would want to ask which are the appropriate prejudices to bring to Scriptural interpretation, what is a healthy tradition to inhabit which is most likely to promote a fusion of horizons? As Heidegger says, the decisive thing is to enter the hermeneutical circle in the right way.[152] At the outset of the next chapter we will address this issue.

6.6 Conclusion

In this chapter we have argued that 'postmodernity' is better understood as a crisis of foundations in late modernity. This crisis is becoming evident in OT studies in terms of hermeneutic pluralism and fragmentation. Although little postmodern work has been done on Ecclesiastes we observed that consistent postmodernism would have radical implications for its interpretation. However, as we have seen, postmodernism is not as radically new as it is often presented and the hermeneutical positions its proponents advocate in OT studies still presuppose metanarratives and epistemologies. The value of postmodernism is its recognition that we have to position ourselves somewhere from which we do our analysis. The problem of postmodernism is its tendency to view all positionings as of equal value or of there being no way of deciding where one *should* position oneself. Gadamer has shown us that prejudices are inevitable in interpretation. The crucial question for biblical scholars is whether or not there are appropriate prejudices for OT interpretation, or are one set as good as another?

---

[150] A.C. THISELTON, *New Horizons in Hermeneutics* (Grand Rapids: Zondervan, 1992) 602-619.

[151] Ibid., 606.

[152] See M. Heidegger, "Understanding and Interpretation," in: K. MUELLER-VOLLMER (ed.), *The Hermeneutics Reader* (1992) 226.

CHAPTER 7

READING ECCLESIASTES

7.1 Introduction

Historical criticism is a product of modernity. Postmodernism problematises this philosophical shaping of historical criticism. Some philosophical shaping is inevitable, but we have seen that at many points the modern worldview is in conflict with a Christian perspective. In this context we have suggested that OT interpretation requires a hermeneutic shaped by a Christian perspective. This is a controversial position to argue for,[1] and so in this chapter we will set out the case for such an approach and then attempt to outline the parameters of such a hermeneutic. Finally we will apply this hermeneutic to Ecclesiastes.

7.2 The Case for a Christian Hermeneutic

The Christian god cannot have a more fundamental witness than Jesus Christ, even antecedent to the commitments of faith; Christian theology cannot abstract from Christology in order to shift the challenge for this foundational warrant onto philosophy. Within the context of a Christology and a Pneumatology of both communal and personal religious experience, one can locate and give its own philosophical integrity to metaphysics, but Christology and Pneumatology are fundamental. If one abrogates this evidence, one abrogates this god.

(M.J. BUCKLEY, *At the Origins of Modern Atheism* [New Haven; London: Yale UP, 1987] 361)

As we have seen modernity sought to bracket out theological presuppositions in the knowledge enterprise and as Ingraffia shows there is a strong anti-theological tendency in postmodern theory.[2] This is a prejudice of modernity and one which, as Gadamer so clearly points out, conflicts with Christianity. In the context of modernity many Christians have sought a synthesis of a Christian with a modernistic perspective in most areas including

---

[1] J. BARTON, *The Future of Old Testament Study* (Clarendon: Oxford, 1993) acknowledges that the argument for a religious hermeneutic is becoming more common but he is very cautious of this direction in biblical studies. A sense of the difference in opinion among scholars at this point becomes apparent by comparing Barton (ibid. and idem, *People of the Book? The Authority of the Bible in Christianity* [2nd ed.; London: SPCK, 1993]) with C.E. BRAATEN and R.W. JENSON (eds.), *Reclaiming the Bible For the Church* (Edinburgh: T&T Clark, 1995).

[2] B.D. INGRAFFIA, *Postmodern Theory and Biblical Theology* (Cambridge: CUP, 1995).

hermeneutics. Krentz, for example, seeks somehow to hold faith and modernistic historical criticism together. As a Jew Levenson clearly demonstrates the antithetical relationship between a modernistic historical approach to the Hebrew Bible and a literary (theological) approach.[3] However, even he still hopes that somehow these antithetical approaches will lead to a larger truth. The problem with this synthesising approach is that it fails to recognise that

> the reason why stories come into conflict with each other is that worldviews, and the stories which characterize them, are in principle *normative*: that is, they claim to make sense of the whole of reality. ... in principle the whole point of Christianity is that it offers a story which is the story of the whole world. It is public truth. Otherwise it collapses into some form of Gnosticism.[4]

Indeed, although many still insist on keeping OT studies distinct from philosophy and theology, there is a growing recognition by a variety of Christian academics that the public nature of the gospel and Christian faith *necessarily* involves actively allowing one's faith to shape one's scholarship.[5] Indeed, within OT studies, I would argue that this is implied in the very name *Old Testament* studies. At the heart of Christianity is the claim to public truth and this claim ought to be given full weight in OT studies, in my view. This is of course, not for a moment to deny the insights that alternative hermeneutics will arrive at or the right of the latter to be practised, but it is to insist that even these insights are not neutral but shaped by their 'storied' roots. This conscious appropriation of my prejudices should not be seen as necessarily inhibiting the critical nature of this work. MacIntyre has, persuasively in my opinion, argued that all rationalities are traditioned[6] and Gadamer has shown the constructive role of prejudices in understanding.[7] The aim of being conscious and up front about our prejudices is that the otherness of the object of study might be focused more, and not less, clearly.

Thus my proposal is that the way ahead philosophically in OT studies is to allow the philosophical scaffolding of OT studies to be shaped by a Christian perspective upon reality, what one might call a Christian worldview.[8] While I

---

3   J.D. LEVENSON, *The Hebrew Bible, the Old Testament and Historical Criticism* (Louisville: Westminister/John Knox, 1993).

4   N.T. WRIGHT, *The New Testament and the People of God* (Minneapolis: Fortress, 1992) 41, 42.

5   Some examples of this tendency are, in philosophy: Dooyeweerd, Wolterstorff and Plantinga. In theology: Newbigin, Frei, Lindbeck (postliberal theology), McGrath. In literary studies: Etchells and Edwards. In aesthetics: Seerveld. See bibliography for titles.

6   A. MACINTYRE, *Whose Justice? Which Rationality?* (London: Duckworth, 1988).

7   H. GADAMER, *Truth and Method* (2nd ed.; London: Sheed and Ward, 1989).

8   A powerful historical case for this type of approach is made by M.J. BUCKLEY, *At the Origins of Modern Atheism* (New Haven; London: Yale UP, 1987). Buckley argues persuasively that the origins of modern atheism in the West resulted to a large extent from the self-alienation of religion in which religion looked to philosophy to establish the existence of God. "In an effort to secure its basis, religion unknowingly fathered its own estrangement" (ibid., 359).

think this is the right way to proceed it is very important that this is not misunderstood to mean that I wish to exclude other approaches from the academy.[9] The sort of religiously shaped approach that I am arguing for is sometimes perceived in this way. What I am arguing for is a *genuine* pluralism in OT studies in which different starting points are allowed to shape OT scholarship so that the real differences can manifest themselves and real dialogue emerge. I do think that my type of approach is the right one but would want to defend the legitimacy of alternative approaches and would want to be in earnest discussion with those approaches in our common quest for the truth. This common quest defeats its object, however, if any of the partners insist that others share *their* starting point. Real academic *freedom* must mean allowing scholars to work from different starting points in different traditions. Too often modernistic scholars insist on a rationalist type of starting point, and 'religious' scholars insists on a religious starting point. A genuine pluralism will make room for both.[10]

It is, of course, no easy matter to decide *how* to give full and critical weight to the public nature of Christianity in scholarship. As Niebuhr points out, there is not one Christian understanding of the Christ-culture relationship but several.[11] Within this investigation there is no room for a detailed evaluation of the different perspectives upon the Christ-culture relationship which underlies any view of what Christian scholarship entails.[12] I must therefore simply declare my view that Niebuhr's transformative paradigm is the most biblical. It is close to the Reformed perspective upon reality (or worldview) which is clearly articulated by Wolters[13] and in general forms the basis from which philosophers like Wolterstorff and Plantinga work.[14] The kind of philosophical direction I am

---

[9]   While I obviously side with those who argue for a religious hermeneutic, it should be noted that I am critical of advocates of both 'secular' and religious OT hermeneutics for their common lack of attention to philosophy. Especially appeals for a *church* hermeneutic seem to me in danger of short-circuiting the philosophical scaffolding of a hermeneutic.

[10] The debate about hermeneutics in OT studies too easily becomes acrimonious with labels like 'liberal' and 'fundamentalist' being slung about, with both sides being reluctant to make room for the other. In my opinion this reflects an inadequate theory of academic pluralism. For a useful analysis of public pluralism see R.J. MOUW and S. GRIFFIOEN, *Pluralisms and Horizons. An Essay in Christian Public Philosophy* (Grand Rapids: Eerdmans, 1993).

[11] H.R. NIEBUHR, *Christ and Culture* (London: Harper Colophon, 1975) 39-44, identifies five approaches to the Christ-culture relationship: Christ against culture; the Christ of culture; Christ above culture; Christ and culture in paradox; Christ the transformer of culture.

[12] For such an evaluation see G. STRAUSS, *Christian Philosophy and the Transformation of African Culture* (Unpubl. MA thesis: University of the Orange Freestate, 1990) 13-35. C. SCRIVEN, *The Transformation of Culture: Christian Social Ethics After H. Richard Niebuhr* (Pennsylvania, Ontario: Herald Press, 1988) represents a recent upgrading of Niebuhr's analysis.

[13] A. WOLTERS, *Creation Regained. Biblical Basics for a Reformational Worldview* (Grand Rapids: Eerdmans, 1985).

[14] N. WOLTERSTORFF, *Until Justice and Peace Embrace* (Grand Rapids: Eerdmans, 1983) 3-22, describes this type of Calvinistic paradigm as "world-formative Christianity."

proposing is the sort advocated by Wolterstorff,[15] Plantinga,[16] Clouser,[17] and Ingraffia.[18]

Within current biblical hermeneutical discussions a number of voices have called for the sort of project I have in mind.[19] Ouweneel proposes what he calls a *Bibliotropic* hermeneutic. In his view the worldview and the theoretical framework through which the Bible is approached and studied should be consistently Christian and in accord with the worldview of the Bible itself.[20] Ouweneel has recently done significant work in re-evaluating the foundations of theology and he has expressed the need for this type of worldview to fund theology by coining a new expression viz. *bibliotropic*.[21] A bibliotropic theology is one which

> not only is faithful to the Bible's own *Selbstverständnis* but which also can
> *critically account* for this faithfulness on the basis of meta-theological or
> philosophical presuppositions which themselves are of a bibliotropic nature.

---

[15] N. WOLTERSTORFF, *Reason Within the Bounds of Religion* (Grand Rapids: Eerdmans, 1984).

[16] A. PLANTINGA, "Advice to Christian Philosophers," *Faith and Philosophy* 1/3 (1984) 253-271.

[17] R. CLOUSER, *The Myth of Religious Neutrality. An Essay on the Hidden Role of Religious Belief in Theories* (Notre Dame; London: University of Notre Dame Press, 1991).

[18] INGRAFFIA, *Postmodern Theory and Biblical Theology*, explores the postmodern opposition to theology, arguing that a continuation of Nietzsche's project of vanquishing God's shadow is central to postmodern theory. Ingraffia examines Nietzsche's, Heidegger's and Derrida's opposition to theology and argues that they all critique the ontotheology that resulted from the Hellenization of biblical theology. Their deconstruction of this is helpful, but they fail to distinguish this ontotheology from biblical theology. The logos of the latter is radically different from the logos of the former and resists the deconstruction that the latter is subjected to by Derrida. Thus Christian thinkers ought not to follow postmodern theory but should reverse the ontotheological route by recovering a theology of the cross, and developing Christian critical theory which is built on revelation and guided by a hermeneutics of faith.

[19] I do not necessarily agree in all details with the examples that follow. For a critique of Watson and Thiselton see C.G. BARTHOLOMEW, "Philosophy, Theology and Biblical Interpretation. Vanhoozer, Wright, Watson and Thiselton" (unpubl. paper, 1995); idem, "Three Horizons: Hermeneutics from the Other End – An Evaluation of Anthony Thiselton's Hermeneutic Proposals," *EJT* 5 (1996) 121-135.

[20] The assumption here is that the Bible does express a consistent perspective upon reality or what we might call a worldview, and that A. WOLTERS, "Gustavo Gutiérrez," in: J. KLAPWIJK, S. GRIFFIOEN, and G. GROENEWOUD (eds.), *Bringing into Captivity Every Thought* (1991) 237, is correct in maintaining that "[b]iblical faith in fact involves a worldview, at least implicitly and in principle. The central notion of creation (a *given* order of reality), fall (human mutiny at the root of all perversion of the given order) and redemption (unearned restoration of the order in Christ) are cosmic and transformational in their implications. Together with other basic elements ... these central ideas ... give believers the fundamental outline of a completely anti-pagan *Weltanschauung*, a worldview which provides the interpretive framework for history, society, culture, politics, and everything else that enters human experience."

[21] W.J. OUWENEEL, *A Critical Analysis of the External and Internal Prolegomena of Systematic Theology* (2 Vols.; unpubl. DTh thesis, University of the Orange Free State, 1993).

Spiritual apostasy may manifest itself not only in liberal but also in conservative theology in so far as the latter is an open fortress, without much *theoretical* resistance to secular philosophy.[22]

Amidst all his work on philosophical hermeneutics and biblical interpretation, Thiselton finds it important to call for a "critique of the cross" in biblical hermeneutics.[23] In a comparable way Watson argues for *a theological hermeneutic* in biblical interpretation.[24] He is quite clear on this:

> The text in question is the biblical text; for the goal is a theological hermeneutic within which an exegesis oriented primarily towards theological issues can come into being. This is therefore not an exercise in general hermeneutics. ... the hermeneutic or interpretative paradigm towards which the following chapters move is a theological rather than a literary one, and the idea that a literary perspective is, as such, already 'theological' seems to me to be without foundation.[25]

Watson's entire text is directed towards the "attempt to formulate in more systematic fashion some of the elements of a *theological hermeneutic*, intended as a framework within which exegesis may proceed."[26]

One of the implications of such approaches to hermeneutics is surely the possibility, in principal at least, of an integrated hermeneutic in OT studies. A transformational Christian perspective[27] in OT hermeneutics is incompatible with the antithetical philosophical pluralism present in the academy. It should be noted that the argument for an integrated hermeneutic is not a position easily arrived at in today's pluralistic context. Contra Barthes anti-theological move[28] which is endorsed by many postmoderns, we insist that the reality of God and the

---

[22] Ibid., I:5.

[23] A.C. THISELTON, *New Horizons in Hermeneutics* (Grand Rapids: Zondervan, 1992) 604-619.

[24] F. WATSON, *Text, Church and World. Biblical Interpretation in Theological Perspective* (Edinburgh: T&T Clark, 1994).

[25] Ibid., 1.

[26] Ibid., 221. For a comparison of Wright, Thiselton, Vanhoozer and Watson see BARTHOLOMEW, "Philosophy, Theology and Biblical Interpretation". WATSON, *Text, Church and World,* does not attend to the theology-philosophy relationship; indeed 'philosophy' does not occur in his index of subjects. However he has written the article on "Philosophy" in the *Dictionary of Biblical Interpretation* (F. WATSON, "Philosophy," in: R.J. COGGINS and J.C. HOULDEN (eds.), *A Dictionary of Biblical Interpretation* [1990] 546-549). In this article he surveys key thinkers in the history of Christianity and concludes that "[t]he influence of philosophy on biblical interpretation has tended to be tangential, and resources for interpretation have generally been drawn from within the Christian tradition or (since the Enlightenment) from the methods of secular historiography and textual scholarship. The present situation is marked by widespread scepticism about the ability of historical-critical scholarship to do full justice to the biblical texts, and increased awareness of the insights provided by the philosophical tradition might help to clarify this issue."

[27] In the sense of Niebuhr's paradigm of Christ as the transformer of culture.

[28] See R. BARTHES, "The Death of an Author," in: D. LODGE (ed.), *Modern Criticism and Theory* (1988) 167-171, who connects textual indeterminacy with an anti-theological move.

existence of humans, texts and history as part of his creation makes determinate meaning principially possible. There is such a thing as the true meaning of a biblical text and this meaning ought to be the goal of interpretation, even if as finite humans we can never be sure we have discovered it in its fullness. We share this commitment to objective truth with historical critics, but our understanding of objectivity is different from theirs, as we will explain below. Thus in the following section we will attempt to outline an integrated hermeneutic model for OT interpretation.

7.3 Towards a Hermeneutical Model for Academic[29] Old Testament Interpretation

If we, as theists, believe that the universe is fundamentally personal in character, it follows that our ultimate understanding will not be in terms of things, which occupy space and may or may not possess certain properties, but of persons, who characteristically do things. Action, not substance, will be our most important category of thought. It is a truth too long neglected by philosophers.

(J. LUCAS, *Freedom and Grace* [London: SPCK, 1976] 111)[30]

The god who is so personal must have the personal as the foundation of his human assertion, and all other reflection that bears upon the existence of this god must have the personal as its critical context.

(M.J. BUCKLEY, *At the Origins of Modern Atheism* [New Haven; London: Yale UP, 1987] 361)

7.3.1 A Communication Model of Old Testament Interpretation

In the light of the above two quotes language and texts are best approached as types of human communication or discourse,[31] so that contra much

---

[29] This section is deliberately headed "for *academic* OT interpretation". Any study of the *Old Testament* i.e. of the OT as Scripture, has to take into account the fact that most of those who 'use' it as Scripture are non-academics. In this sense the *study* of the OT as Scripture is secondary to its pre-theoretical use as Scripture, a hermeneutical principle which has recently been recognised by liberation theologians. The critical question then is, how does theoretical reflection relate to pre-theoretical believing reading of Scripture? Vander Goot's explication of this relationship is the one which I feel most comfortable with (cf. H. VANDER GOOT, *Interpreting the Bible in Theology and the Church* [New York; Toronto: Edwin Mellen, 1984]). He argues for the priority of the 'direct' reading of Scripture and insists that biblical studies should be funded by the same worldview as that of the text. "Only under such circumstances is the Bible's total claim properly acknowledged" (ibid., 83). Biblical theology should deepen insight into and elaborate on the apprehensions of faith that result from the direct use of the Bible in the community of faith.

[30] This statement is quoted by Wolterstorff at the outset of his *Art in Action* (Grand Rapids: Eerdmans, 1980). It was here that the statement attracted my attention.

postmodernism personhood is more basic to reality than language. Ricoeur's approach, which insists that we bring experience to language is of this sort, and is an alternative to deconstruction which makes language fundamental to reality.[32] Such a communication approach to texts positions a text in the hermeneutical framework:

SENDER – MESSAGE – RECEIVER[33]

7.3.2 The Priority of the Text in Exegesis

The contention of this model of exegesis is that the OT texts in the form that we have them should be the focus of interpretation, since it is through *this* text that we get at the message.[34] Lategan is correct when he says that

> the text represents the solidification of a preceding communication event. It is the deposit of a prior encounter between sender (e.g. Moses or Jesus) and receiver (e.g. Israel or the disciples). In the process of becoming a written text, the message may pass through various stages ... *but the text represents also the first stage in the process of reinterpretation. The latter has as its aim a new communication event, this time between text and contemporary receiver.*[35]

---

31 For a philosophical defence of this position see P. RICOEUR, *Interpretation Theory: Discourse and the Surplus of Meaning* (Texas: Texas Christian UP, 1976). From a linguistic position the most well known proponents of this type of model are R. JAKOBSON, "Closing Statement: Linguistics and Poetics," in: T.A. SEBEOK (ed.), *Style in Language* (1960) 350-377; and J.L. AUSTIN, *How to Do Things With Words* (2nd ed.; Oxford: OUP, 1975). Although Ricoeur defends a communication model of interpretation, he is critical of authorial discourse interpretation of texts. See below for a discussion of this.

32 Cf. M.J. VALDÉS (ed.), *A Ricoeur Reader: Reflection and Imagination* (Harvester Wheatsheaf: London, 1991) 5-6.

33 Within Biblical Studies B. LATEGAN, "Hermeneutics," in: D.N. FREEDMAN (ed.), *ABD* Vol. III (1992) 149-154, has applied this model in developing a biblical hermeneutic. According to Lategan, the value of a communication model is that "[w]hen the full scope of the problem ... is taken as the point of departure, it becomes possible to classify methods in terms of the specific aspect they address and to select the most suitable method in each case." L.C. JONKER, *Exclusivity and Variety. Perspectives on Multidimensional Exegesis* (Contributions to Biblical Exegesis and Theology 19; Kampen: Kok Pharos, 1997), likewise argues for a communication model as the hermeneutical framework for a plurality of exegetical methodologies in biblical studies. L. ALONSO-SCHÖKEL, *Apuntes de hermenéutica* (2nd ed.; Colección Estructuras y Procesos; Madrid: Editorial Trotta, 1997), 45ff, also proposes an integrated model with a strong communicative dimension. Similarly THISELTON, *New Horizons in Hermeneutics*, argues for the validity of speech act theory in biblical hermeneutics and N. WOLTERSTORFF, *Divine Discourse. Philosophical Reflections on the Claim that God Speaks* (Cambridge: CUP, 1995) has applied speech act theory to a philosophical understanding of the Bible as divine discourse.

34 In some cases the form of the text is unclear. In this case the different possible 'final forms' will need to be explored. Cf. D.J.A. Clines, *The Esther Scroll. The Story of the Story* (JSOTSup 30; Sheffield: JSOT, 1984) on Esther. WATSON, *Text, Church and World*, 16, helpfully refers to "the relative stabilization of the text."

35 LATEGAN, "Hermeneutics," 152 (the italics are mine).

A communication approach directs us to this new communication event as the focus of interpretation, and clearly the text in its present form mediates the message that is at the heart of the new communication event.

The expression commonly used to refer to this object of interpretation is '*final form*'. I am hesitant about this nomenclature for it may imply that we have access to the earlier forms of *this* text but that we choose to make the final form the object of our exegesis. In this case 'final form' falsely implies that this *same text* existed in a number of different forms. In fact this is never so. We only have the OT texts that we have, and any reconstructed earlier 'forms' are generally speculative and based on readings of the 'final form'. This is particularly problematic when one bears in mind the cultural and time gap between these ANE texts and our era. Furthermore a reconstructed earlier version is a different text; for example the 'Qoheleth' that many scholars reconstruct from the 'final form' of Ecclesiastes is not the same text as Ecclesiastes. 'Final form' also tends to carry with it the synchronic-diachronic tension between historical critical and canonical readings of the OT that is evident in Childs' canonical approach. A text may of course have a very complex pre-history but in its literary form it is far more than the sum of its component parts.

Does such a view of the text as communicative address take sufficient account of the difference between a written and a spoken communication act? According to Ricoeur "no interpretation theory is possible that does not come to grips with the problem of writing."[36] In Ricoeur's view writing differs from an oral speech act in that it fixes the 'said' of speaking, alters the connection of the message to the speaker so that the text becomes semantically autonomous, potentially universalises the message, makes the relation between message and code more complex, and shatters the grounding of reference in the dialogical situation.[37] Nevertheless, in Ricoeur's view, the semantic autonomy of the text is still governed by the dialectic of event and meaning.[38] This is a complex issue but Wolterstorff is correct in my opinion, when he argues that "Ricoeur was right to look for a practice of interpretation located in the space between Romanticism and structuralism. But what occupies that space is not the practice of textual sense interpretation but the practice of authorial-discourse interpretation – a specific version of this being the practice of reading sacred texts to discern divine discourse."[39] Elsewhere Wolterstorff elaborates on this when he writes:

---

[36] RICOEUR, *Interpretation Theory*, 25.

[37] Ibid., 25-37.

[38] Cf. VALDÉS (ed.), *A Ricoeur Reader*, 6.

[39] WOLTERSTORFF, *Divine Discourse*, 152. See pp. 130-152 for a thorough discussion of this aspect of Ricoeur's proposal, and cf. THISELTON, *New Horizons in Hermeneutics*, 361ff, on Ricoeur's rejection of a dialogue model with respect to texts, and the resulting failure to take 'implicature' seriously. See also ibid., 68-75, for theological arguments for reading Scripture as communicative address rather than as disembodied texts. Thiselton prefers the term "address" to

We have to liberate ourselves from the grip of the notion that there is nothing between Romanticism and Structuralism. In addition to an author's intentions, and in addition to an author's text, there is what the author did in fact say by authoring his text. Not what he *intended* to say; what he *did* say. ... So we can set as the goal of our interpretation discerning what an author said.[40]

To privilege the text as the focus of interpretation is not to deny the possibility of a text being so incoherent that it becomes necessary to posit a number of texts rather than a single text.[41] At the end of the day the proof of the pudding of any hermeneutic will be in the eating. As we have seen, though, historical criticism has often been too quick to move in this direction. In this respect NC, as we observed in chapter four, is a helpful reaction to such disintegration by insisting that the focus of literary study should be texts themselves, and that the literary unity of texts is often complex and full of tensions. In OT studies the literary nature of OT texts has been repeatedly confirmed through the application of literary methods to OT texts, thereby showing that what have often been assumed to be contradictions and reduplications are literary features of the text. The history of 'contradictions' in Ecclesiastes is a good example of this.

7.3.3 The *Sender-Message* Relationship: Genetic Criticism

Although in a communication model the text is the focus as the means to the message, such a model is always aware that the directedness of the text is a result of the activity of the sender/s. All texts, and especially OT ones are historically and culturally embedded so that explication of their message will always need to take the sender-message relationship seriously. In reaction to positivism NC often went too far in denying the need to take the historical aspect seriously in interpretation. The type of legacy of this focus on the literary at the expense of the historical in criticism is the tension that many biblical scholars feel today between synchronic and diachronic readings of biblical texts. The weakness of Frei's and Lindbeck's narrative hermeneutic, for example, is its failure to do justice to the referential/historical aspect of biblical texts.[42] The model of OT hermeneutics that I am proposing, while it insists on privileging the OT texts as we have them as the focus of interpretation, refuses to drive a wedge between the synchronic and diachronic aspects of biblical texts. The text as the instantiation of a

---

"communication", since the latter is often linked in people's minds with an unproblematic transfer of information.

[40] N. WOLTERSTORFF, "The Importance of Hermeneutics for a Christian Worldview," in: R. LUNDIN (ed.), *Disciplining Hermeneutics* (1997) 44.

[41] See our comments below on text structure.

[42] As WATSON, *Text, Church and World*, 19-29; and K.J. VANHOOZER, *Biblical Narrative in the Philosophy of Paul Ricoeur. A Study in Hermeneutics and Philosophy* (Cambridge: CUP, 1990) argue.

communication event comes into existence at a certain historical point – in all its synchroneity it is embedded in history, and it is crucial that this historical aspect of the text be taken seriously in interpretation.

The assumption of a tension between synchronic and diachronic readings of texts is common in OT studies today. Levenson is a good example of such a view.[43] He exposes the radical tension between a historical critical as opposed to a literary reading of the OT. In the preface he expresses his "own intuition ... that the two seemingly opposite directions in which these essays move are each indispensable avenues to the larger and more encompassing truth. The dignity both of traditional interpretation and of modern criticism depends on a careful separation of the two and a reengagement on new terms."[44] How these two antithetical approaches might lead to this larger truth is never explained; indeed Levenson has driven a wedge in between the historical and the traditional contexts and what Thiselton says of Morgan should be said of Levenson at this point: "Rather than aim for a shift of emphasis between two paradigms, might not a more constructive task be the welding together of a more comprehensive hermeneutical model which seeks to draw on the strength of each approach while avoiding its distinctive weaknesses?"[45] Sternberg too points in a similar direction in his strong denial that a literary interpretation can avoid historical questions.

However 'welding together' will not be enough if the underlying assumptions of Levenson are not also exposed. In chapter 5 Levenson exposes the Enlightenment underpinnings of the historical method but still tends to affirm its neutral validity in this chapter and the rest of the book.[46] In my opinion this retaining of an area of study as neutral is a legacy of 'positivism' which itself needs to be undermined.

A communication model of textuality alerts us to the need to explore the questions of authorship and readership and their respective worlds in a way that refuses to set the diachronic and the synchronic at odds with each other. With most OT texts, we have no external information in these respects so that we are inevitably pushed back to the text itself for information. The critical question is *how* to take the historical aspect seriously in OT exegesis. Watson (intratextual realism), Wright (critical realism), Vanhoozer (speech act theory) and Thiselton (pastoral hermeneutic) all argue, albeit in different ways, for a 'final form' approach which still takes the historical aspect of biblical texts seriously. Much of Watson's, Wright's and Vanhoozer's concern is with historical narrative texts in which the referential question surfaces in a way that it does not in Ecclesiastes. Historical critical interpretation does however affect the interpretation of

---

[43] LEVENSON, *The Hebrew Bible*.
[44] Ibid., xiv, xv.
[45] A.C. THISELTON, "On Models and Methods. A Conversation with Robert Morgan," in: D.J.A. CLINES (ed.), *The Bible in Three Dimensions* (1990) 341.
[46] LEVENSON, *The Hebrew Bible*, 106-126.

Ecclesiastes in relation to source, form, redaction and tradition criticism in which earlier forms of the text are reconstructed and become the focus of interpretation.

Within OT poetics Sternberg has made what I regard as the most helpful proposals about reconstructing the relationship between source criticism and literary readings of the text.[47] Sternberg regards NC as an unbalanced reaction to the excesses of historical scholarship in that it sought to bracket out historical questions in textual interpretation. This is just impossible according to Sternberg; even to understand Biblical Hebrew requires historical study and "[a]s with linguistic code, so with artistic code."[48] "But is the language any more or less of a historical datum to be reconstructed than the artistic conventions, the reality-model, the value system?"[49] The text has no meaning outside of an historical context: "The appropriate coordinates are historical, and the main trouble with the historical approaches to the Bible is their antihistorical performance."[50]

This antihistorical tendency is clearly seen, according to Sternberg, in the faulty application of source criticism that has been so dominant in OT studies. "Rarely has there been such a futile expense of spirit in a noble cause; rarely have such grandiose theories of origination been built and revised and pitted against one another on the evidential equivalent of the head of a pin; rarely have so many worked so long and so hard with so little to show for their trouble."[51] This is not to deride the question of genesis; "the only point at issue between them is where and how the appeal to the genetic option serves a purpose."[52]

Sternberg maintains that broadly speaking approaches to the Bible are of two sorts: source- and discourse-oriented inquiries.[53] These approaches are distinguished by the object of inquiry. Source criticism is dealt with by the theologian, historian, linguist and geneticist. It focuses on the biblical world (usually part of it) as it really was. The historian, for example, tries to determine what happened in Israelite history. The geneticist focuses on the processes that shaped the biblical text, the passage from oral to written transmission etc. Discourse analysis focuses on the text itself as a pattern of meaning and effect; to pursue this line of questioning is to make sense of the discourse in terms of communication. Discourse-oriented analysis seeks to understand the text as a

> pattern of meaning and effect. What does this piece of language ... signify in context? What are the rules governing the transaction between storyteller or poet and reader? Are the operative rules, for instance, those of prose or verse, parable or chronicle, omniscience or realistic limitation, historical or fictional

---

[47] M. STERNBERG, *The Poetics of Biblical Narrative. Ideological Literature and the Drama of Reading* (Bloomington: Indiana University Press, 1985) 7-23.

[48] Ibid., 12.

[49] Ibid., 10.

[50] Ibid., 11.

[51] Ibid., 13.

[52] Ibid., 14.

[53] Ibid., 14-15.

writing? … To pursue this line of questioning is to make sense of the discourse in terms of communication, always goal-directed on the speaker's part and always requiring interpretive activity on the addressee's.[54]

Sternberg argues strongly for a community of labour; the better we understand the context the better we will understand the text and vice versa. Source analysis is particularly dependent on understanding of the text because apart from the biblical texts we know very little of the context. Thus, "[t]he movement from text to reality cannot but pass through interpretation. If the Bible is a work of literature, therefore, nobody can evade the consequences. As reader, for example, the historian must take into account that every item of reality given in the text may have been stylized by conventions and for purposes alien to historical science."[55]

Discourse and source analysis do not even enjoy temporal priority over each other. "Both the interpreter and the historian must perforce combine the two viewpoints throughout, incessantly moving between given discourse and source in an endeavour to work out the best fit, until they reach some firm conclusion."[56] What varies is the object of study. Where the object is to make sense of the discourse, conjecture about the source operates as an aid to interpretation and discovery of its artful rules. Discourse and genetic analysis only become rivals when they cross their boundaries and, for example, the source critic imposes her reconstruction of the sources and process of composition on the text's structure.

In biblical interpretation, we maintain that the primary object of study is the text as discourse so that source analysis will always be secondary to interpretation of the text. Form, source, redaction and tradition criticism all have their place in the study of the sender-message relationship but understanding of the text as a whole must remain the goal towards which interpretative energies are directed. Clearly the type of model for understanding genetic criticism that Sternberg has proposed has radical implications for traditional genetic criticism as historical critics have practised it. Historical critics have tended to focus on the genetic pole of the genetic-discourse dialectic with often disastrous consequences for discourse analysis. While maintaining the validity of the genetic aspect of biblical interpretation it is vital that the dialectic between source and discourse analysis be recognised.

7.3.4 The Type of Message: Textual Type or Genre

Genre is inseparable from the communicative nature of texts, as some of the metaphors used by scholars to describe genre indicate. Wellek and Warren refer to genre as an 'institution'.

---

54 Ibid., 15.
55 Ibid., 16.
56 Ibid., 19.

One can work through, express oneself through, existing institutions, create new ones, or get on, so far as possible, without sharing in polities or rituals; one can also join, but then reshape, institutions. Theory of genres is a principle of order. ... Any critical and evaluative – as distinct from historical – study involves, in some form, the appeal to such structures.[57]

Other metaphors used of genre are contracts, codes, games, deep and surface structure and patterns of expression.[58] These metaphors point to the character of genres as general, publicly known means of expressing a type of message. Ricoeur helpfully points out that

genres are generative devices to produce discourse as ... Before being classificatory devices used by literary critics to orient themselves in the profusion of literary works, therefore being artefacts of criticism, they are to discourse what generative grammar is to the grammaticality of individual sentences. ... The function of these generative devices is to produce new entities of language longer than the sentence, organic wholes irreducible to a mere addition of sentences. ... Language is submitted to the rules of a kind of craftsmanship, which allows us to speak of production and works of art, and, by extension of works of discourse. Poems, narratives, and essays are such works of discourse. The generative devices, which we call literary genres, are the technical rules presiding over their production.[59]

Consequently, at the macro level one of the major constraints of the way we read texts is the textual type or genre of the text.[60] Morgan argues that

[t]exts, like dead men and women have no rights, no aims, no interests. They can be used in whatever way readers or interpreters choose ... in all cases it is the interests or aims of the interpreter that are decisive, not the claims of the text as such. Any suggestion that the text has rights is a deception concealing someone else's interests.[61]

---

[57] R. WELLEK and A. WARREN, *Theory of Literature* (3rd ed.; London: Penguin, 1963) 226.

[58] T. LONGMAN, *Fictional Akkadian Autobiography. A Generic and Comparative Study* (Winona Lake: Eisenbrauns, 1991) 8-9.

[59] RICOEUR, *Interpretation Theory*, 32, 33.

[60] Cf C. NORRIS, *Spinoza and the Origins of Modern Critical Theory* (The Bucknell Lectures in Literary Theory; Oxford: Basil Blackwell, 1991) 206, 207. Speaking of Spinoza as not belonging to those who regard *interpretation* as the normal mode of literary-critical activity, Norris points out that "[t]his alternative tradition goes right back to Aristotle, with his stress on the virtues of an orderly, disciplined method of approach that starts out from observed regularities of structure in various types of text, and then proceeds inductively to specify the rules or conventions governing that genre. The most obvious heirs of Aristotelian thinking are those modern formalist or structuralist movements which likewise see no virtue in producing ever more sophisticated interpretations of individual texts, but concentrate rather on the various poetic devices ... that characterize literary discourse in general." In this way genre functions as an important part of the resistance of a text to being read in any way.

[61] R. MORGAN with J. BARTON, *Biblical Interpretation* (Oxford Bible Series; Oxford: OUP, 1988) 7. Morgan's view is more nuanced than this quote taken by itself may suggest. See chapter one of *Biblical Interpretation*.

A communicative model, however, refuses to make the aims of the interpreter decisive in this way but insists that the primary responsibility of the interpreter is to read the text along the grain, as it were, in order to discern the message of the text.[62] Texts in this view do have rights, aims and interests, and these need to be taken seriously if the text is to be read and criticised *objectively*. Text are an expression of *interpersonal* communication, and just as we cannot do as we like with people so there are ethics of reading. A communicative model reminds us of the need to respect the otherness of the text and to allow *its* voice to be heard.

This stress on reading biblical texts objectively should not be seen as a reassertion of historical criticism in its classic modern mode. A distinction should, I suggest, be made between *thick* and *thin* notions of objectivity. The thin[63] rationalist understanding of objectivity which reduces the truth of biblical texts to rational propositions and the thin historical-critical approach which generally fails to recognise the literary and kerygmatic nature of biblical texts because of its overwhelming interest in history should be rejected as distorting the biblical texts.[64] However it would be quite wrong to relinquish *any* notion of objectivity or realism, as some postmoderns do. The point is that a reductionistic Enlightenment understanding of objectivity should be rejected because it fails to take into account a variety of factors that influence the acquisition of knowledge,[65] and it yields a narrow view of biblical textuality. A thicker notion of method *and* of biblical textuality is required, since interpretation involves both of these elements. But this means broadening rather than abandoning the quest for objectivity entirely, as some postmodern thinkers are prone to do.

A thicker notion of biblical texts is required which takes into account their historical, literary *and* ideological/theological aspects.[66] Such a notion of textuality needs to be matched by a thicker notion of readers which takes into

---

[62] However important it may be to read texts *against* the grain, before this can be done they first have to be read along the grain.

[63] I am using thin here as a metaphor for reductionistic.

[64] Note that both fundamentalist hermeneutics (propositionalism) and liberal hermeneutics have been deeply influenced by modernity, albeit in quite different directions.

[65] Feminist epistemology, for example, has alerted us to the role of gender and subjectivity in the knowing process. S. HARDING (ed.), *Feminism and Methodology* (Milton Keynes: Open UP, 1987) 9, helpfully points out that "the beliefs and behaviors of the researcher ... must be open to critical scrutiny no less than what is traditionally defined as relevant evidence. Introducing this 'subjective' element into the analysis in fact increases the objectivity of the research and decreases the 'objectivism' which hides this kind of evidence from the public." CLOUSER, *The Myth of Religious Neutrality*, argues for taking religious presuppositions seriously in accounts of theory. In my opinion a thick objectivity or what one might call a *critical* realism needs to take all these factors into account.

[66] In NT studies WRIGHT, *The New Testament and the People of God*, has attempted to develop such a thick notion of biblical texts, and in OT studies STERNBERG, *The Poetics of Biblical Narrative*, has argued along similar lines.

account religion, gender, culture, historical period and so on. In our history-dominated context, careful consideration of the genre of texts can be particularly helpful in resisting imposition of thin methodologies upon texts since it forces one to take the different aspects of the biblical texts seriously.[67]

In discourse analysis of the tagmemic sort some highly creative work is starting to be done on textual types, particularly as these relate to narrative biblical texts.[68] Unfortunately very little of this sort of work has yet been done on wisdom texts. Textual type/genre shapes the entire work so that it is crucial to correct interpretation that the interpreter picks up on the type and is aware of the rules for that genre. As we saw in chapter five, and as we stressed in the section on genetic discourse above, genre determination will be a joint historical-literary venture. The concept of genre also needs to be a flexible one, which refuses to squeeze texts into preconceived patterns and recognises the individual structure of a text.[69] Genre remains however a crucial factor in objective interpretation.

7.3.5 The Individuality of the Message: Text Structure

A communication model of interpretation alerts us to the particularity of each text, and, whereas genre is something that a text shares with other texts, structure is more specific to a text. All texts have some structure. The idea of a text or work carries with it notions of developing unity and coherence. Where these break down completely one would conclude that one is not dealing with a work or unified text. Bradbury argues rightly that

> [a]ll critical theories have some notion of structure: the developing unity of a work. ... I here assume what I think must be assumed for criticism effectively to exist: that every work is a distinct and verbally-created universe and must have a self-created logic or sequence for which the author is responsible. The work will have its own expectations and probabilities which constitute the unity of that universe.[70]

Coherence of relationships, actions, rhetorical devices, and attitudes are part of this unity, as Bradbury points out. Structural analysis seeks to lay bare the way in which these different elements contribute to the developing coherence of a particular text.

Internal (derived from the text itself) and external (derived from outside the text) means exist for gaining access to the coherence of a work. In chapter four

---

[67] As we saw in ch. 5.

[68] See D.A. DAWSON, *Text-Linguistics and Biblical Hebrew* (JSOTSup 177; Sheffield: Sheffield Academic Press, 1994).

[69] Croce's denial of the existence of genre is an extreme position, but it is understandable as a reaction against the '*genre tranché*' of classicism (WELLEK and WARREN, *Theory of Literature*, 233-234). This over reaction correctly recognises the individuality of each text and the importance of an inductive, historical approach to the question of genre.

[70] M. BRADBURY, "Structure," in: R. FOWLER (ed.), *Modern Critical Terms* (1987) 235.

we examined the structuralists' (external) attempt to lay bare the deep structures of different types of literature. This is a helpful area of research provided it is understood as an investigation of what lies behind a text rather than analysis of the text itself. For biblical interpretation the surface structure of the text is more important, and, insofar as the connection between deep and surface structures can be articulated, structuralism has much to offer. Discourse analysis of the way textual type shapes syntax[71] is another example of how external means can be helpful in discerning textual structure. And analyses of the poetics of narrative structure have been found to illuminate the coherence of biblical texts in all sorts of insightful ways.

If it is right to think of deep structure as analysis of genre then what we are after is the way in which a genre/ deep structure has come to the *particular* shape of the text we are examining. In the latter respect the internal means of deriving structure are particularly important, means such as study of the individual texts' rhetorical techniques such as inclusions, repetitions, chiasm and so on. Clearly these cannot be separated either from the content of the text or from 'external' and historical studies of such techniques. Structural analysis will inevitably involve a dialectic between generalised notions of deep structure, genre, discourse-type and rhetoric and the shape of the individual text.[72]

7.3.6 The World of the Message: Intertextuality

I am using intertextuality here not in the polemical sense of *intertextuality* as opposed to *intersubjectivity*[73] but in the sense of pre-understanding and "inner-biblical" exegesis.[74] A communication model of biblical hermeneutics will involve exploring the world of the text and the world of the sender, and their interrelationship. In terms of genetic criticism the OT forms an indispensable part of the historical context of any OT text. However, the OT also comes to us as part of Hebrew and Christian Scripture and this aspect of the text cannot be ignored, as Childs has repeatedly pointed out.[75] An approach to the OT as Christian Scripture would expect a general understanding of the whole to be a helpful prejudice/preunderstanding in approaching the part. In this sense biblical theology and Christian doctrine should form part of the prejudice with which the reader

---

[71] See DAWSON, *Text-Linguistics and Biblical Hebrew*.

[72] STERNBERG, *The Poetics of Biblical Narrative*, 56-57, notes that "[i]n most of the theoretical work that I have done, on narrative and other subjects, the Bible has proved a corrective to widely held doctrines about literary structure and analysis, often a pointer to the formation of alternatives. In my biblical work, conversely, seldom have I found a narrative or strategy proceeding along the theoretically expected grooves or, after the event, failing to illuminate a host of other corpora and traditions."

[73] See THISELTON, *New Horizons in Hermeneutics*, 41.

[74] This is Fishbane's expression (M. FISHBANE, *Biblical Interpretation in Ancient Israel* [Oxford: Clarendon, 1985]; see especially pp. 2-19).

[75] See also WOLTERSTORFF, *Divine Discourse*, 204-208.

comes to the text. However, particular care must be taken that this prejudice is not simply read into the biblical text (eisegesis) but that it allows the text to speak on its own terms. Inner-biblical exegesis can be of help in this respect in examining how a text uses parts of other biblical texts.[76]

7.3.7 The Message of the Text: The Implied Author

A communication model hermeneutic alerts us to discernment of the message as the goal of biblical interpretation.[77] In literary texts, including the OT, the message is not always immediately obvious. This remains true even if we agree with Sternberg that the biblical authors adopted a foolproof method of composition.[78] The movement from the truth to the whole truth of a biblical text is always via the literary contours of a biblical text. A helpful way of getting at this overall message of the text is the notion of the implied author.

The notion of the implied author is developed by Booth.[79] The implied author refers to where the author wants the reader to stand in the world of values. "In short, the author's judgement is always present, always evident to anyone who knows how to look for it."[80] "As he writes, he creates not simply an ideal, impersonal 'man in general' but an implied version of 'himself' that is different from the implied authors we meet in other men's works."[81] Other terms for the implied author are the official scribe, the author's second self.[82] The implied author is not to be confused with the narrator or the "I" of a work, these more commonly refer to the speaker in the work "who is after all only one of the elements created by the implied author and who may be separated from him by

---

[76] See THISELTON, *New Horizons in Hermeneutics*, 39-42, for some helpful comments on Fishbane's inner-biblical exegetical method.

[77] See WOLTERSTORFF, *Divine Discourse*, 183-222, for a very useful discussion of the relationship between interpreting the mediating human discourse and interpreting for the mediated divine discourse. In the hermeneutic method that I am outlining I have not elaborated on this second stage of interpreting the mediated divine discourse. This is not because I regard it as unimportant! Rather, as Wolterstorff makes clear, one gets at the second stage always via the first. "The most fundamental principle, I submit, is this: the interpreter takes the stance and content of my appropriating discourse to be that of your appropriated discourse, unless there is good reason to do otherwise" (ibid., 204).

[78] See STERNBERG, *The Poetics of Biblical Narrative*, 230ff. In conversation with Sternberg it became clear to me that he uses foolproof composition to refer to the basic contours of the narrative rather than specifically to the message of the text. The latter may be located more at the indeterminate margins of the text, and is always arrived at via the poetics of the narrative.

[79] W. BOOTH, *The Rhetoric of Fiction* (2nd ed.; London: Penguin, 1983).

[80] Ibid., 20.

[81] Ibid., 70.

[82] Ibid., 71.

large ironies. 'Narrator' is usually taken to mean the 'I' of a work, but the 'I' is seldom if ever identical with the implied image of the artist."[83]

> Our sense of the implied author includes not only the extractable meanings but also the moral and emotional content of each bit of action and suffering of all the characters. It includes, in short, the intuitive apprehension of a completed artistic whole; the chief value to which *this* implied author is committed, regardless of what party his creator belongs to in real life, is that which is expressed by the total form.[84]

In his work on biblical narrative Sternberg finds Booth's notion of the implied author irrelevant because in biblical narrative the implied author and narrator merge into each other. For Sternberg what is important is that "the distance between the historical writer and the implied author/narrator is so marked, indeed unbridgeable, that they not only can but must be distinguished."[85] However, as we have seen, Fox has suggested that in Ecclesiastes the implied author may be distinct from the narrator, in which case Booth's distinction of the two may still have merit for biblical interpretation. Either way, to think in terms of an implied author or an implied author-narrator is helpful in focusing biblical interpretation on the message of the text. As Sternberg points out this is inevitable:

> [t]he author/narrator exists only as a construct, which the reader infers and fills out to make sense of the work as an ordered design of meaning and effect. ... Where our interpretations differ, so do our reconstructions of his image – ways, means, and all. But reconstruct him according to our lights we must, all of us, not excluding the most dedicated geneticist. For a moment's thought will reveal that the very fragmentation of a biblical tale into sources, documents, etc. presupposes a unity distinctive of some teller, and the triumphant pointing to some version as *the* original form announces his disentanglement from the overall process of transmission.[86]

7.3.8 The Receiver/s of the Message: The Reader and the Text

The reader is the recipient of the message embodied in the text, according to a communication model hermeneutic. The notion of the implied reader fits well with this approach. "The author creates, in short, an image of himself and another image of his reader; he makes his reader, as he makes his second self, and the most successful reading is one in which the created selves, author and reader, can

---

83   Ibid., 73. This is the mistake that Perdue makes (cf. L.G. PERDUE, *Wisdom and Creation. The Theology of Wisdom Literature* [Nashville: Abingdon, 1994] 202). As Booth points out, "In any reading experience there is an implied dialogue among author, narrator, the other characters, and the reader. Each of the four can range, in relation to each of the others, from identification to complete opposition" (BOOTH, *The Rhetoric of Fiction*, 155-158).

84   Ibid., 73-74.

85   STERNBERG, *The Poetics of Biblical Narrative*, 74, 75.

86   Ibid., 75.

find complete agreement."[87] Each biblical text is historically embedded and the way to the message is via the first horizon. As with the sender of the message the initial readership has to be reconstructed mainly via the text. Although the implied author and the implied reader are always constructs of the reader, this approach maximises the constraints of the text in interpretation. Fundamental to the process of biblical interpretation is the attempt to hear the message of the text in this way.

Current methods of interpretation have often undermined this approach to biblical interpretation. Clines has gone so far as to suggest that this approach to interpretation may be unethical, because it may require a reader to position herself against her deepest beliefs.[88] Clines has a point in that Booth is, I think, wrong in suggesting that the most successful reading is always that in which the created selves find complete agreement. Ethically, certain texts are most successfully read when reader and implied author/implied reader are opposed. The point is though, that before one can disagree with a text one has to read it, and to do so along the grain. Feminist and materialist critiques, to mention only two, can *follow* such a reading but should not – indeed cannot – precede it.[89]

Defending the importance of the first horizon in biblical interpretation does not mean ignoring the second horizon. In any textual interpretation the two will be in constant dynamic interaction. As the history of biblical interpretation demonstrates, what is brought to a text influences the way it is read. Subjective and communal factors play a significant role in all interpretation, and critical consciousness of these is vital in biblical interpretation. As Thiselton has argued, biblical interpretation is about the fusion of two horizons, that of the biblical text and that of the reader.[90] Interpretation takes place at the fusion of these horizons

---

[87] BOOTH, *The Rhetoric of Fiction*, 138.

[88] D.J.A. CLINES, "Possibilities and Priorities of Biblical Interpretation in an International Perspective," *BI* 1/1 (1993) 86-87.

[89] For a useful survey of the variety of approaches to the reader in literary theory see S.R. SULEIMAN, "Introduction: Varieties of Audience-Oriented Criticism," in: S.R. SULEIMAN and I. CROSMAN (eds.), *The Reader in the Text. Essays on Audience and Interpretation* (1980) 3-45. Suleiman distinguishes between positive and negative hermeneutics. The former upholds the pervasive notion of the unity and wholeness of the text and the existence and possibility of discovering meaning, the very things which negative hermeneutics deny. This denial of the unity of the text is connected with fragmented views of the self, i.e. with anthropology. As Suleiman perceptively comments, "That there exists a strong correlation between theories of the self and theories of the text has not escaped the more perspicacious of today's literary critics; nor has the correlation between both theories of self *and* of text and larger philosophical issues. Indeed, I think it is the recognition of these correlations and of their consequences that accounts for the passionately polemical tone in the debate between 'positive' and 'negative' theorists of interpretation" (ibid., 42). A positive hermeneutic and the sort of view of the reader I argue follows from a Christian hermeneutical model, in my opinion.

[90] A.C. THISELTON, *The Two Horizons. New Testament Hermeneutics and Philosophical Description* (Carlisle: Paternoster; Grand Rapids: Eerdmans, 1980) 15-16.

and the biblical interpreter needs to be sensitive to the elements in both horizons and how these affect interpretation.

For example, Western individualism and privatised religion have regularly been read into biblical texts, whereas in fact they are concepts deeply alien to biblical religion.[91] I have suggested that there is a certain reader 'baggage' which aids the objective reading of biblical texts, baggage such as a commitment to these texts as Christian Scripture. In this sense Bibliotropic exegesis is the ideal. However, in order to bring hidden baggage to light, interpretations within one community ought to be in dialogue with interpretations of the same text within other communities. In this respect dialogue of Christian interpreters with Enlightenment historical critical readings or other religious readings can be very helpful.

A Christian model of biblical interpretation should ultimately never be individual. Scripture can only be approached as Scripture in community, and this implies a system of checks and balances within the community within which one works. This does not mean however that academic biblical interpretation should all ideally be done within the institutional church. Academic biblical interpretation fits, in my view, within the university, as long as the biblical scholar is genuinely free to allow her religious presuppositions to shape her exegesis.

7.4 *Reading* Ecclesiastes

Such texts as Job, Ecclesiastes, and the parables do not function primarily as raw-material for Christian doctrine. ... Their primary function is to invite or to provoke the reader to wrestle actively with the issues, in ways that may involve adopting a series of comparative angles of vision.

(A.C. THISELTON, *New Horizons in Hermeneutics* [Grand Rapids: Zondervan, 1992] 65, 66)

Our concern in this section is to apply the above communication model of OT exegesis to Ecclesiastes.[92]

7.4.1 Reading *Ecclesiastes*

One of the legacies of modernity in the history of the interpretation of Ecclesiastes is that the present form of Ecclesiastes is hardly ever consciously

---

[91] On the issue of the modern distinction between secular and religious and its relationship to wisdom literature see R.E. MURPHY, "Wisdom – Theses and Hypotheses," in: J.G. GAMMIE, et al. (eds.), *Israelite Wisdom. Theological and Literary Essays in Honor of Samuel Terrien* (1978) 40. Murphy rightly points out that this modern conceptual disjunction is not applicable to OT thought.

[92] It is important to note that what I am proposing are preliminary soundings. The intention of this chapter is not to argue in detail for a definitive interpretation of Ecclesiastes but to show the directions that my hermeneutic proposal might open up.

read as a literary whole.[93] Historical criticism has made a habit of reconstructing *Qoheleth* and then reading this 'earlier form' of the text, with the epilogue (12:9-14) in particular always understood as a later addition to Qoheleth. As I demonstrated in chapter three this remains the dominant way of 'reading' 'Ecclesiastes'. A rare exception to this is Fox who reads Ecclesiastes as a literary unity.[94]

An implication of a communication model of OT exegesis is that exegesis must privilege Ecclesiastes rather than 'Qoheleth',[95] and must take the circular "intent at totality of the interpretative process" seriously.[96] This, as we saw in chapter four, is one of the great strengths of the New Critical approach to literary texts.[97] The hermeneutical circle is involved in all interpretation, including that of the historical critical approach which reconstructs Ecclesiastes before the 'real' interpretation begins. As we saw in chapter three this is the legacy of the application of a wooden source-critical method to the text which ignores its crafted literary character. Even in this hermeneutic, however, there has to be a move from the text in its final form as we have it to the reconstructed text, i.e. a move from trying to read the whole to a conclusion that the whole is incoherent and the text must be divided to be read in layers. Few scholars would still defend the way early historical critical readers of Ecclesiastes came to this conclusion, and yet the legacy of that conclusion lingers, particularly in relation to the epilogue, but *without* the process involved in that initial circular attempt at totality always being made conscious. Indeed, our contention is that the legacy of the early historical critical readings of Ecclesiastes is allowed to occupy the space of that initial circular intent in most modern readings of Ecclesiastes. This is however unacceptable. The conclusion that a text cannot be read as a whole should come at the end (or middle) of a hermeneutic process and not at the

---

[93] Note that this has nothing to do with textual criticism. Cf. R.E. MURPHY, *Ecclesiastes* (WBC; Texas: Word, 1992) xxiv, on the faithful transmission of the text. If the final form of Ecclesiastes is stable, it should be noted however that "[t]he book is exceedingly difficult to translate ... because of our ignorance of the precise nuances of the terminology and of Qoheleth's thought" (R.E. MURPHY, *The Tree of Life. An Exploration of Biblical Wisdom Literature* [NY; Toronto: Doubleday, 1990] 50).

[94] M.V. FOX, *Qoheleth and His Contradictions* (JSOTSup 71; Sheffield: Almond Press, 1989).

[95] קהלת is the Hebrew name for Ecclesiastes, but in critical scholarship this name is often used for the reconstructed text i.e. the words of Qoheleth, which then becomes the focus of interpretation.

[96] This phrase is De Man's (cf. P. de MAN, *Blindness and Insight. Essays in the Rhetoric of Contemporary Criticism* [2nd ed.; London: Methuen, 1983] 31).

[97] De Man (ibid., 27) rightly points out that "[i]t is true that American textual interpretation and 'close reading' have perfected techniques that allow for considerable refinement in catching the details and nuances of literary expression. They study texts as 'forms,' as groupings from which the constitutive parts cannot be isolated or separated. This gives a sense of context that is often lacking in French or in German interpretations."

beginning, as it so often does. The literary character of Ecclesiastes (see below) makes this historical critical short-circuiting of the circular intent at totality in its interpretation of Ecclesiastes particularly damaging, since it excludes the possibility of the full richness of the carefully crafted literary text becoming explicit.

7.4.2 The Genre of Ecclesiastes

We have already given sustained attention to the genre of Ecclesiastes in chapter five, where we concluded that in terms of comparative historical genre Ecclesiastes is a developed wisdom form of the royal testament or fictional autobiography cast in a frame-narrative.

7.4.3 The Structure of Ecclesiastes: Literary Artistry

The more literary a text is the more important it is to attend to its structure in order to penetrate its message. As the quote from Thiselton at the top of section 7.4 above indicates, Ecclesiastes is a text that is carefully crafted in order to draw us into a discussion. Consequently we will arrive at an understanding of its message only via its poetics.

בקש למצא in 12:10 and אזן, חקר and תקן in 12:9 confirm that Ecclesiastes is a carefully crafted text.[98] Recent scholarship has started to recognise this, as treatment of the 'contradictions' in Ecclesiastes indicates.[99] Clements picks up on this literary character of Ecclesiastes when he writes that

> Qoheleth marks a significant milestone in the progress of wisdom. In the first place there are clear signs that, although the author was accustomed to delivering his teaching orally, he has developed characteristically literary structures and woven short epigrammatic sayings into more extended compositions. Individual sayings have been combined into larger structures which serve to modify, and even challenge, the validity of the shorter individual sayings. Some sections display the form of asserting a thesis, seemingly outrageous, which is then skilfully justified.[100]

Our suggestion is that Ecclesiastes is artistically crafted to a greater extent than Clements recognises. Certainly recognition of the literary craftedness of Ecclesiastes is crucial for its interpretation. In the past historical critical scholars have been too certain that they knew what a book is and what it is not. In Good's

---

[98] Wright's mathematical analysis of Ecclesiastes (see ch. 4) and Skehan's mathematical study of Proverbs (P. SKEHAN, "A Single Editor for the Whole of Proverbs," in: J.L. CRENSHAW [ed.], *Studies in Ancient Israelite Wisdom* [1976] 329-340) support the carefully crafted nature of some wisdom texts.

[99] Cf. for example R.N. WHYBRAY, *Ecclesiastes* (NCBC; London: Marshall, Morgan and Scott; Grand Rapids: Eerdmans, 1989) 17-19.

[100] R.E. CLEMENTS, *Wisdom in Theology* (Carlisle: Paternoster; Grand Rapids: Eerdmans, 1992) 34.

words, they thought that a book is "a unified, logically argued and constructed whole."

> When we discover that Qoheleth as it stands does not fit the definition, we are baffled. We are forced to assume, therefore, either that its disunity, lack of construction, and failure of logic are illusions, to be dispelled if we work hard enough, or that somebody has been tampering with the original, which must *ex hypothesi*, have corresponded to our definition of a 'book'. So we search out the 'original', brush aside all that rings falsely with it, and bask in the warm assurance that once again we have justified our definition of a 'book'.[101]

As Good points out, the fact is that we have before us a 'work' and our responsibility is to permit it to speak for itself. To analyse the book's origin is not to solve its problem, and we "must above all avoid the modernizing error of confusing the person of an author with the integrity of the work. In Qoheleth we have to do with the work, not with a hypothetically reconstructible author."[102] Our proposal is that Ecclesiastes is a carefully crafted work and that investigation of its literary craftedness allows the text to speak in all its colours and shades. Research in this area is in its early stages, and what follows is tentative.

7.4.3.1 Irony: "Wisdom" in Ecclesiastes

A great deal of research has been done on irony in literary studies.[103] Lee discerns two major categories of irony, situational and verbal, which can also be classified further as comic or tragic. Verbal irony, which is what we have to do with in Ecclesiastes,[104] Lee defines as, "an art of indirection and juxtaposition,

---

[101] E.M. GOOD, *Irony in the Old Testament* (Sheffield: Almond Press, 1981) 171-172.

[102] Ibid., 172.

[103] See W. BOOTH, *A Rhetoric of Irony* (Chicago; London: University of Chicago Press, 1974) and L. HUTCHEON, *Irony's Edge. The Theory and Politics of Irony* (London; NY: Routledge, 1994) plus their bibliographies for the extensive material available on irony. W. EMPSON, *Seven Types of Ambiguity* (4th ed.; London: Chalto and Windus, 1963) and the New Critics gave sustained attention to irony, as one would expect. Within OT studies GOOD, *Irony in the Old Testament*, examines irony in the OT including Ecclesiastes, and H. FISCH, *Poetry with a Purpose. Biblical Poetics and Interpretation* (Bloomington; Indianapolis: Indiana UP, 1988) has a chapter on Qoheleth as a "Hebrew Ironist". The standard contemporary commentaries on Ecclesiastes rarely deal with irony. A quick survey of G. OGDEN, *Qoheleth* (Readings – A New Biblical Commentary; Sheffield: JSOT, 1987); MURPHY, *Ecclesiastes*; J.L. CRENSHAW, *Ecclesiastes* (OTL; London: SCM, 1988); N. LOHFINK, *Kohelet* (NEB; Würzburg: Echter Verlag, 1993); PERDUE, *Wisdom and Creation*; CLEMENTS, *Wisdom in Theology*; WHYBRAY, *Ecclesiastes* (NCBC); and A. LAUHA, *Kohelet* (Biblischer Kommentar Altes Testament; Neukirchen: Neukirchener Verlag, 1978) reveals that only in Lauha are there a few minor references to irony!

[104] Studies have also been made of irony in Job (see D.J.A. CLINES, *Job 1-20* [WBC; Texas: Word, 1989] xcvii) and to a lesser extent of irony in Proverbs. For the latter cf. for example L. ALONSO-SCHÖKEL, *A Manual of Hebrew Poetics* (Subsidia Biblica 11; Rome: Editrice Pontificio Istituto Biblico, 1988) 165, for a one page discussion of irony in Proverbs. FISCH, *Poetry with a Purpose*, and GOOD, *Irony in the Old Testament*, contain preliminary discussions of irony in Ecclesiastes. J. VILCHEZ LINDEZ, *Eclesiastes o Qohelet* (Estella, Navarra: Editorial Verba Divino,

relying for its success on such techniques as understatement, paradox, puns and other forms of wit in the expression of incongruities."[105] Irony is, according to Lee, a means for unifying the apparent contradictions of experience and is also able to assert the world's diversity.

The common definition of irony is as saying one thing and meaning the opposite. Irony may be taken literally, "Yet a nagging doubt hints at a meaning hidden behind the mask."[106] Irony is criticism which perceives an incongruity in things as they are, but it is distinguished from other perceptions of incongruity by two characteristics. Firstly it is stated by means of understatement or a method of suggestion rather than of plain statement. Secondly the perception comes from a supposed stance in truth.

An ironic mode of speech dominates much of Ecclesiastes.[107] Our aim here is not to do an exhaustive study of irony in Ecclesiastes but merely to show through one central example how an examination of irony in Ecclesiastes potentially opens up the meaning of the text. Our example is חכמה in Ecclesiastes.

חכמה is the specific means by which Qoheleth conducts his search for meaning 'under the sun' (1:13).[108] Reading Qoheleth within the context of the OT wisdom corpus, and especially after Proverbs, one initially tends to read חכמה positively as that practical and intellectual wisdom that is rooted in the fear of Yahweh and handed on from generation to generation. This is what the text appears to say. As Fox points out, in biblical wisdom literature חכמה and דעת are almost always ethically positive.[109] Indeed, some commentators assume that the meaning of חכמה in Ecclesiastes is very much the same as it is in Proverbs and Job. Ogden, for example, says of חכמה in 1:13 that "[t]he tool for this investigation was 'wisdom' ... by which he means the inherited tradition of the wise men together with its method of observation and reflection."[110] Ogden never explores the precise nuance of חכמה in Ecclesiastes. Even those who do not make quite such a strong equation as Ogden still tend to define חכמה in

---

1994) deals with irony at certain points in his exegesis of Ecclesiastes. See especially pp. 201, 274 and 317.

[105] B. LEE, "Irony," in: R. FOWLER (ed.), *Modern Critical Terms* (1987) 128-129. Another useful introductory article is D.E. COOPER, "Irony," in: D.E. COOPER (ed.), *A Companion to Aesthetics* (Oxford: Blackwell, 1992, 1995) 238-242.

[106] GOOD, *Irony in the Old Testament*, 22.

[107] Cf. FISCH, *Poetry with a Purpose*.

[108] For a discussion of the terminology of wisdom see FOX, *Qoheleth and His Contradictions*, 80-85. It has been suggested that חכמה is the object of לדרוש ולתור in v. 13 but wisdom is best understood here as the means by which Qoheleth investigates life (cf. ibid., 175).

[109] Ibid., 82. Two partial exceptions which Fox mentions are Proverbs 3:5 and 21:30.

[110] OGDEN, *Qoheleth*, 34.

Ecclesiastes in quite general terms and to assume that the empiricism of Qoheleth is much the same as that in the other wisdom books.[111]

However, as one proceeds with Ecclesiastes, it becomes apparent that חכמה here means something very different from its predominantly positive usage in Proverbs. One's nagging doubt becomes a strong sense that Qoheleth's חכמה is something very different to the wisdom which is built on the fear of Yahweh. Fox has given sustained attention to חכמה as part of Qoheleth's epistemology in Ecclesiastes.[112] On the basis of 1:12ff Fox insists that we need to carefully examine Qoheleth's epistemology. The problem of knowledge is central to the book, and although Qoheleth's epistemology is unsystematic, it is not chaotic. Qoheleth's ideas form a coherent whole and allow for systematic exposition.

Fox examines חכמה in Ecclesiastes and concludes that Qoheleth adopted an empirical methodology; he seeks to derive knowledge from experience and to validate his ideas experientially.[113] Fox applies 'empirical' to Qoheleth's method by analogy to Western philosophical empiricism, although he recognises that Qoheleth does not offer a philosophical theory: "we can say that he holds a primitive form of the type of empiricism (the 'weak' form) that maintains that all knowledge comes from experience because every proposition is either a direct report on experience or a report whose truth is inferred from experience."[114]

Fox does acknowledge that much that Qoheleth says comes from traditional learning and impulse, and that some of his ideas are formulated *a priori* (e.g., 3:17; 8:12b) or derive from assumptions that lack experiential grounding (e.g., 7:11-12). Nevertheless, Fox maintains that the 'empirical' label is justified, firstly, by Qoheleth's method, which looks to experience as the source *and* warrant of knowledge, and secondly, by his concept of knowledge, according to which knowledge is created by thought and dependent on perception.[115]

---

[111] WHYBRAY, *Ecclesiastes* (NCBC), 49, simply notes that "Qoheleth's intention is to test the adequacy of human wisdom at its best." MURPHY, *Ecclesiastes*, lxi-lxiv, 13, has an extended note on wisdom in Ecclesiastes but fails to detect the serious difference in method between חכמה in 1:13 compared with most of its occurrences in Proverbs. Indeed, Murphy remarkably suggests that, "Qoheleth is often in conflict with wisdom teaching, but his methodology is nonetheless that of the sage. He frequently reminds the reader how he applied himself with 'wisdom'" (ibid., lxiii). See also J.A. GLADSON, *Retributive Paradoxes in Proverbs 10-29* (Ann Arbor, Michigan: University Microfilms International, 1979) 20) for an example of the assumption that wisdom literature shares a common empirical epistemology. Those scholars like Gladson, who use 'empirical' to describe the general method of wisdom use it is an untechnical way to refer to the observational and reflective element in wisdom.

[112] M.V. FOX, "Qoheleth's Epistemology," *HUCA* 58 (1987) 137-155; idem, *Qoheleth and His Contradictions*; cf. Nordheimer in ch. 2.2.

[113] FOX, *Qoheleth and His Contradictions*, 79-120.

[114] Ibid., 85.

[115] D. MICHEL, *Untersuchungen zur Eigenart des Buches Qoheleth* (Berlin; NY: de Gruyter, 1989) 24-28, 35-38; idem, *Qoheleth* (Erträge der Forschung; Darmstadt: Wissenschaftliche Buchgesellschaft, 1988) 33, notes that the verb 'see' occurs 46 times and often means critical

Qoheleth's empirical procedure of discovery is readily confirmed, in my opinion, by an examination of texts like 1:12-18 and 2:1-11. 2:1-11 is concerned with Qoheleth's exploration of pleasure and the process of his enquiry is set out in v. 3-9. The general process of enquiry is set out in v. 3 and the specifics in v. 4-9.[116] The goal of the process is articulated in v. 3bβ as:

עד אשר־אראה אי־זה טוב לבני האדם אשר יעשו תחת השמים.

The goal is to 'see', i.e. to validate through critical observation what is worthwhile and meaningful for humans. This goal is 'achieved' through rational analysis (לבי) and experience. The role of experience is clear in v. 3a and particularly in the numerous first person activities in v. 4-8. Isaksson, as we saw in chapter five, relates the first person Suffix Conjugation forms to the autobiographical nature of Ecclesiastes. This element is present here, but the more dominant element is that of Qoheleth's personal experience as the key to knowledge. The repetition of חכמה in v. 3 and v. 9 should also be noted. These two comments on wisdom function, I suggest, as an inclusion within which the process of inquiry is articulated, and in the process the readers attention is strongly alerted to the method by which *this* wisdom operates.

For Qoheleth investigation of the world with חכמה means that he will use his powers of reason applied to his experience and observations rather than prior knowledge in his inquiry. Fox points out Qoheleth never invokes prior knowledge or anything he heard, as an argument for his convictions. Qoheleth seeks experience, observes it, evaluates it and then reports his conclusions. The methodological orientation in 1:12-13 encompasses all Qoheleth's teaching.

Other scholars have also picked up on this empiricistic epistemology of Qoheleth, although none has examined it as thoroughly as Fox or discerned the ironic contrast with other wisdom literature. Hengel, for example, says of Qoheleth's thought that "[i]ts unprejudiced, detached observation and its strictly rational, logical thought lead to a radical criticism of the doctrine of retribution in traditional wisdom and thus indirectly attack a cornerstone of Jewish piety."[117] As we shall argue below the doctrine of retribution in traditional wisdom is more complex than Hengel suggests, but he has correctly identified the nature of Qoheleth's epistemology. On 2:1 Whybray says: "It is because 'Solomon' has determined to seek it [happiness, contentment] independently for himself that he discovers that, like his corresponding attempt to rely on his own wisdom and

---

observation. He thus suggests that Qoheleth is not registering an empirical datum but is critically evaluating what he has perceived. He argues that Qoheleth is thus not an empiricist, as Fox suggests, who engages in various experiences and notes them down, but a thinker, an epistemological sceptic. MURPHY, *Ecclesiastes*, xxx, notes that the difference between Michel and Fox may just be verbal. However Qoheleth's epistemology has an observatory and a validatory side to it and Michel is mistaken, I think, in restricting Qoheleth's method to the validatory.

116 FOX, *Qoheleth and His Contradictions*, 178.

117 M. HENGEL, *Judaism and Hellenism. Volume One* (London: SCM, 1974) 126.

knowledge (1:13, 17) it proves totally unsatisfactory."[118] Lohfink is very clear that חכמה in Ecclesiastes should not be translated as "Weisheit." "'Wissen', und nicht das übliche 'Weisheit', ist in Koh die sachgemässere Übersetzung des hebr. *hokmah*. ... Es handelt sich um jenes Wissen und Können, das sich in Technik und Herrschaft umsetzen lässt, und um jene Bildung, die gesellschaftliche Stellung verleiht."[119]

The significance of Qoheleth's empiricism is strengthened by examining the epistemology of other wisdom literature.[120] Contrary to a widespread assumption, Wisdom's epistemology is not empirical.[121] Many of the sages' teachings undoubtedly derive from the observations of generations of wise men but always shaped in accordance with prior ethical-religious principles. Whatever the actual source of their teaching, the sages do not, according to Fox, offer their experience as the source of new knowledge and they rarely invoke experiential arguments. The rare appeal to what is seen is a rhetorical strategy and not a fundamental methodological procedure, as with Qoheleth. Fox refers to Proverbs 24:30-34; 7:6-20 and 6:6-8 as examples. The first two passages contain references to what the teacher "saw," in the one case with respect to what happened to a lazy man's field, and in the other he "saw" a woman enticing a youth to fornication. As Fox points out, in Proverbs 24:30-34 the observation is followed by a lesson, but the observation calls the truth to mind rather than the truth being discovered or inferred from the observation. "The sage does not say that he saw a field gone wild, looked for the cause, and found that its owner was lazy, nor does he claim to have looked at lazy farmers and observed what happens to their fields. Rather he came across a field gone wild, and this sparked a meditation on its causes."[122]

In Proverbs 7 the teacher reports observing the seduction but makes no claim to have observed the consequences; these he knows already! Similarly when the wise man exhorts the pupil to "Go to the ant ... consider its ways, and be wise" in Proverbs 6:6-8 the ant is being used as an illustration of diligence. The observation of the ant is used to make the wise man's point emphatic, but not to prove the point in the first place.

---

[118] WHYBRAY, *Ecclesiastes* (NCBC), 52.

[119] LOHFINK, *Kohelet*, 24, 25.

[120] Very little work has been done in this area. J.L. CRENSHAW, "Wisdom and Authority: Sapiential Rhetoric and its Warrants," *VTSup* 32 (1981) 10-29, explores the rhetoric of wisdom along the lines of threefold warrant: ethos, pathos and logos. FOX, *Qoheleth and His Contradictions*, 90, perceptively notes that rhetoric is an expression of an underlying epistemology. Ethos, pathos and logos will be present in any rhetoric, but, as Fox notes, the question is *how* they are realised in specific texts. Fox notes that Crenshaw mentions argument from consensus as the form of logos characteristic in wisdom literature, and thus suggests that, "the seemingly empirical arguments in Wisdom Literature are primarily ways of strengthening ethos by creating consensus." Much work remains to be done in this area. Crenshaw mentions that he is writing a volume on rhetoric in wisdom literature, but it is yet to appear.

[121] FOX, *Qoheleth and His Contradictions*, 90.

[122] Ibid., 91.

Personal experience, Fox points out, is cited more commonly in theodicy.[123] Cf. Psalm 37:25 for example: "I have been young, and now am old, yet I have not *seen* the righteous forsaken or their children begging for bread." Psalm 73:3 is another example: "For I was envious of the arrogant; *I saw* the prosperity of the wicked." However, as Fox perceptively points out,

> Observation in theodicy testifies to old truths; it does not uncover or argue for new ones. ... Qoheleth's use of experience does have certain parallels in theodicy both in the sufferers' complaints and in the defenders' theodicy. He differs in the greater importance he gives to the 'I' and, more significantly, in the reasons for which he appeals to the ego. While the sufferers and defenders try to understand what they observe, they, unlike Qoheleth, do not observe *in order* to gain knowledge.[124]

Qoheleth makes knowledge dependent upon the knower's perceiving it. For Qoheleth there is no body of truth standing outside the individual and demanding assent, no Dame Wisdom who was in existence before mankind and who would exist even if all humans were fools. For Qoheleth wisdom must be justified through the individual's experience and reason. "Qoheleth alone of the sages speaks with 'a voice that justifies itself by reference to the good sense of the individual's reflections on his experiences.'"[125]

Fox does, I think, overstress what one might call 'anti-realism' in Qoheleth, since Qoheleth's project could be thought of as an investigation of whether or not there is such a body of truth out there. But Fox is right about the strong individualism that underlies Qoheleth's empiricism.[126] Crenshaw argues that inherited tradition and individual appropriation are the two essential ingredients of 'ethos' in wisdom's rhetoric. "This bi-polarity of ethos provides an important corrective to the oft-mentioned individualism which characterises wisdom thinking."[127] It is precisely this bi-polarity that is missing in Ecclesiastes; epistemologically the balance has shifted to the pole of individual assessment. In contrast to the other sages, for Qoheleth anything less than certainty is ignorance. "Q seems to start with the expectation that reason can provide certainty, and when he sees that it does not, he is struck by its frailty. The other sages seem more comfortable with the limitations of knowledge."[128]

---

[123] Ibid., 91-92.

[124] Ibid., 92.

[125] Ibid., 95.

[126] Cf. FISCH, *Poetry with a Purpose*, 158. Fisch notes that Ecclesiastes "gives us a radically individualized statement." This is evident in the autobiographical 'I' that dominates Ecclesiastes and is readily seen in 1:12-13 and 2:3-8. Fisch distinguishes the 'I' of Qoheleth from that of the Psalms. The latter may be subjective but it is never autobiographical in Qoheleth's sense. As Fisch points out, Qoheleth could have said with Montaigne, "It is my portrait I draw ... I am myself the subject of my book."

[127] CRENSHAW, "Wisdom and Authority," 19.

[128] FOX, *Qoheleth and His Contradictions*, 106.

Examination of Qoheleth's epistemology and comparison of this with that of other wisdom literature exposes, in my opinion, the ironic use of חכמה in Ecclesiastes. Ironically, even Fox does not recognise this! What one expected to be wisdom rooted in the fear of Yahweh turns out to be a quest for certain knowledge resulting from logical analysis of personal experience and observation. When Qoheleth says חכמה the reader instinctively fills it with a positive content but ironically חכמה comes close to meaning folly![129]

Ironically scholars either, like Murphy and Ogden, pick up that Qoheleth's use of חכמה resonates with the positive use of this word in Proverbs, or they, like Hengel, Lohfink and Fox, pick up that in practice this חכמה is very different from the positive חכמה of Proverbs. However, neither group notices the irony in Qoheleth's use of חכמה! Both meanings are crucial to understanding Ecclesiastes. In 12:9 for example, it is crucial to the understanding of Ecclesiastes that when Qoheleth is described as חכם the reader understands him to be referred to here as in the Proverbs-type tradition in which wisdom is rooted in and based upon the fear of Yahweh. At the same time, for the epilogue to conclude Ecclesiastes, חכם must also here remind the reader of the very unusual empiricist meaning that חכמה appropriated in 1:13ff. And of course in 1:13 it is crucial to the meaning of Ecclesiastes that חכמה first arouse in the readers' mind that Proverb-type meaning of wisdom rooted in the fear of Yahweh, before this is undermined by the empiricist methodology that Qoheleth relentlessly pursues.

לב has also, I suggest, an ironic aspect to it in Qoheleth. The significance of לב in Ecclesiastes is demonstrated by the fact that it occurs some twelve times in 1:12-2:26. A common OT word, לב is "the richest biblical term for the totality of man's inner or immaterial nature. ... Wisdom and understanding are seated in the heart."[130] According to Spykman "[t]he heart represents the unifying center of man's entire existence, the spiritual concentration point of our total selfhood, the inner reflective core which sets the direction for all of our life relationships. It is the wellspring of all our willing, thinking, feeling, acting and every other life utterance."[131] Commenting on Proverbs 4:23, "Keep your heart with all diligence, for from it flow the springs of life", Berkouwer also suggests that "[t]he heart shows forth the deepest aspect of the whole humanness of man, not some functional localization in a part which is supposedly the most important. The term 'heart' deals with the total orientation, direction, concentration of man, his depth

---

[129] Verheij's reading of 2:4-6 according to which Qoheleth acts like God would strongly confirm my reading of חכמה as ironic (cf. A. VERHEIJ, "Paradise Retried: On Qoheleth 2:4-6," *JSOT* 50 [1991] 113-115.).

[130] A. BOWLING, "לבב," in: R. LAIRD HARRIS, G.L. ARCHER, and B.K. WALTKE (eds.), *Theological Wordbook of the Bible*. Vol 1 (1980) 466, 467.

[131] G. SPYKMAN, *Reformational Theology. A New Paradigm for Doing Dogmatics* (Grand Rapids: Eerdmans, 1992) 218.

dimension, from which his full human existence is directed and formed. He who gives his heart to the Lord gives his full life (cf. Proverbs 23:26)."[132]

Admittedly Berkouwer and Spykman are systematic theologians and their comments tend to be totalising rather than focused on the specific uses of לב in Proverbs, Ecclesiastes, etc.[133] However their comments do do justice to those 'heart-sayings' in Proverbs like 4:23 which envision the heart as the source of life or death. According to 4:23 the heart must be guarded 'more than anything which needs to be guarded'[134] because from it flow the influences that lead to 'life.' If the consistent mention of לב in Ecclesiastes is juxtaposed with such Proverbs material then the question of whether Qoheleth's method is really 'wise' becomes acute. לב is mentioned so frequently in 1:12-2:26 because Qoheleth is reflecting on the process of perception and discovery and as Fox says, "He is his own field of investigation."[135] Qoheleth is clearly devoting a huge amount of energy and attention to his לב, as it were, but is this energy directed towards "guarding his heart"? Ironically לב, which is the source of genuine trust in Yahweh (cf. Proverbs 3:5) and thus the seat of חכמה, has become the seat of empirical and thus largely autonomous reason. Qoheleth's understanding of heart becomes like that of Proverbs 28:26 בוטח בלבו הוא כסיל. Van Leeuwen suggests that לב in Proverbs 28:26 amounts to "autonomous 'reason'",[136] and I am suggesting that ironically the לב in Ecclesiastes 1:12ff and similar passages, which is the seat of חכמה, amounts to the same thing. לב is also used in Ecclesiastes in the sense of inner being (cf. 7:3-4; 10:2) but mainly in clearly poetic passages which could be quotes.

לב also occurs a number of times in the concluding section of Ecclesiastes, 11:7ff, and it is here that I think that the irony of Qoheleth's use of לב is revealed. In 11:9 the young man is exhorted to follow his לב and eyes. This deliberately alludes to 2:10 where Qoheleth followed his eyes and heart. In 11:9 however, there is the reminder as it were, that the heart out of which the young man lives needs to be guarded because "God will hold you responsible for all you do."[137]

I would define 'wisdom' in Qoheleth as 'truth derived through observation, experience and analysis i.e. empirically.' This is, as we have seen, a crucially different nuance from Proverbs and Job. However, it is in the epilogue, when Qoheleth is described as 'wise' and this wisdom is associated with fearing God

---

[132] G.C. BERKOUWER, *Man: The Image of God* (Grand Rapids: Eerdmans, 1962) 202-203.

[133] A thorough analysis of לב requires far more detailed consideration of its nuanced uses than these generalised quotes provide. The NRSV, for example, recognises these nuances by sometimes translating לב in Proverbs as 'heart', sometimes as 'sense', and sometimes as 'mind'.

[134] For this translation see WHYBRAY, *Ecclesiastes* (NCBC), 82.

[135] FOX, *Qoheleth and His Contradictions*, 87.

[136] R. VAN LEEUWEN, "Wealth and Poverty: System and Contradiction in Proverbs," *Hebrew Studies* 33 (1992) 34.

[137] This is how FOX, *Qoheleth and His Contradictions*, 347, paraphrases 11:9b.

and obeying his commandments, that the irony attached to חכמה is finally exposed. Fisch expresses this powerfully when he writes of the epilogue,

> the view that would assign these closing verses of Ecclesiastes to another editor or author should be resisted. This skeptical rejection of skepticism is the final twist of Qoheleth's super-irony. It gives us an ego that has ironized itself away and has abdicated the self-sufficient thinking of the *hakam*. Qoheleth never quite says, like the author of Psalm 111, that the *beginning* of *hokma* is the fear of the Lord but his final statement seems to say that the *end point* of *hokma* is the fear of God! ... The proper study of mankind is man, Qoheleth seems to say. But ironically, this penultimate verse of the book explodes such a humanistic pretension. To fear God ... becomes the 'whole of Man' or, we may say, what is left of man when his ego has been ironized away. Read in this way, the verse is utterly integral to the book, its final summarizing statement.[138]

7.4.3.2 The Structure of Repetition in Ecclesiastes

Repetition is common in Proverbs[139] and Ecclesiastes, and yet it has rarely received sustained attention. Snell asserts that "[c]learly, no commentary ever written on Proverbs takes repetitions, clichés, and the shapes of the collections seriously."[140] Snell focuses on repetition in Proverbs but only in order to explore the genesis of Proverbs. He acknowledges that comparative evidence suggests the repetitions are important since no other collection of aphorisms from the ANE has the extensive internal repetition that Proverbs does. He examines the different reasons that are put forward for the repetitions (literary cleavage; final editing; emphasis; poetic and rhetorical motives) and concludes that all these reasons may have a role in the repetition in Proverbs: "A number of important questions remain open, including the questions of why verses are repeated and to what extent proverbial clichés can be used to study affinities within the book."[141]

Ecclesiastes is full of repetition as Murphy, for example, recognises: "While judgement about the peculiar grammatical characteristics of the language is still out ... there can be no doubt about the distinctiveness of Qoheleth's literary style. The poem on the repetition of events in 1:4-11 is as it were a symbol of this style; repetition is its trademark. This repetition is manifest in vocabulary and also in a

---

138 FISCH, *Poetry with a Purpose*, 175.

139 יראת יהוה, for example, occurs fourteen times in Proverbs.

140 D.C. SNELL, *Twice-Told Proverbs and the Composition of the Book of Proverbs* (Winona Lake: Eisenbrauns, 1993) 84. R.N. WHYBRAY, *Proverbs* (NCBC; Grand Rapids: Eerdmans; London: Marshall Pickering, 1994), is the most recent English commentary on Proverbs. He does not refer to Snell, and although he argues for editorial 'unity' his commentary contains no detailed consideration of repetition.

141 SNELL, *Twice-Told Proverbs*, 83.

phraseology that is almost formulaic".[142] Murphy lists 28 favourite words of
Qoheleth.[143] Qoheleth also repeats the following set phrases:

‫מי-ידע, תחת השמש, כל המעשה אשר נעשה, עמל, שתה/אכל, הבל‬.

However, what Snell says of commentaries on Proverbs is true of
commentaries on Ecclesiastes; the way in which this literary device of repetition
manifests itself in the whole book is not generally explored. As part of his
analysis of repetition in Ugaritic and Hebrew poetry Zurro refers to numerous
types of repetition in individual verses in Ecclesiastes.[144] Useful as this analysis
is, it remains at the level of the individual verse, and does not examine the
structure of repetition within a book like Ecclesiastes as a whole. In terms of this
larger analysis Sternberg has done the most thorough work on repetition in
biblical texts, although he limits himself to OT narrative,[145] and clearly there are
some important differences between the structures of repetition in narrative as
opposed to poetic texts.[146] Most relevant to Ecclesiastes is Sternberg's point that
in literary texts, the dismissal of redundancies as 'noise' must be the last resort.
There is a prima facie case in Ecclesiastes, as in biblical narrative, for a functional
approach.[147]

Unfortunately "[n]either literary not biblical study has developed the tools
required even for a formal analysis and typology of repetition structures."[148] This
is certainly true of repetition in Ecclesiastes. We will explore in detail one major
type of repetition in Ecclesiastes, that of the *carpe diem* passages.[149]

In what follows we will examine each of the *carpe diem* passages in
Ecclesiastes. This will take us into detailed exegesis, and it is as well to note that
we will be particularly interested in evaluating Whybray's stimulating suggestion
that the joy (*carpe diem*) passages are answers to the central questions in
Ecclesiastes. This is a fruitful proposal but we will argue that the questions are
answered in two ways, that of ‫ הבל‬ *and* that of joy, and that these contradictory
answers are invariably juxtaposed, thereby creating a gap in the reading that
needs to be filled.

---

[142] MURPHY, *Ecclesiastes*, xxix.

[143] Ibid., xxix, xxx.

[144] E. ZURRO, *Procedimientos iterativos en la poesia ugaritica y hebrea* (Biblica et Orientalia
43; Rome: Pontifical Biblical Institute, 1987).

[145] STERNBERG, *The Poetics of Biblical Narrative*, 365-440.

[146] See ibid., 386, and cf. R. ALTER, *The Art of Biblical Poetry* (Edinburgh: T&T Clark, 1985)
for a consideration of repetition in Hebrew poetic texts.

[147] Contra R.N. WHYBRAY, *Ecclesiastes* (Old Testament Guides; Sheffield: JSOT, 1989) 44,
45) who maintains that "the theory that the material originated as separate, individual pieces ... also
accounts for the frequent repetitions and duplications which are so characteristic of the book. This
feature, regarded in this way, points rather to the literary disunity of the book than to its unity."

[148] STERNBERG, *The Poetics of Biblical Narrative*, 375.

[149] As Robert Alter commented to me, this may not be the most appropriate term for these
passages because it implies a hedonistic attitude which they do not necessarily teach.

1. 2:24-26

2:24-26 is the concluding paragraph of the section 1:12-2:26.[150] Whybray sees 2:24 as the answer to the 'profit' question formulated in 2:22-23.[151] Whybray articulates this answer as follows: "*God* may *give* joy and pleasure; *man* can never achieve it for himself, however hard he may try." The translation of this section is controversial. Murphy translates it as follows:

24 There is nothing [better] for a person [than] to eat and drink and provide pleasure for himself in his toil – this also I saw is from the hand of God.

25 For who can eat or rejoice, if not I?

26 To whomever he pleases God gives wisdom and knowledge, but to the errant one he gives the trouble of collecting and gathering, only to give to whomever God pleases. This also is vanity and a chase after wind.[152]

Whybray stays with the RSV translation.[153] The crucial difference is how v. 25 and 26 are translated. The RSV translates them as follows:

25 for apart from him who can eat or who can have enjoyment?

26 For to the man who pleases him God gives wisdom and knowledge and joy; but to the sinner he gives the work of gathering and heaping, only to give to one who pleases God. This also is vanity and a striving after wind.

For Whybray Qoheleth in v. 26 accepts the orthodox view, realises that it contradicts the experiences he has just narrated and simply states the contradiction.[154] For Murphy v. 26 stresses God's sovereign and enigmatic freedom in imparting gifts. Whybray's understanding seems preferable to me. חוץ ממני is probably better understood as "apart from him", with ממני emendated to ממנו, following the Syriac and Septuagint.[155] Alternatively the more difficult reading ממני could be retained with v. 25 understood as a

---

[150] Most commentators are agreed that 2:24-26 concludes a section. Ogden thinks it concludes 1:3-2:26. LOHFINK, *Kohelet*, 30-33, is an exception. According to him 2:24-26 begins the new section 2:24-3:15.

[151] R.N. WHYBRAY, "Qoheleth, Preacher of Joy," *JSOT* 23 (1992) 88-89.

[152] MURPHY, *Ecclesiastes*, 24.

[153] WHYBRAY, *Ecclesiastes* (NCBC), 62-65.

[154] Ibid., 65.

[155] Following Dahood, C.F. WHITLEY, *Koheleth. His Language and Thought* (Berlin; NY: de Gruyter, 1979) 29, argues that the suffix on ממני is a third person form, but Dahood's examples are not convincing (J. DE WAARD, "The Translator and Textual Criticism [with Particular Reference to Eccl 2,25]," *Biblica* 60/4 [1979] 512). De Waard examines the textual critical and interpretative issues in v. 25 in detail. Because ממני is the more difficult reading he concludes that it is the more original one. However, as he points out, textual critical problems have to be solved at the level of the principles of textual criticism *and* according to criteria provided by the discourse of which the text is a part. On the basis of both of these principles de Waard concludes that ממני is the right reading, but that v. 25 should be read as a quotation with God as the speaker. In substance this amounts to the same as reading ממנו with 'him' referring to God.

quotation of God's words. חורץ מן occurs only here in the OT, and it can either be translated, following Murphy and Crenshaw, as "if not", or as "apart from." Perhaps its more usual meaning is 'apart from', 'outside of',[156] and contextually "apart from him" seems to me to flow more naturally from the reference to "the hand of God" in v. 24 and to connect with enjoyment as the gift of God in v. 26.

The translation and interpretation of v. 26 is the more crucial issue for understanding v. 24-26. Apart from a desire to smooth over the contradiction between this section and the preceding verses, there seems to be no good reason for translating חוטא other than as 'sinner'. Although Murphy maintains that no moral connotation is to be given to טוב and חוטא, even he translates חוטא as "errant one".[157] Like Murphy, Crenshaw argues that "[h]ere, the two terms mean simply 'fortunate and unfortunate, lucky and unlucky.' ... Qoheleth's observations transpose the motif, dear to the sages, that wicked people's wages eventually go to the devout ... Since good people can and do lose their possessions to sinners, the disposer of goods must be indifferent to morality."[158] However, like Murphy, in his translation Crenshaw is constrained to translate these parts of v. 26 as "to the person who pleases him, but to the one who displeases him ..." Thus it would appear that for both Murphy and Crenshaw the text appears to go in one direction, but the logic of the broader passage in another. This tension, which they resolve by forcing v. 24-26 into the logic of the broader text as they understand it, results I suggest from the failure to recognise the juxtaposition of opposites. Furthermore, the more natural reading of כי לאדם שטוב לפניו is, "for to the one who pleases him" rather than as "to whomever he pleases".

These interpretative issues are difficult to decide, and much depends upon one's sense of the whole. Murphy's translation seems to me an attempt to resolve the contradiction present in the text. Ogden follows Whybray's translation but smoothes out the contradiction in a different way from Murphy. He argues that 2:24-26

> stands as the response which Qoheleth makes both to the programmatic question (1.3; 2.22) and the negative answer he offers to that question in 2.11. Thus from 1.3 to 2.24 the author moves, via this ordered structure, from problem to solution. ... Despite the fact that life has this enigmatic dimension, is fraught with problems and pain, to Qoheleth's mind there is only one possible attitude to adopt; enjoy what God gives.[159]

---

[156] This is its common meaning in the Mishnah (cf. WHITLEY, *Koheleth*, 29), and Qoheleth's language is close to that of the Mishnah (WHYBRAY, *Ecclesiastes* [NCBC], 5). F. DELITZSCH, *Commentary on the Song of Songs and Ecclesiastes* (Grand Rapids: Eerdmans, 1970) 252-253, argues that the type of translation which Vg, Tg (and Murphy) adopt, requires יתר instead of חורץ.

[157] MURPHY, *Ecclesiastes*, 26.

[158] CRENSHAW, *Ecclesiastes*, 90, 91.

[159] OGDEN, *Qoheleth*, 48, 49.

Ogden recognises that 2:26 contradicts 2:21. This type of contradiction occurs elsewhere in Ecclesiastes. The answer is that

[t]he wisdom tradition knew full well that no single statement could encompass all truth. Thus it is most likely that 2.26 with its deliberately positive note, is intended to heighten the notion that on occasion the wise is actually better off than the fool, and this despite his occasional bad experience noted in 2.21. Neither 2.21 nor 2.26 can represent the totality of truth, but each may be true given certain circumstances.[160]

Although Ogden covers over the contradiction too quickly, his analysis reveals some penetrating insights. Especially in the series of articles that he has written about Ecclesiastes, Ogden has alerted us to the function of rhetorical questions and of the אין טוב formula in Ecclesiastes,[161] insights which inform his analysis of 2:24-26. The אין טוב formula occurs four times in Ecclesiastes,[162] and each time this is as part of a *carpe diem* saying. Ogden argues that

[t]he form's precise function is to express the advice to enjoy life in light of the negative response to the programmatic question מה יתרון לאדם which initiates Qoheleth's whole undertaking. Set in various contexts ... and with minor variations in expression, the question (מה יתרון) and its response (אין טוב) are integrally related and provide the literary framework around which these portions of the book are built.[163]

Rhetorical questions do play an important part in Ecclesiastes,[164] and positioned where it is, 1:3 is clearly programmatic. Ogden may well be right in seeing 1:3-2:26 as a section, and 2:24-26 introduced as it is with אין טוב as *a* major response to the question posed in 1:3. However it simply is not adequate to see 2:24-26 as *the* answer to the problems posed in 1:4-2:23, to which the consistent הבל conclusion is reached. The repeated references to הבל combined with the stated (2:11) and implied (2:22) conclusion that the answer to the programmatic question of 1:3 is negative cannot somehow flow on to the positive approach of 2:24-26. 2:24-26 contradicts and stands in strong tension to the הבל conclusion, and this tension ought not to be undermined in order to smooth over the text and fill in the gap set up by the tension. It is more accurate to see the two approaches as *juxtaposed* rather than as an orderly progression from 1:3 to 2:24. Particularly noticeable is the fact that God does not feature in 2:1-23, whereas his name occurs three times in 24-26. What we have here is a deliberate juxtaposition of two contradictory approaches.

---

[160] Ibid., 49.

[161] See particularly G. OGDEN, "Qoheleth's Use of the 'Nothing is Better'-Form," *JBL* 98 (1979) 339-350.

[162] See Ecclesiastes 2:24; 3:12; 3:22; 8:15. Variant forms occur in 5:18 and 9:7-10. Apart from Jeremiah 8:15 and 14:19 where it is used simply in the sense of "no good", אין טוב only occurs in Ecclesiastes. See Ogden (ibid.) for an analysis of the form.

[163] Ibid., 350.

[164] There are over thirty rhetorical questions in Ecclesiastes.

The hebel note at the end of 1:3-2:26 indicates, I suggest, Qoheleth's awareness of the tension between 2:21 and 2:26, and perhaps his realisation that with his epistemology even the goodness in creation that he recognises starts to look like הבל. Indeed it is the tension between these two perspectives that gives rise to the impenetrable enigma with which Qoheleth is struggling.

2. 3:10-15

According to Whybray, this section deals with how the human person should behave in the light of his ignorance of the future.[165] V. 13 gives the answer; once again the person who accepts what God gives finds happiness. Ogden's interpretation is much the same; v. 12-13 and v. 14-15 are two positive answers to the rhetorical question in v. 9, each introduced by the marker כי ידעתי. Murphy describes 12-15 as typical of the resigned conclusions found elsewhere, as for example in 2:24. Ogden reads v. 12-15 more positively, suggesting inter alia that v. 15b be translated, "God requests that it be pursued," the "it" being the enjoyment of v. 12-13.[166]

There are a number of difficult issues in these verses: Firstly, how is עולם to be understood. Is it "world" (LXX), "a sense of past and future" (NRSV), "a sense of duration" (Murphy), "ignorance" (Whybray) or "a consciousness of the eternal" (Ogden)? Secondly, should מבלי אשר לא in v. 11b be understood as introducing a purpose clause thus indicating that the presence of עולם ensures that humans will not understand what God is up to, or should it be understood in the sense of "without", i.e. as introducing a result clause and thereby referring to the limitations of human knowledge? Thirdly how should the last part of v. 14 be understood? Is יראו to be understood to refer to fearing/standing in awe (Murphy) or seeing (Ogden)? Ogden translates v. 14b, "God has done (this) so that they might see (what proceeds) from him." And finally how should נרדף־את in v. 15b be translated? Murphy translates v. 15b, "And God seeks out what has been pursued," suggesting that the reference is to the past or events of the past. On the basis of parallels between v. 14b and 15b, Ogden suggests that the את of v. 15b is a truncated version of את אשר (equivalent to ש in v. 14b) which thus introduces a relative clause. V. 15b should thus be translated, "God requests that it be pursued," with "it" referring to the enjoyment of v. 12ff.

In our quest to understand this *carpe diem* section it should firstly be noted that 3:9/10-15 is part of the larger unit 3:1-16.[167] The structure of this unit is clear.

---

[165] WHYBRAY, "Qoheleth, Preacher of Joy," 89-90.

[166] OGDEN, *Qoheleth*, 56-58.

[167] I am following Whybray's divisions here (cf. *Ecclesiastes* [NCBC]). Scholars are not agreed about where this section ends.

V. 1   an introductory comment
V. 2-8   a poem on עת
V. 9   a rhetorical question about the benefit of toil in such a timed world
V. 10-11   observational response to the question
V. 12-13   first confessional (I know) response to the question
V. 14-15   second confessional response to the question

The question of עת is central to this section. In v. 1-8 עת signifies the right occasion for things to take place in a creation ordered by God. Scholars are disagreed as to how positively the author regards this order[168] but there is agreement that as Murphy puts it, "These are *God's* times, not our times."[169] This provides the background for the rhetorical question in v. 9: in such a timed world what is the value and purpose of human labour and toil?

The first response in v. 10-11 is a negative one. Everything may have its divine time but the human cannot discover that time. It is very difficult to know how to translate העלם and there is no agreement among scholars as we noted above. Two contextual clues may help. Firstly, as Murphy notes, the contrast between עת and העלם suggests a temporal meaning, something along the lines of 'duration.'[170] Secondly, it seems to me that we should not ignore the recurrence of עלם in its longer form עולם in v. 14, where it characterises God's activity. These clues suggest that we should think of העלם as something about the way God has made the human person. In a timed world humans recognise that 'there is a time and a place' and that in order to discern this they need a sense of the larger picture, what philosophers might call origin and telos. However, they cannot get access to this 'duration.'

It is very difficult to decide whether מבלי introduces a purpose clause or not.[171] If our understanding of העלם is correct then "without" is probably the better understanding. To translate this clause as "so that" portrays God as deliberately setting up this tension in human experience; an unlikely view in an Israelite context, especially if the author may have Genesis 1 in mind. It is thus the limitation of human knowledge that Qoheleth sees as making the human's toil enigmatic in v. 10-11. The 'gift' (נתן) of העלם is a burden from this angle.

The second and third responses to the question of v. 9 are introduced by ידעתי, whereas Qoheleth's observation that the human person cannot discern God's works is introduced by ראיתי. These two "I know" responses are very different in content to the first "I have seen" response. Here the opportunity that

---

[168] MURPHY, *Ecclesiastes*, 39, speaks of the "strong theological note of divine determinism" in these verses. OGDEN, *Qoheleth*, 51-54, by contrast, sees 3:1-8 as a description of God's good creation order.

[169] MURPHY, *Ecclesiastes*, 39.

[170] Ibid., 30.

[171] For the use of מבלי to introduce a purpose clause see Isaiah 5:13 and Ezekiel 14:15. Its more common OT usage, especially in Job is as "without." See Job 4:24; 6:6; 24:7; 31:19 and Jeremiah 2:15; 9:9-10.

God's order of creation presents for eating, drinking and working is seen as a positive מתת. Murphy recognises the contrast, but then goes on to suggest that the gift of eating and drinking "seems to be a compensation for the העלם."[172] However, a number of factors suggest that what we have here is a juxtaposition of different responses rather than v. 12-15 being a compensation for the negative conclusion of v. 10-11.

Apart from the contradictory content to which we have just referred, there is the fact that the knowledge in v. 12-15 is not arrived at by observation, especially that in v. 14. It is much more of a confessional or traditional nature. The tension between 9-11 and 12-15 is made even stronger if one follows Ogden in translating the last part of v. 14 as "God has done (this) so that they might see[173] (what proceeds) from him,"[174] since this stands in stark contrast to "yet they cannot find out" in v. 11. The juxtaposition of being unable to *find out* and yet *knowing* would strengthen the contrast in this section. However, even if one translates v14bβ along the lines of "stand in awe before him", this still forms a strong contrast with the frustrated hebel-type response of v. 10-11. The recurrence of the opening rhetorical question in v. 9 (cf. 1:3), with its implied negative answer, plus the reference to the harsh task (ענין) that God has given the human person in v. 10, strengthen the הבל focus of v. 9-11.[175]

V. 15, and especially v. 15b, is not easy to interpret. On all accounts it expresses God's sovereignty, but should not be interpreted as a negative expression of this, as Whybray for example does.[176] Whether or not Ogden is right in reading the last part of v. 15 as a reference to God calling humans to joy, v. 15 is a development of v. 14 and both should thus be seen as a positive expression of God's sovereignty.

V. 12-15 is therefore an answer to v. 9, but it is an answer which is *juxtaposed* next to a very different and negative answer in v. 10-11. There is more of a tension in this *carpe diem* passage than a presentation of problem and answer.

3. 3:16-22

This section deals with injustice in the world and not knowing whether or when it will be punished. Whybray notes that out of this depressing state of affairs Qoheleth draws a positive conclusion, humans are to enjoy their work because 'that is their lot' and no one knows the future. The element of contradictory juxtaposition is present in this section in two ways. If we outline the content as follows the juxtapositions become clear.

---

[172] MURPHY, *Ecclesiastes*, 39.

[173] יראו could be the Qal imperfect of ראה (see) or of ירא (fear).

[174] OGDEN, *Qoheleth*, 57.

[175] I agree with Murphy contra Ogden that ענין here, as generally in Ecclesiastes, has a negative connotation.

[176] WHYBRAY, *Ecclesiastes* (NCBC), 75.

V. 16   statement of the problem
V. 17   confessional response – God has an עת for judgement
V. 18-19   הבל response to the problem
V. 20-21   ignorance of what happens to humans after death
V. 22a   אין טוב saying
V. 22b   rhetorical question

In v. 18-19 the injustice of life leads to the הבל conclusion. The injustice that Qoheleth observes is God's means of testing humans to show them that they are but animals. Humans from this perspective have no advantage over animals; they come from dust, return to dust and no one knows what happens to them after that.

V. 18-19 is juxtaposed in a contradictory way to v. 17. Both of these responses to injustice are what אמרתי אני בלבי, but they represent radically opposed responses to the problem. V. 17 picks up on the theme of time in 3:1-8 in a positive way and confesses that there will be a time for judgement which would resolve the problem of injustice. V. 18-19 concludes from observation of life that all is הבל and God is a cruel examiner whose purpose in the injustice is to remind humans that they are only animals.

V. 20-21 mediate between the הבל conclusion and the positive אין טוב saying in v. 22. These two verses deal with the limitations of human knowledge and could, I suggest lead in one of two directions.[177] They could provide further support for the הבל conclusion. In the light of the animal analogy the rhetorical question in v. 21 could imply a negative answer. But the awareness of human limitations could also lead on to the אין טוב saying. And with its close proximity to 3:12-15 and its 'better than' form, v. 22 should not just be read as a statement of positive resignation in the light of human enigmas. The enjoyment here is a positive, shalomic appropriation of the human task in creation, a recognition of the חלק that God has assigned humans.

Like v. 17 the אין טוב saying in v. 22 is juxtaposed in a contradictory way to v. 18-19. Against the idea that v. 22 is the answer to the problem of injustice is the tension between "enjoying their work" and the injustice portrayed in v. 16. V. 22 does not resolve this tension; how is the worker to enjoy life as his portion while being dragged unjustly into the law courts? Similarly the tensions between v. 17 and v. 18-19 are not resolved. The reader is uncertain how the observations leading to the 'God is testing them' conclusion relate to the confession that there is a time appointed for judgement. Both are said in Qoheleth's heart/mind but do the observations deconstruct the former confession? One might think so, but what then of the אין טוב saying? This fits closely with v. 17 and seems to be the conclusion of this brief discussion of injustice. The fact is that the juxtapositions

---

[177] Compare the previous *carpe diem* passage, where the limitation of human knowledge in 3:11ff can lead on to a joyful trust in God, but it can also be the basis of concluding that all is enigmatic.

of contradictory views set up gaps, and the gaps are not filled at this point.[178] The uncertainty with which the reader is left is enhanced by the rhetorical question at the end of v. 22. As with most of the rhetorical questions in Ecclesiastes, this one can be answered in two ways. Like v. 20-21 it could enhance the sense of meaninglessness and enigma. Alternatively, and especially in the light of v. 17, it could imply that even this enigma is under God's control.[179]

4. 5:9-19[10-20][180]

The context of this *carpe diem* saying is that wealth does not satisfy or last and may be lost more quickly than it is gained.[181] According to Whybray v. 17[18] provides the answer.[182] Ogden likewise regards it as Qoheleth's answer to the יתרון question in v. 15[16].[183] There is an element of 'answer' in v. 17[18]. 'Our lot' and the reference to 'few days' support the view that Qoheleth is interacting with the problem of injustice in toil. However a strong tension remains between the response to the problem of toil that leads to darkness, vexation, sickness and resentment, and the 'response' of eating and drinking. They represent radically different ways of approaching life 'under the sun' in which wealth does not last, and the reader is left with a question mark about their relationship, as a comparison of v16[17] with v19[20] makes quite clear. In both v. 16[17] and v. 18[19] there is a reference to eating, but this common activity serves only to contrast the different circumstances of that 'eating.'

As in the other *carpe diem* passages that we have looked at, rather than the *carpe diem* saying being the answer to the problem, we have two contradictory responses to the problem *juxtaposed* and the resulting gap left unresolved. 6:1-6 strengthens the tension between 5:11[12]-16[17] and 5:17[18]-19[20], because although it may be our portion to enjoy life as God enables us to, there are some/many who are unable to enjoy life.

---

[178] See Fox's paraphrase of this section, for a good example of how commentators feel the need to fill the gaps that juxtapositions set up (FOX, *Qoheleth and His Contradictions*, 336-337).

[179] Intriguingly commentators reflect these two options. MURPHY, *Ecclesiastes*, 37, understands v. 22b to refer to humans being unable to see any real future for themselves, whereas OGDEN, *Qoheleth*, 62-63, sees v. 22b as another reason for Qoheleth's positive advice. It is no use inquiring into the future because there is no tangible evidence; nevertheless there is something אחריו and this is part of our יתרון.

[180] Murphy includes 5:9-19 as a section within 4:17-6:9, but he notes that several topics are dealt with in this section and that most commentators deal with these topics separately.

[181] Note that this *carpe diem* passage lacks the אין טוב element present in the others that we have looked at so far. OGDEN, "Qoheleth's Use of the 'Nothing is Better'-Form," 341-342, notes that all the other elements of the form are present and suggests that the non-use of the אין טוב may be deliberate, relating to the fact that 5:17[18] is in a mediate position between 5:12-16[13-17] and 6:1-6. "In the context of life which may issue in these two 'evils' stands the one 'good' which Qoheleth can see."

[182] WHYBRAY, "Qoheleth, Preacher of Joy," 89.

[183] OGDEN, *Qoheleth*, 87.

5. 8:10-15

Scholars are not agreed about how chapter eight should be divided.[184] We follow Murphy and Whybray in seeing 8:10-15 as a section which can be analysed more or less independently. This section deals with the problem of the wicked not being speedily punished. V. 15 in Whybray's view represents Qoheleth's conclusion.[185] Ogden understands v. 15 as closing off the discussion which began in 6:11-12.[186] 8:15 is the last place in Ecclesiastes where אין טוב occurs. Content-wise 8:10-15 develops as follows:

V. 10: description of an enigmatic situation. Qoheleth observes the wicked buried and reflects upon their long life and acclaim within the cultus. This is הבל.

V. 11: explanation of why such a situation is הבל – because the wicked are not seen to be speedily punished human hearts incline towards evil which appears more profitable.

V. 12-13: here Qoheleth *juxtaposes* his confession of what he 'knows' about God's justice next to the prolonging of the sinners' lives. The clear contradiction is left in tact: Compare v. 12a – the sinners do prolong their lives – with v. 13b – they will not prolong their days!

V. 14: another description of an enigmatic situation of injustice.

V. 15: recommendation of enjoyment.

Clearly there are gaps left in the argument as a result of the juxtapositions. The lack of observable justice and the longevity of sinners results in people favouring evil, since such a lifestyle appears to bring about long life and security. Qoheleth is aware of this, and yet he 'knows' that it will be well with those who fear God but sinners will be punished and will not experience longevity! The gap resulting from the deliberate juxtaposition of these contradictory views is left unfilled and in v. 14 Qoheleth proceeds to another example of injustice. What makes this section particularly interesting is that the juxtaposition appears to be done consciously in v. 12, with v. 12a drawing the reader's attention to the contradiction and thereby making the reader aware that the author is aware of the contradiction.[187]

---

[184] WHYBRAY, *Ecclesiastes* (NCBC), 135ff, treats 8:10-15 as the first of a series of sections comprising 8:10-9:12, all of which question the traditional belief that righteousness and wickedness receive their due rewards. MURPHY, *Ecclesiastes*, 79ff, identifies 8:1-17 as a loosely united section under the theme of authority. 8:9-15 is one of the reflections in this section. OGDEN, *Qoheleth*, 139, argues that 8:15 closes off the discussion which began with the questions in 6:11-12. Ogden deals with 8:10-14 as a section.

[185] WHYBRAY, "Qoheleth, Preacher of Joy," 90.

[186] OGDEN, *Qoheleth*, 139.

[187] There is some discussion about how the כי גם in 8:12b is to be interpreted. See, for example, A. SCHOORS, *The Preacher Sought to Find Pleasing Words. A Study of the Language of Qoheleth* (Orientalia Lovaniensia Analecta 41; Leuven: Departement Oriëntalistiek, 1992) 134-136. Murphy and Schoors argue for a concessive understanding of כי גם as "although", but Murphy

Similarly the אין טוב saying in v. 15 is a juxtaposition firstly to v. 14 and to the earlier example and הבל comment insofar as v. 15 concludes this whole section. בעמלו indicates an awareness of the injustice in life, but it should not be thought therefore that the *carpe diem* saying is an answer to the problem of injustice. The question that the juxtaposition raises is precisely *how* one could enjoy life while evil and oppression flourish and the righteous are treated as though they are wicked. How could Qoheleth commend joy amidst all the enigma he observes. The gap created by this juxtaposition is deliberately left open.

6. 9:1-12[188]

For Whybray v. 3b describes a common response to the problem that one cannot know whether one's actions will please God (v. 1b) and that death will come to all (v. 2-3a).[189] V. 4-10 presents an alternative and better response: life is God's gift and one can enjoy life because the fact that God has given one the opportunity for joy means that he has already approved one's actions.

Ogden's view is much the same. He does point out that the *carpe diem* section here is much stronger: "The most striking literary feature of this section is the sudden appearance of a series of imperatives bearing on enjoyment. ... What is new, however, in this section is the move from advice to imperative; it gives the enjoyment theme in this case a more authoritative presentation."[190]

9:1-12 develops in the following way:

V. 1a: a confessional statement about God's sovereignty, stressing that all that the righteous and wise do plus the outcome of their actions is in God's control.[191]

---

does not try and smooth over the resulting contradiction in the way that Schoors, following Gordis, does. Schoors comments, "Reading כי גם as concessive fully fits the context, since, as clearly formulated by Gordis, יודע introduces a restatement of a conventional idea, which Qoheleth does not accept" (ibid., 135). Ogden understands כי גם adversatively as "however." Either way, there is no textual reason for seeing v. 12-13 as not being representative of the view of Qoheleth, unless one is concerned to somehow resolve the tension that this juxtaposition introduces. V. 15 reaffirms the perspective of v. 12-13 as being that of Qoheleth, especially if one bears in mind that v. 15 is an אין טוב saying and that in 3:12-15 enjoyment and the fear of God are held together in an אין טוב saying.

188 Scholars are not agreed as to how to divide up chapter nine. Murphy takes 9:1-12 as a section which he entitles "Reflections." WHYBRAY, *Ecclesiastes* (NCBC), 139, has v. 1-10 as a section which he is "certain" ends with v. 10. Ogden's analysis is preferable because it takes into account the inclusions and introductory phrases that Murphy (inclusions) and Whybray (introductory phrases) refer to (OGDEN, *Qoheleth*, 143ff). According to Ogden 9:1-12 are closely linked, with v. 1-6, 7-10 and 11-12 forming subsections.

189 WHYBRAY, "Qoheleth, Preacher of Joy," 90-91.

190 OGDEN, *Qoheleth*, 151.

191 Cf. ibid., 144. Because of what follows v. 1, Murphy sees ביד האלהים as simply God's control rather than God's benign providence. This is an argument from context which, in my view, fails to recognise the juxtaposition in this section.

V. 1b: an observational enigmatic statement that one does not know whether the future will be love or hate. This deconstructs v. 1a; the righteous may be in God's hands but it is uncertain whether this means that God's love or hate lies ahead for them![192] Murphy puts it most clearly when he writes, "The customary signs of blessing or curse have been displaced, since there is no comprehension of what God is about."[193]

V. 2-6: All is enigmatic because ultimately all share the same destination i.e. death. Some respond to this with evil, a response which experience seems to confirm because the dead have perished and the only certainty of the living is that they will perish.[194] Life may be thought to have some advantages over death but that is like thinking that it is better to be a living dog than a dead lion.[195]

V. 7-10: a very strong imperative to joy.

V. 10-12: no one knows when disaster will strike.

The *carpe diem* section in v. 7-10 opens in a particularly strong way. It looks very much like the other juxtaposed *carpe diem* sayings that we have looked at. The lack of introductory formulae combined with the several imperatives enhance the juxtaposed nature of this advice. There is no אין טוב element, perhaps because of the sharper, imperative nature of the exhortation. God's approval of eating and drinking is however strongly stated in v. 7b,[196] and the festive symbols in v. 8 and the positive reference to marriage in v. 9[197] further embody the positive approach that we are familiar with from the אין טוב sayings. V. 10 is a reminder of how all embracing the *carpe diem* vision of Qoheleth is, because as Whybray points out, "work" here includes 'thought, knowledge and wisdom.'[198]

Significantly though, with this stronger hortatory element there is present a stronger deconstructive element in this *carpe diem* saying than in any of the others. In v. 9 the life that the reader is exhorted to enjoy is כל ימי הבלך, and v. 10b undermines v. 10a by confronting it with the empty reality of שאול. More

---

192 H.W. HERTZBERG, *Der Prediger* (2nd ed.; KAT 17,4; Gütersloh: Gütersloher Verlagshaus Gerd Mohn, 1963) 176, and LAUHA, *Kohelet*, 166, are wrong in suggesting that human attributes are here referred to; in context it is God.

193 MURPHY, *Ecclesiastes*, 90.

194 For Ogden בטחון describes what one may rely on so that Qoheleth here asserts that human beings know only one certain thing, i.e. that they will die. As OGDEN, *Qoheleth*, 148, points out בטחון is a rare word which otherwise occurs only in 2 Kings 18:19 and Isaiah 36:4. In the latter two verses it does have the sense of that which can be relied upon.

195 Cf. ibid., 147-149, on the proverb in v. 4. CRENSHAW, *Ecclesiastes*, 209-210, seems to me right in reading the proverb in v. 4b ironically. The dog functioned as an opprobrious metaphor and in this light it is hard to see what advantage the knowledge that one will die could possibly bring. The proverb should be read ironically.

196 Cf. Ogden and Whybray. Murphy is more cautious but acknowledges that v. 7b refers to God's largesse. All agree on the festive symbolism in v. 8-9.

197 Whybray argues that the woman need not be one's wife, but see Murphy.

198 WHYBRAY, *Ecclesiastes* (NCBC), 145.

than any other of the juxtaposed sections we have looked at, this one witnesses to the enormous tension in the attempt to pursue the logical implications of Qoheleth's epistemology, while also trying to acknowledge the insights of Israelite life and religion. One gets the feeling that the two threaten as it were, to pull each other apart. Once again the exhortation to enjoyment should not just be seen as the answer to the problem of the universality of death. The contradiction remains unresolved: *how* is one to appropriate joy if one is living like a dog?

7. 11:7-12:7/8[199]

Whybray notes that the advice to enjoy life comes at the beginning of the final section of the book and is followed by the description of old age leading to death, expressed in a series of subordinate clauses introduced by עד אשׁר and dependent on the imperative to enjoy life.[200] The description of death is indicative of Qoheleth's stress that his listeners should face reality but the imperative makes the overall tone positive. "It is imperative to enjoy life, because that is the way to 'remember your Creator,' that is, to do his will." Ogden is in basic agreement with Whybray.[201] His structural analysis of this section is most helpful. He notes that 11:8 introduces the two verbs that dominate this section. 'Rejoice' is the imperative that governs 11:9-10 and 'Remember' is the imperative that governs 12:1-8.[202]

Up until this section the *carpe diem* passages have always followed enigmatic sections.[203] This shift to having the *carpe diem* section preface and structure the enigmatic section about death is significant. Previously the two ways of seeing life tend to have been juxtaposed without resolution. This allowing of the *carpe diem* element to shape the whole suggests the possibility of integration and resolution. The proverb in 11:7 that opens this section already says as much. Throughout Ecclesiastes תחת השׁמשׁ is mainly a negative expression disparaging life. But here, perhaps using a quote from Euripides,[204] life under the sun is assessed positively. The bridge element then between the הבל and *carpe diem* poles would be the *remembering* of one's creator in one's youth[205] before (x3) encountering the death and הבל found throughout life.

---

[199] This section is widely recognised as a distinct unit.

[200] WHYBRAY, "Qoheleth, Preacher of Joy," 90-91.

[201] OGDEN, *Qoheleth*, 193-207.

[202] It should be noted that there are many difficulties in the interpretation of 11:7-12:8. In our discussion of this passage I have not attempted to take up all the details since that would make this chapter far too lengthy.

[203] This of course depends upon how one divides up the book. In some cases, as we have seen, the *carpe diem* passages may be sandwiched in between enigmatic sections. The point is that, on my understanding, a *carpe diem* section never opens a new section except here in 11:7ff.

[204] See MURPHY, *Ecclesiastes*, 116.

[205] In a complex article N. LOHFINK, "Freu Dich, Jüngling – doch nicht, weil du jung bist. Zum Formproblem im Schlußgedicht Kohelets (Koh 11,9-12,8)," *BI* 3/2 (1995) 158-189, argues that the address to the youth is part of an initial banquet song form in the poem at the end of Ecclesiastes

זכר means here much more than intellectual acknowledgement of God as creator. It refers to allowing the notion of God as creator to shape one's handling of life's enigmas now. And, if Qoheleth has Genesis 1 in mind, as some scholars suggest, then it is that kind of understanding of God as creator by which Qoheleth calls upon his readers to allow their minds and lives to be shaped.[206] Remembrance, as Wolterstorff recognises, involves consciously allowing the great acts of God, remembered in the tradition, to shape one's perspective in the present.[207] The days of darkness will be many (11:8), but the way to joy in the midst of this darkness (12:2-7) is to remember God as creator. In v. 8 the tension between joy and enigma is still present; the command to rejoice is paralleled by the command to remember the days of darkness. This tension is resolved by changing the object of remembrance in 12:1 and putting the days of darkness in the context of such remembrance, as the threefold use of 'before' makes clear. And just as the description of death is metaphorical[208] so too, it seems to me, should "youth" not be taken too narrowly to refer to only the young. The idea is rather that life needs to be built upon a foundation of such remembrance.

This theology of remembrance of God as creator potentially undermines Qoheleth's empiricist epistemology, because it is tantamount to making the fear of God[209] (here = remember your creator) foundational to Qoheleth's search for wisdom rather than the sort of empiricism he had adopted. Indeed it should be noted that although the reality of death is unequivocal in this section the observational language is absent. Remembrance thus presents the possibility of the resolution of the tension in Qoheleth's juxtapositions of enigma and joy. Ellul puts it this way.

(11:9-12:8). This form is broken and then taken up again in another form, whereby the exhortation to the young to seize life now because it gets so bad in later years is undermined, and all readers are exhorted to enjoy life amidst the presence of death. Whether this is so or not, the description of the teacher in 12:9 indicates that Qoheleth's teaching is relevant to all ages.

[206] On זכר in the OT see H. EISING, "זכר," in: *TDOT* Vol. IV (1980) 64-82, and on the philosophy of remembrance see N. WOLTERSTORFF, "The Remembrance of Things (Not) Past: Philosophical Reflections on Christian Liturgy," in: P. FLINT (ed.), *Christian Philosophy* (1990) 118-161. זכר is not a common word in Ecclesiastes, and while it can be used simply in terms of remembrance as in 9:15 it clearly has a richer nuance in 11:7ff, as the objects of זכר here indicate. Note, for example 11:8b. The remembrance of the days of darkness is far more than mere intellectual acknowledgement, as 12:2-7 makes poignantly clear!

[207] Ibid., 131.

[208] See MURPHY, *Ecclesiastes*, 115-116, for a useful discussion of different approaches to 12:1-7.

[209] Qoheleth does refer to the fear of God, but there is much discussion as to the nuance he attaches to it. See MURPHY, *Ecclesiastes*, lxiv-lxvi. My point here is that "remember your creator" is similar in meaning to "the fear of the Lord" in a text like Proverbs 1:1-7. On the latter text see R.N. WHYBRAY, *Proverbs*, 36, who argues that the acquisition of true knowledge *begins* with the fear of the Lord. In the context of Ecclesiastes 12:1 is making the same sort of point.

Remember your Creator. Only here does Qoheleth call him by this name, and he does so by design! ... You may consider yourself autonomous, but you are incapable of knowing what should be done, incapable of knowing what wisdom is. You are a creature. ... Our problems do not stem from our failure to stay in our garden, like Candide. All the evils, and I choose my words carefully, *all the evils of the world* stem from our taking ourselves to be the Creator.[210]

I have used words like "potentially" and "possibility" deliberately in the above paragraph. The description of death and the הבל saying in v. 8 'balance' the goodness of seeing the light (11:7) and remembrance of the creator with a weighty reminder of the fragility of life. Something of the juxtaposition remains, and the reader is compelled to look to the concluding verses as to whether the "potentiality" of remembrance really does provide the key to resolving the juxtaposition.

Our analysis of these passages would tend thus to confirm Whybray's view that: (1.) these *carpe diem* passages are arranged to state their theme with increasing emphasis and solemnity; (2.)

These seven texts are clearly more than mere marginal comments or asides. They punctuate the whole book, forming a kind of *Leitmotif*; they increase steadily in emphasis as the book proceeds; and the last, the most elaborate of them all, directly addressed to the reader, introduces and dominates the concluding section of the book in which Qoheleth presents his final thoughts on how life should be lived and why. It would be arbitrary to deny that they play a significant part in the exposition of Qoheleth's thought.[211]

However, contra Whybray, I have suggested that the juxtaposition of the *carpe diem* passages with the enigmatic passages creates gaps which have to be filled. I suggest that 'remembrance of God as creator' potentially fills these gaps. For all their penetrating insight Whybray and Ogden fail to recognise the gaps that the juxtaposition creates. Indeed, scholars who view Qoheleth's message as more pessimistic tend to recognise the gaps more easily. The critical question though, is how one fills the gaps. Whybray and Ogden tend to fill in the gaps positively by seeing the *carpe diem* passages as answers. However, as we have seen again and again in our examination of these passages, they would be most inadequate answers. Castellino is much closer to the truth when he insists that "one can not deny the presence of a series of 'antitheses' that makes it difficult to assess the true meaning of the book. Due to these 'antitheses,' exegetes are

---

[210] J. ELLUL, *Reason for Being. A Meditation on Ecclesiastes* (Grand Rapids: Eerdmans, 1990) 278-283. Ellul could well be accused of reading into the text at this point, but if one bears in mind that Qoheleth may have had Genesis 1-3 in mind, then remembrance of one's Creator may well stress the contrast with wanting to become 'like God' by 'knowing good and evil'. The presence of wisdom motifs in Genesis 1-3 has long been recognised (cf. H. BLOCHER, *In the Beginning: The Opening Chapters of Genesis* [Leicester: IVP, 1984]), and Eve's reliance upon what she *saw* rather than what God as creator *said* may well be part of the background here.

[211] WHYBRAY, "Qoheleth, Preacher of Joy."

divided when called upon to judge what fundamental note Qoheleth really strikes. ... There is no denying that both sides could substantiate their judgement through an array of opposite quotations."[212] Failure to recognise the juxtapositions/ antitheses results in scholars endlessly trying to fill in the gap created by them. The gap is always then filled in by making one of the poles the dominant one. Thus Qoheleth either becomes mainly sceptical or mainly positive. Recognition of the juxtapositions grants the insight that he is sceptical and positive! His empiricist epistemology takes him towards scepticism, but his Jewish background and faith provide him with an undeniable, more shalomic perspective upon life.

I have suggested that Ecclesiastes itself gives us clues as to how the gap between empiricistic scepticism and the *carpe diem* perspective is to be filled. The theology of remembrance in 12:1ff is important in this respect, but the epilogue is, I think, crucial in indicating finally how the narrator intends us to fill in the gaps and, I suggest that 12:13-14 confirm my reading of 12:1 as the bridge which positively resolves the tension/gap between the *carpe diem* element and the enigma statements.

As we noted above, Ecclesiastes is full of repetition; the form of the text illustrates the circularity spoken of in 1:3-11. We have only investigated the *carpe diem* element of repetition. Considerably more work remains to be done in this area. For example "under the sun" is a motif that recurs 27 times; "sun" occurs 33 times. It is Qoheleth's way of referring to this-worldly existence. During the course of Ecclesiastes it provides the context for deeply negative (cf. 2:18-23) as well as deeply positive (cf. 5:18) attitudes to life. The proverb (11:7) which opens the 'final' section of Qoheleth tells us that "it is good (טוב) for the eyes to see the sun, thereby encapsulating in proverbial form the message of 11:7-12:7/8 and indicating the side on which Qoheleth finally stands.

7.4.3.3 Juxtaposition and Gaps

We have suggested above that the juxtaposing of contradictory perspectives producing gaps is very much part of the fabric of Ecclesiastes. This has never been consciously studied by commentators,[213] although of course they work with the phenomenon all the time. As we saw, those who see Qoheleth as ultimately positive tend to smooth over the gaps, whereas those who recognise the gaps tend to see Qoheleth as a pessimist with the *carpe diem* passages as hedonistic

---

[212] G.R. CASTELLINO, "Qoheleth and His Wisdom," *CBQ* 30 (1968) 15.

[213] In his examination of the composition of Ecclesiastes, M. EATON, *Ecclesiastes* (TOTC; Leicester: IVP, 1983) 41, says of the 'contradictions', "It is surely more likely that juxtaposed contradictions (e.g. 8:12f.) are calculated to draw our attention to the viewpoint of faith in contrast to that of observation." However, Eaton does not pursue the presence of such juxtapositions in Ecclesiastes as a whole. GLADSON, *Retributive Paradoxes in Proverbs 10-29*, 146, notes that literary juxtaposition is one way the OT handles retributive paradox, and refers to the final chapter of Qoheleth as an example.

resignation or as additions. Good is one of the few to recognise the role of gaps in Ecclesiastes, but even he writes, "The book is not a systematic or complete presentation of theology, a philosophy, an ethic, a way of life. The large gaps that remain, Qoheleth's sardonic wit might have filled delightfully, but we must leave them blank."[214]

Why is it that the gaps in Ecclesiastes have not been attended to? The answer lies in the failure of commentators to take the *literary* nature of Ecclesiastes seriously. As Sternberg points out a literary work *is* a system of gaps which need to be filled.[215] Gaps are not the same as blanks; gaps are relevancies which demand closure. Gaps are created by opposition in juxtaposition: "the narrative juxtaposes two pieces of reality that bear on the same context but fail to harmonize either as variants of a situation or as phases in an action."[216] Gap-filling, according to Sternberg, is not arbitrary but should be controlled by the text's norms and directives. Although they arise from a lack in the telling, gaps move the reader between the truth and the whole truth and thereby give rise to a fullness in the reading.[217]

It is apparent how well this fits with our reading of the *carpe diem* passages in Ecclesiastes. We have shown that the gaps are in fact gaps and that they are created by oppositional juxtaposition. 12:13-14 ensures a foolproof reading of Ecclesiastes but it is only by attending to the gaps that one moves from a true reading to the whole truth.

In this section we have focused on the poetics of Ecclesiastes rather than its overall structure and we will not pursue the complex question of the macro structure of Ecclesiastes further here. However the two are closely related. Wright and Loader, as we saw in chapter four have done important work on the structure of Ecclesiastes, but clearly if our analysis of the structures of repetition is correct then both their analyses would have to be revised. The hebel sayings are part of a large and more complex structure of repetition which Wright's analysis doesn't take adequate account of, and Loader's polar pattern fails to reckon adequately with the gaps that the juxtapositions set up.

7.4.4 Intertextual Analysis

We have already had regular recourse to comparison of Ecclesiastes with Proverbs, indicating the dynamic of intertextuality in all biblical interpretation. Indeed, Qoheleth's relationship to traditional wisdom has featured large in twentieth century interpretation of Ecclesiastes, with Qoheleth regularly seen as reacting strongly against traditional wisdom. Hengel for example, argues that

---

[214] GOOD, *Irony in the Old Testament*, 195.

[215] STERNBERG, *The Poetics of Biblical Narrative*, 186.

[216] Ibid., 243.

[217] See ibid., 186-263, for a detailed discussion of gaps and the reading process in biblical narrative.

Qoheleth's empiricism results in his denying the traditional Jewish doctrine of retribution.[218] Perdue goes so far as to suggest that Qoheleth develops an alternative worldview to that of the sages:

> in his writings the foreground is not occupied by the manifold traditional motives; rather, he transforms them in his extremely individualist criticism by shattering the traditional world-view of earlier wisdom, denying a fixed connection between action and result, and proclaiming the absolute inexplicability of the divine action in nature and history.[219]

And Crüsemann maintains that "[t]his difference between Koheleth and his predecessors must be taken as the starting point for understanding Koheleth."[220] This type of approach to the relationship between Ecclesiastes and the wisdom corpus/movement rests on a developmental reconstruction of wisdom in the OT in which Qoheleth becomes associated with a crisis in wisdom.[221] Preuss is an extreme example of such a position.[222] In his view:

1. Wisdom is marginal to Israel's faith.
2. The God of wisdom is not Yahweh.
3. Wisdom concentrates on the orders in reality.
4. Retribution is one of these orders. The sages sought to discover this mechanical correspondence between action and consequence, as reflected in Proverbs.
5. A deed-consequence viewpoint is the basic dogma of early wisdom.

Clearly if one understands early wisdom in this way, then Qoheleth will be seen as reacting against this mechanical understanding of retribution, and thereby participating with Job in a crisis of wisdom. The critical question is whether or not early wisdom was of this sort, and whether wisdom in Proverbs is of this sort. Murphy points out that although this notion of a wisdom crisis looms almost as large in scholarly discussion as does the exile of 587 BC, the earliest tradition clearly interpreted Qoheleth as working within the wisdom tradition.[223] As he tersely puts it, "There is no record that the book of Ecclesiastes was received with consternation."[224]

The subject of the origin and development of wisdom in Israel is a complex one which we cannot pursue here. However, insofar as inter*textuality* goes, there

---

[218] HENGEL, *Judaism and Hellenism.*

[219] PERDUE, *Wisdom and Creation,* 116.

[220] F. CRÜSEMANN, "The Unchangeable World: The 'Crisis of Wisdom' in Qoheleth," in: W. SCHOTROFF and W. STEGEMANN (eds.), *God of the Lowly* (1984) 61.

[221] See H. GESE, "The Crisis of Wisdom in Koheleth," in: J.L. CRENSHAW (ed.), *Theodicy in the OT* (1983) 141-153; and H.H. SCHMID, *Wesen und Geschichte der Weisheit* (BZAW 101; Berlin: Töpelmann, 1966) on the crisis of wisdom.

[222] MURPHY, *Ecclesiastes,* lxi.

[223] Ibid.

[224] Ibid. For Murphy's understanding of Qoheleth's relationship to traditional wisdom see pp. lxii-lxiv.

are good reasons for rejecting the sort of understanding of the Ecclesiastes-
Proverbs relationship that Preuss advocates. Gladson persuasively argues that
"retributive paradox" occurs in all strands of OT literature.[225] Taken as a whole
Proverbs by no means presents a mechanical act-consequence understanding of
retribution. This has been clearly demonstrated in an excellent article on wealth
and poverty in Proverbs by van Leeuwen.[226]

Van Leeuwen points out that there are large groups of sayings in Proverbs
that assert a simple cause and effect relationship whereby righteousness leads to
wealth and wickedness to poverty. These are examples of the "character-
consequence-nexus". However they do not concern concrete, individual acts and
their consequences: "It is the long-term character and direction of a person or
group (as 'righteous' or 'wicked') which determines life consequences and
'destiny'."[227] It is a failure to recognise this long-term character that leads
scholars to the mechanical view of retribution in Ecclesiastes.

> These proverbs, *when taken by themselves*, are the basis for the view of some
> scholars that the tidy dogmatism of Proverbs does not correspond to reality and
> is doomed to collapse under the weight of reality, as happened in Job and
> Qoheleth. Since the foregoing sayings are not always exemplified in human
> experience, their falsification presumably led to a crisis of faith in Yahweh's
> maintenance of a just world order.[228]

However, proverbs are by their very nature *partial utterances* and this type
of mechanical approach does not do justice to the many sayings in Proverbs
which manifest a more complex understanding of the way God works in creation.
Particularly noteworthy in this respect are the 'better-than' sayings in Proverbs
(cf. 15:16-17; 16:16, 19 etc.) The overall picture is a far more complex one which
van Leeuwen sums up as follows:

> *In general*, the sages clearly believed that wise and righteous behaviour did
> make life better and richer, though virtue did not *guarantee* those
> consequences. Conversely, injustice, sloth, and the like generally have bad
> consequences. The editor-sages who structured Proverbs sought first to teach
> these basic 'rules of life,' thus the heavy emphasis on character-consequence
> patterns in both Proverbs 1-9 and 10-15. We must first learn the basic rules; the
> exceptions can come later. Though very aware of exceptions to the character-
> consequence rule, the sages insisted that righteousness is better than
> wickedness. The most fundamental and profound reason for this is that they
> believed that God loves the one and hates the other. For Israel's sages that
> sometimes seems the only answer. ... the sages knew that there are limits to

---

[225] GLADSON, *Retributive Paradoxes in Proverbs 10-29*.
[226] VAN LEEUWEN, "Wealth and Poverty," 25-36.
[227] Ibid., 27; cf. FOX, *Qoheleth and His Contradictions*, 132-133.
[228] VAN LEEUWEN, "Wealth and Poverty," 28-29.

human wisdom. General patterns may be discerned, but many particular events may be unjust, irrational, and ultimately inscrutable.[229]

Van Leeuwen also notes that there is a future-oriented retribution perspective in Proverbs. Proverbs lacks a doctrine of resurrection and yet insists on the triumph of God's justice. Van Leeuwen regards this as a hallmark of Yahwistic faith. "The sages' stance is to maintain faith in God's justice, even when they personally cannot see it or touch it, even when the recorded past does not verify it. Here religion provides no escape from the pain or absurdities of existence. The book of Job was inevitable, not because Proverbs was too simplistic, but because life's inequities, as reflected in Proverbs, drive faith to argue with the Deity."[230]

Once one recognises that Proverbs' understanding of retribution is more complex than a mechanical deed-consequence notion, then Ecclesiastes relationship to Proverbs and traditional wisdom has to be re-evaluated. Admittedly, van Leeuwen's understanding of this greater complexity is only one possibility among a number. Gladson, for example, makes retributive paradox a function of pluralism and dissent already present in early wisdom traditions. For van Leeuwen, by comparison, "whatever their historical origin, within Proverbs they have come to express *one* broad worldview which acknowledges the conflict of dogma and experience, yet maintains both."[231] Either way, it is clear that Qoheleth's empirical methodology demands a certainty which traditional wisdom was aware that it could not provide. Consequently, rather than Qoheleth representing a crisis in wisdom, he could be seen as focusing on the retributive paradox which Proverbs is aware of and perhaps subsumes under its more general long-term deed-consequence understanding. Because Qoheleth's empiricism is based on observation alone, he moves in the direction of deconstructing the tradition by always focusing on the individual exceptions.

It should also be noted that Ecclesiastes, in our view, does not recommend Qoheleth's empiricism, but ironically deconstructs it and arrives at a "remembering your creator" position which is similar to that "fear of God" which Proverbs declares to be foundational to its wisdom. In this way the focus of Ecclesiastes is far more specific than Proverbs, but the views of wisdom and retribution are not necessarily that far apart.

Another intertextual issue that has featured centrally in the interpretation of Ecclesiastes is the relationship between wisdom and law, especially as this is focused in chapter 12:13b: וְאֶת־מִצְוֹתָיו שְׁמוֹר. For many scholars the introduction of law is alien to the wisdom tradition in which Ecclesiastes is situated, thus indicting that the epilogue, or at least this part of it, is a later attempt

---

[229] Ibid., 32, 33.
[230] Ibid., 34.
[231] Ibid., 26.

to make Qoheleth appear orthodox or to thematize a relationship between wisdom and the commandments in the Law.[232]

However, we have argued that there are good reasons for resisting early attempts to conclude that the epilogue is a later addition.[233] The genre of Ecclesiastes and the circular intent at totality drive us to explore other avenues before concluding that the reference to law must make the epilogue a later addition. And there are indications that the reference to law may not be as alien to Ecclesiastes as some suggest. As Lohfink, for example points out, law is not alien to the fear of God in Qoheleth.[234] He makes the point that 5:6 concludes the section 4:17-5:6. Indeed 4:17-5:6 contain a restatement of the law of Deuteronomy 23:22-24 in 5:3-4 and the background to 5:5 is Numbers 15:22-31. And this section with its allusions to the Torah concludes with the exhortation to "fear God."[235]

This evidence of awareness of pentateuchal cultic legislation needs to be combined with the vocabulary in Ecclesiastes that also appears to relate to the domain of torah, namely 'judgement' (3:17; 11:9), 'sinner', 'sin' (2:26; 5:5; 8:12) 'wicked' and 'righteous' (3:17). These factors, combined with the indications that Ecclesiastes has a strong link with Genesis and several strong links with Deuteronomy, make it more and more difficult to insist that the reference to law means that the epilogue *must* be a later addition.[236] Certainly if Qoheleth had Genesis 1ff in mind, then the use of Elohim and the reference to "your creator" should not be set in opposition to the lawgiver, Yahweh, as Genesis 2 makes particularly clear with its description of God as Yahweh Elohim, thereby stressing that the creator Elohim is the Yahweh of Israel.[237]

---

[232] See G.T. SHEPPARD, *Wisdom as a Hermeneutical Construct* (Berlin; NY: de Gruyter, 1980) 121-129.

[233] The introduction of law does strike the reader as strange, but strangeness is not alien to endings. This century considerable work has been done on the theory of endings and this may provide helpful insights with respect to the epilogue. See F. KERMODE, *The Sense of an Ending: Studies in the Theory of Fiction* (Oxford: OUP, 1966); P. ROGERS, "The Parthian Dart: Endings and Epilogues in Fiction," *Essays in Criticism* XLII/2 (1992) 85-106; and for a fascinating application of this type of theory to Jonah see W.B. CROUCH, "To Question an End, To End a Question: Opening the Closure of the Book of Jonah," *JSOT* 62 (1994) 101-112.

[234] N. LOHFINK, "Qoheleth 5:17-19 – Revelation by Joy," *CBQ* 52/4 (1990) 633.

[235] There is however considerable disagreement as to how to understand Qoheleth's view of the cult. Cf. L.G. PERDUE, *Wisdom and Cult* (SBLDS 30; Missoula: Scholars Press, 1977) 178-188; and OGDEN, *Qoheleth*, 75ff, for two different views. In my opinion Ogden's is the more satisfactory view.

[236] It is, of course, possible to argue that Qoheleth knows the Torah but is very negative towards it. This will depend upon one's understanding of the passages in which this vocabulary occurs.

[237] See J. L'HOUR, "Yahweh Elohim," *RB* 81 (1974) 524-556; and C.G. BARTHOLOMEW, "Covenant and Creation: Covenant Overload or Covenantal Deconstruction," *CTJ* 30/1 (1995) 11-33.

In OT theology the relationship between law and wisdom remains a controversial and difficult issue.[238] Murphy has helpfully suggested that "[t]he problem of the relationship between wisdom literature and other portions of the Old Testament needs to be reformulated in terms of a shared approach to reality."[239] It does need to be remembered that the strong distinction between law and wisdom is a modern construct, and certainly by the third century BC it is likely that wisdom and law would not be considered separate paths to successful living in the minds of teachers and populace since both relate to ordering life in all its dimensions. This becomes particularly clear when one notes that "[a] relationship between religious and secular is not applicable to OT wisdom teaching."[240] Neither is it applicable to torah which also orders all areas of life. How then might these two approaches have been understood to relate to each other?

This is an extremely complex issue and here I simply want to make a suggestion along the lines of Murphy's proposal of a shared reality. The wisdom and legal traditions in the OT are clearly distinct and yet they manifest some awareness of each other, as we have seen with Ecclesiastes.[241] Both have in common the ordering of the life of God's people.[242] Van Leeuwen has analysed the root metaphors of Proverbs 1-9 and argues persuasively that

> underlying the bipolar metaphorical system of positive and negative youths, invitations/calls, 'ways', 'women', and 'houses' in Proverbs 1-9, is a yet more fundamental reality which these images together portray. These chapters depict the world as the arena of human existence. This world possesses two fundamental characteristics. First is its structure of boundaries or limits. Second is the bi-polar human *eros* for the beauty of Wisdom, who prescribes life within limits, or for the seeming beauty of Folly, who offers bogus delights in defiance of created limits.[243]

Van Leeuwen argues that the worldview which Proverbs exhibits is a 'carved' one in that "cultural and personal exhortation is grounded in the reality

---

[238] For a useful discussion of the relationship of these two traditions which both seek to order the lives of God's people see J. BLENKINSOPP, *Wisdom and Law in The Old Testament. The Ordering of Life in Israel and Early Judaism* (Oxford: OUP, 1983).

[239] MURPHY, "Wisdom – Theses and Hypotheses," 38.

[240] Ibid., 40.

[241] See R. VAN LEEUWEN, "Liminality and Worldview in Proverbs 1-9," *Semeia* 50 (1990) 122, for some of the links between Proverbs and Job and the Pentateuch. Van Leeuwen argues that certain texts in Proverbs and Job presuppose the historical tradition of the gift of the land.

[242] MURPHY, "Wisdom – Theses and Hypotheses," is critical of the close association of wisdom with the search for order, arguing that this question is a modern one which focuses on a presupposition of Israel's wisdom approach. However see VAN LEEUWEN, "Liminality and Worldview in Proverbs 1-9," for a powerful defence of taking the tacit presupposition of cosmic order seriously in wisdom literature.

[243] Ibid., 116.

of the created word with its inbuilt normativity."[244] Justice and righteousness are built into the world

This link of wisdom with creation has long been recognised. What is often not noted, though, is that the order that Proverbs finds in the 'carved' creation is not and cannot be simply read out of the creation. This is the point that Fox makes about Israelite wisdom; it is not empirical in the way that Ecclesiastes is, but assumes ethical principles which it uses observation to support. This is the sort of position exemplified in Genesis 1ff. The ordering of creation is not antithetical to instruction from Elohim/Yahweh Elohim. Order and instruction/torah go hand-in-hand, and obedience requires both a good creation and instruction. The point is that wisdom literature assumes certain ethical principles which are not just read off creation but are often very similar to the principles found in the Law. Van Leeuwen, for example, argues that Proverbs 1-9 indicates that it is in "the liquid abandonment of married love" that healthy *communitas* takes place. As van Leeuwen notes, "This reality has its parallel at Sinai."[245]

Thus it can be argued that while wisdom is most closely related to creation it presupposes instruction. Similarly, when the narrative frame within which law always occurs in the final form of the OT is foregrounded, it becomes apparent that the law of Yahweh the redeemer God is also the law of the creator God. This link between Yahweh as creator and redeemer is central to covenant in the OT,[246] and alerts us to the link between law and creation.

My suggestion therefore is that law and wisdom share an underlying and often tacit presupposition of a 'carved' creation order. This is their shared reality. Instruction from Yahweh would therefore not be seen to conflict with the way he ordered his creation, but would provide the ethical principles for discovery of that liminality. If this is even close to the situation that prevailed in Israel then it would confirm our argument for caution about insisting that the epilogue must be an addition because it mentions "keeping commandments."

Many other aspects of biblical intertextuality in relation to Ecclesiastes could be considered. A strong connection between Ecclesiastes and the early chapters of Genesis has long been noted.[247] Alter notes a connection with Psalm 39,[248] and we have noted earlier the similarities between Ecclesiastes and Psalms like Psalm 73. Ecclesiastes cries out for detailed comparison of OT ways of

---

[244] Ibid., 118.

[245] Ibid., 132.

[246] See BARTHOLOMEW, "Covenant and Creation."

[247] C.G. FORMAN, "Koheleth's Use of Genesis," *JSS* 5 (1960) 256-263; D.M. CLEMENTS, "The Law of Sin and Death: Ecclesiastes and Genesis 1-3," *Themelios* 19/3 (1994) 5-8. For example, as Robert Alter pointed out to me in conversation, much of Qoheleth has a very different understanding of time compared with Genesis 1:1-2:4.

[248] ALTER, *The Art of Biblical Poetry*, 68-70.

handling theodicy and of OT views of death and the possibility of life after death. And so one could continue, but we cannot pursue these subjects further here.

7.4.5 The Implied Readership of Ecclesiastes

The shifts in Ecclesiastes between third and first person to second person hortation indicate that the text is designed for instruction, as indeed 12:9-11 says of Qoheleth's teaching. בני (12:12; cf. 11:9) implies a young male readership within Israel, although it is unclear whether this is within the family, school or court.[249] העם (12:9) alerts us to the fact that Qoheleth's teaching was not confined to the young males, but relevant to the whole people of God.[250] The implication is that Ecclesiastes is read within the community of God's people. This is confirmed by the orthodox ending.

One assumes that the readership would identify with the empirical questions that Qoheleth raises and the individualism that he embodies, and the tension that these create with his Israelite perspective upon life. The individualism and empiricism are probably best accounted for by the Greek influence that Jews were being exposed to in the third century BC. Fox suggests that Qoheleth's affinities with Epicureanism is particularly significant, with its view that sensory experience is the ultimate source and arbiter of knowledge.[251] It is notoriously difficult to pin down the specific Greek influences affecting Qoheleth, but I think it is right to imagine a situation in which Jews are increasingly being exposed to the sort of epistemologies that Epicureanism exhibits. Such exposure would tempt them to read their tragic history and present experience along empirical lines. To such Jews the empirical analysis that Qoheleth models, put in the mouth initially of the wise man par excellence, Solomon, but still only running up continually against the enigma of life, would speak with exceptional power. It would be a bomb on the playing field of those seeking a redemptive synthesis in Greek philosophy with the biblical tradition.

Of course Ecclesiastes would appeal immediately to the educated Jew who was being exposed to and tempted by Greek philosophy. In this sense Lohfink may be right in seeing it as a school text book. However, parents and the populace would be increasingly aware of the tension between the pervasive Greek culture and Israelite tradition, and in this sense Ecclesiastes would instruct all the people, as the epilogue notes.

---

[249] Cf. WHYBRAY, *Proverbs*, 7-12.

[250] Cf. VAN LEEUWEN, "Wealth and Poverty," 114-115, who argues that while Proverbs 1-9 are "threshold speeches to those on the verge of adulthood," they also function to 'remind' sages of their basic worldview and strengthen them in it.

[251] FOX, *Qoheleth and His Contradictions*, 16.

7.4.6 The Genesis of Ecclesiastes

It is clear from our reading of Ecclesiastes that careful consideration of the genre and the literary shape of the text makes much of the genetic analysis of Ecclesiastes during this century out of date and inappropriate. Source criticism of Ecclesiastes needs to be revised along the lines Sternberg has suggested. Analysis of individual forms within Ecclesiastes and their *Sitz im Leben* will continue to be helpful to exegesis, but this work has to be related to the present literary shape of the text and its macro-form. The similarity of Ecclesiastes to fictional autobiography makes quests for the historical 'I' of Qoheleth obsolete, and the debate about the genesis of Ecclesiastes will rather need to be focused upon whether with Fox we see one author as responsible for the whole text, or whether we maintain the substantial unity of Ecclesiastes but still see 12:9-14 as the addition of a later hand. However Ecclesiastes reached its present form,[252] I have sought to show that it is the present form that the interpreter should work at understanding. If 12:9-14 is to be excluded from this form, then a strong case which does not just assume the historical critical legacy will have to be made along these lines.

I see no need to depart from the current consensus that Ecclesiastes reached its present form in the fourth or third centuries BC, although it is hard to be certain in this sort of area.[253] Our reading of Ecclesiastes also confirms that it fits very much within a Jewish rather than a Greek background, although the nature of Qoheleth's empirical חכמה indicates the influence of Greek thought upon Israel. This influence is handled critically.

7.4.7 The Message of Ecclesiastes

> *Nothing is further from the spirit of the sages than the idea of an autonomy of thinking, a humanism of the good life; in short of a wisdom in the Stoic or Epicurean mode founded on the self-sufficiency of thought. This is why wisdom is held to be a gift of God in distinction to the 'knowledge of good and evil' promised by the Serpent.*
>
> (P. RICOEUR, *Essays on Biblical Interpretation* [Philadelphia: Fortress, 1980] 88)

Our application of the proposed communication model of hermeneutics has as its goal the explication of the message of Ecclesiastes. However, it needs to be stressed that what has led up to and constitutes the following proposed message

---

[252] It is quite possible that Ecclesiastes has a long history of composition. But neither its genre nor its present shape give any indication that we will be able to recover earlier stages with strong possibility of success.

[253] D.C. FREDERICKS, *Qoheleth's Language: Re-evaluating its Nature and Date* (Lewiston: Edwin Mellen, 1988) has argued that the language of Qoheleth should not be dated later than the exilic period and that it could be dated earlier. But see SCHOORS, *The Preacher Sought to Find Pleasing Words*, 14-16, 222.

of Ecclesiastes is tentative, and needs to be substantiated and tested in much greater detail. In the light of our preceding discussion, I propose that the following might be the message of Ecclesiastes.

Ecclesiastes is written for fourth/third century Israelites who lived in a period when Yahweh's promises seemed to have come to nothing and there was little empirical evidence of his purposes and promises. The Israelites were exposed to pervasive Greek thought and culture at this time and a common temptation especially among the more educated was to apply a sort of Greek (Epicurean) empiricism to their experience of desolation, leading many of their young people to conclude that God's purposes in the world are inscrutable and utterly enigmatic.

Ecclesiastes is crafted by a wisdom teacher as an ironical exposure of such an empiricistic epistemology which seeks wisdom through personal experience and analysis without the 'glasses' of the fear of God. This empiricistic epistemology keeps running up against the enigma of life when pursued from this direction, and it appears impossible to find a bridge between this enigma and the good that is visible and which the biblical tradition alerts one to. The resolution of this paradox is found in the fear of God (rejoicing and remembrance) which enables one to rejoice and apply oneself positively to life in the midst of all that one does not understand, including and especially death. Ecclesiastes exhorts Israelites struggling with the nature of life's meaning and God's purposes to pursue genuine wisdom by allowing their thinking to be shaped integrally by a recognition of God as Creator so that they can enjoy God's good gifts and obey his laws amidst the enigma of his purposes. In this way it is an exhortation to be truly wise in difficult and perplexing situations. This is where the implied author wants the reader/s to stand in relation to the enigmas of life.

7.5 Conclusion

In this chapter we have sought to argue for a Christian hermeneutic in the context of a genuine pluralism in OT studies. We have argued that a communication model of interpretation is a natural extension of a Christian worldview. My argument at this point is similar to Plantinga's approach to epistemology in terms of proper function.[254] He argues that his approach fits with an understanding of humans as 'designed artefacts,' but that it does not fit with naturalism, *despite the fact* that many naturalists hold such a view. In a similar way we are arguing that a communication model is peculiarly appropriate from a Christian perspective.

This may appear commonsensical. However, a cursory reading of Belsey will alert one to the problematic status of 'common-sense' in late modern

---

[254] Cf. A. PLANTINGA, *Warrant and Proper Function* (NY; Oxford: OUP, 1993) 194-215.

scholarship.[255] I am grateful to the postmodern turn for the extent to which it has shown that what may appear as commonsensical is always part of a broader perspective, and that it is difficult to hold onto the 'commonsensical' if you let go of the bigger picture. As Belsey herself says

> there is no practice without theory ... What we do when we read, however 'natural' it seems, presupposes a whole theoretical discourse, even if unspoken, about language and about meaning, about the relationships between meaning and the world, meaning and people, and finally about people themselves and their place in the world.[256]

The proof of any biblical hermeneutic is its ability to allow a text to speak on its own terms and thus the application of our proposed hermeneutic to Ecclesiastes is an important conclusion to this investigation. Our proposed reading of Ecclesiastes needs considerably more testing to establish it as a possible reading. However, we suggest that approaching it as we have done, analysing its genre as a literary unity along literary-historical lines, attending closely to its poetics, setting it in the context of the rest of the OT, does indeed allow its message to be heard in a way that makes sense of the text as a whole.

---

[255] C. BELSEY, *Critical Practice* (New Accents; London: Routledge, 1980).
[256] Ibid., 4.

CONCLUSION

The Bible deals with the whole, the sum total of reality. ... If we confess 'I believe in God, the creator of heaven and earth,' and do not take seriously that every creature is related to God, that God has to do with all creatures, then this confession is an empty phrase. If for us there is a reality which does not have to do with God, then we do not know God, the Creator.

(C. WESTERMANN, "The Contribution of Biblical Thought to an Understanding of Our Reality," in: D.G. MILLER [ed.], *The Hermeneutical Quest* [1986] 48)

This book has sought to investigate the relationship between OT exegesis and hermeneutical theory while using Ecclesiastes as a focus and test case for the investigation. In the introduction we argued that apart from its intrinsic importance such an investigation is particularly relevant at present because of the growing pluralism within OT studies. Analysis and understanding of this pluralism requires exploration of the different philosophies shaping different approaches in OT studies.

In chapter one we surveyed the terrain of philosophical hermeneutics. This survey revealed the diversity within modern philosophical hermeneutics. It became clear that there are different approaches and these will shape interpretative work differently. The postmodern turn in particular has made this diversity apparent. Different hermeneutics work with different understandings of reason, history, the human person etc. We identified Gadamer's hermeneutic as particularly important; it bridges modern and postmodern hermeneutics and raises the question of the role of prejudice and tradition in interpretation. We concluded that if we are to understand different readings of Ecclesiastes and to find a way ahead in the diversity of contemporary OT studies, then we must attend to the different hermeneutical options available and their influence within OT studies. And it was noted from our survey that the relationship of reason to faith is a key issue in modern hermeneutics. Thus, for Christians busy with OT interpretation the question of how a Christian perspective upon reality relates to the different hermeneutical options is an important question.

In chapter two we surveyed the history of the interpretation of Ecclesiastes. We saw that up until the Reformation Ecclesiastes tended to be interpreted allegorically. It was always read as Scripture and with the epilogue as determinative. The Enlightenment and post-Enlightenment period (modernity) marks the watershed in the interpretation of Ecclesiastes. Its effect was to reinforce literal interpretation and to bracket out the constitutive role of faith in the interpretation process. The application of historical method to the OT in the nineteenth century lead eventually to source critical analysis of Ecclesiastes, and then to form critical and traditional critical analyses. Early twentieth century approaches to Ecclesiastes were strongly source critical, but the second half of the twentieth century has seen a recovery of a sense of the unity of Ecclesiastes. However the Epilogue still tends to be regarded as secondary. Newer reading strategies have gradually started to have an impact on the reading of Ecclesiastes.

This survey demonstrated that there is a close relationship between the history of the interpretation of Ecclesiastes and that of hermeneutics. Modernity and its hermeneutical legacy were obviously particularly influential in the interpretation of Ecclesiastes, and yet at the end of the twentieth century there is no agreement about the message of Ecclesiastes. It was concluded that if we are to get a better understanding of Ecclesiastes then it is important to explore the relationship between hermeneutics and the reading of Ecclesiastes more closely.

Because of the importance of modernity for hermeneutics and the interpretation of Ecclesiastes, in chapter three we examined the origin of the historical critical method in modernity and its effect upon the reading of Ecclesiastes. Our analysis confirmed that the historical critical method is a product of modernity and more particularly of nineteenth century philosophies of history. From Toulmin's reassessment of modernity it became clear that the standard account of modernity can no longer be assumed and that, insofar as the historical critical method has been shaped by modernity, we do need to be critically aware of its prejudices. Early twentieth century readings of Ecclesiastes tended to be historically reductionistic and neglected the literary and theological aspects of Ecclesiastes. We argued that an evaluation of historical criticism needed to take account of the anti-Christian nature of some of its roots in modernity. This, combined with the fact that diverse philosophies of history inform the historical critical method and its reductionistic nature led us to conclude that the epistemological foundations of OT studies need re-evaluation.

In the latter half of the twentieth century there have been a number of important reactions to historical criticism in OT studies and we examined these in chapters four and five. Childs' canonical approach represents itself as a theological reaction to historical criticism, and NC and structuralism are reactions to 'positivism' in literary studies. As reactions the value of these approaches was identified in their alerting us to the literary and theological dimensions of the OT texts, aspects which historical criticism tends to neglect. Thus Childs' canonical reading of Ecclesiastes helpfully explores how the epilogue affects the reading of the final form of Ecclesiastes. And NC and structuralism alert us to the fact that Ecclesiastes is a literary text and that exploration of this literary dimension is crucial to its correct interpretation. It was concluded that a hermeneutic is required which accounts for the historical, literary *and* theological aspects of the OT texts.

Chapter five examined Sternberg's narrative poetics which also aims to take the literary dimension of OT texts seriously. Sternberg's sophisticated poetics was a natural bridge to Fox's analysis of Ecclesiastes as a narrative literary whole. We analysed Fox's narrative reading of Ecclesiastes and in this context focused upon the question of the genre of Ecclesiastes. Genre analysis tends to be regarded as more of a historical than a literary question but we concluded that determination of the genre of Ecclesiastes requires close interaction between comparative historical and literary analysis. We argued that Ecclesiastes is a developed wisdom form of the royal testament or fictional autobiography cast in a frame-narrative.

All of these reactions to historical criticism have taken place within the classical humanist paradigm of textuality in which hermeneutics is concerned with the attempt to discern the true meaning of texts. Postmodernism challenges the very possibility of determinate meaning, declares the author dead, and makes textual meaning dependent on the reader. Thus in chapter six we examined the postmodern turn and its implications for OT hermeneutics and the reading of Ecclesiastes. We argued that 'postmodernity' should be understood philosophically as a crisis of foundations in late modernity. We showed that this crisis is becoming evident in OT studies in terms of hermeneutic pluralism and fragmentation. Although little postmodern work has been done on Ecclesiastes we observed that consistent postmodernism would have radical implications for its interpretation.

However, we demonstrated that postmodernism is not as radically new as it is often presented and that the hermeneutical positions its proponents advocate still presuppose metanarratives and epistemologies. The value of postmodernism is its recognition that we have to position ourselves somewhere from which we do our analysis. The problem of postmodernism is its tendency to view all positionings as of equal value or of there being no way of deciding where one *should* position oneself. Thus, it was concluded that the crucial question for biblical scholars is whether or not there are appropriate prejudices for OT interpretation, or are one set as good as another?

In chapter seven it was argued that Christian OT scholars should seek to develop a hermeneutic which is shaped by a religious (Christian) perspective in the context of a genuine pluralism within OT studies. It was argued that an integrated communication model for hermeneutics is a logical development of a Christian perspective and the parameters of such a model were mapped out in a way which attempts to do justice to the historical, literary and theological dimensions of a biblical text.

This model was then applied to Ecclesiastes. It was stressed that such a hermeneutic means taking the circular intent at totality seriously with respect to the whole of Ecclesiastes, including the epilogue. On the basis of our conclusions reached about the genre of Ecclesiastes particular attention was paid to the poetics of the text as the means by which we hear the message of Ecclesiastes. We did not analyse the overall structure of Ecclesiastes but attended to the central role of irony and the much neglected structures of repetition. It was argued that central to the structure of Ecclesiastes is the juxtaposition of the *carpe diem* passages with the enigmatic passages and that this juxtaposition creates gaps which the reader has to fill. Chapter twelve of Ecclesiastes is fundamental to the book in the answer it gives as to how the gaps should be filled, namely by remembering one's creator.

It was concluded that Ecclesiastes is addressed to third or fourth century BC disillusioned Israelites who were in danger of succumbing to Greek scepticism. Ecclesiastes is an ironical exposure of an empiricistic epistemology which seeks wisdom through personal experience and analysis without the 'glasses' of the fear of God. This empiricistic epistemology keeps running up against the enigma of life when pursued from this direction, and it appears impossible to find a bridge between this enigma and the good that is visible and which the biblical tradition alerts one to. The resolution of this paradox is found in the fear of God (rejoicing and remembrance) which enables one to rejoice and apply oneself positively to life in the midst of all that one does not understand, including and especially death.

We began this investigation with a quote from Sternberg about the inter-disciplinary task that biblical studies requires and its superhuman demands. It is well to recall those comments at this stage. Our exploration of the interface between the hermeneutic and exegetical poles of OT studies has meant that we have not been able to examine either pole exhaustively. Certainly our proposed reading of Ecclesiastes, for example, needs to be fleshed out and tested in greater detail. However, this investigation has demonstrated the organic relationship between hermeneutical theory and OT exegesis, as exemplified in the interpretation of Ecclesiastes and, especially in the light of the pluralism and fragmentation in OT studies today, examination of the interrelation of the different elements that constitute OT interpretation needs urgent attention.

Hermeneutical presuppositions are inescapable in exegesis and within modern hermeneutics there are a range of hermeneutical options which will shape one's interpretation differently. We have shown the fundamental role that philosophical hermeneutics play in OT interpretation, and yet very little work has been done in this area. In our opinion if OT scholars are to come to grips with the pluralism in OT studies and to continue to value objective interpretation then awareness of the way in which different hermeneutics shape exegesis will need to receive much greater attention. Of course attention also needs to be given to theological, sociological, linguistic etc. presuppositions, but the epistemological and ontological presuppositions embodied in a hermeneutic are of fundamental importance since they shape the entire knowledge enterprise, and it is here that many of the most fundamental differences among OT scholars are to be located.

At the present time of fragmentation it is vital that these differences are made visible if we are to understand the present and find a way ahead. This is not to suggest that the OT scholar needs to become a philosopher or a theologian, but it is to argue for philosophical and theological awareness by OT scholars and for dialogue with philosophers and theologians about the task of OT scholarship.

OT scholars do also need to reconsider the relationship between faith and scholarship. Much OT scholarship continues to resist allowing religious faith to shape biblical scholarship. In the tradition of modernity faith is privatised and objectivity sought by excluding religious beliefs from the academy. However this is itself a particular prejudice and if OT scholars continue to operate this way they will need to account for their approach. Such an approach can no longer just be assumed to be the right one, and, as the quote from Westermann above makes clear, for those who confess God as Creator it is unacceptable to bracket off OT studies from the reality of God. Of course much thought needs to be given to how one relates biblical studies to God, and we have argued that such a project needs to be theoretically well grounded. However, all scholars bring their ultimate presuppositions to bear on their scholarship and if this were acknowledged then it might be possible to work towards a genuine pluralism in the academy and OT studies. Certainly we need to be wary of a liberal pluralism which presents itself as tolerant but excludes serious academic work shaped by religious presuppositions, just as we ought to be wary of a religious monism which excludes all other approaches.

I would argue that Christian scholars ought to ensure that their scholarship is shaped by Christian presuppositions. Once bodies of OT scholarship start to emerge from within different traditions then the real conversations among different approaches can begin. This would be far more helpful than having presuppositions which do affect OT scholarship being forced underground and thus invisible in the name of objective, rational scholarship.

From a Christian perspective it appears to me that a great challenge for OT studies is to articulate an integrated hermeneutic. This runs counter to many trends in OT studies today but remains essential if hearing the message of the text is to be the focus of exegesis. In chapter seven I have made some preliminary proposals along the lines of a communication model, but clearly an enormous amount of work remains to be done in this area.

The proof of the pudding will always be in the eating, and it has been important to me throughout this project to be able to show how taking hermeneutics seriously does help in the interpretation of a perplexing book like Ecclesiastes. It is still common for readers to attribute the difficulties of Ecclesiastes entirely to the text itself. Our research has shown that this perplexity is as much a product of the reader as it is of the text. Clarity about the extent of the text being interpreted, about what a text is and how the literary, historical and theological elements interrelate go a long way towards clearing the ground for an

objective reading of Ecclesiastes. In particular I suggest that the literary nature of
Ecclesiastes needs renewed attention. Sternberg and others have done great work
on the poetics of narrative but the wisdom texts of the OT have received little
attention in this respect.

ABBREVIATIONS

AB	Anchor Bible
ABD	*Anchor Bible Dictionary* (ed. D.N. Freedman)
AnBib	Analecta Biblica
AOAT	Alter Orient und Altes Testament
AUSS	*Andrews University Seminary Studies*
BASOR	*Bulletin of the American Schools of Oriental Research*
BBR	*Bulletin for Biblical Research*
BDB	F. Brown, S.R. Driver, and C.A. Briggs (eds.), *Hebrew and English Lexicon of the Old Testament*
BETL	Bibliotheca ephemeridum theologicarum lovaniensium
BI	*Biblical Interpretation*
BibSac	*Bibliotheca Sacra*
BN	*Biblische Notizen*
BTB	*Biblical Theology Bulletin*
BZ	*Biblische Zeitschrift*
BZAW	Beihefte zur Zeitschrift für die alttestamentliche Wissenschaft
CBC	Cambridge Bible Commentary
CBQ	*Catholic Biblical Quarterly*
ConBOT	Coniectanea Biblica, Old Testament Series
CTJ	*Calvin Theological Journal*
CUP	Cambridge University Press
EJT	*European Journal of Theology*
ExpTim	*The Expository Times*
FS	Festschrift
GK	*Gesenius' Hebrew Grammar* (ed. E. Kautzsch)
HAR	*Hebrew Annual Review*
HAT	Handbuch zum Alten Testament
HIBT	*Horizons in Biblical Theology*
HTR	*Harvard Theological Review*
HUCA	*Hebrew Union College Annual*
ICC	International Critical Commentary
IOTS	*Introduction to the OT as Scripture* (B.S. Childs)
ITQ	*Irish Theological Quarterly*
IVP	Inter Varsity Press
JAAR	*Journal of the American Academy of Religion*
JBL	*Journal of Biblical Literature*

JETS	*Journal of the Evangelical Theological Society*
JQR	*Jewish Quarterly Review*
JSNT	*Journal for the Study of the New Testament*
JSOT	*Journal for the Study of the Old Testament*
JSOTSup	Journal for the Study of the Old Testament Supplement Series
JSS	*Journal of Semitic Studies*
JTS	*Journal of Theological Studies*
KAT	Kommentar zum Alten Testament
NC	New Criticism
NCBC	New Century Bible Commentary
NEB	Die Neue Echter Bibel
NICOT	New International Commentary on the Old Testament
NIV	New International Version
NRSV	New Revised Standard Version
NY	New York
OTE	*Old Testament Essays*
OTG	Old Testament Guide
OTL	Old Testament Library
OUP	Oxford University Press
RB	*Revue Biblique*
SBL	Society for Biblical Literature
SBLDS	Society for Biblical Literature Dissertation Series
SBT	*Studies in Biblical Theology*
SJT	*Scottish Journal of Theology*
SUNY	State University of NY Press
TB	*Tyndale Bulletin*
TDOT	*Theological Dictionary of the Old Testament* (eds. G.J. Botterweck, H. Ringgren, and H.-J. Fabry; trans. J.T. Willis, G.W. Bromiley, and D.E. Green)
TOTC	Tyndale Old Testament Commentaries
TSF	Theological Students' Fellowship
UF	*Ugarit Forschungen*
UP	University Press
VT	*Vetus Testamentum*
VTSup	Supplements to Vetus Testamentum
WBC	Word Biblical Commentary
WTJ	*Westminster Theological Journal*
ZAW	*Zeitschrift für die alttestamentliche Wissenschaft*

BIBLIOGRAPHY

AARSLEFF, H., *From Locke to Saussure. Essays on the Study of Language and Intellectual History*. London: Athlone, 1982.

ABBAGNANO, N., "Positivism," in: P. EDWARDS (ed.), *The Encyclopedia of Philosophy. Vols 5 and 6*. NY: MacMillan and Free Press, 1967. 414-419.

ABRAMS, M.H., *The Mirror and the Lamp. Romantic Theory and the Critical Tradition*. NY: OUP, 1953.

——, "The Deconstructive Angel," *Critical Inquiry* 3 (1977) 425-438.

——, *Doing Things with Texts. Essays in Criticism and Critical Theory*. NY; London: Norton, 1989.

ALONSO-SCHÖKEL, L., "Hermeneutical Problems of a Literary Study of the Bible," in: *Congress Volume. Edinburgh 1974* (VTSup 28). Leiden: Brill, 1974.

——, "Sapiential and Covenant Themes in Genesis 2-3," in: J.L. CRENSHAW (ed.), *Studies in Ancient Israelite Wisdom*. 1976. 468-480.

——, *A Manual of Hebrew Poetics* (Subsidia Biblica 11). Rome: Editrice Pontificio Istituto Biblico, 1988.

——, *Apuntes de hermenéutica* (2nd ed.; Colección Estructuras y Procesos). Madrid: Editorial Trotta, 1997.

ALSTON, W.A., *Perceiving God. The Epistemology of Religious Experience*. Ithaca; London: Cornell UP, 1991.

ALTER, R., *The Art of Biblical Narrative*. NY: Basic Books, 1981.

——, "A Response to Critics," *JSOT* 27 (1983) 113-117.

——, *The Art of Biblical Poetry*. Edinburgh: T&T Clark, 1985.

——, *The World of Biblical Literature*. London: SPCK, 1992.

ALTHUSSER, L., *For Marx*. London: Allen Lane, 1969.

ANDERSEN, F.I., *The Sentence in Biblical Hebrew*. The Hague: Mouton, 1974.

ANDERSON, B.W. (ed.), *The Books of the Bible: The Old Testament*. NY: Scribners, 1989.

ANDERSON, G.W. (ed.), *Tradition and Interpretation*. Oxford: Clarendon, 1979.

AUFFRET, P., "'Rien du tout de nouveau sous le soleil.' Étude structurelle de Qo 1,4-11," *Folia Orientalia* XXVI (1989) 145-166.

AUNE, D.E., *The New Testament and its Literary Environment*. Cambridge: James Clarke, 1987.

AUSTIN, J.L., *How to Do Things With Words* (2nd ed.). Oxford: OUP, 1975.

BALENTINE, S.E., "James Barr's Quest for Sound and Adequate Biblical Interpretation," in: S. BALENTINE and J. BARTON (ed.), *Language, Theology and the Bible*. 1994. 1-15.

BALENTINE, S.E., and J. BARTON (eds.), *Language, Theology and the Bible. Essays in Honour of James Barr*. Oxford: Clarendon, 1994.

BALTZER, K., "Women and War in Qoheleth 7:23-8:1a," *HTR* 80/1 (1987) 127-132.

BARCLAY, J.M.G., "Mirror-Reading a Polemical Letter: Galatians As a Test Case," *JSNT* 31 (1987) 73-93.

BAR-EFRAT, S., *Narrative Art in the Bible*. Sheffield: Almond Press, 1989.

BARNES, H.E., *A History of Historical Writing*. New York: Dover Publications, 1962.

BARR, J., *The Bible in the Modern World*. London: SCM; Philadelphia: Trinity Press International, 1973.

———, "Childs' *Introduction to the Old Testament as Scripture*," *JSOT* 16 (1980) 12-23.

———, *Holy Scripture. Canon, Authority, Criticism*. Philadelphia: Westminster, 1983.

———, "Exegesis as a Theological Discipline Reconsidered and the Shadow of the Jesus of History," in: D.G. MILLER (ed.), *The Hermeneutical Quest*. 1986. 11-45.

———, "The Literal, the Allegorical, and Modern Biblical Scholarship," *JSOT* 44 (1989) 3-17.

———, "Allegory and Historicism," *JSOT* 69 (1996) 105-120.

BARRÉ, M.L.,"Fear of God and the World View of Wisdom," *BTB* 11-13 (1983) 41-43.

BARTH, K., *Church Dogmatics. Volume 1. The Doctrine of the Word of God. Part 2*. Edinburgh: T&T Clark, 1956.

———, *Protestant Theology in the Nineteenth Century*. London: SCM, 1972.

BARTHES, R., "The Death of an Author," in: D. LODGE (ed.), *Modern Criticism and Theory*. 1988. 167-171.

BARTHOLOMEW, C.G., *The Composition of Deuteronomy: A Critical Analysis of the Approaches of E.W. Nicholson and A.D.H. Mayes*. Unpublished MA thesis: Potchefstroom University, 1992.

———, "Covenant and Creation: Covenant Overload or Covenantal Deconstruction," *CTJ* 30/1 (1995) 11-33.

———, "Review of J. Levenson, *The Hebrew Bible, the Old Testament and Historical Criticism* (1993)," *CTJ* 30/2 (1995) 525-530.

———, "Philosophy, Theology and Biblical Interpretation. Vanhoozer, Wright, Watson and Thiselton," unpubl. paper, 1995.

———, "Three Horizons: Hermeneutics from the Other End – An Evaluation of Anthony Thiselton's Hermeneutic Proposals," *EJT* 5 (1996) 121-135.

———, "New Criticism, Wittgenstein and Barth: In Search of the Roots of Childs' Canonical Approach," unpubl. paper, 1996.

BARTON, G.A., *A Critical and Exegetical Commentary on the Book of Ecclesiastes* (ICC). Edinburgh: T&T Clark, 1912.

BARTON, J., *Reading the Old Testament. Method in Biblical Study*. London: DLT, 1984.

———, "Reading the Bible as Literature: Two Questions for Critics," *Literature and Theology* 1/2 (1987) 135-153.

———, "Should Old Testament Study Be More Theological?" *ExpTim* 100/12 (1989) 443-448.

———, *The Future of Old Testament Study*. Clarendon: Oxford, 1993.

———, *People of the Book? The Authority of the Bible in Christianity* (2nd ed.). London: SPCK, 1993.

BAUDRILLARD, J., *Simulations*. NY: Semiotext(e) Inc., 1983.

BAUMAN, Z., "Is there a Postmodern Sociology?" *Theory, Culture & Society* 5/2-3 (1988) 217-237.

———, *Modernity and the Holocaust*. Cambridge: Polity, 1989.

———, *Intimations of Postmodernity*. London; NY: Routledge, 1992.

———, *Postmodern Ethics*. Oxford: Blackwell, 1993.

BAUMGÄRTEL, F., "Die Ochsenstachel und die Nägel in Koh 12,11," *ZAW* 81 (1969) 98.

BAUMGARTNER, W., "The Wisdom Literature," in: H.H. ROWLEY (ed.), *The Old Testament and Modern Study*. 1951. 210-237.

BEAUCHAMP, P., "Entendre Qohelet," *Christus* 16 (1969) 339-351.

———, *L'un et l'autre. Essai de lecture*. Paris: Seuil, 1976.

———, *L'un et l'autre testament. Vol. 2: Accomplir les écritures*. Paris: Seuil, 1990.

BEAL, T.K., "Ideology and Intertextuality: Surplus of Meaning and Controlling the Means of Production," in: D.N. FEWELL (ed.), *Reading Between Texts. Intertextuality and the Hebrew Bible*. 1992. 27-39.

BEBBINGTON, D., *Patterns in History. A Christian Perspective on Historical Thought*. Leicester: Apollos, 1979.

BECKER, P.J., *Gottesfurcht im Alten Testament* (AnBib 95). Rome: Pontificio Istituto Biblico, 1965.

BECKWITH, R., *The Old Testament Canon of the New Testament Church*. London: SPCK, 1985.

BEHLER, E., *German Romantic Literature*. Cambridge : CUP, 1993.

BEISER, F.C., *The Fate of Reason. German Philosophy From Kant to Fichte*. Cambridge, Mass.: Harvard UP, 1987.

BELSEY, C., *Critical Practice* (New Accents). London: Routledge, 1980.

BENJAMIN, A. (ed.), *The Lyotard Reader*. Oxford: Blackwell, 1989.

BENNETT, B., "Narrative and History: An Assessment of Hans Frei's Narrative Christology," unpubl. paper, 1992.

BERGEN, R.D., "Text as a Guide to Authorial Intention: An Introduction to Discourse Criticism," *JETS* 30 (1987) 327-36.

BERKOUWER, G.C., *Man: The Image of God*. Grand Rapids: Eerdmans, 1962.

BERLIN, A., *Poetics and the Interpretation of Biblical Narrative* (Bible and Literature Series). Sheffield: Almond Press, 1983.

BERNSTEIN, R.J., *The Restructuring of Social and Political Theory*. Oxford: Basil Blackwell, 1976.

BERNSTEIN, R.J. (ed.), *Habermas and Modernity*. Cambridge: Polity, 1985.

BERTENS, H., *The Idea of the Postmodern*. London; NY: Routledge, 1995.

BEST, S., and D. KELLNER, *Postmodern Theory. Critical Interrogations*. Houndmills; London: Macmillan, 1991.

BIANCHI, F., "The Language of Qoheleth: A Bibliographical Survey," *ZAW* 105 (1993) 210-223.

BIRCH, B.C., "Tradition, Canon and Biblical Theology," *HIBT* 2 (1980) 113-125.

BIRIOTTI, M., and N. MILLER (eds.), *What is An Author?* Manchester, NY: Manchester UP, 1993.

BLACKWITH, A.L., *Schleiermacher's Early Philosophy of Life. Determinism, Freedom, and Phantasy* (Harvard Theological Studies XXXIII). California: Scholars Press, 1982.

BLEICHER, J., *Contemporary Hermeneutics. Hermeneutics as Method, Philosophy and Critique*. London: Routledge and Kegan Paul, 1980.

BLENKINSOPP, J., "A New Kind of Introduction: Professor Childs' *Introduction to the Old Testament as Scripture*," *JSOT* 16 (1980) 24-27.

———, *Wisdom and Law in The Old Testament. The Ordering of Life in Israel and Early Judaism*. Oxford: OUP, 1983.

———, "Ecclesiastes 3:1-15: Another Interpretation," *JSOT* 66 (1995) 55-64.

BLOCHER, H., *In the Beginning: The Opening Chapters of Genesis*. Leicester: IVP, 1984.

BODINE, W.R. (ed.), *Linguistics and Biblical Hebrew*. Indiana: Eisenbrauns, 1992.

BOOTH, W., *A Rhetoric of Irony*. Chicago; London: University of Chicago Press, 1974.

————, *The Rhetoric of Fiction* (2nd ed.). London: Penguin, 1983.

BORDO, S., *The Flight to Objectivity: Essays on Cartesianism and Culture*. Albany: SUNY, 1987.

BÖSTROM, L., *The God of the Sages. The Portrayal of God in the Book of Proverbs* (ConBOT 29). Sweden: Almquist and Wiksell, 1990.

BOTHA, M.E., "Framework for a Taxonomy of Scientific Metaphor," *Philosophia Reformata* 53/2 (1988) 143-170.

————, "Understanding Our Age. Philosophy at the Turning Point of the 'Turns'? – the endless search for the universal," *Tydskrif vir Christelike Wetenskap* 30/2 (1994) 16-31.

————, "Does Reformational Philosophy Have an Answer to the Many Guises of Pluralism?" *Koers* 60/2 (1995) 171-188.

BOTHA, R.P., *Challenging Chomsky. The Generative Garden Game*. Oxford: Blackwell, 1989.

BOTTERWECK, G.J., and E.D. GREEN, *Theological Dictionary of the Old Testament* (6 Vols). Grand Rapids: Eerdmans, 1980.

BOWLING, A., "לבב," in: R. LAIRD HARRIS, G.L. ARCHER, and B.K. WALTKE (eds.), *Theological Wordbook of the Bible*. Vol 1. 1980. 466-467.

BRAATEN, C.E., and R.W. JENSON (eds.), *Reclaiming the Bible For the Church*. Edinburgh: T&T Clark, 1995.

BRADBURY, M., "Structure," in: R. FOWLER (ed.), *Modern Critical Terms*. 1987. 235-236.

BRANSON, M.L., and C.R. PADILLA (eds.), *Conflict and Context. Hermeneutics in the Americas*. Grand Rapids: Eerdmans, 1986.

BRAUN, R., *Kohelet und die frühhellenistische Popularphilosophie* (BZAW 130). Berlin: de Gruyter, 1973.

BREMOND, C., "The Narrative Message," *Semeia* 10 (1978) 5-55.

BRETT, M., "Four or Five Things to Do With Texts. A Taxonomy of Interpretative Interests," in: D.J.A. CLINES, S.E. FOWL, and S.E. PORTER (eds.), *The Bible in Three Dimensions*. 1990. 357-377.

————, *Biblical Criticism in Crisis? The Impact of the Canonical Approach on Old Testament Studies*. Cambridge: CUP, 1991.

————, "The Future of Reader Criticisms?" in: F. WATSON (ed.), *The Open Text*. 1993. 13-31.

BRINDLE, W.A., "Righteousness and Wickedness in Ecclesiastes 7:15-18," *Andrews University Seminary Studies* 23/3 (1985) 243-257.

BROOKS, C., *The Hidden God*. New Haven; London: Yale UP, 1963.

————, *Modern Poetry and the Tradition*. NY: OUP, 1965.

————, *The Well Wrought Urn. Studies in the Structure of Poetry*. London, NY: Harcourt Brace Jovanich, 1975.

BROOKS, D., "Modernism," in: M. COYLE, et al., *Encyclopaedia of Literature and Criticism*. 1990. 119-129.

BROWN, F., S.R. DRIVER, and C.A. BRIGGS, *The New Brown-Driver-Briggs-Gesenius Hebrew and English Lexicon*. Peabody, Mass.: Hendricksen, 1979.

BROWN, G., and G. YULE, *Discourse Analysis* (Cambridge Textbooks in Linguistics). Cambridge: CUP, 1983.

BROWN, R.E., J.A. FITZMEYER, and R.E. MURPHY (eds.), *The New Jerome Biblical Commentary* (2nd ed.). London: Geoffrey Chapman, 1990.

BROYLES, C.C., *The Conflict of Faith and Experience in the Psalms. A Form-Critical and Theological Study* (JSOTSup 52). Sheffield: JSOT, 1988.

BRUEGGEMANN, W., "The Triumphalist Tendency in Exegetical History," *JAAR* 38 (1970) 367-380.

——, *In Man We Trust: The Neglected Side of Biblical Faith*. Richmond: John Knox, 1972.

——, *The Prophetic Imagination*. Philadelphia: Fortress, 1978.

——; "Trajectories in Old Testament Literature and the Sociology of Ancient Israel," *JBL* 98 (1979) 161-185.

——, *Hopeful Imagination: Prophetic Voices in Exile*. Philadelphia: Fortress, 1986.

——, "The Social Significance of Solomon as a Patron of Wisdom," in: J.G. GAMMIE and L.G. PERDUE (eds.), *The Sage in Israel and the Ancient Near East*. 1990. 117-132.

——, *Old Testament Theology. Essays on Structure, Theme, and Text* (Ed. P. MILLER) Minneapolis: Fortress, 1992.

——, *Texts under Negotiation. The Bible and Postmodern Imagination*. London: SCM, 1993.

——, "Response to J. Richard Middleton," *HTR* 87/3 (1994) 279-289.

BRUNS, G.L., "Canon and Power in the Hebrew Scriptures," in: R. VON HALLBERG (ed.), *Canons*. 1983, 1984. 65-83.

BUCKLEY, M.J., *At the Origins of Modern Atheism*. New Haven; London: Yale UP, 1987.

BULTMANN, C., "Creation At the Beginning of History: Johan Gottfried Herder's Interpretation of Genesis 1," *JSOT* 68 (1995) 23-32.

BURKE, S., *The Death and Return of the Author. Criticism and Subjectivity*. Edinburgh: Edinburgh UP, 1992.

BURKITT, F. C., "Is Ecclesiastes a Translation?" *JTS* 23 (1922) 22-28.

BURNETT, F.W., "Postmodern Biblical Exegesis: The Eve of Historical Consciousness," *Semeia* 51 (1990) 51-80.

BUTTERFIELD, H., *Man on His Past*. Cambridge: CUP, 1969.

CAPUTO, J.D., *Radical Hermeneutics. Repetition, Deconstruction and the Hermeneutic Project*. Bloomington; Indianapolis: Indiana UP, 1987.

CARR, E.H., *What is History?* (2nd ed.). London: Penguin, 1987.

CARROLL, J., *Humanism. The Wreck of Western Culture*. London: Fontana, 1993.

CARSON, D., et al. (eds.), *New Bible Commentary. 21st Century Edition*. Leicester: IVP, 1994.

CARY, N.R., *Christian Criticism in the Twentieth Century. Theological Approaches to Literature*. London: Kennikat, 1975.

CASHDOLLAR, C.D., *The Transformation of Theology. Positivism and Protestant Thought in Britain and America*. Princeton: Princeton UP, 1989.

CASSIRER, E., *Language and Myth*. New York: Dover, 1946.

——, *The Philosophy of the Enlightenment*. Princeton: Princeton UP, 1951.

CASTELLINO, G.R., "Qoheleth and His Wisdom," *CBQ* 30 (1968) 15-28.

CAZELLES, H., "The Canonical approach to Torah and Prophets," *JSOT* 16 (1980) 28-31.

CERESKO, A.R., "The Function of Antanaclasis (ms' 'to find' // ms' 'to reach, overtake, grasp') in Hebrew Poetry, Especially in the Book of Qoheleth," *CBQ* 44 (1982) 551-569.

CHILDS, B.S., "Interpretation in Faith. The Theological Responsibility of an Old Testament Commentary," *Interpretation* 18 (1964) 432-449.

——, *Biblical Theology in Crisis*. Philadelphia: Westminster Press, 1970.

——, *Exodus* (OTL). London: SCM, 1974.

——, *Introduction to the Old Testament as Scripture*. Philadelphia: Fortress, 1979.

——, "A Response," *HIBT* 2 (1980) 199-211.

——, "Response to Reviewers of Introduction to the Old Testament as Scripture," *JSOT* 16 (1980) 52-60.

——, "Gerhard von Rad in American Dress," in: D.G. MILLER (ed.), *The Hermeneutical Quest*. 1986. 78-86.

——, "Critical Reflections On James Barr's Understanding of the Literal and Allegorical," *JSOT* 46 (1990) 3-9.

——, *Biblical Theology of the Old and New Testaments*. Minneapolis: Fortress, 1992.

——, "Biblical Scholarship in the Seventeenth Century: A Study in Ecumenics," in: S. BALENTINE and J. BARTON, *Language, Theology and the Bible. Essays in Honour of James Barr*. 1994. 325-333.

CLARK, S.H., *Paul Ricoeur*. London; NY: Routledge, 1990.

CLEMENTS, D.M., "The Law of Sin and Death: Ecclesiastes and Genesis 1-3," *Themelios* 19/3 (1994) 5-8.

CLEMENTS, R.E., *A Century of Old Testament Study*. Guildford; London: Lutterworth, 1976.

——, *Wisdom in Theology*. Carlisle: Paternoster; Grand Rapids: Eerdmans, 1992.

——, "Wisdom and Old Testament Theology," in: J. DAY, et al. (eds.). *Wisdom in Ancient Israel. Essays in Honour of J.A. Emerton*. 1995. 269-286.

CLINES, D.J.A., *The Theme of the Pentateuch* (JSOTSup 10). Sheffield: JSOT, 1978.

——, "Methods in Old Testament Study," in: J. ROGERSON (ed.), *Beginning Old Testament Study*. 1983. 26-43.

——, *The Esther Scroll. The Story of the Story* (JSOTSup 30). Sheffield: JSOT, 1984.

——, *Ezra, Nehemiah, Esther* (NCBC). London: Marshall, Morgan and Scott; Grand Rapids: Eerdmans, 1984.

——, *Job 1-20* (WBC). Texas: Word, 1989.

——, *What Does Eve do to Help? And Other Readerly Questions to the Old Testament* (JSOTSup 94). Sheffield: JSOT, 1990.

——, "Reading Esther from Left to Right. Contemporary Strategies for Reading a Biblical Text," in: D.J.A. CLINES, S.E. FOWL, and S.E. PORTER (eds.), *The Bible in Three Dimensions*. 1990. 31-52.

——, "Possibilities and Priorities of Biblical Interpretation in an International Perspective," *BI* 1/1 (1993) 67-87.

——, "Job," in: D. CARSON, et al. (eds.), *New Bible Commentary. 21st Century Edition*. Leicester: IVP, 1994. 459-484.

CLINES, D.J.A., and J.C. EXUM (eds.), *The New Literary Criticism and the Hebrew Bible* (JSOTSup 143). Sheffield: JSOT, 1993.

CLINES, D.J.A., S.E. FOWL, and S.E. PORTER (eds.), *The Bible in Three Dimensions. Essays in Celebration of Forty Years of Biblical Studies in the University of Sheffield* (JSOTSup 87). Sheffield: JSOT, 1990.

CLOUSER, R., *The Myth of Religious Neutrality. An Essay on the Hidden Role of Religious Belief in Theories*. Notre Dame; London: University of Notre Dame Press, 1991.

COGGINS, R.J., and J.C. HOULDEN (eds.), *A Dictionary of Biblical Interpretation*. London: SCM, 1990.

COLLINGWOOD, R.G., *The Idea of History*. Oxford: OUP, 1946.

COLLINS, J.J., "Is a Critical Biblical Theology Possible?" in: W.H. PROPP, B. HALPERN, and D.N. FREEDMAN (eds.), *The Hebrew Bible and Its Interpreters*. 1990. 1-17.

COMSTOCK, G., "Truth or Meaning: Ricoeur Versus Frei on Biblical Narrative," *Journal of Religion* 66 (1986) 117-140.

COOPER, D.E., "Irony," in: D.E. COOPER (ed.), *A Companion to Aesthetics*. Oxford: Blackwell, 1992, 1995. 238-242.

CORETH, E., *Grundfragen der Hermeneutik*. Freiburg: Herder, 1969.

COSTELLO, P., *World Historians and Their Goals. Twentieth Century Answers to Modernism*. Illinois: Northern Illinois UP, 1993.

COYLE, M., P. GARSIDE, M. KELSALL, and J. PECK (eds.), *Encyclopaedia of Literature and Criticism*. London: Routledge, 1990.

CRAIG, K.M., *A Poetics of Jonah. Art in the Service of Ideology*. Columbia: University of South Carolina Press, 1993.

CRENSHAW, J.L., "Method in Determining Wisdom Influence upon 'Historical' Literature," *JBL* 88 (1969) 129-142.

———, "Studies in Ancient Israelite Wisdom: Prolegemonon," in: J.L. CRENSHAW (ed.), *Studies in Ancient Israelite Wisdom*. 1976. 1-6.

———, "In Search of Divine Presence: Some Remarks Preliminary to a Theology of Wisdom," *Review and Expositor* 74 (1977) 353-369.

———, *Old Testament Wisdom. An Introduction*. London: SCM, 1981.

———, "Wisdom and Authority: Sapiential Rhetoric and its Warrants," *VTSup* 32 (1981) 10-29.

———, "Qoheleth In Current Research," *HAR* 7 (1983) 41-56.

———, *A Whirlpool of Torment: Israelite Traditions of God As an Oppressive Presence*. Philadelphia: Fortress, 1984.

———, "The Wisdom Literature," in: D.A. KNIGHT and G.M. TUCKER (eds.), *The Hebrew Bible and Its Modern Interpreters*. 1985. 369-407.

———, "The Acquisition of Knowledge in Israelite Wisdom Literature," *Word & World* VII/3 (1987) 245-252.

———, *Ecclesiastes* (OTL). London: SCM, 1988.

———, "Ecclesiastes, Book of," in: D.N. FREEDMAN (ed.), *ABD* Vol. II. 1992. 271-280.

CRENSHAW, J.L. (ed.), *Studies in Ancient Israelite Wisdom*. NY: KTAV. 1976.

———, *Theodicy in the Old Testament*. Philadelphia: Fortress; London: SPCK, 1983.

CROSSAN, J.D. (ed.), *Semeia 19. The Book of Job and Ricoeur's Hermeneutics*. Chicago: Scholars Press, 1981.

CROUCH, W.B., "To Question an End, To End a Question: Opening the Closure of the Book of Jonah," *JSOT* 62 (1994) 101-112.

CRÜSEMANN, F., "The Unchangeable World: The 'Crisis of Wisdom' in Qoheleth," in: W. SCHOTROFF and W. STEGEMANN (eds.), *God of the Lowly*. 1984. 57-77.

CULLER, J., *Structuralist Poetics. Structuralism, Linguistics and the Study of Literature*. London; Henley: Routledge and Kegan Paul, 1975.

———, *The Pursuit of Signs. Semiotics, Literature, Deconstruction*. London: Routledge and Kegan Paul, 1981.

CULLEY, R.C., "Structural Analysis: Is it Done with Mirrors?" *Interpretation* XXVIII/2 (1974) 165-181.

CUNNINGHAM, V., *In the Reading Goal. Postmodernity, Texts, and History*. Oxford: Blackwell, 1994.

DANBY, H., *The Mishnah*. Oxford: OUP, 1933.

DAVIDSON, R., *The Courage to Doubt*. London: SCM; Philadelphia: Trinity Press International, 1983.

DAWSON, D.A., *Text-Linguistics and Biblical Hebrew* (JSOTSup 177). Sheffield: Sheffield Academic Press, 1994.

DAY, J., R.P. GORDON, and H.G.M. WILLIAMSON (eds.), *Wisdom in Ancient Israel. Essays in Honour of J.A. Emerton*. Cambridge: CUP, 1995.

DE JONG, S., "A Book of Labour: The Structuring Principles and the Main Theme of the Book of Qoheleth," *JSOT* 54 (1992) 107-116.

———, "Qoheleth and the Ambitious Spirit of the Ptolemaic Period," *JSOT* 61 (1994) 85-96.

DELEUZE, G., *Spinoza: Practical Philosophy*. San Francisco: City Light Books, 1988.

DELITZSCH, F., *Commentary on the Song of Songs and Ecclesiastes*. Grand Rapids: Eerdmans, 1970.

DELL, K.J., "Ecclesiastes as Wisdom," *VT* XLIV/3 (1993) 301-329.

DELSMAN, W.C., "Die Inkongruenz im Buch Qoheleth," in: K. JONGELING, H.L. MURRE-VAN DEN BERG, and L. VAN ROMPAY (eds.), *Studies in Hebrew and Aramaic Syntax* (Studies in Semitic Languages and Linguistics XVII). Leiden: Brill, 1991. 27-37.

DE MOOR, J.C. (ed.), *Synchronic or Diachronic? A Debate on Method in Old Testament Exegesis*. Leiden; New York: Brill, 1995.

DERRIDA, J., *Of Grammatology*. Baltimore; London: John Hopkins UP, 1976.

———, *Writing and Difference*. London: Routledge and Kegan Paul, 1978.

———, "The Law of Genre," *Critical Inquiry* 7 (1980) 55-81.

———, *The Ear of the Other. Otobiography, Transference, Translation* (ed. by C.V. McDONALD). NY: Schocken Books, ■■■.

DETWEILER, R., "Generative Poetics as Science and Fiction," *Semeia* 10 (1978) 137-150.

———, *Story, Sign and Self: Phenomenology and Structuralism as Literary-Critical Methods*. Philadelphia: Fortress, 1978.

DE WAARD, J., "The Translator and Textual Criticism (with Particular Reference to Eccl 2,25)," *Biblica* 60/4 (1979) 509-529.

DILLARD, R.B., and T. LONGMAN, *An Introduction to the Old Testament*. Grand Rapids: Zondervan, 1994.

DIRKSEN, P.B., and A. VAN DER KOOIJ (eds.), *Abraham Kuenen (1828-1891). His Major Contributions to the Study of the Old Testament*. Leiden; New York: Brill, 1993.

DOHMEN, C., "Der Weisheit letzter Schluß?" *BN* 63/1 (1992) 12-18.

DONFRIED, K.P. (ed.), *The Romans Debate*. Minneapolis: Augsburg, 1977.

DOOYEWEERD, H., *A New Critique of Theoretical Thought I-IV*. Amsterdam; Philadelphia: Presbyterian and Reformed Publishing Company, 1953-1958.

———, *In the Twilight of Western Thought*. New Jersey: Craig Press, 1960.

DRIVER, S.R., *An Introduction to the Literature of the Old Testament*. Gloucester, Mass.: Peter Smith, 1972.

EAGLETON, T., *Literary Theory. An Introduction*. Oxford: Blackwell, 1983.

EATON, M., *Ecclesiastes* (TOTC). Leicester: IVP, 1983.

EBELING, G., *Word and Faith*. Philadelphia: Fortress, 1963.

EDGAR, A., "Kant's Two Interpretations of Genesis," *Literature and Theology* 6/3 (1992) 280-290.

EDWARDS, M., *Towards a Christian Poetics*. London: MacMillan, 1984.

EISING, H., "זכר," in: *TDOT* Vol. IV. 1980. 64-82.

EISSFELDT, O., *The Old Testament. An Introduction*. Oxford: Blackwell, 1966.

ELIOT, T.S., "Tradition and the Individual Talent", "The Function of Criticism," in: D. LODGE (ed.), *20th Century Literary Criticism*. 1972. 69-84.

ELLERMEIER, F., *Qoheleth I/1: Untersuchungen zum Buche Qoheleth*. Herzberg: Jungfer, 1967.

ELLUL, J., *Reason for Being. A Meditation on Ecclesiastes*. Grand Rapids: Eerdmans, 1990.

EMERTON, J.A., "Wisdom," in: G.W. ANDERSON (ed.), *Tradition and Interpretation*. 1979. 214-237.

EMPSON, W., *Seven Types of Ambiguity* (4th ed.). London: Chalto and Windus, 1963.

ERICKSON, M., *Evangelical Interpretation. Perspectives on Hermeneutical Issues*. Grand Rapids: Baker, 1993.

ESKHULT, M., *Studies in Verbal Aspect and Narrative Technique in Biblical Hebrew Prose*. Uppsala: Uppsala UP, 1990.

ESLINGER, L.M., *The Kingship of God in Crisis. A Close Reading of 1 Samuel 1-12*. Sheffield: Almond, 1985.

ETCHELLS, R., *A Model of Making. Literary Criticism and Its Theology*. London: Marshall, Morgan and Scott, 1983.

EVANS, C.F., *Explorations in Theology 2*. London: SCM, 1977.

EVANS, C.S., and M. WESTPHAL (eds.), *Christian Perspectives on Religious Knowledge*. Grand Rapids: Eerdmans, 1993.

FARMER, K.A., *Who Knows What is Good? A Commentary on the Books of Proverbs and Ecclesiastes* (International Theological Commentary). Grand Rapids: Eerdmans; Edinburgh: Handsel Press, 1991.

FAULKNER, R.O., E.F. WENTE, and W.K. SIMPSON (eds.), *The Literature of Ancient Egypt*. New Haven; London: Yale UP, 1972.

FEWELL, D.N. (ed.), *Reading Between Texts. Intertextuality and the Hebrew Bible*. Louisville, Kentucky: Westminister/ John Knox Press, 1992.

FISCH, H., *Poetry with a Purpose. Biblical Poetics and Interpretation*. Bloomington; Indianapolis: Indiana UP, 1988.

FISH, S., *Is There a Text in This Class? The Authority of Interpretive Communities*. Cambridge, Mass; London: Harvard UP, 1980.

FISHBANE, M., *Biblical Interpretation in Ancient Israel*. Oxford: Clarendon, 1985.

FISHER, S., *Revelatory Positivism? Barth's Earliest Theology and the Marburg School*. Oxford: OUP, 1988.

FLINT, P. (ed.), *Christian Philosophy* (Notre Dame Studies in the Philosophy of Religion 6). Notre Dame: University of Notre Dame Press, 1990.

FODOR, J., *Christian Hermeneutics. Paul Ricoeur and the Refiguring of Theology*. Oxford: Clarendon, 1995.

FORD, D.F., "Barth's Interpretation of the Bible," in: S.W. SYKES (ed.), *Karl Barth – Studies of His Theological Methods*. 1979. 55-87.

——, "On Being Theologically Hospitable: Hans Frei's Achievement," *JTS* 46/2 (1995) 532-546.

FORMAN, C.G., "The Pessimism of Ecclesiastes," *JSS* 3 (1958) 336-343.

——, "Koheleth's Use of Genesis," *JSS* 5 (1960) 256-263.

FOUCAULT, M., *The Order of Things: An Archeology of the Human Sciences*. London: Tavistock, 1970.

——, "What is an Author?" in: P. RABINOW (ed.), *The Foucault Reader*. 1984. 101-120.

FOWL, S.E., "The Canonical Approach of Brevard Childs," *ExpTim* 96 (1985) 173-176.

FOWLER, R., "Literature," in: M. COYLE, et al., *Encyclopaedia of Literature and Criticism*. 1990. 3-25.

FOWLER, R. (ed.), *A Dictionary of Modern Critical Terms*. London; NY: Routledge, 1987.

FOX, M.V., *The Book of Qoheleth and it Relation to the Wisdom School*. Unpublished PhD thesis: Hebrew University, Jerusalem, 1972.

———, "Frame Narrative and Composition in the Book of Qoheleth," *HUCA* 48 (1977) 83-106.

———, "The Identification of Quotations in Biblical Literature," *ZAW* 92 (1980) 416-431.

———, "Job 38 and God's Rhetoric," *Semeia* 19 (1981) 53-61.

———, "The Meaning of *hebel* for Qoheleth," *JBL* 105 (1986) 409-427.

———, "Qoheleth's Epistemology," *HUCA* 58 (1987) 137-155.

———, "Qoheleth 1.4," *JSOT* 40 (1988) 109.

———, "Ageing and Death in Qoheleth 12," *JSOT* 42 (1988) 55-77.

———, *Qoheleth and His Contradictions* (JSOTSup 71). Sheffield: Almond Press, 1989.

———, "The Pedagogy of Proverbs 2," *JBL* 113/2 (1994) 233-243.

FREDERICKS, D.C., *Qoheleth's Language: Re-evaluating its Nature and Date*. Lewiston: Edwin Mellen, 1988.

———, "Life's Storms and Structural Unity in 11:1-12:8," *JSOT* 52 (1991) 95-114.

———, *Coping with Transience. Ecclesiastes on Brevity in Life* (The Biblical Seminar). Sheffield: JSOT Press, 1993.

FREEDMAN, D.N. (ed.), *The Anchor Bible Dictionary*. Volumes I-VI. NY: Doubleday, 1992.

FREEDMAN, H., and M. SIMON, *Midrash Rabbah. The Midrash Volume VIII. Ruth and Ecclesiastes*. London: Soncino Press, 1939.

FREI, H., *The Eclipse of Biblical Narrative. A Study in Eighteenth and Nineteenth Century Hermeneutics*. New Haven; London: Yale UP, 1974.

———, *Types of Christian Theology* (Eds. G. HUNSINGER and W. PLACHER). New Haven; London: Yale UP, 1992.

FREUND, E., *The Return of the Reader. Reader-response Criticism*. London; NY: Methuen, 1987.

GADAMER, H., *Truth and Method* (2nd ed.). London: Sheed and Ward, 1989.

GALLING, K., "Kohelet-Studien," *ZAW* 50 (1932) 276-299.

———, *Der Prediger* (HAT 18). Tübingen: J.C.B. Mohr, 1940.

———, *Der Prediger* (2nd ed.; HAT 18). Tübingen: J.C.B. Mohr, 1969.

GAMMIE, J.G., W. BRUEGGEMANN, W.L. HUMPHREYS, and J.M. WARD (eds.), *Israelite Wisdom: Theological and Literary Essays in Honor of Samuel Terrien*. Montana: Scholars Press, 1978.

GAMMIE, J.G., and L.G. PERDUE (eds.), *The Sage in Israel and the Ancient Near East*. Winona Lake: Eisenbrauns, 1990.

GARRETT, D.A., "Qoheleth On the Use and Abuse of Political Power," *Trinity Journal* 8 (1987) 159-177.

GAY, P., *The Enlightenment. An Interpretation. Vol. 1: The Rise of Modern Paganism*. London: Norton, 1977.

GELLNER, E., *Postmodernism, Reason and Religion*. London: Routledge, 1992.

GESE, H., "The Crisis of Wisdom in Koheleth," in: J.L. CRENSHAW (ed.), *Theodicy in the OT*. 1983. 141-153.

GIDDENS, A., *Modernity and Self-Identity. Self and Society in the Late Modern Age*. Cambridge: Polity, 1991.

GILBERT, M. (ed.), *La Sagesse de l'Ancien Testament* (BETL 51). Leuven: UP, 1979.

GINSBURG, C.D., *The Song of Songs and Coheleth*. NY: KTAV, 1970.

GLADSON, J.A., *Retributive Paradoxes in Proverbs 10-29*. Ann Arbor, Michigan: University Microfilms International, 1979.

GOLDINGAY, J., *Theological Diversity and the Authority of the Old Testament*. Grand Rapids: Eerdmans, 1987.

———, *Models for Interpretation of Scripture*. Grand Rapids: Eerdmans, 1995.

GOOD, E.M., "The Unfilled Sea: Style and Meaning in Ecclesiastes 1:2-11," in: J.G. GAMMIE, et al. (eds.), *Israelite Wisdom: Theological and Literary Essays in Honor of Samuel Terrien*. 1978. 59-73.

———, *Irony in the Old Testament*. Sheffield: Almond Press, 1981.

GORAK, J., *The Making of the Modern Canon, Genesis and Crisis of a Literary Idea*. London: Athlone, 1991.

GORDIS, R., "Quotations in Wisdom Literature," *JQR* 30 (1939-40) 123-147.

———, *Koheleth the Man and His World: A Study of Ecclesiastes*. NY: Schoken, 1968.

GÖRG, M., "זהר," *TDOT* Vol. IV. 1980. 41-46.

GOTTWALD, N., *The Tribes of Yahweh: A Sociology of the Religion of Liberated Israel. 1250-1050 BCE*. Maryknoll: Orbis, 1980.

GRANT, R.M., with D. TRACY, *A Short History of the Interpretation of the Bible* (2nd ed.). Philadelphia: Fortress, 1984.

GREEN, G. (ed.), *Scriptural Authority and Narrative Interpretation*. Philadelphia: Fortress, 1987.

GREENSLADE, S.L. (ed.), *The Cambridge History of the Bible. The West From the Reformation to the Present Day*. Cambridge: CUP, 1963.

GREENSTEIN, E.L., "Theory and Argument in Biblical Criticism," *HAR* 10 (1986) 77-93.

GREENWOOD, D.C., *Structuralism and the Biblical Text* (Religion and Reason 32; Method and Theory in the Study and Interpretation of Religion). Berlin; NY; Amsterdam: Mouton, 1985.

GREGORY THAUMATURGUS, "A Metaphrase of the Book of Ecclesiastes," *The Ante-Nicene Fathers*. Vol. VI. Grand Rapids: Eerdmans, 1978. 9-17.

GREIMAS, A.J., *Structural Semantics. An Attempt at Method*. Lincoln; London: University of Nebraska Press, 1966.

———, *On Meaning. Selected Writings in Semiotic Theory* (Theory and History of Literature 38). Minneapolis: University of Minnesota Press, 1987.

GRIFFIN, D.R., W.A. BEARDSLEE, and J. HOLLAND, *Varieties of Postmodern Theology* (SUNY Series in Constructive Postmodern Thought). Albany: SUNY, 1989.

GRIFFIOEN, S., and B.M. BALK (eds.), *Christian Philosophy at the Close of the Twentieth Century*. Kampen: Kok, 1995.

GRONDIN, J., *Introduction to Philosophical Hermeneutics* (Yale Studies in Hermeneutics). New Haven; London: Yale UP, 1994.

GRUENLER, R.G., *Meaning and Understanding. The Philosophical Framework for Biblical Interpretation* (Foundations of Contemporary Interpretation 2). Grand Rapids: Zondervan, 1991.

GUILLORY, J., "The Ideology of Canon-Formation," in: R. VON HALBERG (ed.), *Canons*. 1983, 1984. 337-362.

GUNN, D.M., *The Story of King David. Genre and Interpretation* (JSOTSup 6). Sheffield: JSOT, 1982.

——, "New Directions in the Study of Biblical Hebrew Narrative," *JSOT* 39 (1987) 65-75.

——, "Reading Right. Reliable and Omniscient Narrator, Omniscient God, and Foolproof Composition in the Hebrew Bible," in: D.J.A. CLINES, S.E. FOWL, and S.E. PORTER (eds.), *The Bible in Three Dimensions*. 1990. 53-64.

GUNTON, C., *The One, the Three and the Many. God, Creation and the Culture of Modernity*. Cambridge: CUP, 1993.

GUYER, P. (ed.), *The Cambridge Companion to Kant*. Cambridge: CUP, 1992.

HABEL, N.C., "The Narrative Art of Job. Applying the Principles of Robert Alter," *JSOT* 27 (1983) 101-111.

HABERMAS, J., *Towards a Rational Society: Student Protest, Science, and Politics*. London: Heinemann, 1971.

——, *Knowledge and Human Interests* (2nd ed.). London: Heinemann, 1978.

——, *The Theory of Communicative Action*. 2 Vols. Cambridge: Polity, 1987.

——, *The Philosophical Discourse of Modernity*. Cambridge: Polity, 1987.

HADIDIAN, D.Y. (ed.), *From Faith to Faith. D.G. Miller Festschrift* (Pittsburgh Theological Monograph Series 31) Pittsburgh: Pickwick, 1979.

HAHN, H.F., *The Old Testament in Modern Research*. Philadelphia: Fortress, 1966.

HARDING, S., *The Racial Economy of Science. Toward a Democratic Future*. Bloomington; Indianapolis: Indiana UP, 1993.

HARDING, S. (ed.), *Feminism and Methodology*. Milton Keynes: Open UP, 1987.

HARLAND, R., *Superstructuralism. The Philosophy of Structuralism and Post-structuralism*. London; NY: Routledge, 1987.

HARRISON, C.R., *Qoheleth in Social-Historical Perspective*. Ann Arbor, Michigan: University Microfilms, 1991.

HARRISON, R.K., *Introduction to the Old Testament*. Grand Rapids: Eerdmans, 1969.

HARRISVILLE, R.A., and W. SUNDBERG, *The Bible in Modern Culture. Theology and Historical-Critical Method from Spinoza to Käsemann*. Grand Rapids: Eerdmans, 1995.

HARVEY, D., *The Condition of Postmodernity. An Enquiry into the Origins of Cultural Change*. Oxford: Blackwell, 1989.

HASSAN, I., "Desire and Dissent in the Postmodern Age," *Kenyon Review* 5 (1983) 1-18.

——, *The Postmodern Turn: Essays in Postmodern Theory and Culture*. Ohio: Ohio State UP, 1987.

HAWKES, T., *Structuralism and Semiotics* (New Accents). London: Routledge, 1977.

HAYES, J.H., and C.R. HOLLADAY, *Biblical Exegesis. A Beginner's Handbook* (2nd ed.). London: SCM, 1987.

HEIDEGGER, M., *Being and Time*. Oxford: Basil Blackwell, 1962.

——, *Poetry, Language and Thought*. NY: Harper and Row, 1971.

——, "Understanding and Interpretation," in: K. MUELLER-VOLLMER (ed.), *The Hermeneutics Reader*. 1992. 221-228.

HENGEL, M., *Judaism and Hellenism. Volume One*. London: SCM, 1974.

HENGSTENBERG, E.W., *Commentary on Ecclesiastes, With Other Treaties*. Edinburgh: T&T Clark, 1860.

HERDER, J.G. von, *Vom Geist der Hebräischen Poesie*. Leipzig: Verlag von Johan Umbrosius Barth, 1825.

HERMISSON, H.J., "Observations on the Creation Theology in Wisdom," in: J.G. GAMMIE, et al. (eds.), *Israelite Wisdom: Theological and Literary Essays in Honor of Samuel Terrien*. 1978. 43-57.

HERTZBERG, H.W., *Der Prediger* (2nd ed.; KAT 17,4). Gütersloh: Gütersloher Verlagshaus Gerd Mohn, 1963.

HESSE, M., "How to be Postmodern Without Being a Feminist," *The Monist* 77/4 (1994) 445-461.

HIRSCH, E.D., *Validity in Interpretation*. New Haven; London: Yale UP, 1967.

HOGLUND, K.G., et al. (eds.), *The Listening Heart. Essays in Wisdom and the Psalms in Honour of Roland E. Murphy, O. Carm* (JSOTSup 58). Sheffield: JSOT, 1987.

HOLM-NIELSEN, S., "On the Interpretation of Qoheleth in Early Christianity," *VT* 24 (1974) 168-177.

——, "The Book of Ecclesiastes and the Interpretation of It in Jewish and Christian Theology," *Annual of the Swedish Theological Institute* 10 (1976) 38-96.

HOLUB, R.C., *Reception Theory. A Critical Introduction* (New Accents). London; NY: Routledge, 1984.

HUGENBERGER, G.P., *Marriage As a Covenant: A Study of Biblical Law and Ethics Governing Marriage, Developed From the Perspective of Malachi*. PhD Thesis, Cheltenham and Gloucester College of Higher Education, 1991.

HUTCHEON, L., *Irony's Edge. The Theory and Politics of Irony*. London; NY: Routledge, 1994.

IHDE, D., *Hermeneutic Phenomenology: The Philosophy of Paul Ricoeur*. Evanston: Northwestern UP, 1971.

INGRAFFIA, B.D., *Postmodern Theory and Biblical Theology*. Cambridge: CUP, 1995.

ISAKSSON, B., *Studies in the Language of Qoheleth With Special Emphasis on the Verbal System* (Studia Semitica Upsaliensia 10). Uppsala: Acta Universitatis Upsaliensis, 1987.

ISER, W., *The Implied Reader: Patterns of Communication in Prose from Bunyan to Beckett*. Baltimore: John Hopkins UP, 1974.

——, "The Reading Process: A Phenomenological Approach," in: D. LODGE (ed.), *Modern Criticism and Theory*. 1988. 212-228.

JACOBSON, R., "The Structuralists and the Bible," *Interpretation* XXVIII/2 (1974) 146-164.

JAKOBSON, R., "Closing Statement: Linguistics and Poetics," in: T.A. SEBEOK (ed.), *Style in Language*. 1960. 350-377.

JAMES, K.W., "Ecclesiastes. Precursor of Existentialists," *The Bible Today* 22 (1984) 85-90.

JAMESON, F., *Postmodernism, or, the Cultural Logic of Late Capitalism*. London, NY: Verso, 1991.

JAPHET, S. (ed.), *Studies in Bible* (Scripta Hierosolymitana XXXI). Jerusalem: Magnes, 1986.

JAPHET, S., and R.B. SALTERS (eds.), *The Commentary of R. Samuel Ben Meir Rashbam on Qoheleth*. Jerusalem: Magnes; Leiden: Brill, 1985.

JASPER, D., *The Study of Literature and Religion. An Introduction* (Studies in Literature and Religion). London: MacMillan, 1989.

——, "The Study of Literature and Theology Five Years On," *Literature and Theology* 6/1 (1992) 1-10.

JASTROW, M., *A Gentile Cynic. Being the Book of Ecclesiastes*. Philadelphia; London: Lippincott, 1919.

JEANROND, W., *Text and Interpretation as Categories of Theological Thinking*. Dublin: Gill and Macmillan, 1988.

———, *Theological Hermeneutics. Development and Significance*. London: SCM, 1994.

JEFFERSON, A., "Autobiography as Intertext: Barthes, Sarraute, Robbe-Grillet," in: M. WORTON and J. STILL (eds.), *Intertextuality*. 1990. 108-129.

JEFFERSON, A., and D. ROBEY, *Modern Literary Theory. A Comparative Introduction* (2nd ed.). London: Batsford, 1986.

JENKINS, K., *Re-thinking History*. London: Routledge, 1991.

———, *On 'What is History?' From Carr and Elton to Rorty and White*. London: Routledge, 1995.

JOBLING, D., *The Sense of Biblical Narrative. Three Structural Analyses in the Old Testament* (JSOTSup 7). Sheffield: JSOT, 1978.

———, "Robert Alter's *The Art of Biblical Narrative*," *JSOT* 27 (1983) 87-99.

———, *The Sense of Biblical Narrative: Structural Analyses in the Hebrew Bible II* (JSOTSup 39). Sheffield: JSOT, 1986, 1987.

———, "Deconstruction and the Political Analysis of Biblical Texts: A Jamesonian Reading of Psalm 72," *Semeia* 59 (1992) 95-124.

JONES, E., *Proverbs and Ecclesiastes*. London: SCM, 1961.

JONKER, L.C., *Exclusivity and Variety. Perspectives on Multidimensional Exegesis* (Contributions to Biblical Exegesis and Theology 19). Kampen: Kok Pharos, 1997.

KAISER, O., *Introduction to the Old Testament. A Presentation of its Results and Problems*. Oxford: Basil Blackwell, 1975.

———, "Qoheleth," in: J. DAY, et al. (eds.), *Wisdom in Ancient Israel. Essays in Honour of J.A. Emerton*. 1995. 83-93.

KAISER, W.C., "Wisdom Theology and the Centre of Old Testament Theology," *Evangelical Quarterly* 50-51 (1978-1979) 132-146.

KATZ, R.C., *The Structure of Ancient Arguments. Rhetoric and its Near Eastern Origin*. New York: Steimatzky, 1986.

KAUTZSCH, E., *Gesenius' Hebrew Grammar* (2nd ed.). Oxford: Clarendon, 1909.

KEARNEY, R., *The Wake of Imagination. Toward a Postmodern Culture*. Minneapolis: University of Minnesota Press, 1988.

KERMODE, F., *The Sense of an Ending: Studies in the Theory of Fiction*. Oxford: OUP, 1966.

———, *The Genesis of Secrecy. On the Interpretation of Narrative*. Cambridge, Mas.; London: Harvard UP, 1979.

KHAN, G., *Studies in Semitic Syntax*. Oxford: OUP, 1988.

KILBANSKY, R., and H.J. PATON (eds.), *Philosophy and History. Ernst Cassirer Festschrift*. London: Harper and Row, 1963.

KITTEL, B., "Brevard Childs' Development of the Canonical Approach," *JSOT* 16 (1980) 2-11.

KLAPWIJK, J., "The Universal in Hans-Georg Gadamer's Hermeneutic Philosophy," *Philosophia Reformata* 50 (1985) 119-129.

KLAPWIJK, J., S. GRIFFIOEN, and G. GROENEWOUD (eds.), *Bringing into Captivity Every Thought. Capita Selecta in the History of Christian Evaluations of Non-Christian Philosophy*. Lanham, NY; London: University Press of America, 1991.

KLEMM, D.E., "Subjectivity and Divinity in Biblical Hermeneutics," *Journal of Literature and Theology* 6/3 (1992) 239-253.

KNIGHT, D.A., "Canon and the History of Tradition: A Critique of Brevard S. Childs' *Introduction to the Old Testament as Scripture*," *HIBT* 2 (1980) 127-149.

KNIGHT, D.A., and G.M. TUCKER (eds.), *The Hebrew Bible and Its Modern Interpreters*. California: Scholars Press, 1985.

KOCH, K., "Is There a Doctrine of Retribution In the Old Testament?" in: J.L. CRENSHAW (ed.), *Theodicy in the Old Testament*. 1983. 57-87.

KOK, J., *Perspectives in Philosophy* (2nd ed.; Syllabus for Philosophy 201). Sioux, Iowa: Dordt College, 1992.

KOLAKOWSKI, L., *Positivist Philosophy. From Hume to the Vienna Circle*. Penguin: Middlesex, 1968/72.

KOVACS, B.W., "Philosophical Foundations for Structuralism," *Semeia* 10 (1978) 85-105.

KRAAY, J., and A. TOL, *Hearing and Doing. Philosophical Essays Dedicated to H. Evan Runner*. Toronto: Wedge, 1979.

KREITZER, L.J., *The Old Testament in Fiction and Film. On Reversing the Hermeneutical Flow*. Sheffield: Sheffield Academic Press, 1994.

KRENTZ, E., *The Historical-critical Method*. London: SPCK, 1975.

KRIEGER, M., *The New Apologists for Poetry*. Westport: Greenwood, 1977.

KRISTEVA, J., *Desire in Language. A Semiotic Approach to Literature and Art*. Oxford: Basil Blackwell, 1980.

——, *Revolution in Poetic Language*. NY: Columbia UP, 1984.

KRONER, R., *Kant's Weltanschaung*. Chicago; London: University of Chicago Press, 1956.

KUGEL, J.L., *The Idea of Biblical Poetry*. New Haven; London: Yale UP, 1981.

KUHN, T., *The Structure of Scientific Revolutions* (2nd ed.). Chicago: University of Chicago Press, 1970.

KUNG, H., *Theology for The Third Millennium*. London: Harper Collins, 1988.

LAIRD HARRIS, R., G.L. ARCHER, and B.K. WALTKE (eds.), *Theological Wordbook of the Old Testament*. 2 Vols. Chicago: Moody Press, 1980.

LAKELAND, P., *Theology and Critical Theory. The Discourse of the Church*. Nashville: Abingdon, 1990.

LAMBERT, W.G., *Babylonian Wisdom Literature*. Oxford: OUP, 1960.

LAMPE, G.W.H. (ed.), *The Cambridge History of the Bible. Vol. 2. The West from the Fathers to the Reformation*. Cambridge: CUP, 1969.

LANDES, G.M., "The Canonical Approach to Introducing the Old Testament: Prodigy and Problems," *JSOT* 16 (1980) 32-39.

LATEGAN, B., "Why So Few Converts to New Paradigms in Theology?" in: J. MOUTON, A.G. VAN AARDE, and W.S. VORSTER (eds.), *Paradigms and Progress in Theology*. 1988. 65-78.

——, "Hermeneutics," in: D.N. *Freedman* (ed.), *ABD* Vol. III. 1992. 149-154.

LATEGAN, B., and W.S. VORSTER, *Text and Reality: Aspects of Reference in Biblical Texts*. Atlanta: Scholars Press, 1985.

LAUE, P., *Das Buch Koh. und die Interpretationshypothese Siegfrieds*. Wittenberg, 1900.

LAUHA, A., *Kohelet* (Biblischer Kommentar Altes Testament). Neukirchen: Neukirchener Verlag, 1978.

LEAHY, M., "The Meaning of Ecclesiastes," *ITQ* 19 (1952) 297-300.

LEAVIS, F.R., *The Common Pursuit*. Middlesex: Penguin, 1952.

——, *The Great Tradition*. London: Chatto and Windus, 1973.

LEE, B., "Irony," in: R. FOWLER (ed.), *Modern Critical Terms*. 1987. 128-129.

LEITCH, V.B., *Deconstructive Criticism. An Advanced Introduction*. New York: Columbia UP, 1983.

LENTRICCHIA, F., *After the New Criticism*. London: Methuen, 1983.

LEVENSON, J.D., *The Hebrew Bible, the Old Testament and Historical Criticism*. Louisville: Westminister/John Knox, 1993.

LEVY, L., *Das Buch Qoheleth. Ein Beitrag zur Geschichte des Sadduzäismus*. Leipzig: Hinrichs, 1912.

LEWIS, C.S., *They Asked For a Paper*. London: Geoffrey Bles, 1962.

L'HOUR, J., "Yahweh Elohim," *RB* 81 (1974) 524-556.

LICHT, J., *Storytelling in the Bible*. Jerusalem: Magnes, 1978.

LINDBECK, G.A., *The Nature of Doctrine: Religion and Theology in a Postliberal Age*. London: SCM, 1984.

LLOYD, C., *The Structures of History*. Oxford: Blackwell, 1993.

LOADER, J.A., *Polar Structures in the Book of Qohelet*. Hawthorne, NY: de Gruyter, 1979.

——, *Ecclesiastes. A Practical Commentary*. Grand Rapids: Eerdmans, 1986.

LODGE, D. (ed.), *20th Century Criticism*. London; NY: Longman, 1972.

——, *Modern Criticism and Theory*. London; NY: Longman, 1988.

LOEWE, R., "Jewish Exegesis," in: R.J. COGGINS and J.C. HOULDEN (eds.), *A Dictionary of Biblical Interpretation*. 1990. 346-354.

LOHFINK, N., "War Kohelet ein Frauenfeind? Ein Versuch, die Logik und den Gegenstand von Koh 7,23-8,1a herauszufinden," in: M. GILBERT (ed.), *La Sagesse de l'Ancien Testament*. 1979. 259-287.

——, "*melek, sallit* und *mosel* bei Kohelet und die Abfassungszeit des Buches," *Biblica* 62 (1981) 535-543.

——, "Kohelet und die Banken. Zur Übersetzung von Kohelet v 12-16," *VT* 39 (1989) 488-495.

——, "'Freu dich, junger Mann ...' Das Schlußgedicht des Koheletbuches (Koh 11,9 – 12,8)," *Bibel und Kirche* 45 (1990) 12-19.

——, "Qoheleth 5:17-19 – Revelation by Joy," *CBQ* 52/4 (1990) 625-635.

——, "Von Windhauch, Gottesfurcht und Gottes Antwort in der Freude," *Bibel und Kirche* 45 (1990) 26-32.

——, *Kohelet* (NEB). Würzburg: Echter Verlag, 1993.

——, "Freu Dich, Jüngling – doch nicht, weil du jung bist. Zum Formproblem im Schlußgedicht Kohelets (Koh 11,9-12,8)," *BI* 3/2 (1995) 158-189.

LONG, B.O., "The 'New' Biblical Poetics of Alter and Sternberg," *JSOT* 51 (1991) 71-84.

LONG, V.P., *The Art of Biblical History* (Foundations of Contemporary Interpretation 5). Leicester: Apollos, 1994.

LONGACRE, R.E., *The Grammar of Discourse*. NY; London: Plenum Press, 1983.

——, *Joseph: A Story of Divine Providence: A Text-Theoretical and Text-Linguistic Analysis of Genesis 37 and 39-48*. Winona Lake: Eisenbrauns, 1989.

LONGMAN, T., "Comparative Methods in Old Testament Studies," *TSF Bulletin* (March-April 1984) 5-9.

——, "Form Criticism, Recent Developments in Genre Theory, and the Evangelical," *WTJ* 47 (1985) 46-67.

————, *Literary Approaches to Biblical Interpretation* (Foundations of Contemporary Interpretation 3). Grand Rapids: Zondervan, 1987.

————, *Fictional Akkadian Autobiography. A Generic and Comparative Study*. Winona Lake: Eisenbrauns, 1991.

LORETZ, O., *Qoheleth und der alte Orient*. Freiburg: Herder, 1964.

————, "'Frau' und griechisch-jüdische Philosophie im Buch Qoheleth," *UF* 23 (1991) 245-264.

LOUGHLIN, G., "At the End of the World: Postmodernism and Theology," in: A. WALKER (ed.), *Different Gospels. Christian Orthodoxy and Modern Theologies*. 1993. 204-221.

LUCAS, J., *Freedom and Grace*. London: SPCK, 1976.

LUNDIN, R., "Our Hermeneutical Inheritance," in: R. LUNDIN, A.C. THISELTON, and C. WALHOUT, *The Responsibility of Hermeneutics*. 1985. 1-29.

————, *The Culture of Interpretation. Christian Faith and the Postmodern World*. Grand Rapids: Eerdmans, 1993.

LUNDIN, R. (ed.), *Disciplining Hermeneutics. Interpretation in Christian Perspective*. Leicester: Apollos, 1997.

LUNDIN, R., A.C. THISELTON, and C. WALHOUT, *The Responsibility of Hermeneutics*. Grand Rapids: Eerdmans; Exeter: Paternoster, 1985.

LUTHER, M., *An Exposition of Salomons Booke, Called Ecclesiastes Or the Preacher*. Aldergate: John Draye, 1573.

————, *Luther's Works Volume 15. Notes on Ecclesiastes. Lectures on the Song of Solomon. Treatise on the Last Words of David* (ed. J. Pelikan). Saint Louis: Concordia, 1972.

LYON, D., *Postmodernity* (Concepts in the Social Sciences). Buckingham: Open UP, 1994.

LYOTARD, J., *The Postmodern Condition: A Report on Knowledge* (Theory and History of Literature 10). Manchester: Manchester UP, 1984.

————, *The Lyotard Reader* (ed. A. Benjamin). Oxford: Basil Blackwell, 1989.

MACDONALD, D.B., *The Hebrew Literary Genius*. Princeton: Princeton University Press, 1933.

MACDONALD, P.J., "Discourse Analysis and Biblical Interpretation," in: W.R. BODINE (ed.), *Linguistics and Biblical Hebrew*. 1992. 153-175.

MACHEREY, P., *A Theory of Literary Production*. London: Routledge and Kegan Paul, 1978.

MACINTYRE, A., "Spinoza, Benedict (Baruch)," in: P. EDWARDS (ed.), *The Encyclopedia of Philosophy*. NY: MacMillan; Free Press. 1967. 530-541.

————, *After Virtue. A Study in Moral Theory*. London: Duckworth, 1981.

————, *Whose Justice? Which Rationality?* London: Duckworth, 1988.

MAKARUSHKA, I., "Nietzsche's Critique of Modernity: The Emergence of Hermeneutical Consciousness," *Semeia* 51 (1990) 193-214.

MAN, P. de, *Blindness and Insight. Essays in the Rhetoric of Contemporary Criticism* (2nd ed.). London: Methuen, 1983.

————, *The Rhetoric of Romanticism*. NY: Columbia UP, 1984.

MANDELBAUM, M., "Historicism," in: P. EDWARDS (ed.), *The Encyclopedia of Philosophy*. Vols. 3 and 4. 1967. 22-25.

MANUEL, F.E., *The Changing of the Gods*. Hanover; London: University Press of New England, 1983.

MARCUS, L., *Auto/biographical Discourses. Criticism. Theory. Practice.* Manchester:
   Manchester UP, 1994.
MAYES, A.D.H., *Deuteronomy* (NCBC). London: Oliphants, 1979.
MAYS, J.L., "What is Written. A Response to Brevard Childs' *Introduction to the Old
   Testament as Scripture,*" *HIBT* 2 (1980) 151-163.
MAYS, J.L., D.L. PETERSEN, and K.H. RICHARDS (eds.), *Old Testament Interpretation.
   Past, Present, and Future.* Edinburgh: T&T Clark, 1995.
MCCONVILLE, J.G., *Law and Theology in Deuteronomy* (JSOTSup 33). Sheffield: JSOT,
   1984.
MCGANN, J.J., *The Textual Condition.* Princeton: Princeton UP, 1991.
MCGRATH, A.E., "Reclaiming Our Roots and Vision: Scripture and the Stability of the
   Christian Church," in: C.E. BRAATEN and R.W. JENSON (eds.), *Reclaiming the
   Bible for the Church.* 1995. 63-88.
MCINTYRE, J., "Historical Criticism in a 'History-Centred Value System,'" in: S.
   BALENTINE and J. BARTON, *Language, Theology and the Bible. Essays in Honour
   of James Barr.* Oxford: Clarendon, 1994. 370-384.
MCKANE, W., *Prophets and Wise Men* (SBT 44). London: SCM, 1965.
MCKENNA, J.E., "The Concept of *Hebel* in the Book of Ecclesiastes," *SJT* 45/1 (1992) 19-
   28.
MCKIM, D.K. (ed.), *A Guide to Contemporary Hermeneutics.* Grand Rapids: Eerdmans,
   1986.
MCKNIGHT, E.V., *The Bible and the Reader: An Introduction to Literary Criticism.*
   Philadelphia: Fortress, 1985.
——, *Post-modern Use of the Bible: The Emergence of Reader Oriented Criticism.*
   Nashville: Abingdon, 1988.
MCNEILE, A.H., *An Introduction to Ecclesiastes With Notes and Appendices.* Cambridge:
   CUP, 1904.
MERQUIOR, J.G., *Foucault* (Modern Masters). London: Fontana, 1985.
MICHEL, D., *Qoheleth* (Erträge der Forschung). Darmstadt: Wissenschaftliche
   Buchgesellschaft, 1988.
——, *Untersuchungen zur Eigenart des Buches Qoheleth.* Berlin; NY: de Gruyter, 1989.
MIDDLETON, J.R., "Is Creation Theology Inherently Conservative? A Dialogue with
   Walter Brueggemann," *HTR* 87/3 (1994) 257-277.
MILBANK, J., *Theology and Social Theory. Beyond Secular Reason.* Oxford: Blackwell,
   1990.
MILLER, D.G. (ed.), *The Hermeneutical Quest. Essays in Honor of James Luther Mays on
   his Sixty-Fifth Birthday.* Pennsylvania: Pickwick Publications, 1986.
MILNE, P.J., *Vladimir Propp and the Study of Structure in Hebrew Biblical Narrative.*
   Sheffield: Almond Press, 1988.
MINTZ, A., "On the Tel Aviv School of Poetics," *Prooftexts* 4 (1984) 215-235.
MITCHELL, B., *Faith and Criticism.* Oxford: Clarendon, 1994.
MORGAN, R., with J. BARTON, *Biblical Interpretation* (Oxford Bible Series). Oxford:
   OUP, 1988.
MOUTON, J., A.G. VAN AARDE, and W.S. VORSTER (eds.), *Paradigms and Progress in
   Theology.* South Africa: Human Sciences Research Council, 1988.
MOUW, R.J., and S. GRIFFIOEN, *Pluralisms and Horizons. An Essay in Christian Public
   Philosophy.* Grand Rapids: Eerdmans, 1993.

MUDGE, L.S., "Paul Ricoeur on Biblical Interpretation," in: P. RICOEUR, *Essays on Biblical Interpretation*. 1980. 1-40.

MUELLER-VOLLMER, K. (ed.), *The Hermeneutics Reader*. NY: Continuum, 1992.

MUILENBERG, J., "A Qoheleth Scroll from Qumran," *BASOR* 135 (1954) 20-28.

MURAOKA, T., *Emphatic Words and Structures in Biblical Hebrew*. Jerusalem: Magnes; Leiden: Brill, 1985.

MURPHY, F.A., *Christ the Form of Beauty. A Study in Theology and Literature*. Edinburgh: T&T Clark, 1995.

MURPHY, R.E., "The Interpretation of the Old Testament Wisdom Literature," *Interpretation* 23 (1969) 289-301.

——, "Wisdom – Theses and Hypotheses," in: J.G. GAMMIE, et al. (eds.), *Israelite Wisdom. Theological and Literary Essays in Honor of Samuel Terrien*. 1978. 35-42.

——, "Qoheleth's 'Quarrel' With the Fathers," in: D.Y. HADIDIAN (ed.), *From Faith to Faith*. 1979. 235-254.

——, "The Old Testament as Scripture," *JSOT* 16 (1980) 40-44.

——, *Wisdom Literature* (The Forms of the Old Testament Literature XIII). Grand Rapids: Eerdmans, 1981.

——, "Qoheleth Interpreted: The Bearing of the Past on the Present," *VT* 32 (1982) 331-337.

——, "Proverbs and Theological Exegesis," in: D.G. MILLER (ed.), *The Hermeneutical Quest*. 1986. 87-95.

——, *The Tree of Life. An Exploration of Biblical Wisdom Literature*. NY; Toronto: Doubleday, 1990.

——, *Ecclesiastes* (WBC). Texas: Word, 1992.

——, "Wisdom in the Old Testament," in: D.N. FREEDMAN (ed.), *ABD* Vol. VI. 1992. 920-931.

NEILL, S., and N.T. WRIGHT, *The Interpretation of the New Testament. 1861-1986*. Oxford: OUP, 1988.

NESTLE, E., K. ALAND, et al., *Novum Testamentum Graece*. Stuttgart: Deutsche Bibelgesellschaft. 1990.

NEWBIGIN, L., *The Other Side of 1984. Questions for the Churches*. Geneva: WCC, 1983.

——, *Foolishness to the Greeks*. London: SPCK, 1986.

——, *The Gospel in a Pluralist Society*. Grand Rapids: Eerdmans, 1989.

——, "Truth and Authority in Modernity," in: P. SAMPSON, V. SAMUEL, and C. SUGDEN (eds.), *Faith and Modernity*. 1994. 60-88.

——, *Proper Confidence. Faith, Doubt and Certainty in Christian Discipleship*. London: SPCK, 1995.

NEWSOM, C.A., "Job and Ecclesiastes," in: J.L. MAYS, D.L. PETERSEN, and K.H. RICHARDS (eds.), *Old Testament Interpretation. Past, Present, and Future*. 1995. 177-194.

NICCACCI, A., *The Syntax of the Verb in Classical Hebrew Prose* (JSOTSup 86). Sheffield: JSOT, 1990.

NICHOLSON, E., *Interpreting the Old Testament: A Century of the Oriel Professorship*. Oxford: Clarendon, 1981.

——, "Story and History in the Old Testament," in: S. BALENTINE and J. BARTON (eds.), *Language, Theology and the Bible. Essays in Honour of James Barr*. Oxford: Clarendon, 1994. 135-150.

NIEBUHR, H.R., *Christ and Culture*. London: Harper Colophon, 1975.

NOBLE, P.R., *The Canonical Approach. A Critical Reconstruction of the Hermeneutics of Brevard S. Childs* (Biblical Interpretation Series 16). Leiden; New York: Brill, 1995.

——, "Synchronic and Diachronic Approaches to Biblical Interpretation," *Journal of Literature and Theology* 7/2 (1993) 130-148.

NOLAN FEWELL, D., "Feminist Reading of the Hebrew Bible: Affirmation, Resistance and Transformation," *JSOT* 39 (1987) 77-87.

NOLAN FEWELL, D., and D.M. GUNN, "Tipping the Balance: Sternberg's Reader and the Rape of Dinah," *JBL* 110/2 (1991) 193-211.

NOLL, M.A., *Between Faith and Criticism. Evangelicals, Scholarship, and the Bible in America*. Grand Rapids: Baker, 1986.

NORDHEIMER, I., "The Philosophy of Ecclesiastes," *American Biblical Repository* XII (1838) 197-219.

NORRIS, C., *William Empson and the Philosophy of Literary Criticism*. London: Athlone Press, 1978.

——, *Contest of Faculties. Philosophy and Theory After Deconstruction*. London; NY: Methuen, 1985.

——, *Derrida* (Modern Masters). London: Fontana, 1987.

——, *Paul de Man: Deconstruction and the Critique of Aesthetic Ideology*. New York; London: Routledge, 1988.

——, *Deconstruction and the Interests of Theory*. Leicester; London: Leicester UP, 1988, 1992.

——, *What's Wrong with Postmodernism?* London: Harvester Wheatsheaf, 1990.

——, "Criticism," in: M. COYLE, et al., *Encyclopaedia of Literature and Criticism*. 1990. 27-65.

——, *Deconstruction. Theory and Practice* (2nd ed.; New Accents). London: Routledge, 1991.

——, *Spinoza and the Origins of Modern Critical Theory* (The Bucknell Lectures in Literary Theory). Oxford: Basil Blackwell, 1991.

——, *The Truth About Postmodernism*. Oxford: Blackwell, 1993.

——, *Truth and the Ethics of Criticism*. Manchester: Manchester UP, 1994.

OGDEN, C.K., and I.A. RICHARDS, *The Meaning of Meaning* (10th ed.). London: Routledge and Kegan Paul, 1949.

OGDEN, G., "Qoheleth's Use of the 'Nothing is Better'-Form," *JBL* 98 (1979) 339-350.

——, "Qoheleth ix 17-x 20. Variations on the Theme of Wisdom's Strength and Vulnerability," *VT* XXX/1 (1980) 27-37.

——, "Historical Allusion in Qoheleth iv 13-16?" *VT* XXX/3 (1980) 309-315.

——, "Qoheleth xi 7-xii 8: Qoheleth's Summons to Enjoyment and Reflection," *VT* XXXIV/1 (1984) 27-38.

——, "The Interpretation of דור in Ecclesiastes 1.4," *JSOT* 34 (1986) 91-92.

——, *Qoheleth* (Readings – A New Biblical Commentary). Sheffield: JSOT, 1987.

O'NEILL, O., "Vindicating Reason," in: P. GUYER (ed.), *The Cambridge Companion to Kant*. 1992. 280-308.

ORIGEN, *The Song of Songs. Commentary and Homilies* (Trans. R. Lawson). Maryland: Westminister, 1957.

OUWENEEL, W.J., *A Critical Analysis of the External and Internal Prolegomena of Systematic Theology*. 2 Vols. Unpubl. DTh thesis, University of the Orange Free State, 1993.

PALMER, R.E., *Hermeneutics. Interpretation Theory in Schleiermacher, Dilthey, Heidegger, and Gadamer*. Evanston: Northwestern UP, 1969.

PATTE, D., "Universal Narrative Structures and Semantic Frameworks," *Semeia* 10 (1978) 123-135.

PERDUE, L.G., *Wisdom and Cult* (SBLDS 30). Missoula: Scholars Press, 1977.

———, "Job's Assault on Creation," *HAR* 10 (1987) 295-315.

———, "Paraenesis and the Death of the Sage," *Semeia* 50 (1990) 81-109.

———, "The Social Character of Paraenesis and Paraenetic Literature," *Semeia* 50 (1990) 5-39.

———, *Wisdom In Revolt. Metaphorical Theology in the Book of Job* (JSOTSup 112). Sheffield: Almond Press, 1991.

———, *The Collapse of History. Reconstructing Old Testament Theology*. Minneapolis: Fortress, 1994.

———, *Wisdom and Creation. The Theology of Wisdom Literature*. Nashville: Abingdon, 1994.

PERRY, T.A., *Dialogues with Koheleth. The Book of Ecclesiastes. Translation and Commentary*. Philadelphia: Pennsylvania State University, 1993.

PHILLIPS, G.A., "Exegesis as Critical Practice: Reclaiming History and Text from a Postmodern Perspective," *Semeia* 51 (1990) 7-49.

PLANTINGA, A., "Advice to Christian Philosophers," *Faith and Philosophy* 1/3 (1984) 253-271.

———, *Warrant and Proper Function*. NY; Oxford: OUP, 1993.

———, "Christian Philosophy at the End of the 20th Century," in: S. GRIFFIOEN and B.M. BALK (eds.), *Christian Philosophy at the Close of the Twentieth Century*. 1995. 29-53.

PLANTINGA, T., "Dilthey's Philosophy of the History of Philosophy," in: J. KRAAY and A. TOL (eds.), *Hearing and Doing*. 1979. 199-214.

———, *Historical Understanding in the Thought of Wilhelm Dilthey*. Toronto: University of Toronto Press, 1980.

PLUMPTRE, E.H., *Ecclesiastes* (The Cambridge Bible for Schools). Cambridge: CUP, 1881.

PODECHARD, E., *L'Ecclésiaste*. Paris: Gabalda, 1912.

POLAND, L., "The New Criticism, Neoorthodoxy, and the New Testament," *Journal of Religion* 65/4 (1985) 459-477.

POLK, D.P., "Brevard Childs' *Introduction to the Old Testament as Scripture*," *HIBT* 2 (1980) 165-171.

POLZIN, R.M., "The Framework of the Book of Job," *Interpretation* XXVIII/2 (1974) 182-200.

———, *Biblical Structuralism. Method and Subjectivity in the Study of Ancient Texts*. Philadelphia: Fortress; Missoula: Scholars, 1977.

PREUS, J.S., "A Hidden Opponent in Spinoza's Tractatus," *HTR* 88/3 (1995) 361-388.

PREZIOSI, D., *Rethinking Art History. Meditations on a Coy Science*. New Haven; London: Yale UP, 1989.

PRICKETT, S., "Biblical Hermeneutics," in: M. COYLE, et al., *Encyclopaedia of Literature and Criticism*. 1990. 653-665.

PRICKETT, S. (ed.), *Reading the Text. Biblical Criticism and Literary Theory.* Oxford: Blackwell, 1991.

PRITCHARD, J.B. (ed.), *Ancient Near Eastern Texts Relating to the Old Testament* (3rd ed.). Princeton: Princeton UP, 1969.

PROPP, V., "Structure and History in the Study of the Fairy Tale," *Semeia* 10 (1978) 57-83.

PROPP, W.H., B. HALPERN, and D.N. FREEDMAN (eds.), *The Hebrew Bible and Its Interpreters.* Indiana: Eisenbrauns, 1990.

PROVAN, I.W., "Ideologies, Literary and Critical Reflections on Recent Writing on the History of Israel," *JBL* 114/4 (1995) 585-606.

PUNTER, D., "Romanticism," in: M. COYLE, et al., *Encyclopaedia of Literature and Criticism.* 1990. 106-117.

RABINOW, P. (ed.), *The Foucault Reader.* London: Penguin, 1984.

RANSOM, J.C., *The New Criticism.* Norfolk: New Directions, 1941.

RANSTON, H., *Ecclesiastes and Early Greek Wisdom Literature.* London: Epworth, 1925.

RAST, W.E., *Tradition History and the Old Testament* (Guides to Biblical Scholarship). Philadelphia: Fortress, 1972.

REAGAN, C.E., and D. STEWART (eds.), *The Philosophy of Paul Ricoeur. An Anthology of His Work.* Boston: Beacon Press, 1978.

REARDON, B.M.G., *Religious Thought in the Nineteenth Century.* Cambridge: CUP, 1966.

——, *Religion in the Age of Romanticism.* Cambridge: CUP, 1985.

RENDTORFF, R., "The Paradigm is Changing: Hopes – and Fears," *BI* 1/1 (1993) 34-53.

——, *Canon and Theology. Overtures to an Old Testament Theology* (trans. and ed. by M. Kohl). Edinburgh: T&T Clark, 1994.

REVENTLOW, H. Graf, *The Authority of the Bible and the Rise of the Modern World.* London: SCM, 1984.

——, *Problems of Old Testament Theology in the Twentieth Century.* London: SCM, 1985.

——, *Problems of Biblical Theology in the Twentieth Century.* London: SCM, 1986.

REVENTLOW, H. Graf, and W. FARMER (eds.), *Biblical Studies and the Shifting of Paradigms. 1850-1914* (JSOTSup 192). Sheffield: Sheffield Academic Press, 1995.

RICHARDS, I.A., *Principles of Literary Criticism.* London; Henley: Routledge and Kegan Paul, 1924.

RICHARDSON, A., "The Rise of Modern Biblical Scholarship and Recent Discussion of the Authority of the Bible," in: S.L. GREENSLADE (ed.), *The Cambridge History of the Bible. The West from the Reformation to the Present Day.* 1963. 294-338.

RICOEUR, P., *The Symbolism of Evil.* Boston: Beacon Press, 1969.

——, *Freud and Philosophy: An Essay in Interpretation.* New Haven; London: Yale UP, 1970.

——, *Interpretation Theory: Discourse and the Surplus of Meaning.* Texas: Texas Christian UP, 1976.

——, "The Critique of Religion", in: C.E. REAGAN and D. STEWART (eds.), *The Philosophy of Paul Ricoeur. An Anthology of His Work.* 1978. 212-222.

——, *The Rule of Metaphor. Multi-Disciplinary Studies of the Creation of Meaning in Language.* London: Routledge and Kegan Paul, 1978.

——, *Essays on Biblical Interpretation.* Philadelphia: Fortress, 1980.

——, *Hermeneutics and the Human Sciences* (Ed. and trans. J.B. THOMPSON). Cambridge: CUP, 1981.

RINGGREN, H., A. WEISER, and W. ZIMMERLI, *Sprüche, Prediger, Das Hohe Lied Klagelieder, Das Buch Esther*. Göttingen: Vandenhoeck and Ruprecht, 1967.

ROBERTSON, D., *The Old Testament and the Literary Critic*. Philadelphia: Fortress, 1977.

ROBEY, D., "Anglo-American New Criticism," in: A. JEFFERSON and D. ROBEY (eds.), *Modern Literary Theory*. 1986. 73-91.

ROGERS, P., "The Parthian Dart: Endings and Epilogues in Fiction," *Essays in Criticism* XLII/2 (1992) 85-106.

ROGERSON, J., "Philosophy and the Rise of Biblical Criticism: England and Germany," in: S.W. SYKES (ed.), *England and Germany. Studies in Theological Diplomacy* (Studies in Intercultural History of Christianity 25). Frankfurt: Peter Lang, 1982. 63-79.

——, "An Outline of the History of Old Testament Study," in: J. ROGERSON (ed.), *Beginning Old Testament Study*. 1983. 6-25.

——, "The World-View of the Old Testament," in: J. ROGERSON (ed.), *Beginning Old Testament Study*. 1983. 55-73.

——, *Old Testament Criticism in the Nineteenth Century. England and Germany*. London: SPCK, 1984.

——, *W.M.L. de Wette. Founder of Modern Biblical Criticism* (JSOTSup 126). Sheffield: JSOT Press, 1992.

ROGERSON, J. (ed.), *Beginning Old Testament Study*. London: SPCK, 1983.

ROGERSON, J., C. ROWLAND, and B. LINDARS, *The Study and Use of the Bible* (The History of Christian Theology). Basingstroke: Marshall, 1988.

RORTY, R., *Philosophy and the Mirror of Nature*. Oxford: Basil Blackwell, 1980.

——, "Postmodernist Bourgeois Liberalism," *Journal of Philosophy* 80/10 (1983) 583-589.

——, *Objectivity, Relativism, and Truth*. Cambridge: CUP, 1991.

ROSE, M., *The Post-Modern and the Post-Industrial. A Critical Analysis*. Cambridge: CUP, 1991.

ROUSSEAU, F., "Structure de Qoheleth i 4-11 et Plan du Livre," *VT* 31 (1981) 200-217.

ROWLEY, H.H., *The Old Testament and Modern Study*. Oxford: OUP, 1951.

RYKEN, L. (ed.), *The Christian Imagination. Essays on Literature and the Arts*. Grand Rapids: Baker, 1981.

RYLAARSDAM, J.C., *Revelation in Jewish Wisdom Literature*. Chicago: University of Chicago Press, 1946.

RYLANCE, R., "The New Criticism," in: M. COYLE, (et al.), *Encyclopaedia of Literature and Criticism*. 1990. 721-735.

SAMPSON, G., *Schools of Linguistics*. California: Stanford UP, 1980.

SAMPSON, P., V. SAMUEL, and C. SUGDEN (eds.), *Faith and Modernity*. Oxford: Regnum Lynx, 1994.

SANDERS, E.P., *Jesus and Judaism*. London: SCM, 1985.

SANDERS, J.A., "Canonical Context and Canonical Criticism," *HIBT* 2 (1980) 173-197.

SAUSSURE, F. de, *Course in General Linguistics* (Trans. W. BASKIN). New York: McGraw-Hill Paperbacks, 1959.

SCHMID, H.H., *Wesen und Geschichte der Weisheit* (BZAW 101). Berlin: Töpelmann, 1966.

SCHOLDER, K., *The Birth of Modern Critical Theology*. London: SCM, 1990.

SCHOORS, A., "La structure littéraire de Qohéleth," *Orientalia Lovaniensia Periodica* 13 (1982) 91-116.

———, *The Preacher Sought to Find Pleasing Words. A Study of the Language of Qoheleth* (Orientalia Lovaniensia Analecta 41). Leuven: Departement Oriëntalistiek, 1992.

SCHOTROFF, W., and W. STEGEMANN (eds.), *God of the Lowly*. NY: Orbis, 1984.

SCHÜRER, E., *The History of the Jewish People in the Age of Jesus Christ*. Vol. 1 (2nd ed.; rev. and ed. G. VERMES and F. MILLAR). Edinburgh: T&T Clark, 1973.

SCOBIE, C., "The Place of Wisdom in Biblical Theology," *BTB* 14/2 (1984) 43-48.

SCOTT, R.B.Y., *Proverbs, Ecclesiastes* (AB 18). Garden City: Doubleday, 1965.

———, "The Study of the Wisdom Literature," *Interpretation* 24 (1970) 20-45.

SCRIVEN, C., *The Transformation of Culture: Christian Social Ethics After H. Richard Niebuhr*. Pennsylvania, Ontario: Herald Press, 1988.

SCRUTON, R., *Kant* (Past Masters). Oxford: OUP, 1982.

———, *Spinoza* (Past Masters). Oxford: OUP, 1986.

SEARLE, J.R., *Speech Acts. An Essay in the Philosophy of Language*. Cambridge: CUP, 1969.

SEBEOK, T.A. (ed.), *Style in Language*. Cambridge, Mas.: MIT Press, 1960.

SEERVELD, C., *Benedetto Croce's Earlier Aesthetic Theories and Literary Criticism. A Critical Philosophical Look at the Development During the Rationalistic Years*. Kampen: J.H. Kok, 1958.

———, "Review of H.G. Gadamer, *Truth and Method*," *Criticism* 36/4 (1978) 487-490.

———, "Towards a Cartographic Methodology for Art Historiography," *Journal of Aesthetics and Art Criticism* 39/2 (1980) 143-154.

———, *A Christian Critique of Art and Literature* (2nd ed.). Toronto: Toronto Tuppence Press, 1995.

SELDEN, R., and P. WIDDOWSON, *A Reader's Guide to Contemporary Literary Theory*. London: Harvester Wheatsheaf, 1993.

SHEPPARD, G.T., "The Epilogue of Qoheleth as Theological Commentary," *CBQ* 39 (1977) 182-189.

———, *Wisdom as a Hermeneutical Construct*. Berlin; NY: de Gruyter, 1980.

SIEGFRIED, C., *Prediger und Hoheslied* (HAT). Göttingen: Vandenhoeck and Ruprecht, 1898.

SIM, S. (ed.), *The A-Z Guide to Modern Literary and Cultural Theorists*. London: Prentice Hall; Harvester Wheatsheaf, 1995.

SIMEON, C., *Simeon's Works, Volume VII, Proverbs to Isaiah XXVI* (ed. T.H. Horne). London: Henry G. Bohn, 1844.

SIMS, S.P., *Qoheleth – Critic of Post-Exilic Beliefs*. Unpublished DPhil thesis: Oxford University, 1994.

SIMPSON, W.K., *The Literature of Ancient Egypt. An Anthology of Stories, Instructions, and Poetry*. New Haven; London: Yale UP, 1972.

SKA, J.L., *"Our Fathers Have Told Us." Introduction to the Analysis of Hebrew Narrative* (Subsidia Biblica 13). Rome: Pontifical Biblical Institute, 1990.

SKEHAN, P., "A Single Editor for the Whole of Proverbs," in: J.L. CRENSHAW (ed.), *Studies in Ancient Israelite Wisdom*. 1976. 329-340.

SMALLEY, B., *The Study of the Bible in the Middle Ages* (3rd ed.). Oxford: Blackwell, 1983.

SMEND, R., "Questions About the Importance of the Canon in Old Testament Introduction," *JSOT* 16 (1980) 45-51.

——, "The Interpretation of Wisdom in Nineteenth-Century Scholarship," in: J. DAY, et al. (eds.), *Wisdom in Ancient Israel. Essays in Honour of J.A. Emerton.* 1995. 257-268.

SNELL, D.C., *Twice-Told Proverbs and the Composition of the Book of Proverbs.* Winona Lake: Eisenbrauns, 1993.

SONTAG, S., "Against Interpretation," in: D. LODGE (ed.), *20th Century Criticism. A Reader.* 1972. 652-660.

SONTAG, S. (ed.), *A Barthes Reader.* London: Jonathan Cape, 1982.

SOSKICE, J.M., *Metaphor and Religious Language.* Oxford: Clarendon, 1985.

SPINOZA, B., *A Theologico-Political Treatise. A Political Treatise* (trans. R.H.M. ELWES). NY: Dover, 1951.

——, *Ethics.* London: Everyman, 1993.

SPIVEY, R.A., "Structuralism and Biblical Studies. The Uninvited Guest," *Interpretation* XXVIII/2 (1974) 133-145.

SPYKMAN, G., *Reformational Theology. A New Paradigm for Doing Dogmatics.* Grand Rapids: Eerdmans, 1992.

STEINER, G., *Real Presences.* London: Faber and Faber, 1989.

STERNBERG, M., *The Poetics of Biblical Narrative. Ideological Literature and the Drama of Reading.* Bloomington: Indiana University Press, 1985.

——, "Biblical Poetics and Sexual (?) Counterreading," *JBL* 111/3 (1992) 463-488.

STRAUSS, D., "The Modern Scientific Dispensation and the Spiritual Climate of Contemporary – 'Postmodernism'," unpubl. paper, 1995.

STRAUSS, G., *Christian Philosophy and the Transformation of African Culture.* Unpubl. MA thesis: University of the Orange Freestate, 1990.

SUELZER, A., and J.S. KSELMAN, "Modern Old Testament Criticism," in: R.E. BROWN, J.A. FITZMEYER, and R.E. MURPHY (eds.), *The New Jerome Biblical Commentary.* 1990. 1163-1129.

SULEIMAN, S.R., "Introduction: Varieties of Audience-Oriented Criticism," in: S.R. SULEIMAN and I. CROSMAN (eds.), *The Reader in the Text. Essays on Audience and Interpretation.* 1980. 3-45.

SULEIMAN, S.R., and I. CROSMAN (eds.), *The Reader in the Text. Essays on Audience and Interpretation.* Princeton: Princeton UP, 1980.

SYKES, S.W. (ed.), *Karl Barth – Studies of His Theological Method.* Oxford: Clarendon, 1979.

TALSTRA, E., *Solomon's Prayer. Synchrony and Diachrony in the Composition of 1 Kings 8, 14-61.* Kampen: Kok Pharos, 1993.

TATE, A., *The Man of Letters in the Modern World. Selected Essays 1928-1955.* NY: Meridian, 1955.

——, *Collected Essays.* Swallow: Denver, 1959.

TAYLOR, M., "The Eventuality of Texts," *Semeia* 51 (1990) 215-240.

TENNYSON, G.B., and E.E. ERICSON (ed.), *Religion and Modern literature. Essays in Theory and Criticism.* Grand Rapids: Eerdmans, 1975.

THIELICKE, H., *The Evangelical Faith. Volume One. Prolegomena. The Relation of Theology to Modern Thought Forms.* Edinburgh: T&T Clark, 1974.

THISELTON, A.C., *The Two Horizons. New Testament Hermeneutics and Philosophical Description.* Carlisle: Paternoster; Grand Rapids: Eerdmans, 1980.

——, "On Models and Methods. A Conversation with Robert Morgan," in: D.J.A. CLINES (ed.), *The Bible in Three Dimensions.* 1990. 337-356.

——, *New Horizons in Hermeneutics*. Grand Rapids: Zondervan, 1992.

——, *Interpreting God and the Postmodern Self. On Meaning, Manipulation and Promise*. Edinburgh: T&T Clark, 1995.

TORRANCE, T.F., *The Ground and Grammar of Theology*. Charlottesville: University Press of Virginia, 1980.

——, *The Hermeneutics of John Calvin*. Edinburgh: Scottish Academic Press, 1988.

TOULMIN, S., *Cosmopolis. The Hidden Agenda of Modernity*. Chicago: University of Chicago Press, 1990.

TRACY, D., *The Analogical Imagination. Christian Theology and the Culture of Pluralism*. London: SCM, 1981.

TRIBLE, P., "Ecclesiastes," in: B.W. ANDERSON (ed.), *The Books of the Bible: The Old Testament*. 1989. 231-239.

TRIGG, R., *Reason and Commitment*. Cambridge: CUP, 1973.

——, *Rationality and Science. Can Science Explain Everything?* Oxford: Blackwell, 1993.

TUCKER, G.M., *Form Criticism of the Old Testament* (Guides to Biblical Scholarship). Fortress: Philadelphia, 1971.

VALDÉS, M.J. (ed.), *A Ricoeur Reader: Reflection and Imagination*. Harvester Wheatsheaf: London, 1991.

VAN AARDE, A.G., "Historical Criticism and Holism. Heading Toward a New Paradigm," in: J. MOUTON, A.G. VAN AARDE, and W.S. VORSTER (eds.), *Paradigms and Progress in Theology*. 1988. 49-64.

VANDER GOOT, H., "The Modern Settlement: Religion and Culture in the Early Schleiermacher," in: J. KRAAY, and A. TOL (eds.), *Hearing and Doing*. 1979. 173-197.

——, *Interpreting the Bible in Theology and the Church*. New York; Toronto: Edwin Mellen, 1984.

VAN LEEUWEN, R., "Proverbs 30:21-23 and the Biblical World Upside Down," *JBL* 105 (1986) 599-610.

——, *Context and Meaning in Proverbs 25-27* (SBL Dissertation Series 96). Atlanta: Scholars Press, 1988.

——, "Liminality and Worldview in Proverbs 1-9," *Semeia* 50 (1990) 111-144.

——, "Wealth and Poverty: System and Contradiction in Proverbs," *Hebrew Studies* 33 (1992) 25-36.

——, "In Praise of Proverbs," in: L. ZUIDEVAART and H. LUTTIKHUIZEN (eds.), *Pledges of Jubilee*. 1995. 308-327.

VAN NIEKERK, M.J.H., "Response to J.A. Loader's 'Different Reactions of Job and Qoheleth to the Doctrine of Retribution'," *Old Testament Essays* 4 (1991) 97-105.

VANHOOZER, K.J., "A Lamp in the Labyrinth: The Hermeneutics of 'Aesthetic' Theology," *Trinity Journal* 8 (1987) 25-56.

——, *Biblical Narrative in the Philosophy of Paul Ricoeur. A Study in Hermeneutics and Philosophy*. Cambridge: CUP, 1990.

VENTER, J.J., *Pieke en Lyne In die Westerse Denkgeskiedenis. Band II: 'n Geskiedenis van Moderne Westerse Leidende Ideë*. Potchefstroom: PU vir CHO, 1991.

VERHEIJ, A., "Paradise Retried: On Qoheleth 2:4-6," *JSOT* 50 (1991) 113-115.

VIA, D.O., "A Structuralist Approach to Paul's Old Testament Hermeneutic," *Interpretation* XXVIII/2 (1974) 201-220.

VILCHEZ LINDEZ, J., *Eclesiastes o Qohelet*. Estella, Navarra: Editorial Verba Divino, 1994.

VON HALLBERG, R. (ed.), *Canons*. Chicago; London: University of Chicago Press, 1983, 1984.

VON RAD, G., *Wisdom in Israel*. London: SCM, 1972.

WALHOUT, C., and L. RYKEN (eds.), *Contemporary Literary Theory. A Christian Appraisal*. Grand Rapids: Eerdmans, 1991.

WALKER, A. (ed.), *Different Gospels. Christian Orthodoxy and Modern Theologies*. London: SPCK, 1993.

WARNKE, G., *Gadamer. Hermeneutics, Tradition and Reason*. California: Stanford UP, 1987.

WATSON, F., "Philosophy," in: R.J. COGGINS and J.C. HOULDEN (eds.), *A Dictionary of Biblical Interpretation*. 1990. 546-549.

——, *Text, Church and World. Biblical Interpretation in Theological Perspective*. Edinburgh: T&T Clark, 1994.

WATSON, F. (ed.), *The Open Text: New Directions for Biblical Studies?* London: SCM, 1993.

WEBER, J.J., *L'Ecclésiaste: Le livre de Job-L'Ecclésiaste. Texte et commentaire*. 1947.

WEINFELD, M., *Deuteronomy and the Deuteronomic School*. Oxford: Clarendon, 1972.

WEINSHEIMER, J.C., *Gadamer's Hermeneutics. A Reading of 'Truth and Method.'* New Haven; London: Yale UP, 1985.

WEISS, M., *The Bible from Within: the Method of Totality Interpretation*. Jerusalem: Magnes, 1984.

——, "The Contribution of Literary Theory to Biblical Research. Illustrated by the Problem of She'ar-Yashub," in: S. JAPHET (ed.), *Studies in Bible*. 1986. 373-386.

WELLEK, R., *Concepts of Criticism* (ed. and with an introduction by S.G. NICHOLS). New Haven; London: Yale UP, 1963.

WELLEK, R., and A. WARREN, *Theory of Literature* (3rd ed.). London: Penguin, 1963.

WENHAM, G.J., "Method in Pentateuchal Source Criticism," *VT* XL/1 (1991) 84-109.

WEST, G., *Biblical Hermeneutics of Liberation. Modes of Reading the Bible in the South African Context*. Pietermaritzburg: Cluster, 1991.

WESTERMANN, C., "The Contribution of Biblical Thought to an Understanding of Our Reality," in: D.G. MILLER (ed.), *The Hermeneutical Quest*. 1986. 47-57.

WESTPHAL, M., "Christian Philosophers and the Copernican Revolution," in: C.S. EVANS and M. WESTPHAL (eds.), *Christian Perspectives on Religious Knowledge*. 1993. 161-179.

——, "Deconstruction and Christian Cultural Theory: An Essay on Appropriation," in: L. ZUIDEVAART and H. LUTTIKHUIZEN (eds.), *Pledges of Jubilee. Essays on the Arts and Culture, in Honor of Calvin G. Seerveld*. 1995. 107-125.

WHITE, H.C., "The Value of Speech Act Theory for Old Testament Hermeneutics," *Semeia* 41 (1988) 41-63.

WHITLEY, C.F., *Koheleth. His Language and Thought*. Berlin; NY: de Gruyter, 1979.

WHYBRAY, R.N., *The Intellectual Tradition in the Old Testament* (BZAW 135). NY; Berlin: de Gruyter, 1974.

——, *Two Jewish Theologies: Job and Ecclesiastes*. Hull: University of Hull, 1980.

——, "The Identification and Use of Quotations in Ecclesiastes," *VTSup* 32 (1981) 435-451.

——, "On Robert Alter's *The Art of Biblical Narrative*," *JSOT* 27 (1983) 75-86.

———, "Ecclesiastes 1:4-7 and the Wonders of Nature," *JSOT* 41 (1988) 105-112.

———, *Ecclesiastes* (NCBC). London: Marshall, Morgan and Scott; Grand Rapids: Eerdmans, 1989.

———, *Ecclesiastes* (Old Testament Guides). Sheffield: JSOT, 1989.

———, "Today and Tomorrow in Biblical Studies: II. The Old Testament," *ExpTim* 100/10 (1989) 364-367.

———, *Wealth and Poverty in the Book of Proverbs* (JSOTSup 99). Sheffield: Sheffield Academic Press, 1990.

———, "Qoheleth, Preacher of Joy," *JSOT* 23 (1982) 87-98.

———, *Proverbs* (NCBC). Grand Rapids: Eerdmans; London: Marshall Pickering, 1994.

———, "The Wisdom Psalms," in: J. DAY, et al. (eds.), *Wisdom in Ancient Israel. Essays in Honour of J.A. Emerton*. 1995. 152-160.

WILLIAMS, J.G., *Those Who Ponder Proverbs. Aphoristic Thinking and Biblical Literature*. Sheffield: Almond Press, 1981.

WILSON, G.H., "'The Words of the Wise': The Intent and Significance of Qoheleth 12:9-14," *JBL* 103/2 (1984) 175-192.

WILSON, L., "The Book of Job and the Fear of God," *TB* 46/1 (1995) 59-79.

WIMSATT, W.K., *The Verbal Icon. Studies in the Meaning of Poetry*. Lexington: University Press of Kentucky, 1954.

WIMSATT, W.K., and M.C. BEARDSLEY, "The Intentional Fallacy," in: D. LODGE (ed.), *20th Century Criticism*. 1972. 334-345.

———, "The Affective Fallacy," in: D. LODGE (ed.), *20th Century Criticism*. 1972. 345-358.

WIMSATT, W.K., and C. BROOKS, *Literary Criticism. A Short History. Volume 3. Romantic Criticism*. London: Routledge and Kegan Paul, 1957.

WINDELBAND, W., *A History of Philosophy*. London; NY: Macmillan, 1901.

WINK, W., *The Bible in Human Transformation*. Philadelphia: Fortress, 1973.

WITHERINGTON, B., *Jesus the Sage. The Pilgrimage of Wisdom*. Edinburgh: T&T Clark, 1994.

WITTGENSTEIN, L., *Philosophical Investigations*. Oxford: Blackwell, 1958/67.

WOLTERS, A., "On Vollenhoven's Problem-Historical Method," in: J. KRAAY and A. TOL (eds.), *Hearing and Doing*. 1979. 231-262.

———, *Creation Regained. Biblical Basics for a Reformational Worldview*. Grand Rapids: Eerdmans, 1985.

———, *The Song of the Valiant Woman (Prov 31:10-31): A Pattern in the History of Interpretation (To 1600)*. Unpublished MA thesis: McMaster University, 1987.

———; "Gustavo Gutiérrez," in: J. KLAPWIJK, S. GRIFFIOEN, and G. GROENEWOUD (eds.), *Bringing into Captivity Every Thought*. 1991. 229-240.

WOLTERSTORFF, N., *Art in Action*. Grand Rapids: Eerdmans, 1980.

———, *Until Justice and Peace Embrace*. Grand Rapids: Eerdmans, 1983.

———, *Reason Within the Bounds of Religion*. Grand Rapids: Eerdmans, 1984.

———, "The Remembrance of Things (Not) Past: Philosophical Reflections on Christian Liturgy," in: P. FLINT (ed.), *Christian Philosophy*. 1990. 118-161.

———, *Divine Discourse. Philosophical Reflections on the Claim that God Speaks*. Cambridge: CUP, 1995.

———, "The Importance of Hermeneutics for a Christian Worldview," in: R. LUNDIN (ed.), *Disciplining Hermeneutics*. 1997. 25-47.

WOOD, A.W., "Rational Theology, Moral Faith, and Religion," in: P. GUYER (ed.), *The Cambridge Companion to Kant*. 1992. 394-416.

WORTON, M., and J. STILL (eds.), *Intertextuality: Theories and Practices*. Manchester: Manchester UP, 1990.

WRIGHT, A.G., "The Riddle of the Sphinx: The Structure of the Book of Qoheleth," *CBQ* 30 (1968) 313-334.

——, "The Riddle of the Sphinx Revisited: Numerical Patterns in the Book of Qoheleth," *CBQ* 42 (1980) 38-51.

——, "Additional Numerical Patterns in Qoheleth," *CBQ* 45 (1983) 32-43.

——, "Ecclesiastes (Qoheleth)," in: R.E. BROWN, J.A. FITZMEYER, and R.E. MURPHY (eds.), *The New Jerome Biblical Commentary*. 1990. 489-495.

WRIGHT, E., "Modern Psychoanalytic Criticism," in: A. JEFFERSON and D. ROBEY (eds.), *Modern Literary Theory*. 1986. 145-165.

WRIGHT, G.E., *The Old Testament Against Its Environment* (SBT 2). London: SCM, 1950.

——, *God Who Acts. Biblical Theology as Recital* (SBT 8). London: SCM, 1952.

WRIGHT, N.T., *The New Testament and the People of God*. Minneapolis: Fortress, 1992.

WRIGHT, T.R., *The Religion of Humanity. The Impact of Comtean Positivism on Victorian Britain*. Cambridge: CUP, 1986.

ZAHRNT, H., *The Question of God. Protestant Theology in the Twentieth Century*. London: Collins, 1969.

ZIMMERLI, W., "The Place and Limit of Wisdom In the Framework of Old Testament Theology," *SJT* 17 (1964) 146-158.

——, "Das Buch des Predigers Salomo," in: H. RINGGREN, A. WEISER, and W. ZIMMERLI, *Sprüche, Prediger, Das Hohe Lied Klagelieder, Das Buch Esther*. 1967. 123-253.

——, "Concerning the Structure of Old Testament Wisdom," in: J.L. CRENSHAW (ed.), *Studies in Ancient Israelite Wisdom*. 1976. 175-207.

ZIMMERMAN, F., *The Inner World of Qoheleth*. NY: KTAV, 1973.

Zohar. The Book of Enlightenment (trans. and introduction D.C. Matt). London: SPCK.

ZUCK, R.B., "God and Man in Ecclesiastes," *BibSac* 148 (1991) 46-56.

ZURRO, E., *Procedimientos iterativos en la poesia ugaritica y hebrea* (Biblica et Orientalia 43). Rome: Pontifical Biblical Institute, 1987.

INDEX OF BIBLICAL REFERENCES

INDEX OF NAMES

SUBJECT INDEX

Finito di stampare il 20 ottobre 1998
Tipografia " Giovanni Olivieri "
Via dell'Archetto, 10 - 00187 Roma